BRITISH RESIDENTS AT THE DARBAR OF BENGAL NAWABS AT MURSHIDABAD (1757–1772)

BRITISH RESIDENTS AT THE DARBAR OF BENGAL NAWABS AT MURSHIDABAD (1757–1772)

By

Dr. Subhas Channdra Mukhopadhyay

GYAN

ISBN : 978-81-212-0200-8

Published, 2018

Published by

Gyan Publishing House
5, Ansari Road
Daryaganj, New Delhi-110002
Phone: 011-47034999, 9811692060
www.gyanbooks.com
E-mail: books@gyanbooks.com

Printed at: G. Print Process, Delhi.

INTRODUCTION

The British Residents at the *darbar* of Bengal Nawabs at Murshidabad played a vital role in moulding the destiny of the *subah* and the consequent fate of its people from 1757 to 1772. While Murshidabad remained a seat of power, it was they, who helped gain the political suzerainty for the English Company by adopting means, both fair and foul. Consequently the Residents were responsible for infusing a new spirit, that of political hegemonism, towards establishing England's colonial empire. This urged the London authorities to attempt to control the activities of the English Company in Bengal that enjoyed sanction for monopoly trade but did not have the licence to intercede and get embroiled in political conflicts and controversies.

While sitting in judgment, the historians should be impartial in their approach. Our historians, also claim for themselves, at least occasionally, the impartiality of judges. Professor R.C. Majumdar, a doyen in the field, observes: "The purpose of the historian is the ascertainment of the Truth. His only duty is to determine guilt or innocence in the fashion of a judge in a law court."[1] Thus the plain truth is that the apparently simple English traders of the mid-seventeenth century in Bengal, changed their colour completely in the mid-eighteenth century. The adventurers who had landed for purely

---

1. Majumdar, R.C., "Bharat Itihaser Nutan Sanskaran", *Itihas*, Vol. VI No. 2, 1362 B.S. (1955-56).

commercial pursuits, began to craze for and actively pursued the goal of political predominance.

In the spirit of political adventurism as well as being oppressed by the *subahdars* of Bengal, the officials of the East India Company often came into disputes with the Mughal authorities at the end of the seventeenth century. During this time, almost every English merchant in India had a double occupation—the trade on the Company's account as well as his own private individual trade. Realising this, Shaista Khan—the *subahdar* of Bengal under Aurangzeb prevented such illegal trade. But the officials of the Company on account of their superior skill and craft established a successful maritime trade of their own. However, making of illegal profits was not confined to them alone, because the *subahdars* also extracted money from the people by unlawful means and filled their own coffers. Shaista Khan himself took with him nine crores of rupees from Bengal, while Azim-us-Shan eight crores. Under such conditions of extortion and anarchy, the English became the *Zamindar* of three villages and this occupation of a *Zamindari* created a gradual change in their outlook.

India at that time was seething with discontent. Aurangzeb closed his aged-eyes in death in 1707. His death led to the quick process of disintegration of the Mughal Empire in the first half of the eighteenth century. His unworthy successors lacked the ability to control the situation and with the erosion of their power there was anarchy almost everywhere in the empire. Rebellion was in the air. The Sikhs, the Jats, the Rajputs, the Rohillas, the Marathas and the Pathans jumped into the fray and jockeyed for power. The Marathas in various parts of India and the Sikhs at Lahore established their respective independent rules. Asaf Jah in Hyderabad, shujauddaulah in Oudh and Murshid Quli Khan in Bengal, usurped powers for themselves. The Jats fought for their own supremacy, while the Rohillas sought for their own homeland. In such a free-for-all situation, the European traders began to fish in the troubled waters.

In the mid-eighteenth century, the English Company wanted to consolidate their position in Bengal as the base of their prosperity in near future. Both the expansion of their economic activities and their successes in the south against the French gave them a great boost. Thus a great craving for power arose among them. The vast increase in the Company's export trade from Bengal consolidated their economic gains and, hence, flushed with success, the Company's officers thought themselves powerful enough to build their own fortune by playing the diplomatic game for their own benefit.

Thus, at a time when India was advancing gradually to the death of the long-languishing political and social order, the British star began to rise. The chaotic condition in the country marked also the fateful augury of the ushering in of British political hegemony over the whole of this sub-continent for two centuries, till the birth of free India. The period was dark, confused and anarchical. But this dark chapter of human history also carried the forces from which history was made. It had many things in it to learn from because it was the time when the first steps were taken, which finally moulded the shape of a nation and gave a new turn to its history. Thus, essentially, the period was one of transition marked by internals feuds, conspiracies and also of ferment and germination. The historical importance of the period thus can hardly be gainsaid.

Sirajuddaulah had to accept a British Resident at his *darbar* early in February, 1757, under the precarious circumstances of duress when the news of Ahmad Shah Abdali's proposed incursion to Bengal had reached him. Later this proved to be a false scare. But it was due to this mistake that the young Nawab unconsciously sowed the seed of his own ruin, as well as sealed the fate of his own countrymen. Throughout the period from 1757 to 1772, the activities of the Residents at the *darbar* may be divided into two broad-based phases. In the first phase, they adopted devious but successful ways of intrigue and became a constant check on the powers of the Nawabs and a thorn in his flesh till the grant of *diwani* in 1765. In the second phase, they confined their activities to complete the fruits of the *diwani* and hence tried to lay the foundation of British imperialism in India. They abolished the village-based economy of Bengal and introduced a system akin to their own. They discarded the old revenue system by which revenue was previously collected in terms of produce from a village unit. The revenue system was now based on cash collection. Moreover, every individual of a village community was made responsible to pay the due revenue in the accepted currency. In the upshot of this the peasants of Bengal became poorer, as sometimes they had to sell their entire harvest in order to pay their dues to the Company.

In preparing the present study, an attempt has been made to show in the first chapter, how the British came to Bengal in the guise of a mercantile community, but taking advantage of the situation, tried to acquire unlicensed trade privileges in Bengal from the end of the seventeenth century. This chapter extends the discussion to the death of Alivardi in 1756 when the traders from Albion were still looked upon as traders. This chapter has purposively been made brief since it aims at drawing just the backgrounds of the English traders, and more so, as a connecting link with their future plans and programmes.

The second chapter deals with the English activities in the *subah* during the time of Sirajuddaulah when they repeatedly defied the order of the Nawab. This led to the eventual showdown between the two forces and the ruin of the English establishment at Calcutta. But by the advent of Clive, the English merchants regained their position and forced the Nawab to accept a British Resident at his *darbar*.

The third chapter discusses the role of the Resident at Murshidabad, his subsequent diplomacy to capture the stronghold of Chandernagore from the French, as well as to form a party at the Nawab's *darbar*. A successful conspiracy was hatched by the Resident with the help of the malcontents at the *darbar* against Sirajuddaulah. This ultimately forced the latter to accept defeat at Plassey at the hands of the English army.

The fourth chapter deals with the accession of Mir Jafar on the *masnad* with the help of the English. The Resident received the so called presents from the Nawab with other

English officers who also shared in the largesse. The Residents forced Mir Jafar during his brief rule to become their puppet. Mir Jafar struggled hard to rescue himself from this position of disgrace but the Residents did not allow him any such opportunity. On the other hand, Mir Jafar was eventually deposed from the *masnad* on various charges of which, unfaithfulness was one of the most important.

The fifth chapter deals with the installation of Mir Qasim on the *masnad*. But soon, after having been disillusioned about the Nawab, the Company tried to curb his independent attitude. Though a Resident was proposed to be appointed at his *darbar* at Mungher, the Nawab rejected this idea. Similarly on the question of internal trade privileges also the cold war between them resulted in the battle of Buxar.

The sixth chapter discusses about the restoration of Mir Jafar by which his powers were further impounded by the new treaty. Mir Jafar had to accept a British Resident and so too his son, Najmuddaulah. Najmuddaulah had to accept even a Regency controlled by the Resident. During this time, the Company obtained the *diwani* of Bengal and the helpless Nawab, by an arrangement with the Resident, became a pensionor on an annuity. The Resident now began to control even the household affairs of the Nawabs of Bengal.

The seventh chapter deals with the activities of the Residents, who became the administrators of all revenue collections. As the Residents were on the spot, the Select Committee at Calcutta had to pay due regard to their views. Some Residents carried on their own private inland trade, though it was repeatedly forbidden by the Home Government. In this process, the Residents became seekers of fortune and amassed huge wealth by questionable means.

The eighth chapter deals with the drought, epidemic and famine in Bengal that followed in rapid succession from 1769. Lakhs of people died in this devastating famine ever-known in the history of humanity. But the officials under the Resident continued their loot and they extorted money from the poor *raiyots* up to the last penny. The English authorities at Calcutta could not follow any firm and planned course of action. They only tried to preserve the lives of their own men. The Controlling Councils of Revenue established at Murshidabad and Patna failed to chech this kind of 'privateering' by the Company's officials. As there was a complete failure of dyarchy, the Court of Directors decided strongly to stake their claim as the *diwan* of Bengal, in which they succeeded. Hence the capital of Bengal was transferred from Murshidabad to Calcutta with most of its necessary offices.

In conclusion, an attempt has been made to show that the Residents played a vital role in consolidating the British power in Bengal. As things stood at the time, the office of the Resident was of great weight, next only to the Governor. During 1767 to 1772 the practical operation of the *diwani* rested with the Residents and in this context, the success or failure of dyarchy rested not on the Governor or his select committe, but on the Residents at Murshidabad.

While working on this study, I have carefully gone thorugh the original unpublished records preserved in the National Archives, New Delhi and the State Archives of west Bengal, Calcutta. I have also consulted materials from the English and Bengali sources, as well as from translated French and Persian sources. I have also studied in the National Library, Asiatic Society of Bengal and Bangiya Sahitya Parished Library in Calcutta. Besides, I have consulted the Central Library of Banaras Hindu University for a long period of time. I have also consulted materials from Dhaka University liberary as well. I express my deep sense of gratitude to the staff of all the above academic centres, who rendered valuable co-operation and help to me.

The study has been completed after strenuous and continuous efforts for a long period of ten years. My gratitude is also due to the concerned authorities of the University Grants Commission, New Delhi, who sanctioned me financial grant in 1975 for this project. I have also derived one more advantage from this grant. Besides my Ph. D. work that I have completed my subsequent work enitled "*Diwani in Bengal 1765*,,. The latter book, since its publication in 1980, has received wide popularity. Meanwhile my another research work on *the Agrarian Policy of the British in Bengal, 1698-1722* since its publication in 1987 from Allahabad, has recieved wide popularity among the scholars.

I am indebted to many persons. I express my deep sense of remorse at the demise of my father, late Bholanath Mukherjee, who always remained a symbol of love and confidence, unfortunatily, he could not see the publication of my present research work. I am very fortunate that the topic of research had been approved by Dr. K.K. Datta, the then Vice-Chancellor of Patna University, when I met him (14 April, 1970 at his village home at Jhikarhati, Santhal Pargana, Bihar. My relation with him dates back from December, 1967, down to his death in March, 1982. He suggested many improvements on all my research works, inculding the persent one. I pay my humble respect to this departed scholar whose eminence in this field has been universally acknowledged. Besides, I express my gratitude to professor B.K. Roy, retired Professor and Head of the Department of History L.N. Mithila University, Darbhanga. My relation with him dose not require any explanation in writing, who had been helping me in various ways for more than two decades. I also express my gratitude to Professor Hiralal Singh. formerly Head of the Department of History, Banaras Hindu University, Professor Sukumar Ray, formerly Head of the Department of Islamic History and culture, calcutta University, Prof. Bimal Prasad of Jawaherlal Nehru University and Prof. Irfan Habil, Professor and Chairman, Aligarh Muslim University, for their valuable suggestions and encouragements to me from time to time. My gratitude is also due to Shri I.B. Banerjee of Calcutta and Smt. Sandhya Mukherjee of Varanasi, for their generous encouragement.

S. C. Mukhopadhyay.

DEPARTMENT OF HISTORY
BANARAS HINDU UNIVERSITY
VARANASI.

ABBREVIATIONS

Aitchison, *A Collection of treaties. etc.*	Aitchison, C.U., *A Collection of Treaties, Engagements and Sanads.*
Auber, *Rise*	Auber, P., *Rise and Progress of the British Power in India.*
Bandopadhyay, *Banglar Itihas*	Bandopadhyay, Rakhaldas, *Banglar Itihas O Ashtadash Satabdir Nababi Amal.*
Beveridge, *Hastings in Lower Bengal*	Beveridge, H., *Warren Hastings in Lower Bengal.*
Beveridge, *A Comprehensive History*	Beveridge, H., A *Comprehensive History of India.*
Bhattacharya, *The East India Company*	Bhattacharya, Sukumar, *The East India Company and the Economy of Bengal.*
Bolts, *Considerations . .*	Bolts, William, *Considerations on Indian Affairs.*
Brome, *Bengal Army . .*	Broome, A., *History of the Rise and Progiess of the Bengal Army.*
Bruce, *Annals . . . .*	Bruce, John, *Annals of the East India Company.*
B.M.P.	*Bengal and Madras Papers.*
B.P.P.	*Bengal Past and Present.*
B.S.C.	Bengal Secret Consultations.

Caraccioli	Caraccioli, C., *The Life of Robert Lord Clive.*
Chaudhuri, *Trade* . .	Chaudhuri, Susil, *Trade and Commercial Organisation in Bengal.*
C.C.C.	*Colonel Clive's Correspondence*
C.P.C.	*Calendar of Persian Correspondence.*
Debrit, *Transactions*	Debrit, J., *Transactions in India*
Dodwell . . .	Dowell, Henry, *Dupleix and Clive.*
Elphinstone, *The Rise* . . .	Elphinstone, M., *The Rise of the British Power in the East.*
Feiling, *Hastings*	Feiling Keith, *Warren Hastings*
Firiminger *Fifth Report* . .	Firminger, W.K., *Fifth Report*
Forrest, *Clive* . .	Forrest, G. *The Life of Lord Clive.*
Foster *The Embassy of Sir Thomas Roe.*	Foster, W., *The Embassy of Sir Thomas Roe to The Court of the Great Mugal.*
F.W,I.H.C.	*Fort William India House Correspondence.*
Gleig's *Clive* . . .	Gleig, G.R., *The Life oj Rabert First Lord Clive.*
Geleig, *Hastings*	Gleig, G.R., *Memoirs of the Life of Right Hon'ble Warren Hastings.*
Hill . . .	Hill, S.C., *Bengal in 1756-57*
Hill, *Three Frenchmen* . .	Hill, S.C., *Three Frenchmen in Bengal.*
Hill, *Abstract* . .	Hill, S.C., *An Abstract of the Early Records in the Foreign Department.*
Holwell, *Importants Facts* . .	Holwell, J.Z., *Important Facts Relating to the E.I. Co.'s Affairs in Bengal.*
Holwell, *Tracts* . . .	Holwell, J.Z., *India Tracts.*

Hunter, *Indian Empire* . . .	Huter, W.W., *The Indian Empire.*
Hunter, *Annals* . . .	Hunter, W.W., *Annals of Rural Bengal.*
Iv's *Voyage* . . .	Ive, Edward, *A Voyage from England to India.*
Law, *Memoire* . . .	Law Jean, *Memoire sur Quelques Affairs De L'Empire Mogol.*
Long, *Unpublished Records*	Long, J., *Selections from the Unpublished Records of the Government.*
L.C.B., Natore . . .	Letter Copy book of the Supervisor of Rajshahi at Natore.
Maitra, *Sirajuddaulah.*	Maitra, A.K., *Sirajuddaulah.*
Malcolm, *Clive* . . .	Malcolm, John, *The Life of Robert Lord Clive.*
Malleson, *Hastings* . . .	Malleson, G.B., *The Life of Warren Hastings.*
Malleson, *Decisive Battles*	Malleson, G.B., *The Decisive Battles of India.*
Majumdar, *Musnud* . . .	Majumdar, P,C., *The Musnud of Murshidabad*
Mill, *British India* . . .	Mill, James, *The History of British India.*
Mukhopadhyay, *Rai- Durlabh*	Mukhopadhyay, S.C,, *The Career of Rajah Durlabhram Mahindra (Rai-Durlabh).*
Mukhopadhyay, *Diwani in Bengal*	Mukhopadhyay, S.C., *Diwani in Bengal, 1765.*
Mukhopadhyay, *The Agrarian Policy*	Mukhopadhyay, S.C., *Th Agrarian Policy of the British in Begal, 1698-1772.*
Original Papers	Vansittart, H., *Original Papers Relative to the Disturbances in Bengal.*

Orme, *Indostan* . . .	Orme, R., *A History of the Military Transactions of the British Nation in Indostan.*
P.C.C.R.M. . . .	Proceedings of the Controlling Council of Revenue at Murshidabad.
P.S.C.	Proceedings of the Select Committee.
Rameshwar Rachanavali . . .	Chakraborty, Panchanan, *Rameshwar Rachanavali.*
Reginald, *Robert Clive* . . .	Reginald, Gatty *Robert Clive and the founding of the British Empire.*
Resident at the Durbar	Copy book of the letter of the Resident at the Durbar.
Riyaz . . .	Salim, Ghulam Husain, *Riyazu-s-salatin.*
Roy, *Mir Jafar* . . .	Roy, A.C., *The Career of Mir Jafar Khan.*
Roy, B.K., *Maharaja Nanda Kumar*	Roy, B.K., *The Career and Achievements of Maharaja Nanda Kumar.*
Sarkar, *History of Bengal*	Sarkar, J. N. *The History of Bengal.*
Scrafton's *Reflections*	Scrafton, Luke, *Reflections on the Government of Indostan.*
Scrafton, *History of Bengal* . . .	Scrafton, L., *A History of Bengal Before and After Plassey.*
Seir . . .	Husain, Ghulam, *The Seir Mutagherin.*
Stewart, *History of Bengal*	Stewart, Charles *History of Bengal.*
S.C.R.	Select Committee Records.
S.C.P. . . .	Select Committee Proceedings.
S.D.R.	Secret Department Records.
S.D.	Secret Department.

Tarikh . . .	Blochmann, H. *Tarikh-i-Mansuri*
Thornton, *British Empire*	Thorntonn, Edward, *The History of the British Empir in India.*
Transition, . . .	Khan, Abdul Majed, *Transition in Bengal.*
Vansittart, *Narrative* . . .	Vansittart, H., *A Narrative of the Transactions in Bengal*
Verelst, *View* . . .	Verelst, Harry, *A View of the Rise, Progress and the Present State of the English Government in Bengal*
Walsh, *Murshidabad*	Walsh, J.H. T., *A History of Murshidabad District.*
Watts, *Memoirs*	Watts, William, *Memoirs of the Revolution in Bengal.*
Wheeler, *Early Records.*	Wheeler, J.T., *Early Records of British India.*
Wilson, *Early Annals* . . .	Wilson, C.R., *The Early Annals of the English in Bengal.*

CONTENTS

1

THE BACKGROUND : AN OUTLINE OF THE EAST INDIA COMPANY'S TRADE IN BENGAL

"Bengal is a kingdom in Asia, very rich, on the gulf of the same name. '[1] It was also known as "The paradise of India" —an epithet found in the writings of Europeans as well as in the official papers of the Mughal Empire up to the middle of the 18th century. Bengal produced cotton and silken cloth of all kinds, most beautiful muslins, opium and saltpetre. The ground produced, in great abundance, very fine corn. Everything necessary for life was found in plenty; "very good beef, excellent mutton and perfect vegetables."[2] Thus its wealth attracted the attention of the foreign travellers, who began to visit the land from the 15th century. Successful navigators of Europe, mostly Italians, Spaniards, Portugese and Dutch, paved the way of direct trade establishment with the East Indies. From them, the English came to know about the wealth of Bengal that became legendary in the medieval period. For many centuries, the English remained satisfied with supplies from Bengal at second hand from some Italian maritime states.[3] Thus they became eager, after the Renaissance, to come to this "Paradise of Nations."

By the middle of the 17th century, the European Companies were able to establish their trade centres and

---

1 Hill, S.C. (Edt.), *Bengal in 1756-57*, Vol. III (London, 1905), p. 215.

2 *Ibid.*, p. 216.

3 Beveridge, Henry, *A Comprehensive History of India, Vol. I*, (Reprint, New Delhi, 1974), p. 257.

factories in Bengal. It was due to the fact that the commodities produced in Bengal were cheap, much cheaper than the ones from other parts of India. The *subah* of Bengal enjoyed political stability which helped the growth and development of trade and commercial pursuits. There had already grown up a number of important ports that suited the purpose of the foreign traders. Among them Satgaon served as the most important port of Bengal from the ancient times till about the middle of the 16th century. It was the chief emporium of trade in the western part of the *subah*. The port used to attract so much foreign trade that it often found its place in foreign travellers' tales. The merchants of Satgaon never left their home town. International trading vessels brought all commodities at their doors. As it was the chief mart of Bengal, Satgaon attracted merchants from different parts of India and abroad. As such, it became the royal port of Bengal till the emergence of Hugli in the middle of the 16th century. Hugli was the chief emporium of Portugese trade since 1537.[4]

But with the passage of time, the external trade of Bengal deserted Satgaon and was diverted to Hugli, where, though there were limited activities of a few Arab and Indian traders, actually the major portion of its overseas trade were controlled by the Portuguese. Even in inland trade, Hugli took its place officially in 1632 as the royal port. This change of fortune aroused the jealousy of the Mughals at Satgaon. The Hugli port developed with much rapidity under the Portuguese after its foundation by them in 1537. It soon rose to the position of the richest trading port in Bengal. But the glorious days of the Portuguese in Hugli did not last long. In 1632, Qasim Khan—the General of Emperor Shan Jahan, defeated the Portuguese at Hugli, since the latter had so long molested the Muslims.[5] The Portuguese were expelled from Hugli and it

4 Chaudhuri, Susil, *Trade and Commercial Organisation in Bengal*, 1650-1720 (Calcutta, 1975) pp. 6-7.

5 Salim, Ghulam Husain, *Riyazu-S-Salatin* (Eng. Trans. Reprint, Delhi 1975), p. 410 f.n. But, G.B. Malleson in his book *The Life of Warren Hastings* (London, 1894), p. 10) wrongfully tells us that Hugli was captured in 1637.

became the royal port of Bengal, where the Mughal authority was firmly established. This blow was too severe for the Portuguese to revive; and, as a consequence, their pre-eminent position in Bengal was lost for ever. Even though the Portuguese trade declined, the trade in Hugli flourished unabated. Soon after, the Dutch and the English East India Companies started their trade directly with Bengal and established their factories in Hugli in the middle of the 17th century.

The indigenous merchants of Bengal had a long and glorious tradition in overseas trade that remained alive upto the 17th century. They had traded with different Asian countries. They were most powerful and influential, and frustrated the first attempt of the Dutch to open up their trade with Bengal in 1632, after the fall of the Portuguese. As a matter of fact, the Bengal trade was most tempting before the foreign traders for its cheapness as well as for the political stability in the region. It was against this background, that the English East India Company became tempted to establish their trade in Bengal.

Many English attempts had been made to find out a passage to the East Indies from 1576. In 1577, Sir Francis Drake circumnavigated the globe and on his way home, touched at Ternate; the king of that island agreed to supply England the commodities that was locally produced. But the first modern Englishman known to have visited India was Thomas Stephens in 1579. His letters to his father were said to have created great enthusiasm and interest in England to trade directly with India.[6] This enthusiasm reached its pitch after the accession of Queen Elizabeth, when the English had their own agents in different parts of the Levant. Soon after in 1581, she granted a charter of exclusive privileges to a mercantile association which assumed the name of Levant Company. This Company did not remain satisfied by confining its connections to the ports of Levant only, but extended them far into the interior. They sent out many

---

6 Hunter, W.W., *The Indian Empire* (Third Edn., Delhi, 1973), p. 427.

agents whose travels furnished valuable information with regard to Indian trade.[7]

Some years passed before any British expedition could reach the East, due mainly to some political events. Philip II of Spain had fitted out his boasted Armada and Queen Elizabeth, in her heroic efforts, tried to defeat him. Accordingly in October, 1589, the very year after the invincible Armada was defeated, a body of English merchants, presented a memorial to the Lords in Council, in the name of "divers merchants" for the royal permission to send three ships, on a voyage to India. They prayed for permission after a rapid survey of the Portuguese settlements in the East. This expedition was the first of its kind in which India was its immediate destination, though its object was not trade, but perhaps to plunder. The ships were fitted out in April, 1591, less than eighteen months from the date of its application. But before they could reach the Cape of Good Hope, disease had made such ravages that one vessel had to be sent back home with the sick. The other two had not long doubled the Cape, when the principal ship was lost in a storm. In the remaining vessel, Captain James Lancaster sailed to the West Indies, where he lost his ship and returned home with great difficulty.[8]

While a sense of despair prevailed in the minds of the English, the Dutch sent, in 1595, four ships to trade with India by the Cape of Good Hope. This created jealousy in the minds of the English, who, in September, 1599, formed an association, raised a fund amounting to £ 30,133,65,8 d, shared by 101 adventurers.[9] It was agreed to apply to the Queen for a warrant to fit out three ships and also for a charter of privilege of Indian trade. A committee of fifteen was chosen to manage the affair.[10] The subscribers, known

7 Beveridge, *A Comprehensive History*, Vol. I, p. 258.

8 Mill, James, *The History of British India*, Vol. II (Reprint, New Delhi, 1972), p. 14.

9 *Ibid.* Also, Beveridge, *A Comprehensive History* Vol. I, p. 275.

10 This marked the foundation of the Court of Directors.

as the adventurers, became impatient and presented a memorial before the Queen.

Towards the end of the year 1600, the adventurers renewed their efforts. They went on preparing post haste for an Indian voyage, though the consent of the government was still under consideration. Meanwhile, the government directed the adventurers for the employment of Sir Edward Michalbourne in the expedition. On 8th of October, five ships were provided. Captain James Lancaster, whose difficult return from a predatory expedition had raised his stock high, was chosen to command the fleet. Meanwhile, the Queen was convinced by the zeal of the adventurers, and on the 31st of December, 1600, the English East India Company was incorporated by Royal Charter, under the title of "The Governor and Company of Merchants of London trading to the East Indies." The Queen granted this charter to the Company for a period of fifteen years, empowering them to trade in those places of India not claimed by other European nations, to punish the offenders of Her Majesty's subjects who might engage in the Indian trade without a licence, and to purchase lands from the Indians for their factories.[11]

In the early years of its trade, the English East India Company, it is seemed, had no intention of beginning their trade direct with Bengal. It was due to the apprehension that the Portuguese, who had become the absolute masters of the Bengal ports, might act against the English in opening up trade in that *subah*. In 1615, Sir Thomas Roe was sent to India for strengthening the English alliance with the Mughals. Roe was invested with power to act as an ambassador from the king of England, James I. In September 1615, Roe arrived at Surat. Before Roe should go to the Court of Jahangir, Captain Keelingurged him for the necessity of opening up overland trade with Bengal.[12] But it seems that Roe was not very much enthusiastic about establishing maritime trade with Bengal.

11 Elphinstone, M., *The Rise of the British Power in the East* (London, 1887), p. 30.

12 Foster, W., *The Embassy of Sir Thomas Roe to the Court of the Great Moghul, 1615-1619.* (London, 1899), p. 79.

Sir Thomas Roe betook himself to the Imperial Court at Ajmer and opened negotiations. He had the first audience at Court on 16 January 1616, where he was graciously received. At the court, Roe lost no opportunity of furthering the interests of the Company and the Emperor Jahangir also replied graciously[13] to the letter of James I. Roe obtained a permission from Jahangir[14], authorising the English to trade in Bengal. The importance of this permission thus granted, appears to have got no immediate appreciation, for the English were little inclined to settle a factory in Bengal. It remained pending for the time being and the Surat Council wrote to the Company on 2 November, 1616, that though they had been permitted to trade with Bengal, due to the want of small ships, no such venture could be fitted out for that purpose.[15]

The Surat-based English merchants were, however, eager to procure a *farman* for Bengal and particularly to establish a factory at Piply and requested Roe to procure a *farman* to that effect. Roe, however, failed to obtain a *farman*, though he was given a promise by Asaf Khan. Out of disgust, Roe wrote a letter to the Court of Committees on 14 February 1618: "Bengala hath no ports but such as the Portingalls possess for small shipping; it will vent nothing of yours".[16]

Though the English Company failed to establish their first foothold in Bengal, they never gave up the idea altogether. Gradually they felt the necessity settling a factory in Bengal for the pressing necessity of procuring more quantities of calicoes for their home markets. The immediate attention of the Surat Council fell on Patna, a city of large infiuence. In 1620, the East India Company had despatched an agent to visit and report upon the facilities which Bengal offered for commerce.

---

13 Bolts, William, *Considerations on Indian Affairs* (Second Edn., London, MD CCLXXII), p. 57.

14 Roe obtained not a treaty or grant of privileges that he proposed, but limited trade privileges for the English.

15 Chaudhuri, *Trade*, p. 13.

16 Foster, *The Embassy of Sir Thomas Roe*, p. 434.

The English agent, Robert Hughes, reached Patna on 3 July. On his arrival, he realised the need of establishing a factory at Patna but at the same time, advised the Surat Council to send an assistant and with more money to be invested for goods, within a short time. John Parker joined Hughes in September and soon they started their business. Within a few days the English agents realised the necessity for the establishment of a factory at Patna. But the English factors at Agra gave some discouraging reports that although the raw materials were cheaper at Patna, when the cost of transport and charges of the factory were added, the total cost rose very high. Though Hughes and Parker suggested that the factors should be sent to Murshidabad where silk could be procured in great quantity, the Company became doubtful whether it would not be better to buy them at a higher rate at Agra, nearer the seat of political power, than to maintain a factory at Patna. These considerations, led the Company to withdraw its agents from Patna. In March 1621, the house occupied by the English was burnt and so the enthusiasm of the factors was cooled down. The Surat Council, however, directed Hughes to proceed to Agra,leaving Parker at Patna. These twin developments forced the decision promptly to close the Patna accounts, and finding that the situation was becoming worse instead of better, they had to quit the place. Thus the first attempt at establishing a factory in Bengal resulted in failure.[17]

The famine of 1630 in Masulipattam and Madras, caused a dearth of cloth, which again attracted the attention of the factors of the Bengal, the only other possible source of supply. From this time onwards, there were constant attempts to establish factories in Bengal, to obtain silk and cotton from this unexplored region. The famine brought the Company into the coastal trade. In 1633, the Masulipattam factors thought it a necessity to obtain a liberal supply of cloth in Bengal and to that end despatched eight Englishmen by

---

17 Temple, R.C. *Documents Relating to First Commercial Mission to Patna*, 1620-21. (1914), pp. 83-230. Also Malleson, G.B., *The Life of Warren Hastings*, (London, 1894), pp. 9-10.

country boat to the coast of Orissa.[18] This attempt was made in pursuance of the more ambitious object of setting up of a petmanent factory in Bengal.

The endeavour made in 1633 was not wholly unsuccessful. The Englishmen, headed by Ralph Cartwright reached Hariharpur in Orissa. A few days later, they went to the fort of Barabati in Cuttack to meet the Nawab of Orissa, Aga Muhammed Zaman. The Nawab received the Englishmen in the audience-hall, turned his head to Cartwright and "offered his foot to the English merchant to kiss," which was twice refused, but at last complied with. The Nawab then granted the English a *parwana* to trade and to build houses for their factories.[19] The Englishman came down to Hariharpur with much hope,summoned all the persons that were with them and started to set up a factory there. Thus the earliest factory of the Company was established on 14 May, 1633 at Hariharpur on the Mahanadi delta.[20] In the same month Cartwright founded a factory at Balasore.[21]

When the English were in the midst of both hope and despair, it is said that a fortuitous development suddenly gave them some privileges of trade in Bengal. In 1644[22] Jahanara,

---

18 Firminger, W.K., *Fifth Report* (Reprint, Calcutta, 1962), p. 65.

19 *Riyaz*, p. 410 f.n.

20 *Ibid.* Also Chaudhuri, *Trade*, p. 22. But Charles Stewart, in his *History of Bengal* (First Indian Reprint, Delhi, 1971), p. 244, wrongly states that it was at Piply, the English established their first factory in Bengal.

21 *Ibid.* Also Bhattacharya, Sukumar, *The East India Company and the Economy of Bengal* (Calcutta, 1969), p. 10.

22 Writers have widely differed about the year of this accident. But Bruce, who had access to all the official papers, gives the date in 1644, which seems mostly correct. (Vide, Bruce's *Annals of the East India Company*", Vol. I, p. 406). Accordingly, most of the writers followed the date of Bruce ; such as Malleson in *The Decisive Battles of India*, p. 10, Broome in his *History of the Rise and Progress of the Bengal Army*, Vol. I, p.4, etc. On the other hand Orme in *A History of the Military Transactions of the British Nation in Indostan*, Vol. II p. 8, gives the date as 1636, Wheeler in *Early Records of British India*, p. 149, fixes it at 1640, and Stewart in *The History of Bengal*, p. 251, gives the date in 1636.

a daughter of Emperor Shah Jahan met with a serious accident; her clothes had caught fire and she was severely burnt before the flames could be extinguished. When the Indian doctors or *hakims* could not cure her, an English Surgeon Dr. Gabriel Boughton immediately hastened to Agra and fortunately cured the young princess. This success rendered Boughton a great favourite with the Emperor. When the Emperor desired him to name his own reward, he did not seek for any private emolument but requested that his nation might have the liberty to trade in Bengal, free from all duties and to establish factories in that province. The boon was granted and a *farman* was issued. Boughton was also furnished with the means of travelling across the country to Bengal. He immediately hastened to Rajmahal.[23]

The boon was granted to Boughton at a time when the Company's agents in India were in a fix—whether they should continue the Bengal trade or abandon it. They referred the matter to the Court of Committees in London for decision. The Company finally resolved that due to the unrewarding condition in the south, the Company's trade in Bengal should be stepped up. Accordingly, the ship *Lioness* was sent to Bengal under the command of Captain Brookhaven, who was given almost a *carte blanche*: "setting a factory at Hugli with acquisition of the Prince's *farman* for free trade, was wholly referred to the same Captain's discretion."[24]

Brookhaven, after reaching Balasore, directed James Bridgemen and other merchants in December 1650, to go to Bengal for establishing a factory at Hugli. In these instructions, the Captain laid stress on obtaining a *nishan* from Prince

---

23 Wheeler, J.T., *Early Records of British India* (New Imp. London. 1972), p. 129. Also Orme, R., *A History of the Military Transactions of the British Nation in Indostan*, Vol. II (Indian Reprint, New Delhi, 1971), p. 8. Also, Stewart, *The History of Bengal*, p. 244. Also Broome, A., *History of the Rise and Progress of the Bengal Army*, Vol. I (London, 1850), p. 4.

24 Yule, H. (Edt.), *Diary of William Hedges*, Vol. III (London, 1887-89), p. 187.

Shuja for free trade in Bengal.[25] During this time, Boughton arrived in the court of Prince Shuja at Rajmahal. The circumstance rendered him favourite with Prince Shuja also.[26] The Prince, with his liberal and grateful disposition, afforded full assistance to Boughton in establishing trade in Bengal, and protected English traders during the whole period of his government of Bengal till 1657. However, these privileges granted by Shuja to Boughton, were personal and not general to the English Company. Later John Beard, the Company's agent in Bengal (1684-85), stated; "He (Prince Shuja) offers Mr. Boughton that if he would trade, he should be free from paying custom and all other duties and gave Mr. Boughton two *nishans* to that end."[27] Thus, it is clear that the *nishan* of Shuja was personal to Boughton. However, Bridgemen arrived at Rajmahal within a short time. He was introduced to the Prince by Boughton; the Prince received him with great cordiality. It was James Bridgemen, who secured the first *nishan* in August 1651, for the Company's trade in Bengal,[28] founded upon a *farman* procured by Boughton from Shah Jahan.[29] The English took immediate

25 Brookhaven's instruction about the necessity of a *nishan* from Shah Shuja for free trade in Bengal made the question doubtful whether the company at all obtained the privileges of free trade by Shah Jahan's *farman*.

26 Broome, A., *History of the Rise and Progress of the Beneal Army* Vol. I (London, 1850), p. 5. Also, Nolan, E.H., *The History of the British Empire in India and the East*, Vol. II (London) p. 13.

27 Factory Records, Fort St. George, Vol. 30, f. 36 (quoted in Chaudhuri, *Trade*, pp. 29-30.

28 Yule, H. (Edt)., *Diary of William Hedges,* Vol. III (London, 1887-89), pp. 159-160. It is probable that it was due to Boughton's influence that the English obtained a *nishan* from shuja, and by the terms of this *nishan*, the English were obliged to pay a *peshkash* of three thousand rupees and permitted to trade duty-free.

29 The English claimed that the original *farman* of Shah Jahan was lost by Weldegrave in 1654 on his journey from Bengal to Madras. Thus the Indian historians express doubt whether any *farman* for Bengal trade was at all obtained from Shah Jahan.—Huq Mazharul, *The East India Company's land Policy and Commerce in Bengal* (Dacca, 1964) p. 4. Also, Mukhopadhyay, S.C., *The Agrarian Policy of the British in Bengal* (Allahabad, 1987), p. 2

advantage of this, and settled a factory in Hugli in 1651 which laid the foundation of their commerce in Bengal. The foundation of the Engiish factory at Hugli was of great importance to the immediate interests of the East India Company. But during the unsettled condition of Bengal, due to the war of succession among the sons of Shah Jahan, the French established their factory at Chandernagore, the Dutch at Chinsurah and the Danes at Sreerampore. The English also prepared themselves for defence. Besides Hugli they had established agencies at Patna and Kasimbazar.[30] A little later, in 1668, a new factory was opened at Dacca, then the capital of Bengal, which was the main market for cotton and cotton goods in the *subah*. Soon after, two factories at Malda and Rajmahal were also established.[31]

During the time of Aurangzeb, Mir Jumla occupied Rajmahal and settled the western part of Bengal. Dacca soon became his headquarters[32] as he became the *subahdar* of Bengal. It became the usual practice of the Company to procure a *parwana* for custom-free trade from each succeeding *subahdar* of Bengal. Hence, during the time of the Mir, they represented about the loss of Shah Jahan's *farman*, that gave them such a concession. But while the Dutch offered help to Mir Jumla against Shuja, the English Company followed a policy of 'wait and see.' Thus, the *subahdar* levied a duty of 4% on all English exports. In the upshot by the end of November, 1659, the English trade in Bengal was brought practically to a standstill position.[33] However, on the representation of Trevisa.[34] Mir Jumla gave the Company a *parwana* in 1660 for duty-free trade.

But this state of things did not continue for long. A dispute soon arose between the government of Mir Jumla and

---

30 Malleson, *Hastings*, p. 12. The factory at Kasimbazar was established in 1658.

31 Bruce, *Annals*, Vol. II, p 451.

32 Stewart, *History of Bengal*, p. 286,

33 Sarkar, J.N. (Edt.), *The History of Bengal* (Patna) 1973), p. 383.

34 The English agent in Bengal

the English Company as the latter refused to pay Rs. 3,000 demanded in 1658 by the Governor of Hugli in lieu of annual customs. It was the first open conflict with the Company, and the c:ux of the matter was that the new *subahdar* had an extensive private trade of his own. He had business transaction with the Company too. Highly irritated at this, Mir Jumla stopped the English boats, laden into saltpetre and much injured their trade at Patna.[35] As a retaliative measure, the Engllsh agent at Hugli, resolved to take the remedy into his own hands, seized a country vessel in 1661, belonging to Mir Jumla. Thus,when Mir Jumla threatened to retaliate upon their inland agencies as well as their factory at Hugli, the English agent, Trevisa, apologised and returned boats seized to the subahdar Mir Jumla. But this dispute marked the beginning of a new chapter in the history of the Company. The English now began to think seriously how best they could protect their trade in Bengal, irrespective of the favour of local officials.

After the death of Mir Jumla in 1663-64, the governmence of Bengal was conferred on Shaista Khan, a great magnate of the Imperial Court, and a maternal uncle of Emperor Aurangzeb.[36] The Muslim historians believe that during the government of Shaista Khan in Bengal, tle commerce of the English continued to flourish. But on the other hand, the Company's officials complained that Shaista Khan frequently stopped the English trade, seized on their saltpetre and instead of the annual payment of three thousand rupees, he exacted from the English the same duties as were paid by the Hindus, that he compelled the English soldiers to attend on him in his war against Arakan and that his officers were guilty of a thousand exactions. The fact was that, like Mir Jumla, Shaista Khan

35 Stewart, *History of Bengal*, p. 286.

36 Shaista Khan was the son of the celebrated *wazir* Asaf Jah and the nephew of the Empress Nur Jahan. He had not then recovered from the wounds that he had received at Poona from Shivaji. Thus he was permitted to govern the *subah* of Bengal through his deputy, Daud Khan, and did not proceed to Bengal till 1663-64 He held the *subahdari* of Bengal till 1677 and again, after two years' gap, from 1679 to 1689,

also tried to monopolise the saltpetre trade and even once directed the English Company not to sell any imported goods to anyone except him, at a lower price which is to be decided by his agents. Though he confirmed Prince Shuja's *nishan* yet the order was little observed in practice.[37] So in May 7, 1677, the Governor of Madras, wrote to Shaista Khan that if the latter continued his practice of oppression to the English and that, if the English were not better treated, they would entirely withdraw from Bengal.[38]

So long as the Company's trade was small and adequate bribes were forthcoming from them, the Mughal officials did not interfere much in the affairs of the Company. But after the final victory of Aurangzeb over his rivals and the restoration of Charles II in England, the English trade in Bengal began to increase. By 1680 the Company's export from Bengal had risen to £ 1,50,000 and the next year to £ 230,000[39] The factors of the English Company on the resignation of Shaista Khan from his first *subahdari*, and during his absence from Bengal (1677-79), had sent an agent to the Imperial Court to procure a *farman*. The agent after much expense and perseverance, succeeded only in obtaining the Emperor's vague *farman* and returned to Hugli on 8 July, 1680.[40]

In obedience to the regulations of Aurangzeb, Shaista Khan enforced the *jiziya* or poll tax on the Hindus. At Hugli, the Mughal officials demanded payment of this tax from the Christians as well,[41] but when the English and the Dutch

---

37 Chaudhuri, *Trade*, p 36.

38 Stewart, *History of Bengal*, pp. 301-302. Also, Wheeler, *Early Records*, p. 161.

39 Sarkar, *History of Bengal*, p. 383. The money was distributed as follows: £ 140,000 to Kasimbazar, £ 14,500 to Patna, £ 32,000 to Balasore, £ 15,000 to Malda and £ 12,000 to Hugli.—see also Beveridge, *A Comprehensive History*, v. I, p. 423.

40 Stewart, *History of Bengal*, p. 308.

41 At Surat the Englisn Company paid a duty of 30 percent on its goods and thus a similar duty was also claimed in Bengal.—Elphinstone, *The Rise*, p. 56.

refused to pay it, they were subjected to regular insults. William Hedges, the newly appointed Chief found at Hugli "several affronts, insolences and abuses" daily put up on the English by Balchand,[42] that became unbearable. The English agent and his council at Hugli tried to get redress of their grievances, and "it was agreed that the only expedient now left was for the Agent to go himself in person to the Nawab and *Diwan* at Dacca,"[43] and to lay a complaint before Sha'sta Khan so as to arrive at some definite adjustments concerning the customs. At the capital, Hedges spent some six weeks in negotiations with the *subahdar* and returned to Hugli with his supposed successes.[44]

But in no time his expectations proved illusory. The Mughal officials at Hugli continued to follow the same mode of oppressions, by seizing the Company's boats and their goods.

The affairs of the Company had, for some years, been much disturbed by many other tantrums as well, and so, the home authorities in Fngland, di-ected their agent at Hugli to try to obtain some permanent place of defence and it was decided that the English agent should apply to Shaista Khan or, even if necessary, to Aurangzeb, for some better place within the *subah*, that could be satisfactorily fortified.[45] Accordingly, Gyfford, the English agent at Hugli, made an application to Shaista Khan, for permission to erect a fortification on the bank of the Ganges, to prevent the ships of those called 'interlopers' from entering the rivers. But Shaista Khan did not want to see the increase of power of the foreigners and hence, he not only refused the requests but ordered the English Company to pay 3½ per cent duties on all their imports, instead of the annual payment of three thousand rupees.[46]

---

42 The Customs Collector at Hugli.
43 Sarkar, *History of Bengal*, p. 383.
44 Firminger, *Fifth Report*, p. 73.
45 Broome, *Bengal Army*, v. I, p. 11.
46 Stewart, *History of Bengal*, p. 311.

At last the English Company lost all patience with the Mughal government and came to the conclusion that if their trade in Bengal was to prosper, they must take recourse to arms against the exactions and harassment by the *subahdar* and his officials. In a letter written on 21 December, 1683, the Court observed:"Some of our captains tell us there is no way to mend our condition but by seizing and fortifying one of these pleasant Islands in the Ganges about the Braces"; but "some others have pronounced us the seizure upon a Toune called Chittogong in the easternmost mouth of the River Ganges, upon or near the coast of Rackan (Arakan).[47]

The Court of Directors obtained permission from king James II to retaliate their injuries by declaring war against Shaista Khan and Aurangzeb. Job Charnock.[48] who became the English agent at Hugli in 1685, received previons notice of these intentions and was directed to be ready with all the English subjects, to join with the English army at Balasore. It was also decided to proceed and surprise the city of Chittagong, "where they were immediately to fortify themselves."[49]

This decision of the court for an open conflict with the Mughals in Bengal was the outcome of a number of complaints it had received from the Company's officials in India. The first advocate of this policy was Gerald Aungier, who became the governor of Bombay in 1669, and recommended a vigorous policy to ensure the stability of the Company's trade in India. The advice of Aungier was acceptable to the Company. The decision was further strengthened by the recommendation of Josiah Child, who later on became the governor of Bombay. It was resolved to take resort to a "forward policy" and Hedges, the then English agent in

---

47 Quoted by Forrest, G , in *The Life of Lord Clive*, Vol. I (London 1918) p. 281.

48 In 1658, Job Charnock was made the first member of the Council at Kasimbazar and in 1679, he was promoted Chief of Kasimbazar factory.

49 Orme, *Indostan*, v. II, p. 12.

Bengal, urged the Company to fortify settlements of the protection of the English trade. Thus the Court of Directors promptly fitted out a fleet of ten ships, the command of which was given to Captain Nicholson, elevated to the rank of Vice-Admiral and instructed him to transfer the command of the land forccs to Charnock, the Company's agent in Bengal, now given the title of Admiral.[50]

Nicholson was also instructed to proceed to Balasore and after joining with the Company's forces, he was to continue his journey to Chittagong. In order to facilitate this enterprise, he was directed to enter into an alliance with the king of Arakan, with whom, it was supposed, the Mughals had rivalry, and in this case, he would readily join with the English. Nicholson was also, at the same time, instructed to enter into alliance with the Hindu Chiefs or *zamindars* in the neighbourhood of Chittagong, to collect revenues and to render Chittagong a place of arms for the English on the eastern side of Bengal.[51] It was decided that after the capture of chittagong, the English army would proceed to Dacca and would demand from the *subahdar* the privileges of Bengal trade for the Company.[52]

Of the fleet, delayed by storms and other difficulties on the way, only three could reach on the Bay of Bengal. Instead of proceeding to Chittagong, the fleet entered on the western bank of the Ganges and anchored at Hugli in September 1686. Job Charnock had received reinforcements of 400 soldiers from Madras and had raised a second company of Portuguese infantry, known in those days as *topasses*. After the arrival of the English army, Charnock showed every determination to carry out the orders that he had received from England.[53]

The arrival of such a force at Hugli, immediately roused the suspicion and excitement of the *subahdar*, Shaista Khan.

---

50 Melleson, *Hastings*, p. 12.

51 Stewart, *History of Bengal*, pp. 312-313.

52 Beveridge, *A Comprehensive History*, v. I, pp. 426-427.

53 Malleson, *Hastings*, p. 13. Also. Stewart, *History of Bengal*, p. 314.

He had "concentrated 3,000 foot and 300 horses" at Hugli to guard the town. The command of these troops had been bestowed on the *faujdar* of Hugli. Meanwhile, to gain time, the *subahdar* offered to compromise the differences with the English and to submit the dispute to arbitrators appointed by mutual consent.[54] But actually this was a ruse for gaining time to call up reinforcements.

Shaista khan became more angered than alarmed by the news of the first English resistance and retaliation in Bengal. He ordered confiscation of all the English factories in Bengal, particularly, Patna, Dacca, Kasimbazar and Malda. At the same time, he ordered a very considerable body of his army, both infantry and cavalry, to proceed immediately to Hugli, to drive the English out of Bengal.[55]

In the face of a large-scale army movement. Job Charnock and members of his council did not think it prudent to remain in an unfortified position. They were afraid, the attack might overpower them. The English took with them all the stores and movable property of the Company and with all the ships of the fleet moved down from Hugli on 20 December, to a village called Sutanuti.[56] At Sutanuti, Charnock began to construct some huts for temporary residence.

From Sutanuti, Charnock continued his negotiation with Shaista Khan but instead, the latter sent a considerable army under Abdul Samad Khan, to destroy the rising settlements. Abdul Samad was instructed to expel the English from Bengal or to destroy them.[57] As successful defence was impossible, Charnock moved from Sutanuti on 9 February, with his stores and garrisons to Hijli, a low island, separated from the main land by a narrow channel. At Hijli, the English established themselves with their men and guns. On their way to

54 Stewart, *History of Bengal*, p. 314.

55 Stewart, *History of Bengal*, p. 315.

56 Sutanuti was situated, at the present site of Calcutta from the Mint to Sobha Bazar.

57 Malleson, *Hastings*, p. 14

Hijli, the English had already captured the Imperial Fort of Tanna.[58]

Even at Hijli, Charnock and his party were pursued by Abdul Samad. In the middle of May the latter arrived with 12,000 soldiers. He at once erected batteries where the channel was narrowest. His heavy batteries opened fire across the Rasulpur river on the English. on 28 May a considerable portion of the Mughal army, consisting of 700 cavalry with 200 gunners, crossed the river before Hijli, and then seized and burnt the town. The deadly malaria of the place also helped Abdul Samad. Among the English soldiers, two hundred had already died of the disease and only a hundred, weakened by fever, survived.[59] Among the forty English officers, only five survived. But though the English were reduced by disease and their provisions ran out, they tenacio-usly continued the fight. At last the English negotiated for peace and on 11 June, they evacuated Hijli with their artillery.[60]

When the English accepted the terms of Abdul Samad, hostilities ceased, and an armistice was concluded between them. Not wishing to return to Hugli without the ships of war, the English now hastened to Uluberia. There the Chief began to construct docks and build houses; but after residing there for a period of three months, he found the locality inconvenient. He applied for and obtained the permission to return to Sutanuti.[61] in November, 1687. At Sutanuti, Charnock remained for about a year. He saw a new prospect for the English at Sutanuti and thus on 27 June, 1688, he

58 Modern Garden Reach facing Matia Burj.

59 Stewart, *History of Bengal*, p. 317. Stewart humorously observes: "For in three months more than half of the European troops died, and the remainder were only fit subjects for an hospital".

60 Sarkar, *History of Bengal*, p. 385. The fight was indecisive. And though Firminger observes in the *Fifth Report* (p. 75) that the English went out of the forth with their "drums beating and flags flying", it seems unbelievable. There is no record to prove that the English became victorious.

61 Broome, *Bengal Army*, v. I, pp. 18-19.

observed in his letter to the governor of Madras : "We are in great hopes of obtaining Chuttanuttee to settle in with three or four other adjacent townes which doubtless may be in some years so improved as to be very profitable to the Right Honoble Comp and possibility may be gradually improved to a considerable strenth."[62]

When the intelligence of the failure of the English factors in Bengal reached England, the court became much dissatisfied with the conduct of their servants in India and threw the whole blame on them. The Bengal officials of the Company were censured for their timid conduct and were charged for pursuing their own selfish interest, without paying any regard to the honour of the king of England as well as the Company. The Home Government of the Company threatened them with expulsion from service, if their main object of conducting the war should not be accomplished. The home authority, therefore, despatched a large ship, called *Defence*, under the command of Captain Heath to Bengal, fully armed, carrying on board 160[63] Soldiers. Captain Heath arrived at Sutanuti, in October, 1688. His brief was either to prosecute the war with vigour or to bring away the Company's servants at Madras.[64] Though Charnock asked him not to recommence war in Bengal, Heath did not listen to him; instead he directed all the Company's servants to embark at Sutanuti and on 8 November, started for Balasore.[65] From Balasore, Heath started for chittagong and reached there on 17 January, 1689.[66]

Heath intimated his landing at Chittagong to the Mughal *subahdar* of Bengal and informed him that he wanted to assist the *subahdar* against the king of Arakan; thus he tried to gain time for an attack on Chittagong.[67] He then starred negotiation with the king of Arakan, who, it was supposed, for his

62 Quoted in Forrest, *Clive*, v. I, p. 288.

63 Quoted in Beveridge, *A Comprehensive History*, y. I, p. 430.

64 Stewart, *History of Bengal* p. 319.

65 *Ibid.*, pp. 319-320.

66 *Ibid.*, p. 321. Also, Firminger, *Fifth Report*. p. 76.

67 Firminger, *Fifth Report*, p. 76.

enmity with the Mughals, might grant the Company a locality in his territory. Heath thus applied to the king for the same purpose, but the latter, however, had no use for the services of the English. So when Heath did not get any reply, after waiting for 15 days, he became disgusted with his new ally, and without waiting for the result of his proposals, sailed away with the whole of his fleet to Madras.[68] Heath arrived at Madras on 4 March, carrying with him the English factors in Bengal, Charnock and his council. There he apologised to the Governor for not having achieved anything.[69]

The war had been fought by the Company not only in Bengal but in the south also under John Child. These exasperated Aurangzeb and the latter's vendetta exposed the Company s establishment to ruin in every part of India. The Emperor, in consequence, directed his commanders to expel the English from his dominions, and to seize or destroy their property everywhere.[70] In consequence of these orders Shaista Khan seized all the English property in Bengal and arrested the Company's agent at Dacca.[71]

By 1689, the Company' forces had been completely defeated and hence they sued for peace and pardon from Aurangzeb. For this purpose they sent from Bombay two English representatives, George Weldan and Abraham Navarro, to the Court of Delhi, where they were brought before Aurangzeb's presence"with their hands tied up by a sash," and were obliged to prostrate themselves.[72] Aurangzeb, However, realised the utility and importance of the English commerce in Bengal and "it was understood well enough that the British Commerce was productive of gains which the imperial treasury

---

68 *Ibid.* Also Stewart, *History of Bengal*, pp. 321-322. Also, Beveridge, *A Comprehensive History*, v. I, p. 431.

69 Stewart, *History of Bengal*, p. 322.

70 *Ibid.*, p. 322.

71 *Ibid*, Others say that the offilciating *subahdar* of Bangal, Bahadur Khan, after the departure of Shaista Khan, committed this act.

72 Bolts, *Considerations*, p. 59. Also, Gupta, B.K. *Sirajuddaullah and the East India Company* (Leiden, 1966), p. 5.

could ill-afford to forego."[73] Thus, The Emperor informed Ibrahim Khan, the new *subahdar* of Bengal that the former had been pleased to pardon the "irregularities" of the English and hence, directed the latter to invite the English to return to Bengal.[74] The Emperor also directed him that after their return to Bengal, they should not be molested but allowed to continue their trade as in former days.[75]

In consequence of the permission from the Emperor, Ibrahim Khan immediately wrote a letter to the Mardras Council, inviting the English to return to Bengal,[76] and to re-establish all the Company's factories. He also assured them fair treatment, promising that the English would be placed as "the most favoured foreign nation.[77] As a result of this invitation, Charnock with his whole party, attended by some soldiers, returned on 24 August 1690 to Sutanuti, where he was received by the *faujdar* of Hugli with much cordiality.[78] Meanhile, the Emperor forwarded to Ibrahim Khan the following *farman*, dated 23 April, 1690: "You must understand, that it has been the good fortune of the English to repent them of their irregular past proceedings; and they; not being in their former greatness, have, by their *vackeels*, petitioned for their lives, and a pardon for their faults, which, out of my extraordinary favour towards them, have accordingly, been granted [79]

But the Emperor granted them the *farman* only when the English promised to pay a fine of Rs. 1,50,000, to restore all plundered goods and behave themselves no more in such a way. The Emperor thus accepted their submission but granted

73 Firminger, *Fifth Report*, p. 76.

74 Stewart. *History of Bengal*, p. 325.

75 Firminger, *Fifth Report*, p. 76.

76 Wheeler, *Early Records*, p. 162, Also, Firminger, *Fifth Report*, p. 76 Also, Sarkar, *History of Bengal*, p. 386. Also, Roy, N.N., *Murshidabader Itihas* (in Bengali, Calcutta, 1309 B.S.), p. 286.

77 Stewart, *History of Bengal*, p. 325.

78 *Ibid*, p. 326. Also, Firminger, *Fifth Report*, p. 76. The 24th day of August is known as the foundation day of the city of Calcutta.

79 Quoted in Stewart. *History of Bengal*, Appen. No. VI, pp. 540-541.

them the *farman* on condition that "Mr. Child, who did the disgrace, be turned out and expelled."[80] Next year, on 10 February, 1691, an *hasb-ul-hukm* was issued under the seal of the *wazir*, Asad Khan, authorising the English to continue their trade in Bengal, on an annual payment of Rs. 3,000, in lieu of all dues.[81]

Though, so much freedom of trade had been granted to the English its agents were still oppressed by the lower-order officers of the Bengal *subahdar*. Thus the Company began to think about obtaining the jurisdiction of the *subahdar* of Bengal. For this reason, they established a factory at Sutanuti and tried to acquire some places, adjacent to it.[82] This opportunity, all of a sudden, came at last due to an event that disturbed the tranquillity of the *subah* of Bengal.

A rebellion broke out in Bengal during 1695-96, headed by sobha Singh—a *zamindar* of Midnapore, against the *zamindar* of Burdwan, Krishna Ram Roy. It is said that in 1694, Krishna Ram Roy, obtained the *zamindari* right of Burdwan by a *farman* from Emperor Aurangzeb. He promised to pay all the taxes, including the *jiziya*, which became the cause of dissatisfaction among his Hindu subjects.[83] Besides this, Sobha singh had some personal causes of dispute with the *zamindar* of Burdwan. However, in this campaign of Sobha Singh, some of the Hindu *taluqdars* and Rajahs of the adjoining districts, like Raghunath Singh—the *taluqdar* of Chandrakona and Gopal Singh—the Rajah of Bishnupur also joined with him.[84] The party was further strengthened by joining with them, Rahim Khan—an Afghan Chief of Orissa.

---

80 *Riyaz*, p. 411. f.n.

81 Sarkar, *History of Bengal*. p. 392. Also Stewart, *History of Bengal* p. 326.

82 Stewart, *History of Bengal*, p. 327.

83 Chakraborty, Panchanan (Edt.) *Rameswar Rachanavali* (Calcutta, 1965), pp. 87-88. But most of the European writers, except Stewart observe that the *zamindar* of Burdwan revolted against the Mughal authority in Bengal, is fundamentally wrong.

84 *Ibid.*, p. 94. Also Mitra, S.K. *Hugli Zelar Itihas O Banga Samaj*, part-II (Third Edn., Calcutta, 1965), p. 631.

The large body of rebels began to advance towards Burdwan and in the skirmish that followed the *zamindar* of Burdwan was easily defeated and slain. His eldest son, Jagatram, somehow escaped from Burdwan and went to Dacca, to narrate the catastrophe to his family, to Ibrahim Khan—the *subahdar*. Ibrahim Khan directed Nurullah Khan—the *faujdar* of Hugli, to suppress the rebels. But the victory at Burdwan instigated the rebels to plunder the adjoining districts, and they, within a short time captured Hugli. Nurullah Khan, who advanced with his force to meet the rebels, escaped, out of fear, from Hugli on July 22, 1696, and retreated to Jessore.[85]

For this great disorder in Bengal, the three European settlements, the Dutch at Chinsurah, the French at Chandernagore and the English at Sutanuti, began to guared their properties. They professed themselves friends of the Bengal government requesting permission from the *subahdar* to defend their factories against the enemy. The *subahdar* directed them, in general terms, to defend themselves and hence, all the European settlers began to raise walls and bulworks round their respective factories.[86]

After the death of Sobha Singh[87] the rebel army, unanimously chose Rahim Khan as their leader, who now assumed the royal title of Rahim Shah. Under Rahim Shah, the rebellious party took possession of Rajmahal and Malda, plundered Murshidabad, laid siege to Sutanuti and Tanna, The news of this rebellion alarmed Aurangzeb, who became astonished as well as indignant at the lack of firmness in the conduct of Ibrahim Khan. He immediately appointed his own grandson Prince Azim-us-Shan to assume the charge of the united government of Bengal, Bihar and Orissa. He however, directed the *subahdar* of Bengal to remain at his post till the

---

85 *Ibid.*, pp 36-37.

86 Stewart, *History of Bengal*, p. 329.

87 It is said that Sobha Singh was murdered by Sayabati, the daughter of the deceased *zamindar* of Burdwan, who retaliated the crime for the death of her falher-Rameswar Rachanavali, p. 98.

arrival of his successor. But in the meanwhile, it was also directed that Zabardast Khan—the *subahdar*'s son, should immediately be despatched against the rebels.[88] The Emperor also issued orders to the *subahdars* of Oudh and Allahabad, to co-operate with the Bengal army.

Zabardast Khan, a tried and gallant soldier, immediately marched aga nst the rebels and defeated them at Rajmahal. He was hot on the trails of the rebels from place to place and the greater part of their plunder was retaken. At last the rebels were finally defeated and their camps were plundered by the Mughal army. In the month of May, 1697, Zabardast Khan announced his victory, when Azim-us-Shan arrived in Bengal. The latter, however, directed Zabardast Khan to refrain from further hostilities.[89]

The Prince Azim-us-shan remained at Burdwan for a period of three years. The Prince had an eye on the *masnad* of Delhi; so he came to Bengal with a determination to amass wealth. During this time, the Dutch made a representation that while they were liable to pay a duty of 3½ per cent on all their commerce, the English had paid only a nominal sum of Rs. 3,000 annually. Therefore, the Dutch solicited that they might be placed on the same footing.[90]

The English also deputed Walsh[91] as their envoy, not only to oppose the intrigues of the Dutch but to procure the grant of three villages of Sutanuti, Govindpur and Calcutta. Walsh was accompanied by Khwajah Sarhad, who after some years, accompanied John surman to the court of Farruk-Siyar.[92] However, the English envoys represented the restitution of the Company's property that had been plundered by the

---

88 *Ibid*, p. 334. Also Broome, *Bengal Army*, v. 1., p. 29.

89 Broome, *Bengal Army*, v. I, p. 29.

90 Stewart, *History of Bengal*, p 341.

91 Malleson in his book *The Life of Warren Hastings* (p. 16), wrongly states that it was Stanley, a member of the council, who was deputed to Prince.

92 Firminger, *Fifth Report*, p. 80.

rebels and the grant of the Prince's special *nishan*, confirming the freedom of trade, without payment of any duties. The envoys could not effect the object of their mission till the month of July, 1698, when, after the present of a considerable sum of money to the Prince, his order for the purchase of three villages had been procured.[93] But the *zamindars* of these three villages refused to make over the lands to the Company, threatening to complain before the Emperor about the injustice of the Prince. Finding them in constant opposition, it was agreed, "that 1500 rupees be paid them, provided they will relinquish their titles to the same towns, and give it under their hand in writing, that they have made over the same to the Honourable Company.[94]

By virtue of the Prince's *nishan* the three villages were purchased from the *zamindars*[95], that extended about three miles. The English, then hastened to erect a fort to protect these united villages. The fort was completed in 1700, and in compliment to the reigning king of England it was named as Fort William.[96] As such, the united villages, subsequently known as Calcutta, were becoming prosperous and that attracted a large number of inhabitants within a short time. The English Company thus acquired a legel status within the Mughal dominion.

But the flourishing trade of the Company in Bengal began to decline from the competition of a new Company during the beginning of the 18th century. The new Company was formed in England in 1698; it obtained a charter from the King, on condition that they would supply a loan of two crore of rupees to the government of England. As such, William Norris was sent to the court of the Mughal Emperor

---

93 Stewart, *History of Bengal*, p. 342.

94 Wilson. C.R., *Old Fort William in Bengal*. Vol. I, pp. 39-40,

95 Malleson mentions that the English, by a bribe of sixteen thousand rupees obtained the grant of these villages. It required another payment of eight hundred rupees to secure the actual transfer—Malleson, *Hastings*, p. 17. Also, Mukhopadhyay, *The Agrarian Policy*, pp. 8-9.

96 Malleson, *Hastings*, p. 17. Also, Stewart, *History of Bengal*, p. 346.

to abtain privileges for this Company, and to solicit a *farman* for that purpose. Norris landed at Masulipattam in September 1699. He went to the Emperor's camp, but his efforts in obtaining concession for the new Company became fruitless. Auranzgeb did not grant a *farman* to this new Company due to the news of the frequent acts of plundering by the English pirates, called 'interlopers.'[97] Thus, on 29 April, 1702, Norris embarked a ship and a few days after, sailed for England. But the advent of Norris and the mutual rivalry of the two English Companies in India, created worse suspicions and "the English fell everywhere into discredit."[98] The Emperor himself became much incensed. At last the officials of the two Companies, both homebased and abroad, started negotiation and the dissensions were terminated by the union of the two Companies in 1702-1703. The Company became known as the "United Company of Merchants trading to the East Indies."[99]

To assist his inefficient grandson—Azim-us-Shan, the Emperor had nominated in 1701 Kar Tulb Khan or Muhammed Hadi, a recent convertite to Islam, to the important post of *diwan* of Bengal, with the title of Murshid Quli Khan.[100] Murshid Quli, after his appointmet, soon proceeded to Dacca. In a short period, he ascertained that the revenues of Bengal amounted to one crore of rupees and so appointed his own collectors in different districts of Begal. The jealousy of Azim-us-Shah was excited by this nomination, and it added fuel to his belligerent temper, when he found that his favourites and courtiers were constantly controlled by the *diwan*. Thus, Azim-us-Shan tried to depose Murshid Quli by any means, if it

97 Bandopadhyay, Rakhaldas, *Banglar Itihas O Astahdash Satabdir Nababi Amal* (in Bengali, 1315 B.S.), p. 116.

98 Wilson, C.R. *The Early Annals of the English in Bengal* (Vol. II, Part II, Reprint, Calcutta, 1963), p. VIII.

99 Stewart, *History of Bengal*, p. 351, f.n. Also, Malleson, G.B., *The Decisive Battles of India* (New Edn., New Delhi, 1969), p. 38.

100 Murshid Quli was previously, the son of a poor Brahmin, who had become a Muslim and rose to the highest post in the *subah* of Bengal by his merit.

could be effected without risking the displeasure of Aurangzeb.[101] Even the *subahdar* tried secretly to assassinate murshid Quli, but it failed. Thus, after consulting his friends, Murshid Quli deemed it unadvisable to remain in the same place with the Prince, and resolved to fix his residence at Mukhsudabad. He made Mukhsudabad the capital of Bengal, but he grafted it on his own name and called Murshidabad, the city of Murshid. Thus he handed down his own name to posterity.[102]

In 1706, the Prince Azim-us-Shan departed for Delhi and his son, Farruk-Siyar was appointed in his place in Bengal, but the *diwan* paid little attention to his nomination. This departure was in a way a blessing to him; it gave the *diwan* an unlimited control over the three provinces.[103] Meanwhile in February 1707, Aurangzeb breathed his last. The officials of the Company realised that during the war of sucession, confusion and disorder would prevali in the *subah* and as such, the local officials as well as the *zamindars* would try to oppress the Company's officials resulting in loss of trade in Bengal. So all the English officials were directed to return to Calcutta and the Company began to fortify fort William.[104]

As the seat of government was transferred from Dacca to Murshidabad, which was in the ceatre of the *subah* and nearer to Calcutta. Murshid Quli was better able to take cognizance of the Company's affairs. Hedges—the Chief of the Kasimbazar factory[105] went to Murshidabad in 1710 to offer his respect to the *diwan*. But Murshid Quli demanded money from him. According to his order, the English boats began to be seized in different places. At last the Company was forced to pay him thirty thousand rupees. The Company also promised to

101 Malleson, *Hastings*, p. 17. Also, Stewart, *History of Bengal*, p. 354.

102 *Ibid.* p. 17.

103 Stewart, *History of Bengal*, p. 369.

104 Bandopadhyay, *Banglar Itihas*, pp. 119-120.

105 In 1713, Hedges was promoted to the post of Governor of the English Company in Bengal.

pay him Rs. 22,500, if the *diwan* could bring *farman* for the Company's trade privileges from the Emperor.[106]

Murshid Quli Khan clearly understood that Bengal owed much of its wealth to its external commerce. But the Mughal and Arabian merchants had to pay the prescribed duties of 2½ per cent. He used to say that the English had obtained *farmans* and *nishans* by means of bribery and corruption. Therefore, he demanded from the English Company, either the same duties of presents that were paid by the Hindus or a constant renewal of presents, both to himself and to the inferior officials. Thus, every year, his administration was marked by extraordinary and increasing extortions. Such conduct irritated the officials of the English Company, who forwarded a detail of their grievances to the Directors of the Company and proposed that an embassy of complaint, supported by valuable presents, should be sent to Delhi.[107]

Negotiations for sending an embassy to Delhi were revived, when in 1710, Ziaud-din who became friendly to the English, was sent to Bengal as *faujdar* of Hugli and Admiral in the Bay.[108] In 1712, the presents were carefully packed in boats, ready to go up the river. In March 1713, the Emperor Farruk-Siyar was informed by the Calcutta Council that the presents[109] and embassy were now ready to set out for Delhi. The English at that time, thought of sending a great Armenian merchant of Calcutta, Khwajah Sarhad, as one of the members of the embassy, to enter into private negotiation with the court through Padre Daniel and various others of his fellow countrymen in Delhi. Khwajah Sarhad had a great mastery of the Persian language to conduct the negotiation. He also

---

106 *Ibid.*, p. 124.

107 Stewart, *History of Bengal*, pp. 394-395.

108 Bandopadhyay, *Banglar Itihas*, p. 123.

109 "There were goods and varities comprised in the kings' presents valued at Rs. 1,02,472-11-4. Other goods valued at Rs. 1,08, 248-11-3 were intended principally for presents to court nobles. A third set of goods, valued at Rs. 29,958-4-0, consisted of cloth and other articles needed for the personal service of the embassy."—Wilson, *Early Annals*, II, p.XXI.

enjoyed the confidence of the English.[110] At the same time he had personally become known to Farruk-Siyar.

The nomination of the members of the embassy was left to Hedges—the Governor of Calcutta, who selected John Surman—Chief, Khwajah Sarhad-Second, Edward Stephenson-third, and Hugh Barker—Secretary. William Hamilton would accompany the embassy as a surgeon.[111] The embassy took with them the originals of the most important grants made to the English in Bengal.

The embassy arrived at Delhi on 8 July, 1715, after a continuous march of three months. They became the guests of Saiyyad Salabat Khan who conducted them to the Imperial Palace. At the palace, they were presented to their patron, Khan Duran.[112] When the Emperor showed himself in the hall of audience,Khan Duran introduced the members. The embassy then presented to the Emperor, the rare and costly things that they had brought as well as Governor Hedges' letter.[113]

From the time of his accession to the *masnad*, Farruk-Siyar was suffering from continuous illnes and towards the end of 1715 the Emperer's complaints reached the point of crisis. The disorder of the Emperor's health lingered, and the Emperor became impatient for the delay, because he was waiting for the celebration of his marriage with the daughter of Ajit Singh—the Rajput king of Jodhpur. At last, in consequence of the recommendation of Khan Duran, the Emperor allowed Hamilton to attend him. In a few week's time, the Emperor was sufficiently restored to health. Thus, Hamilton became a

---

110 Khwajah Sarhad knew something of the English language, though he was not able to read or write it. He had been to England at one time with his uncle. In 1697-98, he had taken a prominent part in the negotiation with Prince Azim-us-Shan that resulted in the acquisition of three villages,—Wilson, *Early Annals*, II, pp. XV-XVI.

111 Wilson, *Early Annals*, II. XVII and XIX.

112 This Khan Duran was previously as Khoja Hussain, who had accompanied Farruk-Siyar from Bengal. When Farruk-Siyar ascended to the *masnad*, he obtained the title of Khan Duran, and became a great favourite of the Emperor.

113 Willson, *Early Annals*, II, p. XXXIX.

great favourite with the Emperor, who publicly presented Hamilton with a jewelled plume, a vest, two diamond rings, an elephant, horse and five thousand rupees.[114] The Marriage ceremony and various rituals of the Emperor continued during the whole month of December,[115] during which all the business of the state was interrupted. The embassy was obliged to wait for six months before they could obtain opportunity of presenting their petition.

The petition was at last presented in the month of January 1716. It contained nineteen articles of which the first eight related to Bengal; the other articles were related to various complaints from Bombay and Madras. The most important articles that related to Bengal were ; that a *dustuck* or passport, signed by the President of Calcutta, should exempt the goods it specified from being stopped or examined by the officers of the Bengal government, under any pretence.

That the officers of the mint, at Moorshudabad, should at all times, when required, allow three days in the week for the coinage of the English Company's money.

That all persons, whether Europeans or natives, who might be indebted or accountable to the Company, should be delivered up to the Presidency at Calcutta, on the first demand.

That the English might purchase the lordship of thirty-eight towns, with the same immunities as the Prince Azeem Ooshan had permitted them to buy Calcutta, Chuttanutty and Govindpore."[116] The *farman* was finally handed over to the embassy and they took leave of the Emperor in July 1717, just two years after their arrival at Delhi.

At the success of the embassy, Murshid Quli Khan became much irritated. It added to his indignation, when it

114 *Ibid*, p. XIIV.

115 In this marriage festival also, Hamilton received on 28 December, a dress of honour, horse and one thousand rupees from the empress-mother. (*Vide*, Wilson, *Early Annals*, p. XIV).

116 Quoted in Stewart, *History of Bengal*, p. 398.

beeame known to him that the English had been empowered, by the grant of the *farman* to purchase thirty-eight villages adjacent to Calcutta. But as he could not dare openly to oppose the Imperial order, he privately directed the concerning *zamindars* under the threat of severe consequences, not to part with their land to the English on any favourable terms that might be offered to them.[117] Thus, he evaded the *farman* and frustrated the design of the English to purchase thirty-eight villages. These villages were valued by the English because they were situated around Calcutta. The villages were situated on both sides of the river Hugli extending from Baranagore in the north to Kidderpore in the south, and as such the *subahdar* foresaw that the acquisition of the villages would enable the Company to have complete control on the river.[118] The Company wisely gave up this point. They tried to conciliate the *subahdar* by making occasional presents to him and thus the English affairs enjoyed a long interval of prosperity. The English, unable to purchase the villages by direct method, adopted indirect tactics. Some of these villages were purchased by the Company's brokers. Thus a system of questionable transfer of ownership of these villages and the unsettling of their revenues up to 1757, resulted in confusion [119] Murshid Quli's successful defiance of the imperial *farman* proved the fatal weakness of the Mughal administrative machinery.

The English Company also gained little success to use the mint at Murshidabad. In 1724, the English made some futile efforts to gain this, by offering to pay forty thousand rupees to the *subahdar*, but the latter refused this on the simple ground that the subordinate officer who operated it, was dangerously ill.[120] In this way, Murshid Quli frustrated

---

117 *Ibid.*, Also Broome, *Bengal Army*, v. I, p. 36.

118 Broome, *Bengal Army*, v. I. 36.

119 Bhattacharya, *The East India Company*, p. 31.

120 The real opposition to the use of the mint came from Jagat Seth Fateh Chand. He successfully opposed the efforts of the English to win over the *Subahdar* to the execution of this measure.—*Ibid*, p. 24.

both these designs of the English Company. He did not want to see foreigners too strong in the *subah* of Bengal.

But the return of the embassy gave a great impetus to the growth of Calcutta, though the Company had been denied the privileges of the *farman*. The Company had given licence to a large number of private English merchants, but, besides them Calcutta, within a short time, became populous by the infiltration of Portuguese, Armenian, Mughal and Hindu merchants, who carried on their commerce under the protection of the English flag. Thus, many individuals amassed wealth, without injuring the Company's trade or incurring the displeasure of the *subahdar* of Bengal. As Stewart observes "...the inhabitants of Calcutta enjoyed, after the return of the embassy, a degree of freedom and security unknown to other subjects of the Mughal Empire; and that city, in consequence, increased yearly[121] in extent, beauty and riches."[122] During this time, a successful voyage of the Austrian-Netherlands also encouraged a set of German merchants to establish an East India Company at Ostend. The Emperor of Germany granted them permission, in 1723, to trade to the East Indies under the name of the Ostend Company.[123]

As Murshid Quli Khan was also desirous of introducing more rivals to the English, he granted the prayer of Ostend Company and assigned them the village of Bankibazar, fifteen miles above Calcutta on the bank of the river, for the residence of the Germans. In 1724, an Ostend ship arrived in Bengal and the officers of the ship took possession of Bankibazar and erected temporary houses. The English and the Dutch became jealous of the growth of this Ostend Company, tried to influence the *subahdar* against the Germans. They bribed the *faujdar* of Hugli to make a false representation about their strength at Bankibazar and the danger allowing the

---

121 After 1700, Calcutta grew in importance and wealth. In 1704, its population was that of 15,000, but in 1750—it became more than one lakh. Sarkar, *History of Bengal*, pp. 411-419.

122 Stewart, *History of Bengal*, p. 403.

123 *Ibid.*, p. 422.

Germans to remain within a few miles from the royal port The English also took the initiative and captured one German ship out of two, on the river Hugli, the other escaped to Bankibazar.[124]

The *faujdar* of Hugli thus undertook prompt action and directed the Ostend Company to dismantle its fortification. This gave rise to a violent dispute in 1733, during the time of Shujauddin, between the German agent and the *faujdar* of Hugli. A body of troops were sent against this German Company by the *faujdar*, under the command of an officer named Mir Jafar, who besieged their factory. The Chief of the Ostend Company after the arrival of one of its ships from Germany anchored down the river and immediately proceeded to Europe.[125] Meanwhile, the Mughal troops, under Mir Jafar levelled the fortifications of the factory and delivered Bankibazar to the *zamindar.*

Shujauddin or Shuja Khan became the acknowledged *subahdar* of Bengal in September 1727, with the confirmation from the court of Delhi. The New Nawab assured the English Company of his sympathy and encouraged them to carry on their business as usual. The Company also did not think it proper to risk an open conflict with him as that might go to augment the trade of other European nations. It might also unite the French and the Dutch Companies with the Nawab to frustrate the objects of the English in Bengal. Very often the English conciliated themselves with the government of Shujauddin by the payment of occasional presents of money to him.[126]

In his relation with the Europeans, Shujauddin followed the policy of Murshid Quli Khan. He occasionally demanded money from them. All the European traders in Bengal, the English, the French, the Dutch and the Ostenders, were taken

---

124 Sarkar, *History of Bengal*, p. 429.

125 Stewart, *History of Bengal*, p. 425. Even after this flight, the Ostend Company continued their trade, when in 1748, Alivardi Khan drove them out of Bengal—Orme, *Indostan*, II, p. 45.

126 Sarkar, *History of Bengal*, p. 431.

to task, at one time or the other. As such the Nawab's good relations with the English did not continue for long and soon it became embittered on the question of trade in salt. Thus, some boats of the English merchants proceeding to Patna were seized by the officers of his government, and a huge quantities of salt was unloaded by them at Bhagalpur. The English at Murshidabad made strong representation before the Nawab to regain the possession of salt. Shujauddin not only refused but demanded of them not to trade in salt in future.. The government accused the English Company that their trade had of late increased on much and that they dealt with so many other commodities than in the past that the trade of the Indian merchants has much declined, and unless an effective restraint was imposed upon their inland trade, the English would engross the whole trade of the *subah* and thereby deprive a vast number of Indian people of their means of livelihood.[127]

Another dispute arose during his time, when Shuja Quli Khan the *faujdar* of Hugli, demanded high duties from all the European settlers—the English, the French and the Dutch. When the European traders tried to resist him, the *faujdar* decided to chastise them. He seized some bales of raw silk and clothes that belonged to the English but these were soon recovered by a body of English troops.[128] But the *faujdar*, with a party of his soldiers, stopped all supplies to the English in Calcutta and Kasimbazar. In this extreme situation, the Chief of the English factory at Kasimbazar tried to conciliate the Nawab by promising to pay him a *nazar* of three lakhs. The Calcutta Council expressed their opinion that in relation to the position of the government it would be most advisable "to submit to the expenses by making presents, now and then, to the under officers of the *durbar* and those that have authority in several other places.[129]

127 Bhattacharya, *The East India Company*, p. 41.

128 Stewart, *History of Bengal*, p. 426.

129 Ouoted in Sarkar, *History of Bengal*, p. 431.

Though the English tried to cultivate better relation at the *darbar* of the Nawab by presenting a handsome horse to Sarfaraz, the son of the Nawab,[130] they could not change the Nawab's prejudices against the English, and he ordered the Indian merchants not to have any further dealings with the English. He prohibited the Indians to supply the English with grain at Calcutta or any of their subordinate factories.[131] The reason of this fresb dispute with the Nawab was the alleged issue of *dastacks* by the English for goods sold to merchants other than the inhabitants of Calcutta. The Calcutta Council therefore decided in January 1736, to accommodate matters with the Nawab. At last, by the mediation of Haji Ahmad, the English Company were able to satisfy the Nawab by the payment of Rs. 55,000 and on 6 July 1736, they obtained *parwana* for their trade.[132] As the English also apologised for their misconduct before Shujauddin,[133] they remained on a very good terms with him

In March 1739, Sarfaraz Khan became the Nawab of Bengal after the death of his father, Shujauddin. The English wanted to cultivate good relation with the new Nawab. But Sarfaraz Khan could neither control the administration of the *subah*. nor was he a match for the intriguing and ambitious nobility at the *darbar*. Meanwhile, Nadir Shah's invasion at Delhi discredited the Mughal Empire. His coins already came to be minted at Murshidabad and Fateh Chand would not lend to the Company any other but Nadir Shah's *siccas*. Haji Ahmad, whose influence with Sarfaraz was great, threatened to stop all business of the Company unless they would procure a new *farman* from Delhi. The old royal family had been vanquished, and unless a new *farman* was obtained from the New Emperor, English would not be allowed their trade privileges.[134] The English protested that no one had replaced

130 Sarfaraz was at that time the nominal *diwan* of Bengal.

131 Stewart, *History of Bengal*, p. 426.

132 Sarkar, *History of Bengal*, p. 432.

133 Stewart, *History of Bengal*, p. 426.

134 Consultations, 11 and 31 May, 1739. (Vide Bhattacharya, *The East India Company*, p. 64.)

Muhammed Shah, neither was there intimation of any settled government at Delhi. But at the same time, the English Company tried to keep the Haji pacified on reasonable terms.

Alivardi became the Nawab of Bengal in 1740, after defeating Sarfaraz. But the earlier years of his rule were weaked by frequent Maratha ravages in Bengal, the 'Bargis', who invaded the *subah* on the plea of collecting *chauth*. In course of their incursions, the Marathas began to plunder the wealth of the people, burnt many important towns and villages. Hence these invasions not only created panic among the people but brought untold miseries. As a result, a number of Indian inhabitants, of the eastern side of the river Hugli, came to Calcutta under English protection. To save themselves from any further injury from the Marathas, the Indian inhabitants of Calcutta requested Alivardi to dig a ditch at their own cost, round the Company's territory, from the northern part of Sutanuti to the southern part of Govindpur. This work would extend about seven miles. Alivardi, as he was himself greatly harassed by the Marathas, did not make any objection to this work.[135] Within a period of six months three miles were dug. But when the inhabitants noticed that the Nawab with his army had vigorously prevented the incursions of the Marathas within sixty miles of Calcutta, they discontinued the work. As the people of Calcutta dug a ditch of three miles, it began to be called the 'Maratha ditch'. In the same year, Alivardi also permitted the English to raise a rampart with bastions of brickwork round their factory at Kasimbazar.[136]

To repel the repeated Maratha invasions into Bengal, Alivardi's government ran short of money. His army bill alone amounted to one crore and eighty lakhs of rupees annually. Thus the Nawab's government became bankrupt and he was forced to raise money by all possible means. So in 1743, Alivardi had levied a war tax of Rs. 2,000 from each of the

---

135 Hunter, *Indian Impire*, p. 448. Also, Orme, *Indostan*, II, p. 45

136 Orme, *Indostan*, II, p. 45.

three European nations. Early in July 1744, he made an extraordinary demand on the English Chief of Kasimbazar, intimating that the English had to pay "two months pay for his troops", amounting to nearly thirty lakhs of rupees. But when Alivardi did not receive any prompt reply, he, after three days from the despatch of his instruction, set peons on the European merchants at Murshidabad and directed them to stop their trade within the *subah* of Bengal.[137]

The Nawab began to torture the officials of the English Company. He went on arresting and whipping every person connected with the Company whom he could lay hands on. After sometime, the Nawab referred the matter of the English Company to Chin Ray and Jagat Seth Fateh Chand. These two high dignitaries informed the English that, "the Nawab does not expect this sum (nearly 30 lakhs) from the Company, but expects that they raise it among the merchants under their protection and from the number of rich persons (who have) fled to Calcutta during (these) troubles...That the Nawab, to pay his troops, had spent the revenues of the province, his own wealth, and was forced to take money from his relations and servants and, therefore, thought it highly reasonable (that) the inhabitants of Calcutta should pay a share.[138]

In order to reopen their business in the *subah* cf Bengal, the English Company in October, 1744, were forced to pay the Nawab three and a half lakh of rupees, besides which they had to pay Rs. 30,500 to his officers at Murshidabad, Rs. 8,000 at Patna and Rs. 5,000 at Dacca.[139]

The Marathas, during their wars with the Bengal Nawab, committed at least one act of considerable depredation on the English trade. In 1748 they stopped a fleet of boats coming

---

137 Sarkar, J.N. *Fall of the Mughal Empire*, Vol. I (Calcutta 1932), p. 108.

138 Bengal Letter, 8 November, 1744 (quoted in *Ibid.*, p. 109).

139 Ibid., 9 February, 1745 (quoted in *Ibid.*, pp. 109-110).

from Kasimbazar to Calcutta. Three hundred bales of raw silk, belonging to the Company, were plundered by them.[140]

The Nawab's officials also tried to exact money from the English merchants, sometimes by adopting a coercive policy. Thus the factors of Malda complained in April, 1748, before Edward Ezles, the Chief of Kasmbazar, that they had been ill-treated by the Nawab's officials when the former refused to comply with the demands of the latter' for a large sums of mony. The Nawab's officials threatened the Malda factors with plunder of everything if they would resist. Seized with fear the English merchants of Malda immediately wrote a letter to Nawazish Muhammad and Chin Ray, requesting them to inform the Nawab about the above threat. But these two officials of the Nawab did not interfere in the matter.[141]

Another incident of rupture took place when in 1748, Commodore Griffin and some of his squadron, captured some trading boats of the Armenian and Mughal merchants in Bengal. The Armenians lodged a complaint and appealed to the Nawab for redress. The Nawab immediately sent a *parwana* to Barwell; the Company's governor at Fort William to the following purport : "The Sayds, Moghuls, Armenians etc., merchants of Hughly, have complained that lakhs of goods and Treasure with their ships you have seized and plundered, and I am informed from foreign parts that ships bound to Houghly you seized on under pretence of their belonging to the French. The ship belonging to Antony with lakhs on Board from Mochel'[142] and several curiosities sent me by the Sheriff of that place on that ship you have also seized and plundered. These merchants are the Kingdom's benefactors, their Imports and Exports are an advantage to all men, and their complaints are also grievous that I cannot forbear any longer giving ear to them. As you

---

140 But the European commerce derived great advantages out of the distressed condition of the *subah*, as the price of every article increased considerably.—Orme, *Indostan*, II., p. 46.

141 Consultations, May 2, 1748. Also, Long, J., *Selections from Unpublished Records of Government* (Reprint Calcutta, 1973), p. 7.

142 The Red sea port in Western Arabia.

were not permitted to commit piracies therefore I now writ you that on receipt of this you deliver up all the merchants' goods, and effects to them as also what appertains upto me, otherwise you may be assured a due chastizement in such manner as you least expect."[143]

Barwell, did not comply with the Nawab's order,[144] and as such, the Nawab became much angry. He sent his troops, who stopped the English trade and surrounded the English factory at Kasimbazar. The English tried through the Seths to reach a compromise, but the latter demanded a large amount of money for themselves and four lakhs of rupees for the Nawab. In the meantime, however, the English were able to satisfy the Armenians and as such the Nawab seemed pacified, at least for the time being. But still the English had to pay a large amount of money to the Nawab through the Seths.[145]

In August 1752, Prince Sirajuddaulah, whom Alivardi nominated as his successor had arrived at Hugli. On his arrival, the officials of the French and the Dutch Company went to meet him. The English officials of Calcutta also were in attendance to greet him. The English were "received with utmost politeness and distinction far superior than was paid to the Dutch or French". The various articles that the English presented to Siraj, were valued at nearly Rs. 1600.[146] From this time, the crown-prince was permitted to have almost a free hand in the affairs of the government of Bengal. Nawab Alivardi also seemed to be pleased with the English and in recognition thereof, he despathed a *parwana* to Darke, the English Governor of the Company, which arrived at Calcutta on 8 October. "I am extremely pleased and delighted with you and a thousand thousand times remain sensible of it, and

143 Consultations, January 11, 1749 (Long, *Unpublshed* p. 20).

144 Long, *Unpublished Records*, p. 20 f.n.

145 Consultations, August 31, 1749 (Long, *Unpublished Records*, p. 23).

146 Walsh, J.H.T., *A History of Murshidabad District* (London, 1902), p. 149.

in return by the grace of God the Company's business I will be very favourable to."[147]

But the extraction of money from the English officials continued in different *chowkies* of the *subah*. Thus the Calcutta Council directed the Chief[148] and the members of the Kasimbazar factory, to make a representation at the *darbar* about the complaints of the English merchants. The Calcutta Council also further received information that the *faujdar* of Bakarganj prohibited the importation of rice to Calcutta and hence the council also directed the gentlemen at Kasimbazar to obtain a *parwana* from the Nawab for the free importation of grain to Calcutta. But the gentlemen at Kasimbazar could not obtain a *parwana* without making a *nazar* of Rs. 3,000 to the *chuta-nawab*' and his *diwan*, which the council, after mature consideration, directed the gentlemen at Kasimbazar not to comply with.[149]

To remove the interruption of the Company's business, the factors of Kasimbazar went to the *darbar* and after a discussion of the matter, Watts obtained a *parwana* from the '*chuta-nawab*' forbidding all impositions and unjust levies of money from boats belonging to the English Company. But it was realised that this *parwana* would meet but little success, unless Hukumbeg[150] directed to the *chowkies* under his jurisdiction, to pay a due regard to it. But Hukumbeg did not agree to this, as he would sustain a great financial loss thereby. Watts, therefore, thought and the Calcutta Council should agree to pay ten to twelve thousand of rupees to Hukumbeg if his promise would have the desired effect and "this present would not be made use of as a precedent and be demanded by his successors as a right". When this decision of the Calcutta

---

147 Consultations, 11 October, 1752, *Uupublished Records*, p. 44).

148 William Watts was appointed Chief of the Kasimbazar factory in 1752.

149 Letter to Court, 4 January, 1754 (*Fort William-India House Correspondence*, Vol. I (Delhi, 1958), pp. 726-737, Edt. by datta, K.K.)

150 Accountant for the Purchases of Sugar.

Council was intimated to Hukumbeg. he gave strong assurances to Watts that his order would be strictly complied with.[151] In this way, by offering presents and bribes to different officials, the English Company carried on their trade in Bengal. The *faujdar* of Hugli obtained a fixed amount of present from the Company every year, that amounted to Rs. 2750. Rajah Rajballabh, the *naib* of Nawazish Muhammad, who had become all powerful at Dacca, extracted in 1754, from the English and French Companies Rs. 4300 by forcible method.[152]

Relatively speaking the Europeans were very little molested during the time of Alivardi. He permitted them to carry on their trade according to the terms of the *farmans*, upon making the usual presents. As such, under Alivardi, the English prospered greatly. When Mustafa Khan, the principal general of Alivardi urged the Nawab to expel the English from Bengal and to seize all their property within the *subah*, the Nawab did not agree with him.[153]

But this prosperity of the English trade in Bengal came to a half, followed by an open conflict between them and the Nawab during the time of sirajuddaulah. This rivalry with the English it is stated was due to the instruction of Alivardi to his heir-designate, Sirajuddaulah. According to Holwell,[154] Alivardi had warned the young Prince to reduce the power of the Europeans. This statement of Holwell does not seem true. Holwell was in the habit of inventing stories to serve his own purpose. Contemporary English officials, such as Richard Becher who was at that time the Chief of the English factory at Dacca, completely doubted the veracity of any such instruction given by Alivardi. Another official, Mathew Collet,

---

151 F.W.I.H.C., I, p. 987.

152 Bandopadhyay, *Banglar Itihas*, pp. 182-183.

153 Stewart, *History of Bengal*, pp. 490-491.

154 Holwell assumed the office of the Collector in July, 1752.

who was the second of the factory of Kasimbazar remarked about this as a "specious fable''.[155] Additionally, we come to know from the persian sources that Alivardi forbade Sirajuddulah "not to fight with the English.''[156]

155 Stewart, *History of Bengal*. pp. 490-491

156 Singh, Kalyan, *Khulasat-ut-Tawarikh* (Eng. trans., published in the *Journal of Bihar and Orissa Research Society*, vol. V., 1919, p. 231.)

2

RETALIATION AGAINST SIRAJUDDAULAH AND THE APPOINTMENT OF WILLIAM WATTS—THE FIRST BRITISH RESIDENT AT MURSHIDABAD

The rivalry between Sirajuddaulah and the English Company started some days before the death of Alivardi. For this rivalry, the European writers laid the whole blame on Sirajuddaulah. Sirajuddaulah was "young in years but old in vice." observes one writer, while the other depicts him as a youth of cruel disposition who "gave way to every description of vice and profligacy without any check."[2] Charles Stewart observes about him that Sirajuddaulah "associated with none but infamous and profligate companions and at their head, used to patrole the streets of Murshidabad." This character of the young Prince was known to Alivardi but the "old man was so infatuated" with the prince that "he took no measures to correct his flagitious conduct."[3] The French writer. Jean Law, who was for sometime at the court of Sirajuddaulah also did not spare him and observes that "before the death of Alivardi Khan the character of Sirajuddaulah was reputed to be one of the worst ever known. In fact he had distinguished himself not only by all sorts of debaucheries but by the revolting cruelty."[4]

---

1 Busteed, H.E., *Echoes from Old Calcutta* (Cal, 2nd Edn., 1888), p. 4.

2 Broome, *Bengal Army*, I, p. 46.

3 Stewart, *History of Bengal*, p. 495.

4 Law, Jean, *Memorie Sur Quelques Affairs De l' Empire Mogol* 1756-61 (Translated by Hill, S.C., *Bengal in 1756–57*, Vol. III, p. 162).

Thus it seems that the European writers painted the character of Sirajuddaulah as black as they could do. Was the character of Sirajuddaulah as black as they have narrated ? Or was it a malice against him that led them to make such remarks ? We must be cautious to verify the causes that led to the rivalry of the English Company with the young Prince. In fact, Sirajuddaulah was a creature of circumstances, over which he had no control. It was the English who provoked him to fall on them.

Though Alivardi had nominated his grandson Sirajuddaulah early in 1752 as his suceessor, yet just before the death of the former, many persons bagan to entertain an idea that the latter could never become the Nawab. The English began to think and act in this way as they noticed two rival groups, one led by Ghasiti Begam—the eldest daughter of the old Nawab, and other by Shaukat Jang, the Governor of Purnea, opposing the succession of Sirajuddaulah. So the English "never addressed themselves to Sirajuddaulah" when they used to go to Murshidabad for transacting their business during the fatal illness of Alivardi. On the contrary, they "avoided all communication with" the young prince.[5]

Nawazish Muhammad khan—the eldest son-in-law of Alivardi, died issueless in December 1755, leaving the riches and property to his widow, Ghasiti Begam. Rajah Rajballabh who was the *diwan* of Nawazish Muhammad, made common cause with his widow and he became the chief agent of Ghasiti Begam's affairs. Rajballabh was at Murshidabad during the last illness of Alivardi, when Sirajuddaulah became the *de facto* ruler of the *Subah*. Siraj brought charges against Rajballabh for the embezzlement of public money and called for an account of his administration of the Dacca finances. When Rajballabh failed to give a satisfactory account, he was imprisoned,[6] or he was placed under a strict surveillance,[7]

5 Law. *Memorie*, p. 162.

6 Watts' reply to Holwell's charges to the Court of Directors,30-1-1757 (F.W.I.H.C., II, pp. 182-183) informing them that Rajballabh's arrest before the death of Alivardi was a fabricated story, rather Rajballabh was employed by Alivardi for giving an account of Nawazish Muhammad Khan's riches to the latter.

7 Hill, I., p. XIIV.

but Alivardi somehow managed to save the life of the Dacca *diwan* pending the auditing of his accounts.

It appeared to the English that the two contesting parties would likely unite to overthrow Sirajuddaulah. It created much confusion among the Company's officials as they gradually formed an idea that the young Prince would not have sufficient influence to sit on the *masnad* and as such the former carried on a secret correspondence with Ghasiti Begam.[8] Rajballabh, the *diwan* of Ghasiti Begam readily allied himself with the Begam to oppose the succession of Sirajuddaulah. The ripe old age, combining with the fatal illness of Alivardi greatly alarmed the Begam's group. Rajballabh realised that his own family as well as the "greatest part of his wealth were exposed to danger at Dacca;" his only consideration was to remove them to a place of security.[9] Ghasiti Begam also, just before her father's death, raised a force around her.[10]

During these undercurrent cold war of palace-politics, Willlam watts was the Chief of the fortified English factory at Kasimbazar, the place situated about two miles south of Murshidabad. The affairs of the Kasimbazar factory were managed by a council, presided over by the first in Council called the Chief, who was subordinate to the Governor and council in Calcutta. This Chief of the Kasimbazar factory practically represented the British interests at the *darbar*, of the Bengal Nawabs.[11] William watts believed in Rajballabh, a friend of the English, because while the Rajah was the *diwan* of Nawazish Muhammad at Dacca, the English had some dealings with him. So during this rivalry, watts thought that Rajballabh might be "useful to them" and "might be more so" in future as well.[11] Sensing this attitude of the English,

8 Law, *Memoire*, p. 163.

9 Holwell's letter to Court, 30 November, 1756.

10 Watt's reply to Holwell's Charges. Letter to Court, 30 January, 1757. (F.W.I.H.C., Vol. II, Edt. by Sinha, H.N., Deihi, 1957, pp. 182-187).

11 Watts' letter to Court, 30 January, 1757 (*Ibid*). Watts was an active and courageous man. His wife, Frances, had two husbands before Watts. Incidentally, his daughter by Frances, formed an important link in British Indian politics by marriage to Charles Jenkinson.—Feiling, Keith, *Warren Hastings* (Lond., 1955), p. 18.

Rajballabh intstructed his son, Krishnadas, to travel by boat with his women and valuable treasures, on the plea of proceeding to the temple of Jagannath at Puri. As the wife of Krishnadas became ill on the way, Rajballabh obtained a recommendatory letter from Watts, for his son's admission into Calcutta, until the wife of Krishnadas became fit to proceed on her journey. Watts complied with the request of Rajballabh without consulting his council and handed over a letter to him addressed to the Governor at Calcutta for the admission of Rajballabh's family.[12] Another letter of the same purpose he wrote under a closed seal to Manningham.[13] Later on, Watts argued in his self-defence after the Company's recapture of Calcutta to the Court of Directors on 30 January 1757: "The Rajballabh's son's wife was taken ill on her way to Jaggernaut; therefore Rajabullub desired she might be admitted into Calcutta for a month till she was brought to bed as she was ready to lie in."[14]

Holwell also could not frame a definite charge against watts[15]but he argued that it was only because of the recommendatory letter from watts that Krishnadas's family were received in Calcutta and were "treated with all possible regard."[16] When Krishnadas arrived in Calcutta, the President at the settlement, Governor Roger Drake was at Balasore to recover his ill-health and as such, this family was received by Manningham on behalf of the Governor.[17] When the spies of the Nawab reported the fact to Murshibabad, the young Prince was naturally excited and he became suspicious about the

12 Hill, I, XIV.

13 Watts' letter to Court, 30 January, 1757 (F.W.I.H.C., II, pp. 182-187).

14 *Ibid.*

15 Holwell's letter to Court, 30 Nov., 1756 (Holwell, J.Z., *Important facts relating to the East India Company's affairs in Bengal* (Lond., 1774), p. 272.

16 *Ibid.* Also, F.W.I.H.C., Vol. I, p. 1044. Also, Caraccioli, C., *The Life of Lord Clive*, Vol. III (Lond., 1775), p. 37. Krishnadas brought with him a treasure estimated at Rs, 5,300,000.

17 *Ibid.*

motive of the English to protect the family "of a man reputed to be under his displeasure."[18]

This protection to Krishnadas, not only wounded the pride of Sirajuddaulah, but he also became enraged against the English. He immediately informed Alivardi about the Englishis design to support the claim of Ghasiti Begam. During tht time, Dr. Forth, the surgeon of the English factory a Kasimbazar, was present at Alivardi's bedside. The old Nawab did not reply to the query of the young Prince but interrogated Dr. Forth about the report. Dr. Forth completely denied the charges, characterising them "groundless", answering before them, that these wild rumours might have raised by the enemies of the English to create a bitter feeling against them at the *darbar*, adding that "the English had no other ambition than to be merchants in his country." Alivardi seemed to be convinced by this argument, told Sirajuddaulah that he should give no credit to this information. But Sirajuddaulah was not pacified and he continued his search about the design the English[19] against the Nawab.

This suspicion of Sirajuddaulah against the English became strong as days rolled on. Within a few days befofe the death of the old Nawab, the former summoned to the *darbar* the agents of the English, the French as the Dutch, who were interrogated on three consecutive days. The French and the Dutch agents were asked if they knew anything about the conspiracy of the English with Ghasiti Begam. To this question, they pleaded their ignorance on the matter.[20] On the other hand, when there seemed no hope of Alivardi's recovery, Ghasiti Begam quitted Murshidabad and surrounded with her ten thousand soldiers stationed herself at *Moti-jhil*[21] to face the situation. Thus the atmosphere of Murshidabad became tense.

18 Hill, I, p. XIV.
19 Orme, *Indostan*, II, p. 51.
20 Law, *Memoire*, p. 164.
21 Orme, *Indostan*, II, p. 50.

When Sirajuddaulah's accession to the *masnad* seemed, assured, a few days before the old Nawab's death, watts wanted to reverse the earlier politics of the English in Bengal. Watts sent a note of warning to Drake at Calcutta: "That there was a multitude of the government spies at Calcutta; that the small strength of its fortifications and garrison, and the easy capture of it, were the publick discourse of the city and *Durbar*; and that it behoved Mr. Drake to be upon his guard, and by some means prevent the government's spies bringing daily intelligence to the *Durbar* the weak situation of the place."[22] Upon the receipt of this letter, Drake became cautious and instructed Holwell to keep a close watch on the settlement. Anybody suspected within the settlement might be turned out from Calcutta, he directed. Holwell obeyed this instruction immediately and no person was admitted into the town without a strict examination.[23]

Drake recieved another letter from Watts in Which the latter also reversed his earlier opinion about Rajballabh and suggested to the former, "That Kissendass and the rest of Raagbullob's family should have no longer protection in Calcutta, as it was very uncertain what a turn things would take after the demise of the *Suba*.[24]

This opinion of Watts was supported by Holwell and Manningham as they did not want to take any risk against the unpredictable move of the young prince,[25] but Drake remained firm in his resolution and continued to protect Krishnadas at Calcutta. Becher also thought on the same line as watts and observed that "the first admission of Kissendass and his wealth was wrong" and that Rajballabh "had given much trouble" to the English as well as there was "no probability of success" of Ghasiti Bagam. But later on, when Calcutta was recaptured by the English and even when Mir Jafar was seated on the

22 Holwell's letter to Court, 30 November, 1765 (F.W.I.H.C., Vol. I, pp. 1044-1045). Also, Hill, II, p. 5.

23 *Ibid.*

24 *Ibid.* Also, Holwell, *Important Facts*, p. 272.

25 Hill, I, p. XLVI.

masnad by them, Holwell changed his earlier contention and wrote to the Court of Directors that it was not a wrong policy to protect Krishnadas "as things were then circumstanced."[26] This conduct on the part of the governor of the Company as well as some members of his council, to protect Krishnadas, afterwards, gave rise to the suspicion that some of the members of the Calcutta Council had received bribes to protect the family of Rajballabh.[27]

After the death of the old Nawab, Alivardi, on 10 April, Sirajuddaulah succeeded him on the *masnad*. Governor Drake did not forget to congratulate Sirajuddulah on the eve of his accession. The young Nawab, till then, did not nurse any particular hostility against the English, on the other hand he extended his "favour and protection" to the Company.[28] But the firs. care or Sirajuddaulah, just after his accession, was to secure the *masnad* for himself. Accordingly Siraj ordered a number of his forces to march to *Moti-jhil* against Ghasiti Begam. It was the plan of Sirajuddaulah "to confine her in some other place, after which the commanding officer was to seize everything belonging to her."[29] Ghasiti Begam wanted to resist but when her mother, the widow of Nawab Alivardi persuaded her, She surrendered without any resistance. She was ordered to retire to the harem, while her wealth was confiscated by the Nawab[30] This happened within ten days after Alivardi's death. Thus the immediate opposition against the young Prince came to an end.

Sirajuddaulah, within a few days after his aceession, sent Narain Singh, brother of Ramram Singh—the *faujdar* of Midnapore and the head of the spies--to Calcutta, with a letter to the president of Calcutta, demanding the delivery of

---

26 Holwell's letter to Court, August 1757, (Holwell, *Important Facts*, p. 343).

27 Hill, I, p. XIVII.

28 Datta, K.K., *Sirajuddaulah* (Calcutta, 1971), p. 6.

29 Husain, Ghulam, *The Seix Mutaqherin*, Vol. II (Eng. Trans. Calcutta 1902, p. 185).

30 Hill, I, p. xivii

Krishnadas and his family. The spy came in a small boat and landed in Calcutta in the disguise of a European on 14 April, and lodged in the house of Omichand. As the governor, Drake, was absent, having gone to Barasat, and Manningham was at his country residence on that day, Omichand came to Holwell and apprised him about the matetr. Holwell received the messenger with great respect but he pleaded his inability to take any decision on the order of the Nawab, pending Drake's arrival at Calcutta.[31]

On the next day, Drake returned to Calcutta with Manningham and Frankland. The members of the council felt greatly embarrassed and did not know how to act on this occasion. The last intelligence received from Murshidabad about the state of things between the young Prince and Ghasiti Begam, seemed to them dubious. It was finally concluded by the council that the "messenger was an engine" prepared by Omichand to alarm the English and "restore his own importance." Thus the result of the deliberation was that."As Narran Singh had stole like a thief and a spy into the settlement the President should not receive him or his *perwannah*." Thus the President ordered one of his servants to turn Narain Singh out of Calcutta, which was done accordingly,[32] But at the same time, letters were sent to Watts to guard against any evil consequence from this proceeding. Upon receiving this intelligence, Watts became apprehensive that this action "might occasion some trouble," and immediately wrote to some of the *darbar* officers to scotch any complaint against the English and see to it that the affair was hushed up.[33] But Sirajuddaulah concealed his resentment against the English for the time being. And when the Nawab learnt from Watts, agent that the English had turned out Narain Singh as an imposter, showed no sign of displeasure. After that event, the young

---

31 Holwell's letter to Court, 30 Nov., 1756 (F.W.I.H.C., Vol. I, p. 1045). Also, Orme, *Indostan*, II, pp. 53-54.

32 F.W.I.H.C. Vol. I pp. 1045-1046.

33 Watts' letter to Court, 16 July, 1756 (F.W.I.H.C., Vol. I, p. 1008).

Nawab gave no instructions to Watts or Drade concerning the surrender of Krishnadas.[34]

The final rupture between the Nawab and the English came when the Nawab's spies informed him that the English and the French were fortifying their settlements at Calcutta and Chandernagore. In fact, a war had broken out in Europe between these two nations and hence they, began to perpare and fortify their settlements in Bengal. The French were making efforts at Chandernagore to fortify one of the bastions of their fort, while the English were as busily engaged in digging a great ditch round their settlement and in rebuilding some masonry works. Hence the Nawab gave orders to the *vakils* of both the nations to appear at the *darbar* In their presence Sirajuddaulah ordered the French *vakil* "to pull down all the works made" since the death of Alivardi, and to the English, to fill up the ditch as well as to demolish the work of fortifications.[35] The French gave a polite reply, while the English *vakil* replied in a rather tactless manner.[36] The English *vakil* returned from the *darbar* and acquainted Watts about the order of the Nawab. Accordingly Watts wrote a letter to the Nawab in which he completely denied any knowledge of English fortifications of Calcutta.[37] To this letter, the Nawab sent no reply to Watts, but sent a *parwana* to Calcutta to "desist from fortifying and to level what new works they had begun."[38]

---

34 Orme, *Indostan*, II, p. 54.

35 Law, *Memoire*, pp. 164-165.

36 Reginald, Gatty, *Robert Clive and the Founding of the British Empire* (London, 1927), p. 146.

37 Watts was fully aware about the English fortifications of Calcutta. The fortifications had begun at least one year earlier. The Calcutta Council in their letter to the court, requested the latter to send some engineers, "carrylng on in the most regular manner Plans of Fortifications" —Letter to Court, 22 August, 1755. Aiso, Maitra, A.K., *Sirajuddaulah*, 1304 B.S., p. 120, f.n.

38 Watts' and Collet's letter to Court, 16 July, 1756 (F.W.I.H.C., I, p. 1008).

This led to the hostility between the English and the Nawab of Bengal. Otherwise, Sirajuddaulah was in no way against the English trade in Bengal. The Nawab did not provoke them. On the contrary, in 1752, after his becoming the heir-designate, when the young Prince had arrived at Hugli, the agents of the three nations viz., the Dutch, the French and the English waited upon him. The English President was received by Sirajuddaulah, "with the utmost politeness and distinction far superior than was paid the Dutch to the French."[39]

But this attitude of the Nawab gradually changed because the English betrayed excessive indulgence in the political affairs of Bengal. It was due to the advice of Watts, before the accession of Sirajuddaulah, that the English began to fortify Calcutta without the permission of the Nawab.[40] The Nawab's cause of dissatisfaction against the English was fully known to Watts. The Nawab could not approve of the English fortifications of Calcutta and, before the factory of Kasimbazar was surrendered, Watts had informed the Calcutta Council about the intention of the Nawab: "For he (Sirajuddaulah) looked upon us only as a set of merchants, and therefore if we chose to reside in his dominions under that denomination we were extremely welcome, but as the Prince of the country he forthwith insisted on the demolition of all those new buildings we had made."[41]

After ordering the English governor of Calcutta to demolish the new fortifications, the Nawab immediately left Murshidabad to march against Shaukat Jang of Purnea. This order of the Nawab reached Calcutta before 12 May, and Drake, without consulting his council sent the following reply to Watts at Kasimbazar, who forwarded it to the Nawab: "That the Nabab had been misinformed by those who had represented to him that the English were building a wall

39 Letter to Court, 18 September, 1752.

40 Letter to Court, 3 September., 1755 (F.W.I.H.C., I, pp. 883–884).

41 Hasting's MSS in the British Museum, Vol. 29209. Quoted in Maitra *Sirajuddaulah*, p. 134, f.n.

round the town:... that in the late war between England and France, the French had attacked and taken the town of Madrass, contrary to the neutrality which it was expected would have been preserved in the Mogul's dominions: and that there being at present great appearance of another war between the two nations, the English were under apprehension that the French would act in the same manner in Bengal, to prevent which, they were repairing their line of guns on the bank of the river."[42]

When the Nawab received this letter at Rajmahal, he became extremely furious and immediately ordered his troops to turn their bayonetes against the English factory at Kasimbazar. The Nawab himself followed with his whole army.

On the eve of the capture of Kasimbazar factory, Sirajuddaulah said to have written a letter on 28 May to the principal merchant at Hugli: "It has been my design to level the English fortifications raised within my jurisdiction on account of their great strength; as I have nothing at present to divert me from the execution of that resolution, I am determined to make use of this opportunity; for which reason I am returning from Rajahmaul."[43]

Forrest states that at the bottom of this letter, the Nawab wrote in his own handwriting that he swore before God and the Prophet that unless the English would consent to his proposals, he would expel them totally out of his country. But this observation of Forrest was not supported by any other evidence. Even Watts, who was imprisoned at Kasimbazar by the Nawab did not believe that the Nawab "intended to drive the English out of his dominions."[44] Omar Beg—one of the Nawab's officers, believed that the Nawab merely intended to frighten the English.[45]

On the approach of the Nawab's army at Kasimbazar,

42 Orme, *Indostan*, II, p. 56.

43 Quoted in, Eorrest, *Clive*, I p. 294.

44 Watts' Letter to Court, 30 January, 1757 (Hill, III, p. 336).

45 Little, J.H., *House of Jagat Seth* (Calcutta, Reprint, 1967), p. 162.

Watts, the Chief, and his two colleagues, Collet and Batson wrote a letter to the Calcutta Council that the Nawab had become extremely angry with the English, had sent order to Rai-Durlabh to put a stop to the English business at Kasimbazar and to Mohanlal, to put a stop to the English business at Dacca. As the Nawab was advancing with 400 horses, the Kasimbazar officers requested the governor at Calcutta to help them against the Nawab with a supply of soldiers and arms. The Kasimbazar Council became much frightened when they did not get any reply from Calcutta and so they again appealed to Calcutta on 31 May "either to fill up the ditch and pull down the new works", or to supply them with soldiers as the defenee of the factory was "very weak" But at the end of the letter, they concluded that it would be better for the English to write a letter to the Nawab immediately.[46]

But the attitude of the Fort william authorities in Calcutta was one of resistance to the Nawab as well as to disobey his orders. The Nawab still entertained hopes of compromise and sent Khwajah Wajid to Calcutta for a settlement. Tooke observes in his Narrative: "The Nobab at the same time sent to the President and council Fuckeer Tougar (Khwajah Wajid), with a message of the same purport, which as they (the English) did not intend to comply with, looking upon it as a most unprecedented demand, treated the messenger with a gerat deal of ignominy and turned him out of their bounds, without any answer at all."[47]

Khwajah Wajid even after his disgrace, sent his *diwan* "four times" to Calcutta to persuade the gentlemen "to pasify" the Nawab but was threatened by the English at Calcutta "to be used ill if he came again on the same errand."[48] Thus the Calcutta Council deliberately threw away all chances of compromise with the Nawab.

46 Ram Gopal, *How the British Occupied Bengal* (New York, 1963)p.74

47 William Tooke's Narrative, 10 November, 1757,

48 Watt's and Collet's Letter to Court, 16 July (F.W.I.H.C., I, pp 1011-1012).

On 22 May, the vanguard of the Nawab's army under Rai-Durlabh appeared before the factory of Kasimbazar and it was encamped[49] at once. But Rai-Durlabh committed no hostilities until the arrival of the main body of the army under the Nawab himself, who joined with the former on 1 June. According to Watts, the whole of the Nawab's army consisted of 10,000 horses and 20,000 Rajputs and other men with a large train of artillery, whereas with in the Kasimbazar factory there were only "fifty soldiers most of which were Portuguese."[50] Thus the factors at Kasimbazar made no effort to defend the fort against the Nawab. Though Drake wrote in reply to a demand for the assistance of Kasimbazar that that were "sufficient for the purpose required" and that "the garrsion was to make the best defence possible, and was only to retreat should it find the place untenable."[51] Watts rightly thought that the place could not be defended and that any attempt to maintain it would not only be useless but might damage the fortunes of the English. Hence he wrote to the court: "Had we attempted to resist, our factory must inevitably had fallen into their hands, we being in no condition to make a defence against so large a force."[52]

After reaching Kasimbazar, Sirajuddaulah wanted to have a conference with Watts, the Chief of that factory. Accordingly, Rai-Durlabh wrote a letter to Watts that if the latter "might come out with great safety and no harm would happen" to him, the *diwan* would introduce him to the Nawab. Watts then called a meeting of the members of the factory, but meanwhile, he wrote a letter to Durlabhram to desist from an attack.[53] In the meeting of the council opinion was divided. But finally Watts had to agree to the demand of the Nawab for the sake of

---

49 Holwell's Letter to Court, 30 Nov. 1756 (Home-Public, 1755-57).

50 Watts' and Collet's letter to Court, 16 July 1756 (F.W.I.H.C., I, 1008-1009).

51 Malleson, *Hasting*, p. 30. But the reply of Draxe was not received by watts.

52 Watts' and Collet's letter to Court 16 July 1756 (F.W.I.H.C., I, p. 1009).

53 Hill, II, pp. 60-61. Also, Mukhopadhyay, S.C., *The Career of Rajah Durlabhram Mahindra,—Rai-Durlabh, Diwan of Bengal.* Varanasi, 1974,p.33).

his (Watts') wife, as she became "distracted with terror and weeping in fear."[54] Thus Watts set out to the Nawab's camp accompanied by Dr. Forth. When he reached the gate, the guard refused him to pass. Mrs. Watts ran up with her two babies in arms and by her tears, persuaded the guard to admit her husband in the camp. This Watts entered the camp with the surgeon and when they advanced near to the Nawab's tent, they were disarmed and their hands were tied up. This was unexpected and Watts became surprised to find that they had been arrested.[55]

After the arrest of Watts, the Nawab insisted that Watts should write a *muchelka* (obligation) that within fifteen days the members of the Calcutta Council would level the new works they had raised, would deliver up the Nawab's subjects who had fled for their protection and for the abuse of the Company's *dastacks* "by giving them to those that had no right to them"; the English should pay back what the "Government had suffered by loss of duties. "Watts informed the Nawab that his signing of the *muchelka* was of "no consequence" without the approval of other members of the factory.[56] Accordingly Collet and Batson were called for to make "an end of the affairs." They were brought before the Nawab, but because it was not a convenient place to discuss the articles proposed to them,"they signed on *muchelka* blindly with that of watts on condition that the supreme council at Calcutta should approve of what did not come within their powers."[57] when they signed the *muchelka* jointly, Collet and Mrs. Watts were imprisoned, while Batson was sent back to

54 Hill, III, p. 222.

55 Watts entered into the tent of the Nawab weeping. He could say nothing except that he was the slave of the Nawab. "Toumar Golam, Tomar Golam", he only uttered these words before the Nawab.—Extract from a translated manuscript entitled *Revolutions in Bengal*, (quoted in Hill, III, p. 222).

56 Watts' and Collet's Letter to Court, 16 July, 1756 (F.W.I.H.C., I. p. 1009). Also. Hill, III, p. 223.

57 *Revolutions in Bengal* (Hill, III, p. 223).

the factory.[58] The Nawab directed the *godowns* of Kasimbazar to be sealed, while Watts and Collet were carried as prisoners with the Nawab. Mrs. Watts wlth her children were released on the request of Law[59], but at the same time a number of men became prisoners[60] in the hands of the Nawab. On 4 June, the factory of Kasimbazar was surrendered and the Nawab took possession of the cannon, ammunition and military stores.[61]

Watts never contemplated hostilities with the Nawab. He thought that some suitable presents to the Nawab might bring the hostilities to an end. With this in view, before the final blow on Kasimbazar, Watts went to Sri Babu-Khwajah Wajid's *diwan* at Chinsurah from whom he came to know about Drake's reply. Drake had told Sri Babu that sooner the Nawab came to Calcutta, the better, for then he "would make another Nawab."[62] These insinuations and disobedience of Drake, threw the Nawab into a tremendous rage; the Nawab determined to march to Calcutta for a totol submission by the English.

On June 6 a rumour spread in Calcutta about the surrender of Kasimbazar, which was confirmed by a letter from Collet, early in the morning on 7 June. The English further learnt that the factory had been delivered to Rai-Durlabh, but it was not plundered and the Nawab was "determined to march with his whole army to Calcutta'[63], to take revenge against the English.

---

58 Watts' and Collet to Court 16 July 56 (F.W.I.H.C., I, p.1009)

59 Hill, p. 223 Mrs. Watts and her children were permitted to live in the French Factory at Kasimbazar.

60 Besides Watts and Collet, some other persons like Hastings, Watts junior, Sykes, Marriot Chambers and about fifty soldiers were arrested at Kasimbazar-Scots Magazine, Vol. XIX, May, 1757 (qoted in Hill, III.p.101)

61 Letter to Court, 17 July, 1756.

62 Watts' and Collet's letter to Court, 17 July, 1756 (F.W.I.H.C., I, 1024).

63 Holwell' Letter to Court, 30 November, 1576 (Home-Public, p. 258)

The first reaction of Drake when he learnt about the Nawab's advance to Calcutta, was one of oppositian. As a preparatory measure, he immediately directed, on 7 June, to the Chiefs of the subordinate factories to withdraw : "Advice early in the morning was received at Calcutta of the loss of Cassimbazar factory, and that the Nabob was upon full march, with all his forces, for Fort William. The same day orders were sent to the Chiefs of Dacca, Jugdea and Ballasore to withdraw and quit their factories, with what effects they could secure."[64]

Watts and Collet accompanied the Nawab's army to Calcutta. On their way, Rai-Durlabh was frequently sent to Watts for a compromise with the English and as such the *diwan* informed the Chief that the dispute could be settled, if the Company would pay one crore of rupees to the Nawab. On this formula of compromise, Watts assured the *diwan* that the "Company's whole estate did not amount to that sum". To this reply from Watts, Rai-Durlabh lessened the demand to twenty lakhs of rupees. Watts then answered again that the Company's annual trade to Bengal did not amount to that sum. Even then, the *diwan* pressed Watts to ascertain how much money the English would be able to pay. Watts replied again that he had no power to deal with this matter alone, but if he be permitted, he might write to Calcutta to know about the decision of the council. This request of Watts to write to Calcutta was rejected by Rai-Durlabh but the latter informed the former that if any proposals of accommodation were made first from Calcutta, Watts then might inform the *diwan* "as often as he pleased" But Watts and Collet did not get any opportunity to write to Calcutta as they were all the time surrounded strictly by the Nawab's soldiers. This went on till they reached a place opposite to Hugli, where they wrote to the Dutch Director to forward their letters to Calcutta, wherein they informed Drake and his cocncil to send a proper person to the camp or to empower them to act on

---

64 Hastings' MSS. Vol-29209. (Quoted in Maitra, *Sirajuddaulah*, p. 163 f.n.)

behalf of the Calcutta Council to settle the dispute with the Nawab for a sum of money. To this letter from Watts, Drake and his council replied that "after the disgrace the Company had suffered at Cossimbazar by the taking of their factory and imprisoning their servants," they resolved "not to come to any agreement" with the Nawab.[65] In fact, Kasimbazar and Calcutta became thus symbols for ambivalent policies.

The Nawab on his way to Calcutta took further measure against the English. He directed all the *zamindars* around Calcutta to stop the supply of all provisions to the English. Between 10 to 13 June; the Nawab's army took possession of the fort of Tanna and hence cut off the English communication on the river. This news alarmed the English at Calcutta, who immediately sent letters to Madras and Bombay for reinforcements. But at any length, they could not expect assistance within a month. So, for a relief nearer at hand, the assistance of the Dutch as well as the French was solicited, as a common cause to enter into a defensive alliance āgainst the Nawab. The Dutch positively refused to help the English by saying that they were directed by their nation to "remain neuter in all disputes" with the Nawab; while the French added further insult by advising the English to come to Chandernagore, in which case they promised them their protection.[66] Hence no avenues remained open before the English but to rely on their own strength,

When the Nawab's forces had arrived at Ranaghat, which was about two days' march from Hugli, Khwajah Wajid-the principal merchant at Hugli-again tried in his own way, to make a settlement of affairs. As such, he again sent his *diwan* Shri Babu to Calcutta, but when the latter reached Baranagore, he received a message from his *gomastah* in Calcutta, not to proceed any further, as there was a possibility

65 Watts' and Collet's Letter to Court, 16 July, (1756 (F.W.I.H.C., I, p. 1011). Also. Watts' Letter of Csurt, 30 January, 1757 (Home-Publc, p. 425).

66 Holwell's Letters to the Governcr of Bombay, 17 July 1756 (F.W.I. H.C.,I, pp. 1019-1023). Also, Stewrt, *History of Bengal*, p. 500. Also, Orme, *Indostan*, II, p. 59.

of his arrest at Calcutta. Hence Shri Babu returned to Hugli without venturing any new effort,[67]

But when the final blow of the Nawab was expected any moment, Governor Drake and his council came to their senses as it seemed to them absurd to resist so large a force of the Nawab. Accordingly, they judged it advisable to demolish all the works they had made and wrote a letter to Watts to appease the Nawab. But this letter was not received by Watts.[68] Another effort of Sri Babu for a compromise also failed, for when he was in the camp of the Nawab at Bankabazar, he wrote a letter to Drake but the reply of this letter arrived when the Nawab's forces were at Kellsall's gardens and hostilities had already been commenced. Sri Babu delivered this letter of Drake to the Nawab, but it was too late, as the Nawab became highly incensed against Drake.[69]

When the Nawab surrounded the Fort William on 15 June, there were a very few soldiers to defend it,[70] On the morning of 18 June, the outworks of the fort were attacked. To defend themselves, the English then sent small parties to the "tops of some of highest houses," but in this enterprise, Charles Smith, Robert Wilkinson and some others were killed by the Nawab's snipers. Only Mons. La Bonne with a few soldiers defended the jail bravely for six hours until he was wounded and obliged to retire. In the evening, the Nawab's army killed and wounded several of the English army and surrounded them from all sides. The English army then retreated from the outworks of the fort and during the night they sheltered themselves in the church as well as in the Company's houses.[71]

---

67 Watts' and Collet's letter to Court, 17 July, 1756 (P.W.I.H.C., I, p. 1025).

68 Letter to Court, 17 Sept., 1756 (F.W.I.H.C., I, p. 1033).

69 Watts' and Colleter to Court, 17 July 1956 (F.W.I.H.C., I, p. 1025).

70 About 1500 men and native troops deserted the English after the first day of war against the Nawab (Stewart, *History of Bengal*, p. 501); only 264 of regular force remained with Holwell to defend the fort.—Forrest, *Clive*, I, p. 296.

71 Oray's Junior Account of the loss of Calcutta (F.W.I.H.C. I, p. 1015).

On the morning of 19, the war continued again and the Nawab's army killed as well as wounded several of the English soldiers. The English soldiers were directed to retire from the church. The ladies and the wounded men somehow escaped and were sent on "board the ships". Then followed a ruch among the English to save their own lives. Governor Drake with the company of several soldiers and officers fled on board the ships, that greatly disspirited the other English soldiers who remained within the fort.[72] Those who fled from the fort, could save nothing belonging to the Company, not even their books and papers.[73] Immediately after the retreat of Governor Drake and some others, Holwell was unanimously chosen in his place, who made a public declaration of Drake's cowardly flight.[74] But the soldiers could not stand to resist the fort and during the night of 19 June, 1756, English soldiers deserted the fort. The others who still remained in the fort, obtained the liquors and wine of the deserted soldiers, soon became drunken and disobeyed the command of Holwell. Thus when the soldiers became unruly, disorder and confusion followed within the fort. This opportunity was taken up by the Nawab's army, who rushed upon them, applied ladders to the walls and were soon in possession of the fort. Before that Holwell had hoisted a flag of truce to cease hostilities.[75] Thus Fort william was captured by the Nawab on 20 June and most of the men, officers and soldiers were carried as prisoners to Murshidabad.[76]

On 21 June, the surrender of Calcutta was followed by Universal pillage. The Nawab, at five in the afternoon,

---

72 *Ibid.*

73 Watts' and Collet's letter to Court, 16 July, 1756 (F.W.I.H.C., I, 1010).

74 Gray's (Junior) account of the loss of Calcutta (*Ibid.*, p. 1085).

75 Holwell threw a letter from the rampart, written by Omichand, addressed to Manikchand, who commanded a body of troops before the fort, requesting him to cease hostilities.—Stewart, *History of Bengal*, pp. 502-503.

76 Watts' and Colles's letter to Court, 16 July, 1756 (F.W.I.H.C., I, p. 1010), Holwell with Burdett, Court, Walcott and Ensign were carried as prisoners to Murshidabad (*Vide, Ibid.*)

entered Fort William, surrounded by his generals and principal officers, and received their congratulations. The Company's warehouses as well as the dwelling places of the chief English, Hindu and Armenian merchants were plundered by the army of sirajuddaulah.[77] The English treasury at the fort had been searched, and to the Nawab's infinite disappointment, it contained only Rs. 50,000.[78] The Nawab then ordered Omichand and Krishnadas to be presented before him and when they were brought, the Nawab received them with civility[79]. Sirajuddaulah then, after making proper arrangements for the administration of Calcutta by appointing Manikehand as its governor, returned to Murshidabad with his army.

The English had been humiliated. Governor Drake, with other English gentlemen, who had escaped from Calcutta, had now taken their shelter on board country ships at Falta. They were presumably comtemplating flight to Madras. But the Nawab did not disturb the English refugees at Falta and allowed them to remain there. Meanwhile. on the news of the fall of Calcutta, the Nawab's forces at Dacca surrounded Richard Becher—the English Chief, and the members of his council. They were made prisoners and then were sent to the French factory at Dacca, but lost all their "books and papers", along with the Company's eflects and money.[80] But Peter Amyatt—the English Chief at Lakhimpore and Thomas Boddam of Balasore somehow escaped and saved about sixty thousand and six thousand rupees respectively in money and goods of the Company's property. Both of them joined the Englishe refugees at Falta.[81] Later on, after remaining in the

---

77 *Selr*, II, p. 190.

78 Beveridge, *A Comprehenstve History*, I, p. 689. Law in his *Memoire* states that during all his investigations, the Nawab could not prccure more than two or three lakhs of rupees (Hill, III, pp. 171-172).

79 *Ibid.* Also, Stewart, *History of Bengal*, p. 503.

80 Becher's letter to Court, 18 July, 1756 (F.W.I.H.C., I, pp.1029-1030).

81 Watts' and Collet's letter to Court, 16 July, 1756 (*Ibid.*, p. 1012).

French factory at Dacca for a period of nearly two months, Richard Becher with his subordinates and the English ladies were sent to Falta, by M. Courtin—the Chief of the French Factory at Dacca. They reached Falta on 26 August,[82]

When the Nawab's army crossed the river at Hugli, he sent detachmehts to the Dutch and the French settlements asking both to assist him with money. The Nawab threatened to extirpate them both, as he had already done the English, unless they would pay him a large sum of money immediately. When they repeatedly assured their full submission to his will, the Nawab consented to accept from the Dutch a sum of Rs. 4,50,000 and from the French Rs. 3,50.000. The Nawab demanded less money from the French, because they supplied him two hundred chests of gunpowder during his march to Calcutta.[83] There at Hugli, the Nawab released Watts and Collet on 28 June and delivered them to Renault—the French governor at Chandernagore. The Nawab then took a receipt for these two Englishmen from Renault and directed him to send them safe to Madras.[84] Watts and Collet, it transpired, had received "the most humane treatment" at Chandernagore.[85] The Nawab then slcwly marched to Murshidabad, where he arrived on 11 July.

On 30 June, when the Nawab was on his way to the capital he wrote a letter to George Pigot—the governor of Madras informing him that the Nawab "had no intention to remove the mercantile business of the Company" in Bengal, but he had to do it due to governor Drake, "a very wicked and unruly man," who protected those persons who had the charges

---

82 Hill, S.C., *Three Frenchmen in Bengal* (Lond., 1903) pp. 134-135.

83 Stewart, *History of Bengal*, pp. 505-506.

84 Nawab's letter to Renault, 28 June 1756 (Hill, I, pp. 196-197).

85 Watts' and Collet's letter to Court, 16 July (F.W.I.H.C., I, p. 1014) Some English soldiers and sailors, numbering abouts 110 were admitted in the French hospital at Chanderhagore and they were provided with diet and clothing.—*vide, Ibid.*

of the defalcation of government money against them.[86] He pointed out that this protection had been given to them despite the Nawab's repeated instructions to the governor. The Nawab gave the assurance that he did not intend to put a stop to the mercantile business of the English because as he pointed out, he had allowed the English to remain at Falta and did not disturb them from there.

The loss of Culcutta brought the English to a miserable strait. The fugitives at Falta passed their days with great agony, due to want of provisions and proper shelter. They tried to secure some assistance from the adjoining Hindu *zamindar*, Rajah Nabkrishna of Sobhabazar. Food was occasionally supplied to them by the Dutch at Chinsurah.[87] But these were far from sufficiene to meet their needs. The English, thus finding no otner alternative, tried to open negotiations with the Nawab for their re-settlement at Calcutta. Eor this purpose, the English refugees at Falta tried to get help from Khwajah Wajid as well as his *diwan* Sri Babu and Bisdom—the Dutch Director at Chinsurah. Governor Drake and his adjourned council met at Falta and through the help of Sri Babu, they wrote a letter to Bisdom—forwarding copies of the letter to Watts and Collet at Chandernagore, requesting them to be delivered to Khwajah Wajid, Rai-Durlabh, Manikchand and Ghulam Husain Khan, "desiring their interest with the Nabab to be admitted again into Calcutta." Upon the receipt of this letter, Bisdom took prompt action and informed Khwajah Wajid his desire to have a conference with the Nawab. To this Khwajah Wajid replied that the Nawab at the moment, might take "umbrage at any private meeting." He also hinted it to Bisdom that even if the Nawab permitted the English to re-establish at

86 Letter from the Nawab to Pigot—Governor of Madras, 30 June, 1756 (Hill, I, p. 196.)

87 After many discussions the Dutch came to a secret resolution on 20 Juld, in consideration of the close alliances with the English "to provide the Fulta fugitives with more food and clothes intending to charge it to the English Company."—Hill, I, pp. 302-308.

Calcutta, it would not be any on better conditions than those allowed to the Portuguese and Armenians to trade in Bengal.[88]

But Watts and Collet remained very oftuse in their reaction to Drake's entreaty to the Nawab that the English be admitted again into Calcutta. They even refused in their letter of 8 July, to acknowledge the authority of Drake and his council as still in office, and hence declined to deliver the letters to the principal men at Murshidabad. They even became much enraged with Drake and his council and wrote to the following purport : "Had your Honours etc. thought proper to treat before the Nabob reached Calcutta we are pretty certain a sum of money would have made all easy, prevented the loss of the settlement and the ruin of many thousands and we wrote to your Honours etc. to that purpose when we were off Hughley, the only opportunity we have while in the camp."[89]

Expressing their stern refusal to accept Drake's authority, they wrote to Drake: "We likewise think that after your Honour and the majority of you had quitted Fort William, which still hold out, your power as a Governor and Council from that moment ceased and we are of opinion that you have no authority to indemnify us for acting by your orders."[90] Naturally Drake and his council at Falta reacted sharply to Watts and Collet for the latter's *volte face*. During this time there were exchanges of letters between Watts and Holwell, containing charges and counter-charges on each other and each held the other responsible for the catastrophe of the English in Bengal. Holwell wrote to the Court of Directors that the factory of Kasimbazar was surrendered to the Nawab without any resistance. "A defence of only 24 hours would in its consequences have retarded in all probability his march to Calcutta for many days", observed Holwell in his letter and added that "a detention of his Army before Cossimbazar for two or three days would have brought on dirty rainly weather in his march

88 Watts' and Collet's letter to Court, 17 July, 1756 (F.W.I.H.C. I, p. 1025). Also, Hill, I. p. cxi.

89 *Ibid.* (*Ibid.*, p. 1026).

90 *Bengal and Madras Papers*, Vol. II (Calcutta, 1928), p. 61.

towards us", but the easy possession of Kasimbazar enabled the Nawab to march against Calcutta "without loss of time."[91]

This charge of Holwell greatly angered Watts. He replied to the Court of Directors that the resistance offered by Holwell and his men was next to nothing. They had practically done nothing to defend Calcutta even when the number of soldiers and military stores of the English at Calcutta were "above ten times more" than the factory of Kasimbazar. The Kasimbazar factory, he pointed out, consisted of only 51 or 52 men out of whom six were sick. "With this force.", observed Watts, "we had orders to resist an army of thirty thousand men." But if the Kasimbazar factory could not be defended "we were to make the best retreat in our power" replied Watts, "a retreat of above a hundred miles over land, through an enemy's country and in the face of so large an army."[92] On these charges, Holwell observed in his letter to court that the nature of the fortifications of Calcutta and Kasimbazar and the force brought against both these places, were not equal. Pointing out the discrepancies in Watts' report, Holwell pointed out that on 1 June, Watts reported to Calcutta that the Nawab was marching with 12,000 troops but subsequently he informed that 30,000 troops were brought against Kasimbazar. Holwell thus expressed the view that Watts was guided more by malice than truth.[93]

Due to the indignation of Drake and his council at Falta Watts and Collet at last agreed to deliver the letters to the Indian personages. They employed the good offices of Bisdom, and the latter again employed Khwajah Wajid and Sri Babu. Khwajah Wajid then advised them to translate the letters into Persian and then send them back to Drake to have his seal put on them and then to return these letters for delivery. But at the same time, Sri Babu informed Watts that all these

91 Holwell's letter to Court, 30 Novmber, 1756 (F. W.I. H.C.. I,p 1051).

92 Watts' letter to Court, 30 January, 1757 (*Ibid.*, II, p. 184).

93 Holwell's letter to Court, August, 1757 (Holwell, *Important Fact*, p. 358)

endeavours would have no good result. Therefore, if the English wanted to re-establish themselves in Calcutta on creditable terms, the only methods would be to go to Madras for military help and "to return with strength sufficient to enforce any petitions we had to make."[94]

Watts and Collet also shared the same opinion. For military help, which was the only method of restoration, they wrote to Fort Saint George: "We shall do all in our power to get permission to re-establish the settlement but are without any hopes of obtaining it during the life of the present Nabob. We therefore know of no other method but that of a military force which we hope your Honour and C. will be able to send sufficient to attack the Nabob even in his Metropolis."[95]

The council at Falta opened this negotiation with the Nawab with the hope that if the latter were amenable, it would relieve the English from their distress at Falta where they were in the utmost want of all necessities of life. But strict orders had been issued by the Nawab to the local people, not to supply any provisions to the English.[96] But when they realised that there was no chance of reconciliation, they sent Manningham to Madras, early in July, asking for military help. At the same time, they wrote a letter to the President and Council at Madras: "You will support us with the whole force you can obtain on your coast, military and marine, together with a sufficient quantity of ammunition, cannon and all other warlike stores,...... which may enable us to re-establish ourselves in these provinces."[97] Drake and his council from Falta also wrote a letter to the President and Council of Bombay for the supply of troops and hoped that if these two presidencies would supply the English at Falta with military help, they would be able to re-establish their honour in Bengal "upon a secure and respectable footing."[98]

94 Watts' and Collet's letter to Court, 17 July, 1757 (F.W.I.H.C. Vol. I, p. 1026)

95 Watts' and Collet's letter to Fort St. George, 7 July 1756, Hill, I, pp. 58-59).

96 B.M.P., II, pp. 71-72.

97 *Ibid.*

98 Letter to Court from Drake and his Council at Falta, 17 Sept. 1756 (F.W.I.H.C., I, pp. 1035-1036).

The hostility in Bengal with the English Company, resulting in the surrender of Kasimbazar reached Madras on 13 July from a letter of the President and Council of Calcutta. As the disturbances with the country powers were very common, it did not excite much surprise in Madras and it was supposed that the attack on Kasimbazar was a temporary phase and that the wrath of the hostile Prince might be appeased in due course of time. So Madras Council resolved on 14 July to send a re-inforcement of 200 men to Bengal under the command of Major Killpatrick.[99] The Madras Council, at the same time wrote a letter to the Select Committee at Bombay *about their decision* of reinforcement to Bengal and requested the latter to send troops to Madras "as much as possible."

Major Killpatrick with his troops arrived at Culpee on 28 July and reached Falta on 31 of the same month. On the news of the arrival of re-inforcement, members of the council who so long remained scattered in different places began to arrive at Falta and within 13 August, Watts Collet, Pearkes and Holwell had arrived there. On 26 August Becher with other gentlemen had also arrived from Dacca.[100]

At Falta, the Major found himself placed in a very bad situation. He had insufficient troops and ammunition with him and owing to the prevalence of sickness among his soldiers, he could not venture to undertake a war against the Nawab. He had to wait for further re-inforcements from Madras. and meanwhile, to gain time, he opened correspondence with the Nawab on 15 August. The Major wrote a letter to the Nawab, assuring him about the good intention of the English that "the British did not bear malice for what had happened in the past," and requested for a supply of provisions to the English refugees at Falta. This letter was sent to Hastings for delivery to the Nawab, who was still at Kasimbazar. At the same

99 B.M.P., II, p. 81. Also, Hill, I, p. CXIII. Captain Lin, Captain Godwin, Lieutenant Eidman, Ensigns Vouga and Flaction were appointed for this expedition to Bengal.

100 Hill, I, pp. CXII-CXV.

time, Khwajah, Petrus and Abraham Jacobs brought with them a letter from Omichand, advising Killpatrick to write friendly letters to Manikchand, Khwajah Wajid, Rai-Durlabh and Jagat Seth, which was done accordingly by the Major.[101] Omichand, who tried to negotiate with the Nawab, on behalf of the English, after receiving these letters from the Maior to be delivered to the respective persons, returned them to the Major, advising him that "some small presents" from the Major would be useful as well as acceptable to those, whom the English wanted to employ in this negotiation.[102]

Meanwhile, Drake and his council at Falta, wrote two letters to the Madras Council on 18 and 19 August, informing the latter about the fall of Calcutta and the arrival of Killpatrick for their assistance in Bengal. But as it seemed to them that the forces under Killpatrick were too small to undertake any expedition, they requested the Madras authorities to send "a sufficient force both military and marine." In their second letter on 19 August they further acquainted the Madras Council that about seven thousand troops of the Nawab were stationed at Calcutta, Tanna and Budge Budge.[103]

The English refugees at Falta did not remain satisfied by merely communicating their position in Bengal to the Madras authority and asking for military help from the latter, but also watched closely the politics of the *subah*. On 31 August, they appointed Dr. Forth to procure intelligence from the Dutch as well as the French about their intention towards the English. At the same time, they directed Hastings to watch the politics at Murshidabad and to keep a secret correspondence with the Major "by every opportunity."[104]

According to these instructions to Dr. Forth as well as to Hastings, the former intimated to the English at Falta on 2 September, the account of a dispute between the Nawab and

101 Consultations on Board the Pnoenix Schooner, Falta, Aug. 22, 1759 (Long, *Unpublished Records*, pp. 92-93).

102 Consultations, Falta. September 5, 1756 (Long, *Unpublished Records*, p. 95).

103 B.M.P., II, p. 89.

104 Consultations, Falta, August 31 (Long, *Unpublished Records*, pp. 93-94.)

the Jagat Seth. The Nawab had rebuked Jagat Seth for not procuring a *farman* from Delhi in favour of the former and asked the latter to raise from the merchants three crores of rupees for the purpose. But Jagat Seth refused to raise the money from the "already oppressed people" and as such was confined by the Nawab. Hastings also informed Forth on 26 August from Kasimbazar about the appointment of the Purnea Nawab as the *subahdar* of Bengal, which had created much confusion at Murshidabad and that Siraju-ddaulah was making preparation for a war against Shaukat Jang of Purnea. It was further informed that most of the adjoining Rajahs of Purnea had made their common interest with Shaukat Jang.[105]

Tidings of the fall of Calcutta reached Madras on 16 August which "created more horror and resentment than consternation and perplexity." [106] On August 18, a despatch was sent to Fort St. David requiring Clive's immediate presence at Madras. The Madras authorities then began to decide, for some days, their future course of action. This event wholly changed the aspect of affairs. The council at Madras decided to send the whole naval squadron and all the available land forces to retake Calcutta and requested Admiral Watson-Commander of the king's ships, and Colonel Aldercron-Commander of the king's men for their co-operation. Admrial Watson at once responded and pledged his ready assistance in the matter.

The Madras Council was fully aware of the risk and, therefore, the question of sending re-inforcement was earnestly debated. Some members proposed to send a small force to Bengal which would after joining with Killpatrick's troops be able to retake Calcutta and would harass the Nawab so that he would be forced to come to an agreement with the English. But this was strongly opposed by Robert Orme-the historian, then a member of the council at Madras. He maintained the necessity of despatching a force, sufficient to act with

105 Consultations, Falta, September 5 (*Ibid.*, pp. 95-96).

106 Thornton Edward, *The History of the British Empire in India* (Lond., 1841-48), p. 45.

courage. After facing much opposition, this view, at last, prevailed.[107]

After spending more than a month in debate the Madras Council decided on 22 September for "re-establishing the Company in their Rights and Priviledges at Bengal", the whole squadron should proceed with 600 men and the detachment of His Majesty's artillery "under the command of Captain Hislop" and the whole command by Colonel Clive[108], with full power for the conduct of the treaties to be made with the Nawab. The Madras authorities decided to take this bold step, when they learnt from the Company's ships that arrived from England that there was no news about any actual outbreak of war with France.

When Charles Manningham had arrived from Bengal in the morning of 29 September, the question of sending expeditions, the rights of the defunct Bengal Council at Falta, the rights of the officers of the expeditions presently formed at Madras were all discussed. With regards to the powers given to Watson as the Admiral of the naval forces, the Madras Council requested him to assert the "Company's Ancient settlements in that Province, upon the former or if possible, a better footing ; that this must be done by Treaty with the Nawab". But this treaty which would safeguard the Company's rights and privileges can be conducted only by the Company's representatives in Bengal. The military part of the said treaty would undoubtedly be conducted by a council of war, composed of officers of the sea and land forces both. Watson then desired to know what powers he was to be vested with. In reply the council held that the "powers he had from His Majesty were quite sufficient" to do the needful. Then the second question was put before the council, who were the proper representatives of the Company in Bengal ? Whereupon it was resolved that Drake, Lawrence when present, Watts, Manningham and Becher would form the select Committee

107 *Ibid.*

108 Colonel Lawrence was the most qualified for the command of the land forces and as such, his name was proposed. But as Lawrence was ill, Orme suggested the name of Clive, which was accepted also by Lawrence—Thornton, *British Empire*, p. 45.

of Bengal. And this select Committee, when joined by Clive, would be regarded as the proper representative of the Company in Bengal. This committee would deliver to Clive "a plan for the conduct of such Treaty as they shall recommend to be made for the best advantage of the Company with the Nabob of Bengal." The council had an entire confidence in Colonel Clive's abilities of faithfully implementing their plans in Bengal and requested Watson, in reply to his question, "to pay the same attention as you have hitherto done to us."[109] Thus on 16 october, after a dispute and debate at Madras for more than two months, five men-of-war under Watson, with 2,400 soldiers and 900 Europeans under Colonel Clive sailed from Madras for Bengal.[110]

On 5 December Watson anchored his squadron in Balasore road, where Watts and Becher had arrived to congratulate him and to apprise him with the situation of the English in Bengal.[111] On 12 December the Admiral reached Hugli and on 13 Culpee, where Drake and Holwell received him. On 15 December, Watson arrived at Falta with three ships *Kent Tyger* and *Walpole* and on the same day Clive also landed at Falta with his forces.[112]

Immediately after his landing at Falta, Clive wrote a letter to Manikchand-the Governor of Calcutta and tried to delude the Rajah with friendly correspondence. He wrote : "Upon my arrival in these parts from Madras, I was informed that you had shown a great friendship and regard for the English Company for which I write to return you thanks. I doubt not as you have hitherto professed a desire to serve the Company, you will at this time, when their affairs most require it, retain the same disposition in their favour."[113]

109 Consultations, Fort, St. George, From 29 Sept. to 1 Oct., 1756 (B.M.P., II, pp. 91-92).

110 Reginald, *Robert Clive*, p. 149.

111 Watts, William, *Memoire, of the Revolution in Bengal* (Lond., 1764), p. 15.

112 Forrest, *Clive*, I, pp. 333-334.

113 Clive's letter to Manikchand, 15 December, 1756 (*Colonel Clive's Correspondence*, Book No. 10, *vide*, B.M.P., II p. 2) Also, Forrest *Clive*, I, p. 334.

In reply to Clive, Manikchand informed him: "Your great abilities and dignity I was before well informed of, and I sincerely rejoice to hear of your safe arrival in these parts,...Your letter has determined me more than ever in the same sentiments, and in my desire of serving the Company which I shall continue to do to the utmost of my power."[114]

Watson also wrote a letter directly to the Nawab on 17 Deceber from his ship *Kent* at Falta : "The King, my master (whose name is revered among the monarchs of the world) sent me to these parts with a great fleet, to protect the East India Company's trade, rights and privileges...I doubt not you will consent to make them a reasonable satisfaction for the losses and injuries they have suffered and by that means put an amicable end to the troubles."[115]

Clive also wrote a letter to the Nawab. He sent this letter to Manikchand for delivery : "You may already have heard that there are forces arrived in Bengall.... That by doing good to the English you will do good to and establish the trade of your own country,... and that by your favour they may again be admitted to remain in your dominions and to trade as formerly."[116]

When Manikchand received this letter for delivery to the Nawab, he asked Clive to write the letter in a milder tone, which was at once refused by Clive. Thus, on December 25, Clive wrote to Manikchand that "however proper it might have been before the taking of Calcutta, would but ill-suit with the present time," when the English came to Bengal to demand satisfaction for the injuries done to them by the Nawab.[117]

While the English preteneded friendship with Manikchand, they also started their belligerent operations in Bengal. On 27 December the English troops attacked Budge Budge'[118] and

114 Manikchand's letter to Clive, 19 December (*Ibid.*)

115 Watson's letter to Nawab, 17 December (Quoted in Maitra, *Sirajuddaulah*, pp. 261-262).

116 Clive's letter to Nawab, 21 December [C.C.C. *vide*, B.M.P., II p. 3].

117 C.C.C. [B.M.P., II p. 6]

118 Thornton, *British Empire*, p. 47.

captured it. The following three days were spent in a series of minoractions against the Nawab's forces. On 29 December, Clive learnt from Watts the weak position of the Tanna fort as well. On 30 December, the English forces had arrived at Mayapur and on that day, a skirmish took place with Manikchand in which the latter escaped to Calcutta after a short resistance, receiving a shot on his turban. On the same day the Tanna fort was captured by the English forces.[119] Then the English forces began their march for the capture of Calcutta. Manikchand, on his part, tried to defend Calcutta with about 2,000 horses.[120]

The English army then attacked Calcutta on 2 January, 1757, where Manikchand tried to defend the fort. But the skirmishes at Budge Budge and Mayapur reminded him of the English valour and "not fiinding in himself courage enough to stand an engagement," fled away from Calcutta.[121] The English thus gained an easy victory. On the next day on 3 January, Watson enabled Drake and the members of the council to take possession of Calcutta. Within the fort all the effects, guns, military stores and other were restored.[122] Having restored Calcutta the Select Committee asked Watson to declare open war against Sirajuddaulah, on behalf of his Majesty for the losses and "injuries committed against the subjects of Great Britain."[123] Thus, at Clive's insistence, on 3 January, Drake, on behalf of the Company, and Watson, on behalf of the king of England, declared war against the Nawab At the same time, Clive hinted to Manikchand that the English had come to Bengal to obtain justice. If this was refused by the Nawab "it will occasion the utmost trouble in his country and produce a terrible scene of confusion."[124]

119 Stewart, *History of Bengal*, p. 514.

120 Hill, II, pp. 76-77. Also F.W.I.H.C., II, p. 189.

121 *Seir*, II, p. 221.

122 Letter to Court, 8 January, 1757 [F.W.I.H.C., II, p. 175]. Also Hill, S.C., *An Abstract of the Early Records of the Foreign Department*, Part-I [Calcutta, 1901], p. 9.

123 Select Committee's letter to Watson, 3 January, 1757 [F.W.I.H. C. II, p. 83]. Also, Hill, II, p. 83.

124 Clive's letter to Manikchand, 8 January, 1757 [C.C.C. p. 7]

As a follow-up action after the easy victory of Calcutta, as well as to strike terror into the heart of the Nawab, the English determined to attack Hugli. The Nawab's army began to defend the town but they could not resist for long against the naval and land forces of the English and hence the town was captured on 11 January.[125] The English soldiers destroyed some stores of rice and returned to Calcutta on 19 January, having destroyed the granaries at Bandel on the way.[126]

Apparently the Nawab was a silent spectator to the latest developments in Bengal. But he had realised after the expulsion of the English from Calcutta that his revenues showed a steep fall. But when the news reached Sirajuddaulah about the English forces' sack of Hugli, him became indignant and ordered all his troops to assemble at Murshidabad, from where he planned to march on Calcutta, with a determination to punish the foreigners who had dared that much.

Evidently the English had undertaken their attack on Hugli with a view to making the Nawab alarmed. But on the news of the Nawab's march to Calcutta, the anger of the English was replaced by fear and Clive took every measure of defence as well as for negotiations. When he expressd his views before the committee Clive used every legitimate argument in favour of conciliation. It seemed to him the most expedient policy for the English to follow the path of peace with the Nawab at that juncture.[127]

The English thought of the mediation through the French but the renewal of their war in Europe prevented Clive to seek the French intercession. Hence Clive sought negotiations with the Seths but the latter refused unless the English stopped all acts of hostility. The Dutch offered their mediation for a settlement with the Nawab but Watson did not agree to the Dutch proposal. Thus, Clive requested both Khwajah Wajid and the Seths for their intervention in the affair and sent his proposals

125 Gleig, G.R., *The Life of Robert First Lord Clive* [Lond., 1907], pp. 65-66.

126 Hill, *Abstract*, p. 9.

127 Gleig's *Clive*, p. 66.

to the former. Meanwhile Admiral Watson received a letter from the Nawab in which the latter accused Drake for having acted contrary to the order of the Nawab. Accordingly the Nawab ordered Drake's expulsion from Bengal but he desired that the English might carry on their trade as formerly, "had another Chief been sent here."[128] In reply, Watson wrote to the Nawab, "was it becoming the justice of a prince to punish all for one man's sake?" He further observed in the same letter, saying that the "great princes delight in acts of justice and in showing mercy."[129] In reply, the Nawab again wrote to Watson: "You have taken and plundered Houghley and made war upon my subjects, these are not actions of becoming merchants. I have therefore left Muxadabad and am arrived near Houghley." He further observed that if the English were desirous of peace, they should "send a person of confidence to me, who can make your demands, and treat with me upon this affair." But he gave the dire warning that if the English did not want a compromise and wished to keep the dispute alive and were determined of an war "it is no fault of mine to prevent the fatal consequences of a ruinous war."[130]

From the tone of Sirajuddaulah's letter it seems that he was desirous of settling disputes with the English, if the latter professed to remain like peaceful merchants. But the Nawab continued his march to Calcutta and crossed the river ten miles above Hugli on 30 January. On the same day, the Nawab wrote a letter to M. Renault, the Director-General of the French Company, that if he would assist him by sending "the ships of War" against the English, "I abolish for ever the annual imports on your commerce, and I give you the right to establish a mint at Chandernagore."[131] But unfortunately for the Nawab the French did not assist him. The

128 Nawab's letter to Watson, 23 January, Also. Ive, Edward, A voyage from England to India [Lond, 1773] p. 108.

129 Watson's letter to the Nawab, 27 January (*Ibid.*, p. 109].

130 Ive's *Voyage*, p. 110.

131 Nawab's letter to M. Ranault, 30 January [Forrest, *Clive*, I, p 352).

French thus lost a good oppcitunity of crippling their rivals in Bengal.

While advancing to Calcutta with his army, the Nawab continued his policy of settlement with the English and asked Clive on 1 February to "send a person of trust" to him who might accommodate matters with him. "I will allow you the same freedom in Calcutta and your factories as you enjoyed formerly,"[132] observed the Nawab in his letter. When Clive received this letter from the Nawab he also professed his inclination for restoring peace and accordingly informed the Nawab on 3 February his desire of sending Watts and Scrafton, the two deputies of the Company to attend upon him. Meanwhile on the same day, the Nawab marched with his army to Omichand's garden situated at a distance of two miles from Calcutta, where the two deputies, accompanied by Khwajah Petrus arrived before the Nawab's tent on 4 February. The English deputies were introduced by Ranjit Rai to the *diwan* Rajah Durlabhram, who sought for an interview with the Nawab. Durlabhram suspected them and insisted on their being searched in order to ensure the security of the Nawab. The English deputies felt insulted by the behaviour of the *diwan* and refused to submit under such humiliation. At last Durlabhram had to stop the search and the English were then led to the Nawab. Before the Nawab, the English deputies presented a paper to conclude a peace treaty. The Nawab read it and then handed it over to the *diwan* to settle the matter and then dismissed the deputies.[133] After this unsuccessful interview, when the English deputies were about to leave, they vwere warned by Omichand that the Nawab "was only waiting for his artillery" to attack them.[134] The English became alarmed and immediately ordered their attendants to extinguish the light. Under the cover of darkness they hastened off, without waiting for any further interview.

Watts and Scrafton hastened back to Clive and apprised him about the whole situation. Clive immediately decided to

132 Nawab's letter to Clive, 1 Feb. [C.C.C., p. 8].

133 Mukhopadhyay, *Rai-Dur'abh*, pp. 43-44.

134 Scrafton Luke, *Reflections on the Government of Indostan* (Lond., 1763), p. 71.

make a surprise attack on the Nawab's camp to preempt any move on the latter's part. Accordingly, he rapidly sent a messenger to Watson apprising the latter of his design and requesting the Admiral's assistance of a reinforcement from the fleet. Orders were also issued to several officers to furnish Clive with troops and as such an army consisting of 569 men, armed with muskets, were assembled under the banner of Clive [135]

The next day, on 5 February, at about 5 A.M., Clive made a surprise attack in thick fog on the Nawab's tent, for which the Nawab's army were totally unprepared. Clive wanted to arrest the Nawab in person but luckily for the Nawab, he was shifted to another tent by Rai-Durlabh. In a skirmish that followed, many of the Nawab's soldiers were killed and wounded, while the English also lost some of their men.[136] But in the morning when the sky became clear, Clive had to withdraw from the Nawab's camp. The Nawab and his army also did not think it safe to remain near the English camp and so they went to Dum Dum, where they reached on 6 February. On the same day, Watson sent the following letter to the Nawab: "Evidences so full and positive, of your bad intentions towards us, that however strong my inclinations might be towards peace, I could no longer entertain any reasonable hope of seeing it accomplished. I therefore desired Colonel Clive to show you what an army of Englishmen was capable of doing, that before it was too late you might agree to the proposals, which would be made to you."[137]

The letter was written with a view to threatening the Nawab. In the Nawab's camp his soldiers were also not willing to continue the fight any longer. Even his father-in-law, Irez Khan, and the principal commanders of his army, asked the Nawab to listen to the proposals for peace. Just at that time,

---

135 Broome, *Bengal Army*, I. p.96.

136 M. Law tells us that 1200 to 1500 men were killed on the side of the Nawab, while the English lost 200 men, black and white. Law, *Memoire* (Hill, III pp. 182-183).

137. Watson's letter to the Nawab, 6 February (Ive's *Voyage*, p. 113).

the Nawab heard about the victory of Ahmad Shah Abdali over the Mughal forces of Delhi and became apprehensive of the invader's advance towards Bengal. Thus, confusion within and the fear of a danger from outside, induced the Nawab to agree to the proposals for peace. Accordingly, Ranjit Rai sent a letter to Clive through Khwajah petrus on 6 February: "What has happened will occasion no difference in this affair. If you want to accommodate matters send a letter to the Nabob with your proposals and I will get them signed and sent them back to you......After this the Nabob will decamp and march to Muxadabad."[138]

So Clive wrote a letter to the Nawab on 7 February along with the terms of the treaty. In this letter, Clive assured the Nawab of his faith for peace and asked the Nawab to affix his seal and signature. There were altogether seven articles in the proposed treaty in which the English mainly asked from the Nawab the assurance that the Company's servants would no longer be molested on any account in regard to the privileges that had been granted by the *farman*: that all goods belonging to the English Company should pass freely by land or by water within the *subah* of Bengal without payment of duties; that restitution be made to the Company for their losses suffered in the settlements of Calcutta, Kasimbazar and Dacca etc; that the Company be allowed to fortify Calcutta in such a manner as that the Company would think proper; that *siccas* be coined at Calcutta in the same manner as at Murshidabad; that these proposals be ratified in the strongest manner in the presence of God and his Prophet and that Admiral Watson and Colonel Clive promised on behalf of the English nation and the English Company to observe general peace and friendship with the Nawab.[139] After a thorough discussion with his officers, the Nawab affixed his signature on the proposed treaty on 7 February, along with the signatures of Mir Jafar and Rai-Durlabh.[140]

138 Ranjit Rai's letter to Clive, 6 February (C.C.C., p. 10).

139 Terms of Articles sent by Clive to the Nawab, 7 February, 1757 (C.C.C., p. 11). Also, Aitchison, C.U., *A Collection of Treaties, Engagements and Sanads*, Vol. I (Calcutta, 1909), pp. 181-182.

140 Aitchison, *A Collection of Treaties* etc., Vol. I, p. 182.

The Nawab handed over this treaty to Ranjit Rai who sent it to Clive on 9 February through Khwajah Petrus and requested Clive to affix his signature as well.[141] On the same day, the Nawab wrote a letter to Watson to the following purport: "He (Clive) desires me to get the articles of the treaty now made, ratified by my great men and principal officers, I have complied with his request. It will be proper likewise for you and the Colonel on one part, and myself on the other, to execute an agreement, that hostilities between us shall cease, that the English will always remain my friends and allies, and that they will assist me against my enemies."[142]

The English acknowledged the receipt of the treaty. It was duly sealed and signed by the Governor and Council. Admiral Watson and Colonel Clive promised to maintain friendship with the Nawab as long as these articles were kept in force and remained unviolated.[143] After the conclusion of the treaty, the Nawab sent to Clive, Drake and Watson each a jewel, a robe of honour and an elephant. Drake and Clive accepted the gift, while Watson as representative of the king, refused to accept the present.[144]

In the treaty of 9 February, though there was no provision for the appointment of a British Resident at the *darbar* at Murshidabad, the Nawab had to accept in a *de facto* manner a British Resident at his *darbar*. On 12 February, when the question arose about an alliance "offensive and defensive against all enemies", Omichand was instructed by Clive to sound the Nawab if he would permit the English to attack the French settlement of Chandernagore. The Nawab did not like the idea but gave an evasive reply by requesting the English that they might prevent the French from entering into

141 Ranjit Rai to Clive, 9 February (C.C.C., p. 13)

142 Nawab's letter to watson, 9 February (Ive's *Voyage*, p. 114).

143 Bolts, *Considerations*, Appen. I. Also, Orme, Indostan, II pp. 135-136. Also, Scrafton's *Reflections*, pp. 71-72 ; Also, Hill, II, p. 217.

144 Forrest, *Clive*, I, p. 366. Also, Scrafton's *Reflections*, p. 72.

Bengal.[145] As a further disguise, the Nawab sent a letter to Clive on 14 February through Omichand, requesting him that William Watts[146] might be appointed the Company's Resident at the *darbar* at Murshidabad,[147] who might be accompanied by 25 artillery men with him for the seivice of the former.[148]

Watts evidently enjoyed a better status in the eyes of the Nawab. From his easy surrender of Kasimbazar, the Nawab had concluded that "he must be a person of feeble character, who might be easily duped"[149] and in his letter to Pigot, written some months earlier, the Nawab spok about Watts, "a helpless, poor and innocent man."[150] Clive become happy when he learnt about Watts' appointment as Resident at the *darbar*. He immediately wrote a letter to Ranjit Rai, soliciting the latter's "friendly assistance and advice" to Watts at the *darbar* for promoting the interest of the Company.[151]

Though the Nawab formed a very poor opinion about Watts, the members of the Calcutta Council were fully aware of his diplomatic skill. Scrafton wrote about him: "Mr. Watts well versed in the country language, and in their politics and customs accompanied the *soubah* to attend the fulfilling of the treaty."[152] The report of the council of war also decided that the choice of Watts was just. This report instructed the select Committee as well not to renew hostilities with the Nawab, but to gain their objects by diplomacy.[153] The Court of Directors also approved this idea of the appointment of a civil servent at the *darbar* of the Nawab. "In this appointment" the court observed "the abilities and qulifications of the per-

145 Orme, *Indostan*, II, p. 136.

146 William Watts joined the Company's service on 2 May, 1737.

147 Nawab's letter to Clive, 14 February, 1757 (C.C.C., p. 17).

148 *Ibid.* Also, Forrest, *Clive*, I, p. 359.

149 Hill, I, p. Clvii.

150 Nawab's letter to Pigot, 17 August, 1756 (Hill, I, p. 196).

151 Clive's letter to Ranjit Rai, 16 February (C.C.C., p. 18).

152 Scrafton, Luke. *A History of Bengal before and after Plassey* (Reprint, Calcutta, 1975), p. 74.

153 Hill, I, p. Clvii.

son should be chiefly regarded and we suppose you had these in view in the choice of our present Resident, Mr. Watts."[154]

Many points without which the treaty was of little consequence had to be adjusted by Watts. The Select Committee instructed him on 16 February about his mode of functioning. He was asked to apply to the Nawab on the following matters:

"1. The privileges granted by the Emperor were to be entered in the Emperor's book: strict obedience to them to be publicly ordered: the villages granted to the British by the *farman* to be delivered to them.

2. The Article of Mint to be explained and extended.

3. The British to be allowed to punish any of the Nawab's officers infringing their *dastaks* without waiting to complain to the *darbar*.

4. Strict enquiries to be made into the losses of the Company's servants and private Europeans, and restitution made either by the Nawab or those of his principal men who had plundered the Europeans without his knowledge. Any servant of the Company who had taken advantage of the troubles to defraud the Company to be arrested. Manikchand to refund the fines he had inflicted.

5. In cases restitution for private losses were refused, the Nawab to pay all debts due by the British to his people.

6. The courts of justice established by Company's Charter to be allowed by the native government.

7. European Agents of the Company to be received politely at the *Darbar* and without being required to make any presents to the Nawab or his officer.

8. The Nawab to erect no fortifications on the river below Calcutta.

9. The Patna factory to be reopened without payment of any present to the *Darbar*.

---

154 Letter from Court, 15 February, 1765 (F.W.I.H.C., Vol. IV, Edt. by C.S. Srinivasachari, Delhi, 1962, p. 82).

10. The Nawab to order his officers to restore all books, papers and accounts belonging to the English."[155]

Watts was accompanied by Omichand to assist the former in representing the Company's interest at Murshidabad. Watts started for Murshidabad on 17 February[156] with Omichand, having in mind the arduous task of fulfilling the objects of the Company. On the same day, when Watts arrived at Hugli, he sent Omichand to meet Nandkumar the *faujdar* of the place to sound the latter about his attitude towards the French. Thus Watts started the career of an intriguer from the very beginning of his appointment as a Resident. On 21 February Watts reached the camp of the Nawab which was about 40 miles south of Murshidabad and has an interview with the Nawab. After the interview was over, Watts immediately bribed Rajaram, the Nawab's head spy, to ascertain from him the Nawab's secret intentions and his desire of fulfilling the promises.[156] Thus it was clear enough that the treaty that had been signed by the Nawab with the English Company on 9 February had begun to be doubted from the very start by the Company's Resident at Murshidabad.

---

155 Hill, I, p. Clviii.

156 Hill, I, p. Clviii. It is stated that Omichand bribed Rajaram in favour of Watts.

3

WATTS' INTRIGUES FORCE SIRAJUDDAULAH TO ACKNOWLEDGE DEFEAT

Watts went to the *darbar* at Murshidabad with a definitely motivated aim and the success or failure of the English in Bengal, depended much on his handling the intricate problems of the Company in his favour. The assignment certainly required both cunning and courage because he had to engineer intrigues against the ruling Prince of the *subah*. Fortunately for the English Company, it was Watts and no other man; in fact Watts appeared at Murshidabad as an agent of corruption, who did not lack either craft or daring in handling this dirty business.

Watts' was a really difficult task when he was sent to Murshidabad. He had not only to obtain the ratification and implementation of the treaty made with the Nawab but to interpret it in favour of the English and also to induce the Nawab to offer several other advantages to the Company, that were not included in the actual treaty. At the *darbar* he had to deal with the French intrigue, who were supported by Jagat Seth and some other influential men; and Watts quickly realised that he must neutralise all French manoeuvres "by opposing corruption to corruption." Having come to realise that this was the only way of gaining his end at the *darbar*, he had no hesitation, in collaboration with Omichand, in playing a foul game[1] at Murshidabad.

The first aim of the English in Bengal, after the conclusion of the treaty of 9 February, was to expel the French out of the *subah*. From Bombay had come information about the proclamation of the state of war between England and France. The Calcutta Council had been definitely advised by the authorities of Fort St. George to dispossess the French of Chandernagore at the first possible opportunity.[2] The plea came to them when the French deputies arrived at Calcutta on the question of maintaining a neutrality within the Ganges. The English did not give any positive answer to the French on this point.[3] The English, in truth, thought it their ',legitimate right'' to recommend the attack on Chandernagore. The Calcutta authorities wrote to the Court of Directors that this attack on the French might "not be disagreeable to the Nabob" and hence, they further instructed Watts to obtain permission from the Nawab, and if possible, "to expel that nation out of the settlements of Bengal."[4] It was known that neither in the treaty of 9 February with the Nawab, nor in the instructions of the Select Committee on 16 February to Watts, it was mentioned that the English should attack the French. Moreover no offensive-defensive alliance with the Nawab had been concluded. Evidently the anti-French move was an after-thought; it was an additional plea of the English and it was only at the time of Watts departure that they advised him verbally to undertake this arduous task.

---

1 Hill, S.C, *Bengal in 1756–57*, Vol. I (Lond., 1905). p. CIX.

2 *Ibid.*,p.302.

3 The treaty of a neutrality was proposed by the French. The English agreed to this on condition that the French should join them against the Nawab. The French did not accept this and so the treaty of neutrality could not be concluded – Dodwell, H.H., *Dupleix and* Clive (Gorakhpur, Reprint, 1962). p. 138.

4 Letter to Court, 22, February, 1757 (F. W. I. H. C., II, p. 203).

Clive slyly suggested this point, of driving the French out of Bengal, to Ranjit Rai, but met with no response from him. Therefore, Omichand was entrusted along with Watts to secure permission from the Nawab. Omichand went to the camp of the Nawab and returned from him with a letter written on 14 February, in which the Nawab not only made the request to send Watts at the *darbar* with 25 artillery soldiers but also desired that the English "would prevent the French from entering his kingdom by land or water." The English thought it a permission for attacking the French at Chandernagore and hence they advised Watts to have further consultation on this point with the Nawab.[5]

Watts was very zealous in fulfilling his intended mission of driving out the French from Bengal and it has already been noted that on his way to the Nawab, he halted near Hugli on 17 February and sent Omichand to Nandkumar, the *faujdar* of the place, to ascertain the attitude of the latter and, if possible, to drag him to the side of the English. Omichand learnt from the *faujdar* that the Nawab had already sent two messengers, Sri Babu[9] and Mathura Mal[7] to the French with a present of one lakh of rupees. He further learnt that Nandkumar was directed to assist the French with all his forces, in case the English would attack Chandernagore or if the French would attack the English. So Omichand realised that in no case the Nawab would allow any escalation of the quarrels of these two nations in Bengal. He felt that if the English wanted to be aggressive and on the winning side, they must take time by the forelock.

Thus after his visit to Nandkumar, Omichand advised Watts on 18 February of "attacking Chandernagore immediately." In such a case the English would have to face not more than three hundred matchlockmen in Hugli. He also intimated that as per his secret arrangement with Nandkumar,

---

5 Forrest, *Clive*, I, p. 369.

6 *Diwan* of Khwajah Wajid.

7 Nephew of Narain Singh.

the latter had promised to delay matters and would prevent any assistance coming to the French from the Nawab. As such according to him this venture of the English would not at all be risky. Thus in his letter to Clive, Watts wrote : "Omichand has promised in behalf of the English that if Nuncomar keeps neuter, and by his policy prevents any assistance arriving from the Nawab to the French, that we will then make him a present of ten or twelve thousand rupees, and use our interest to continue him in the government of Hughley."[8]

Watts further added in his letter that if Clive would approve of this present to Nandkumar, he would say to the bearer of the letter, the coded words "*Golaub que foul*" or a rose flower, so that Nandkumar would be assured about his verbal agreement with Omichand. Omichand and Watts were of opinion that "if the man proves faithfully" this money might be given to him. Omichand further informed Watts that the French were indebted to the Seths to the tune of thirteen lakhs of rupees, which would prevent the Seths from joining the English against the French. It was further learnt that Manikchand as well as Khwajah Wajid had gone over to the French side. Thus Watts informed Clive that if these proposals were agreeable to him, he should immediately send a messenger to Nandkumar.

Watts' proposals to Clive were accepted and the word "Rose" was conveyed to Nandkumar.[9] The contemporary English writers, then involved in the service of the Company in Bengal, observed that Nandkumar was bribed by the English for a promise of Rs. 12,000 only, "a striking instance of the extreme venality which prevails even amongst the highest ranks in Indostan; for the annual emolument of the *phousder* amounted to 2,50,000 rupees."[10] Scrafton observed that a "well applied bribe to Nuncomar removed all obstacles."[11] But the

8 Watts' letter to Clive, 18 February (Hill, II, p. 228).

9 Forrest, *Clive*, I, p. 371.

10 Orme, *Indostan*, II, p. 137.

11 Scrafton's *Reflections*, p. 75.

modern Indian authors have invariably expressed great doubt about the authenticity of this offering of bribe to Nandkumar.[12]

On 18 February, the day on which Watts sent these proposals to Clive, the Engiish forces under the latter began to move towards Chandernagore, crossed the Ganges and encamped opposite to Barnagal. Clive expected the naval forces to join him on 25 of the month.[13]

On the news of the English forces' march, the Nawab called omichand to his camp near Agradip on 20 February and told him that the English had broken the agreement with him and were marching with their forces. To this Omichand replied by asking from whom the Nawab got this information and what part of the agreement had been broken by the English. To this the Nawab replied and asked if there was ever any fighting before among the Europeans along the river. Further if any complaints were made to him of this nature. was he not obliged to redress them? To this Omichand again replied that the English had received news about the Nawab's promise of giving Hugli to the French, that the Nawab had already presented the French one lakh of rupees and had promised them to grant a mint. He added that because of

12 Satya Charan Sasti. in his *Clive Charit* (p. 97) says that Nandkumar had given a loan of Rs. 57,000 to the French Council at Chandernagore and as such the Maharajah maintained a good relation with the French. It is highly illogical that Nandkumar was prepared to sacrifice Rs. 57,000 for Rs. 12,000. Prof. B.K. Roy in his book *The Career and Achievement of Maharaja Nanda Kumar* (Calcutta, 1969) tries to prove (pp. 18-21) that Nandkumar did not receive bribe from the English. During the Anglo-French war for the capture of Chandernagore, the Maharajah kept neutral for various reasons. As a further proof, the author had obtained an original record from the India Office Library. London (India Office Records, Vol. 193, sec 6, no. 63) which conclusively proves that Nandkumar did not know anything even before some days about the English attack on the French. On 18 March, Nandkumar wrote to Clive : "I am not informed that 400 soldiers and Tellinghas are arrived, am unacquaindted with what Intent they are come......inform me immediately of this affair."

13 Clive's letter to court, 22 February F.W,I.H.C., II, pp. 201-202),

these reports the English had become much concerned and discussed how the French could merit such favours from the Nawab when they had contravened the Nawab's call for their help. Omichand further told the Nawab that the English were much exercised and anxious over the possible motives of the French commander M. Bussy's coming to Bengal with a large force. Omichand then tried to convince the Nawab about his reports by saying that "he (Omichand) had lived under the English protection these forty years, never knew them (the English) once to be guilty of breaking their word."[14] To give a religious sanctity of his reports Omichand "took his oath by touching a Brahmin's foot" and told the Nawab "that if a lie could be proved in England on any one they were spit upon and never trusted."[15] Watts wrote to the Select Commitee that upon this the Nawab was well pleased with the English and recalled the orders he had given for Mir Jafar's going to the assistance of the French. At the same time, the Nawab sent a message to Watts through Omichand writing to the English that the men had already been sent out to Hugli to garrison it and that the Nawab would give orders to his forces not to molest the English.[16]

When Omichand apprised Watts of his conversation with the Nawab, Watts wents to the Nawab in the evening of 21 February and was graciously received. The Nawab then told Watts to come to him on the next day, when he would present Watts with a robe of honour and would send Narain singh with him for the delivery of the factory of Kasimbazar. At that time Watts did not reply but later on, he sent a message through Omichand to the Nawab desiring that the factory might be delivered to him by Jagat Seth at Murshidabad. The Nawab agreed to this and told Watts that "he might depend on his keeping the agreement he (the Nawab) had made with us

14 Select Committee Records, 25 February, pp. 3-5.

15 *Ibid.* Also, Watts' letter to the Select Committee, 21 February (H.Il, II, pp. 231:232), Also, Hill, *Abstract*, p. 11. Also, long, *Unpublished Records*, p. 109.

16 *Ibid.*, Also, Hill, II, pp. 231-232.

(the English) and hoped we would not infringe it on our part. He deisred we would not listen to any stories we might hear from others." Thereafter the Nawab turned out Hukum Beg and his family from the *subah* of Bengal for misrepresenting before the Nawab about the English. Further, the Nawab desired English assistance when asked for. To this, Watts replied: "While the English name lasted he (the Nawab) might be sure of adhering to the treaty strictly. That we never listened to any stories and that he might depend on all the assistance in our power."[17]

Though Sirajuddaulah was assured of friendly assistance from Watts, he did not want to turn the *subah* of Bengal into an arena of warfare between the two European nations. And as there was no mention in the treaty of 9 February about an offensive and defensive alliance with the English, the Nawab absolutely forbade the English to commence hostilities with the French. If the English would attack the French againgt the will of the Nawab it would be considered as an attempt of violating the treaty and in such case, the Nawab would assist the French with all his forces.[18]

This letter from the Nawab totally disappointed Clive. So long as he was eagerly expecting a singal from Watts to attack the French. Thus Clive wrote to Sirajuddaulah on 22 February, expressing his surprise why the Nawab seemed to be not fully trusting the English. It must have been due to, as he added, the representations of the French, "who never have paid the least regard to truth:" In the same letter he wrote to the Nawab not to listen to "all these bad stories" which had been concocted by designing men. "I will lay aside all thoughts of attacking the French", observed Clive, "let them enter into a peace with us in your dominions directly."[19]

---

17 Watts' letter to the Select Committee, 22]February (S.C.R., 25 February,). Also, Watts, *Memoirs*, pp. 31-32. Also, Hill, *Abstract*, p. 11.

18 Clive's letter to Court, 22 February (F.W.I.H.C., II, p. 202).

19 Clive's letter to the Nawab, 22 February (C.C.C., pp. 18-19).

During this time, the Select Committee at Calcutta received a letter from the Director and Council Chandernagore requesting the English once again for the preservation of neutrality within the Ganges.[20] The Select committee at Calcutta discussed this matter thoroughly and thought it advisable to agree to the proposals, rather than risk a rupture with the Nawab. Accordingly they replied to the French at Chandernagore that if they (the French) were empowered to make such a treaty, that could be guaranteed by the Nawab as well, the English were ready to act accordingly.[21] The English were evidently playing a cautious game. Thus the Select Committee directed Watts not to mention anything about it at the *darbar*.[22]

On 25 February, three deputies from Chandernagore, Fournier, Nicolaas and Le Conte, attended a meeting of the Select Commiittee at Calcutta and they were asked whether they could conclude a treaty of neutrality without the permission from the supreme council of Pondichery and whether such a treaty could be binding on all Frenchmen. And whether they could restrain the French ships from attacking the English. To these questions, the French deputies asked for time to reply. On the same day, however, the French deputies sent an answer in writing that as all the councillors of Chandernagore were the members of the council at Pondichery, they were entitled to conclude such a treaty. The French Council at Chandernagore would direct M. Law to obtain the Nawab's guarantee, if Watts would do the same on the part of the English.[23] The French deputies further enquired in their letter about the power of the English in Bengal to conclude a treaty of neutrality and to what extent another Admiral would be bound by Watson's pledge. To

---

20 S. C. R., 25 February, pp. 3–5. Also, Hill, II, p. 250.

21 Clive's letter to the Secret Committee of London, 22 February, (Forrest, *Clive*, Vol I, p. 372).

22 Letter from Select Commrttee, Calcutta, to the Secret Committee. London, 24 February (Hiil, II, p. 250).

23 Forrest, *Clive*, Vol I, pp. 372-373

this query from the French, the Select Committee at Calcutta concluded that they would instruct Watts jointly with M. Law to apply to the Nawab for a guarantee and that until this had been obtained, the French must stop all works on their fortifications. They further resolved that the treaty of a neutrality must be concluded as early as possible.[24]

But in fact Watts wanted to play at Murshidabad a double game of intrigue against the French, as also against the Nawab. Though the Select Committee at Calcutta favoured a treaty of neutrality with the French, and Clive as well as Watson were hesitant to attack the French without the written permission from the Nawab, Watts turned down all these views. He duped the Nawab as well by working up in the latter a scare about what he described as the imminent invasion of the *subah*, by the Afghans. In doing all these on his own Watts justified himself for his better understanding of the situation than any other, saying that as he was on the spot he "watched every motion of the *suba*, (and) knew exactly the character of his (the Nawab's) courtiers and Principal Ministers, and had the most certain Intelligence of everything that passed"; hence he continued to press home the point of expeditiously attacking Chandernagore:[25] This "judgment" of Watts, Scrafton observed, was "well founded," as Sirajuddaulah had always shown his favour to the French and had entered into a private negotiation with the French Governor, where in the Nawab promised him the government of Hugli, a mint and other advantages.[26]

The treaty of 9 February did not say anything about the expulsion of the French from Bengal, but the English thought that as there subsisted a treaty between them with the Nawab, the latter would help them in their mission. The threat of an Afghan invasion and the Nawab's request to help him in such a case, placed the English in high hopes that Sirajuddaulah would give them the permission to attack.

24 S. C. R., 26 February (Hill, *Abstract*, pp. 11-12).

25 Watts' *Memoirs*, p. 35.

26 Scrafton's *Reflections*, p. 74.

But as it turned out the Nawab was very unwilling to sacrifice the French. He looked upon them as the only power that was capable of counterbalancing the English, but he was equally unwilling to offend the latter.[27]

Within a few days at Murshidabad, Watts realised that the French intrigue at the *darbar* was very strong and that they were supported by a number ef principal officers. But when the Nawab was alarmed by the news of the advance of Ahmad Shah Abdali into Bengal, he dropped some hints to Watts for assistance. Accordingly, Clive, on receipt of this news, crossed the Ganges with a view to marching to Murshidabad for the Nawab's help or, if found opportune, to Chandernagore for attacking the French. Watts at that time fully utilised his cunning. He kept alive the Nawab's fear of the reported Afghan invasion and passed on the hint to Clive to move towards Chandernagore.[28] In this way Watts tried to maintain good relations with the Nawab and at the same time successfully prevented the English army from coming to any help to the Nawab.

Within 25 February, Watts became confirmed about the end of all talks about a treaty of a neutrality with the French and, thus emboldened, he again urged the English to attack Chandernagore. In a letter to Walsh, on the same date, Watts informed him with "utmost concern" about the Nawab's direction of not attacking the French but he believed that his letter of 21 to the Select Committee would alter their resolution and that they would "request the Admiral and Colonel to proceed on the attack." He further observed that he would again try to persuade the Nawab not to assist the French, but if he would fail in this enterprise, there was "no reason to be alarmed," as Watts believed that the Nawab in any way would "never assist the French. If the English became successful in defeating the French, they would derive "great advantage to the nation and Company". Watts knew it well that "fear" was predominant in the Nawab's

27 Glei 's *Clive* p. 75.

28 Scrafton's *Reflections* p. 73.

mind. The aggressive stance of the English would keep him cowed down. "The more powerful we make ourselves the greater compliance we shall meet with him", observed watts in his letter, "whereas if the neutrality goes on and the squadron leaves us, he will shuffle and delay doing us justice or complying with his agreement till the French have a force arrive and then probably he will finish his contract with us by joining them and driving us out of the country, for by what I can learn there is no faith to be put upon either his word or oath." Watts further observed in the same letter with a warning, "judge you what must be our fate when the squadron leaves us. He finally concluded that it was the mutual interest of the French and the Nawab to destory the English.[29]

On the same day Watts informed the Select Committee about his confirmed view as well as the assurances of Omichand that the Nawab would not assist the French, if the English would attack them. Omichand had advised Watts to attack Chandernagore immediately, if, of course, the English were fully confident of taking that place. The Nawab's fear complex was a fact and, therefore, as Watts saw it, "if we attack and take Chandernagore every part of our agreement will be fulfilled." About the treaty of a neutrality with the French, Watts observed in the same letter, "if a neutrality is concluded with the French no chicanery, artifice or cunning will be left untried to delay putting us in possession of what the Nabob was assented to." According to Watts' estimate of the situation, within a few days, the Nawab would leave for Patna with his forces to meet the challenge of the Afghans and during his absence Mohanlal would transact the business at Murshidabad on his behalf. From Mohanlal, no friend of the English, the latter would get only obstacles and difficulties. Watts concluded his letter again with a warning that from Monanlal, "we shall never be able to get a public order or leave to attack the French."[30]

---

29 Watts' letter to Walsh, 25 February (Hill, II, pp. 254-255).

30 Watts' letter to Select Committee, 25 February (*Ibid.*, pp. 255-256),

This letter of Watts made Clive very doubtful about the Nawab's intention, yet he was not absolutely hopeless. He wrote a letter to Watts from the camp asking Watts how he (Clive) could attack the French, when the Nawab had positively asked the English not to attack them. Clive's contention was that the Nawab should at least give a hint to him or to Watts that in case the English started an action against the French, the Nawab would not interfere. Only then could Clive commence the attack which, the Colonel thought, "is not yet too late". Thus Clive directed Watts to obtain the Nawab's favour[31] about this matter. In another of his letter to Watts on 1 March, Clive repeated the same thing. How could he attack the French when the Nawab positively forbade the English to do so? This opinion of Clive was shared by the members of the Select Committee as well. And accordingly the Select Committee decided to settle the matter of neutrality very soon, of course, in such a way as would give the English greater strategic leeway in the Bengal trade. Thus Clive requested Watts that the latter should take the fullest advantage of the situation in order to get a guarantee from the Nawab in favour of the English. In concluding his letter, Clive did not fall in the same tune as of Watts about the Nawab's sincerity and observed: "I cannot be of your way of thinking that the Nabob will not abide by any part of the agreement so solemnly sworn to, as it does not appear that such an opinion is backed by any proofs."[32]

But Watts was not willing to yield before Clive. He again wrote to the Select Committee intimating them the Nawab's verbal approval of the English troops, attacking Chandernagore on the condition that the English should assist the Nawab against the Afghans. At the same time, Watts presented a translation of a letter from the Nawab in which the latter sought assistance from the English against the Afghans. These two letters led to the idea that the

31 Clive's letter to Watts, 25 February (*Ibid.*, p. 245).

32 *Ibid.*, 1 March (*Ibid.*, p. 265).

situation was propitious for the English. It was almost taken for granted in the English camp that the Nawab would not intervene if the English attacked the French at Chandernagore. The members of the Select Committee now more or less shared the opinion of Watts and hence the question of writing again to Watson, who was so long averse to attacking the French, was raised.[33] They decided to reject the proposal for a treaty of neutrality and, instead, determined to attack the French.[34]

When the refusal of a treaty of neutrality was decided upon, Clive wrote a letter to the commitee that in such an event, the Fernch would immediately assist the Nawab in case the latter had any designs against the English. In such a case Clive observed, "that success against the Nawab and the French together will be very precarious, notwithstanding the arrival of the Bombay troops." Thus Clive requested the commitiee to join with him in directing Watson "a third time" immediately to attack chandernagore by water, as Clive was ready to do with his landforce. If Watson "refuses this likewise", Clive further observed, "he becomes responsible for every misfortune that may happen to the Company's affairs."[35] Thus the hesitant Clive was also won over by Watts.

The news of Ahmad Shah Abdali's intended march to Bengal created great terror and anxiety in the mind of Sirajuddaulah and, as the days rolled on, it gradually increased. Thus,

---

33 S.C.R., 6 March (Hill, *Abstract*, p. 14) Becher was strongly in favour of a neutrality with the French, informing the Admiral that the treaty of 9 February was concluded with his consent and that now he would be responsible for its results (*Vide, Ibid.*).

34 When the treaty of neutrality was drawn up and was sent to Watson for signature, he objected to it on the ground that it must be sent to Pondichery for approval. As this would involve delay of two months during which the English fleet would be away, no reliance could be placed on the Nawab's guarantee. Thus the council changed their opinions and resolved to attack Chandernagore-.Long, *Unpublished Records*, p. 111, fn.

35 Select Committee Proceedings, 4 March (Long, *Unpublished Records*, p. 111).

the Nawab wanted to have a good understanding with the English in order to ensure non- belligerence from the latter's side. The English, however, went on playing the game of cunning and did not take any tangible step to help the Nawab. Sirajuddaulah even went to the extent of making an offer to the English in which he requested the latter to assist him with their forces; he informed them that he would march to patna and if the English would assist him, "I will allow you every month a lakh of rupees, during the time you contiune with me, for the maintenance of your army". When no reply came to this letter, the Nawab again made the same offer to Watson. On 4 March, Watson replied that if the English forces would join the Nawab during his march to patna, the French would get the opportunity of destroying the English in Bengal. Therefore, the Admiral informed the Nawab, "let us take Chandernagore and secure ourselves against any apprehensions from that quarter, and then we will assist you with every man in our power and go with you even to Delhi if you will."[36]

The Nawab did not reply to this letter of Watson. He did not want to abandon the French at the mercy of the English. Thus when the English offered only conditional help to the Nawab, the latter invited Bussy to come to his assistance against the Afghans. This news enraged Watson so much that he wrote a menacing letter to the Nawab, observing that if Bussy would come to Bengal, "I will kindle such a flame in your country as all the water in tne Ganges shall not be able to extinguish."[37]

The anger of the Nawab "waxed hot" on the receipt of Watson's threatening letter to him. But his immediate problem was to face the Afghan invader. So he did not want to show his temper to the English, rather he wanted to reconcile them bv executing some of the articles of the earlier treaty. During this time, even Watts was convinced of the Nawab's sincerity and on 6 March, he wrote to the Select Committee

36 Forrest, *Clive*, I, p. 377
37 *Ibid.*, p. 378.

at Calcutta, "if we keep firm to our agreement made with the Nabob in every particular and grant him the assistance he requirers, all matters will end well and to the greatest advantage for the Company."[38] Watts also enclosed a copy of his letter to the Nawab, informing the committee that during the *Holi*, no business would be attended to because, according to custom, "all the Nabob's Ministers having obtained permission to be absent." So watts did not get a *parwana* or even a letter "till the *Holy* days were over." On 7 March watts again informed the committee about the delivery of the factory of Kasimbazar to him by the Nawab's officers.[39] On 10 March, Watts waited upon the Nawab about the further execution of the treaty. The Nawab showed a favourable disposition and directed Jagat Seth to pay the English Resident 40,000 gold *mohars* from the Nawab's treasury. The Nawab then directed his subordinate officers to expedite the matter of delivering over to the Resident "the goods and effects" that were in his possession. The writers of the Nawab, thus prepared *parwanas* according to the terms of the treaty. The Nawab also desired to execute the *farman* of the Mughal Emperor[40], and would send his directions to the *zamindars* to sell 38 villages to the English. The Nawab also permitted the English to coin *siccas* in Calcutta. He further assured Watts that "he would comply with every part of his contract." Watts also took the necessary steps. He desired that the Select Committee should send him an item-wise account of the treasury in the factory, when the place was seized by the Nawab. He also wanted to know from the committee an account of the "money, jewels and effects" belonging to private people. Likewise Watts further requested the committee to send to him the comastahs of several aurungs belonging both to the Company and the private people, or tenants of calcutta so that he could learn from them what were taken by the Nawab's army and what were plundered by others. He further informed them that Omichand had told

---

38 Watts' letter to the Select Committee, 6 March S.C.R., 12 March, pp. 49-51). Also, Hill *Abstract*, p. 14.

39 Watts' letter to the Select Committee, 7 March (*Ibid.*)

40 This *farman* was granted by Farruk-Siyar to the English in 1717.

the governor, the Colonel and himself, that Ranjit.Rai, acting *vakil*, expected commission at the rate of 10 per cent on 3 lakhs of rupees obained, and they had consented to allow this percentage to Ranjit Rai. According to Watts, Ranjit Rai deserved this 10 per cent from the English, "as they used to get on payment" this type of commisson-money for their work. Furthermore as Watts added, Ranjit Rai "is a men of sense and weight and in great favour with the Nabob and has it much in his power to expedite their business without whose assistance we shall meet with many obstacles from the Nabob's ministers."[41]

Subsequently the Nawab fairly kept his promises and performed most of the articles of the treaty with the English. He intimated it to Clive and observed, "in compliance with my promises to you I have delivered to Mr. Watts the three lakhs of rupees, and I will finish the rest of this business in ten or twelve days."[42] Thus it seemed that the Nawab had an ardent desire to fulfil his promises to the English. This was also admitted by Clive, who observed in his letter to the Committee on 11 March that the Nawab had restored the Kasimbazar factory to the English "with a considerable quantity of goods."[43]

Though in this way, the Nawab tried to cultivate good relation with the English, the latter did not forget their earlier design to attack the French at Chandernagore and thus dupe the Nawab as well. In the midst of all the above settlements with the Nawab Clive began to advance his forces on 8 March towards Chandernagore. At the same time he also tried to soothe the mind of the Nawab by assuring him that he would not attack Chandernagore without the latter's permission.[44]

---

41 Watts' letter to the Select Committee, 10 March S.C.R., 12 March, pp. 49-51).

42 Nawab's letter to Clive, 10 March (C. C. C., p. 22).

43 Hill, II, p. 282.

44 Lawford, James p. , *Clive, Proconsul of India* (Lond. , 1976), p. 207.

Clive's approach towards Chandernagore with a large force was known to the French, who represented the matter to Sirajuddaulah. The French urged the Nawab to use his good offices for the maintenance of neutrality between them and the English in Bengal. The Nawab quickly responded and both Law and Watts were asked to meet him. The Nawab thus tried once again, to chalk out a plan of neutrality.

Law went to the Nawab, apprised him of the danger posed by the situation and pressed for reinforcements. The Nawab asked Law to remain with him, until they could meet Watts. When Watts appeared at the *darbar*, the Nawab told him in presence of Law that he would not allow the two nations to start warfare in Bengal and was determined to preserve the state of neutrality. To this Watts, at least outwardly, agreed. Then the Nawab asked Watts to send reports to him about the progress made so far as the treaty of neutrality was concerned. Watts, however, introduced the element of diplomatic polemics by telling the Nawab that the French at Chandernagore had no authority to conclude such a treaty. Law immediately objected to it stating that the English did not want neutrality, and they were itching for trouble after the arrival of substantial reinforcements from Bombay. He pointed out that in fact the English were reluctant to enter into such a treaty, for, otherwise, the negotiations for the treaty would have been completed much before when Watson actually "had promised to sign the treaty." As a formula of settlement and to put a stop to such wrangling the Nawab proposed to draw up a paper in which Law would promise that the treaty of neutrality would be approved by the authorities at Pondichery. To This Law agreed. Then the Nawab told Watts to draw up a paper promising that the English would not attack the French and would in the meantime get the approval of the competent English authorities for a no-hostility pact with the French within the Bengal *subah*. Watts apparently agreed to this[45] At that

45 Watts at that time knew about the Select Committee's resolution on 6 March for attacking Chandernagore.

time Law asked Watts if the latter could assure the Nawab that Watson would be bound by his (Watts') promise. To this Watts replied that he could not say anything about Watson's approval. The Nawab immediately said that he would then write to Watson for a treaty of neutrality. Law then represented before the Nawab that his letter to Watson woulc have the same fate as the earlier ones. The English Admiral, he said "would certainly not pay more attention to this letter than to the preceding ones." This wounded the Nawab's vanity. He insisted that both Law and Watts should forthwith draw up the paper as aforesaid. The Nawab stressed that he would write to the Admiral in strong terms for maintenance of neutrality, and he would send his own emissary to smoothen and expedite the progress of negotiations between these two nations.[46] Thus both Law and Watts departed from the Nawab after this settlement and the Nawab asked his secretary to prepare the necessary instructions to the parties along with a draft of the proposed treaty of neutrality between the two nations.

When these documents were going to be written out by the Secretary on behelf of the Nawab, behind the latter's back, Watts made handsome presents to the secretary and asked him to draw up the proposal in such a manner that it would indicate permission to the English to attack the French, and then to despatch it without delay.[47] This was done and the Nawab hastily affixed his seal to the letter which was sent to Watson at once.[48] The Nawab thus sent 'his' views on 10 March, stating *inter alia*: "My forbidding war on my borders was because the French are my tenants, and upon this affair desired my protection: on this I wrote you to make peace, and no intentions had I of assisting or favouring them...........You have understanding, and generosity: if your enemy with an upright heart claims your protec-

46 Law, *Memoire*, (Hill, II, pp. 194-196).

47 Watts, *Memoirs*, p. 39. Also, Hill, III, p. 191 f. n. Also, Forrest, *Clive*, I, p. 382. Also, Scrafton, *Reflections*, p. 74.

48 The Nawab never read this letter, which he directed to be written by his secretary. Hill, *Three Frenchmen*, p. 89, f. n.

tion, you will give him his life, but then you must be well satisfied of his intentions; if not, whatever you think right, that do."[49] A careful eye could not but miss how the letter had been tampered.

As Watts had expected, Watson and Clive regarded the last paragraph as a permission to attack Chandernagore.[50] Thus Watts' cunning once gain gained him his end. It was now easy for him to persuade Watson for an attack on the French and change him from his previous position in which he had been averse to attack them without the Nawab's permission. To instigate the English further, Wãtts, after this bribe to the Nawab's secretary, sent a mendacious report to the Select Committee at Calcutta on 10 March that since the Nawab could not write he had desired Watts to inform the English that if they were determined to attack the French, the Nawab would neiter interfere, nor would assist the French.[51]

On receiving these two letters, one from the Nawab and another from Watts, Admiral Watson held a council of war to consider what was most proper to be done. These letters had "put an end to the debate"[52] and almost flagged off Watson to undertake war. Watts by his intrigue had also the Nawab in his toils, as is evident from the fact that on 11 March the Nawab wrote to Clive that the former was impatiently waiting for the arrival of the latter at Murshidabad. In This letter the Nawab said nothing about Chandernagore.[53]

---

49 Hill, II, p. 279.

50 Scrafton obserxes that "the letter may be well understood as consent to our attacking Chandernagore though it certainly was never meant as such."--Scrafton's *Reflections*, p. 75.

51 Watts' letter to the Select Committee, 10 March (S.C.R., 12 March, pp. 49-51).

52 Watts, *Memoirs*, p, 43. Also, quoted in Forrest, *Clive*, I, p. 383.

53 Hill, II p. 280. It is a further proof that the Nawab did not give his consent to the English for attacking the French.

Clive acted according to the decision of the Select Committee[54] and, accordingly, quickly moved up with his land forces and finally encamped near Chandernagore on 12 March. He received the fullest encouragement from Watts. Next day, on 13 March, Clive directed Renault,—the French Governor of Chandernagore, to surrender the fort.[55] But when the French Governor refused to surrender, Clive attacked Chandernagore on 14 March. At that time also, the Nawab waited for a reply from Watson but got no immediate response. On 15, Law received the news of the attack.[56] Quite naturally it upset him and filled his mind with misgivings. He immediately took the matter up with the Nawab.

As soon as Chandernagore was attacked, urgent French messages were sent to Murshidabad and Law begged before the Nawab immediately to rush reinforcements. But Watts tried to prevent the issue of any such order. On the other hand though the Nawab had a strong force at Murshidabad, ready to march under the *diwan*, Durlabhram, yet the *diwan* had serious hunches in regard to a military action against the English.[57] With the deepening crisis Law was at his wit's end. He requested the Nawab to send him the services of a native officer with one hundred musketeers.[58] The Nawab again tried for peace and worte to Clive on 15 March: "I have often before wrote to you that you should not make war with the French.........Let there be peace between you in some manner, and I shall be very well pleased, if not I shall be displeased."[59]

When the English army continned their siege on Chandernagore, the Nawab despatched his forces with cannon and

---

54 Becher still declined to agree with the committee as it was contary to his way of thinking.--Letter to Court, 26 March (F.W.I.H.,C. II,p. 212).

55 Forrest, *Clive*, I, p. 383.

56 Law, *Memoirs* (Hill, III, p. 196). Also, Hill, *Three Frenchmen*, p. 94.

57 Hill, *Three Frenchmen*, p. 33.

58 *Ibid.*, p. 95.

59 Nawab's letter to Clive, 15 March (C.C.C., p. 24).

other wariike weapons to assist the French. It was reported to Watts that the Nawab intended to march himself but on the receipt of a letter from Nandkumar that the French would not be able to defend the place and that on the arrival of their ships the English would surely carry the day, the Nawab ordered his forces to return.[60] But at the same time the Nawab became very angry with Khwajah Wajid who had given him to understand that the French were superior to the English. Still the Nawab did not want war and hinted it to Watts, who observed in his letter on 16 March to the Select Commitee that "the Nabob forbids positively our warring with the French."[61]

In the midst of his war upon the French, Clive replied to the letter of Nawab, which the Nawab had written to him on 15 March forbidding him to attack the French. Clive became surprised to notice the change in the Nawab's tone. He received the Nawab's latest letter "with the greatest displeasure". Clive observed that this change of attitude of the Nawab was due to the machinations of self-interested men who were not actuated by the welfare of the Nawab but to serve their own benefit. Clive reminded the Nawab by observing that "there is not a man in your *Durbar* who is more sincere and zealous in his attachment to your interest and welfare than myself."[62]

On Sirajuddaulah's part, though he became greatly agitated over the English attack on Chandernagore, he did not forget to fulfil his own duty. He proceeded towards the settlement of the other outstanding issues in the

---

60 Watts' letter to the Select committee, 16 March (S.C.R., 9 April p. 58-60). This army of the Nawab was under the command of Durlabhram. While the *diwan* was twenty miles away from Hugli, he recerved a letter from Clive, that made him stop with fear and surprise. Though Law promised him to pay two lakhs of rupees for his assistance to the French, Durlabhram could not muster enough courage to move forward.—Mukhopadhyay, *Rai-Durlabh,* pp. 49-50.

61 *Ibid.*

62 Clive's letter to the Nawab, 20 March (C.C.C., p. 24).

light of the treaty already signed. Watts informed the Select Committee that he had received three lakhs of rupees but could not understand what to do about Ranjit Rai's claim of commission to the tune of 10 per cent, neither could he send the money with safety to Calcutta "till the disputes with our enemies were settled." He was sending goods daily to the factory; still, as he intimated, "another application to the Nabob from the Admiral and the Colonel with regard to the ready money taken in Calcutta", and other subordinate factories and *aurungs*, was necessary. Watts had also received a general *parwana* for trade; and a special *parwana* for the *aurungs* was also in the process of preparation. Further, Watts obtained a letter from the Nawab written to Ramnrain, the *naib* of patna, for opening up the usual English trade at that place. The Resident further informed the committee that he was looking for the people for the establishment of a mint, for he would get another *parwana* for the currency of the *siccas*.[63]

Sirajuddaulah did not want that his *subah* should be a scene of warfare. It was not only his favourable disposition to the French, but as Watts observed, the Nawab "would not have war made in his country, by which the people under his government must suffer, the king's Revenues be lessened, and the Tranquility of his Dominions disturbed." Thus evidently in great rage and anguish the Nawab wrote "letter after letter to Colonel Clive who is said to have received no less than ten of them in one day." However, Clive did not stop the war but continued his duplicity with the Nawab, assuring him again of his sincere attachment to the terms of the late treaty.[64]

On 23 March, when there was no definite news about the fall of Chandernagore, the Nawab again sent a strong note to Clive observing that he (the Nawab) on his part had complied with all that watts had proposed before him "except a very few articles which I hope will be finished by the 15th of the month."

63 Watts' letter to the Select Committee, 18 March (S.C.R. 9 April pp. 58-60). Also, Hill, *Abstract*, p. 15.

64 Watts, *Memo irs*, P. 48.

But notwithstanding this, the English had done many things "contary to the treaty" and the English soldiers had devastated the town of Hugli as well as the areas of Burdwan and Nadia.[65]

But the English defied several instructions of the Nawab and Chandernagore was invested by land and sea. Finally on 23 March the fort was surrendered to Admiral Watson.[66] Captain Latham was despatched by Watson to receive the keys of the fort and Clive entered into the fort with his troops at about 5 in the afternoon.[67] Most of the French escaped from the fort; about one hundred persons became prisoners of war.[68] Thus the capture of Chandernagore, a scheme originally proposed by Watts, became possible by the English officers' playing a foul game of duplicity and bribery.

After the fall of Chandernagore, Clive wrote a letter to the Nawab. He described the success of the English and prayed for the blessing of the Almighty. He further added in his letter, quite evidently with extreme mockery: "My heart is earnest in your interest, and I shall be always ready with my own life and that of my own army to drive away your enemies."[69] When the Nawab received this letter he concealed his feelings and outwardly maintained joy. He sent through Watts a congratulatory letter to Clive for the success of the English.[70] But this success of the English brought about a sharp realignment of forces in the *darbar* politics at Murshidabad. The Seths were so long averse to the English. But now when the rising sun could not be ignored any more, Jagat Seth wrote a congratulatory letter to Clive by observing: "Mr. Watts shows me great favour; what-ever he desires me regarding the Company's business I look on the trouble attending it as a

---

65 Nawab's letter to Clive,23 March (C.C.C., P. 27).

66 Letter to Court, 26 March (F.W.I.H.C., II, p. 212).

67 Watts,*Memoirs*, p. 45.

68 Gleig's *Clive*, p. 76.

69 Forrest, *Clive*, I, p.399.

70 Watts' letter to Clive. 26 March (Hill, II, p. 294). Also, Scrafton's *Reflections*, p. 77.

real pleasure. I have always the greatest pleasuae in Mr. Watts' goodness and firiendly behaviour. I hope that you will always look on me as your sincere friend and favour me with your kind and friendly letter, which will always give me the greatest pleasure."[71]

The tone of Sirajuddaulah also began to cool down after this event but still he continued his policy of protection to the French. It was reported to Watts that the French had applied to the Nawab for their protection at the French factory at Kasimbazar, which had been granted to them. But the Nawab had also informed Watts that the request of the English about the French would be complied with. Watts also informed Clive about Omichand's indefatigable service for the cause of the Company, by observing : "He is always with me, and as I am convinced of his superior understanding I always consult him, and am persuaded he is sincere and hearty in the cause of the English." In concluding his letter to Clive, Watts observed about the Nawab's desires of granting assurance to Nandkumar and the people of Hugli by saying: "He or the tenants of Hughly need be under no apprehensions, and that you will give him any assisstance he wants. Your treating Nuncomar kindly will have a good effect, as his letters are of weight here, and he has been of great service to us already."[72]

About the restitution money of the English, the Nawab became very particular. And so Watts wrote to the Select Committee on 28 March that he had received Rs. 1,50,000 for the money taken at Kasimbazar and Dacca. It seemed to him a great risk of keeping so much money at Kasimbazar factory. He also wanted that a servant of the Company might be sent to take charge of the Dacca goods delivered to him. Watts further informed the committee that he had been forced to appoint a *vakil* to carry on the business and that he had failed

71 Letter from Jagst Selh to Clive, Rd. 29 March C.C.C., p. 28).

72. Watts' letter to Clive, 26 March (Hill, II, pp. 294r295). This last sentence about Nandkumar was due to his remaining neutral in the war.

to get back the cannon taken from Kasimbazar by the Nawab's soldiers.[73]

Thus Clive, became satisfied in respect of the Nawab's intention of fulfilling the articles of the treaty. Accordingly, he wrote a letter to Pigot—the Governor of Madras, on 29 March : "He (the Nawab) has already performed almost every article of the treaty : paid Mr. Watts the three lacs of rupees, delivered up Cossimbazar, and all the other Factorys, with the money and goods therein taken. The Gentlemen write from thence that little or nothing is wanting."[74]

The Select Committee of Calcutta also received letters from the 'gentlemen' of Kasimbazar and Dacca factories and learnt from them that there were "little or no sufferers there." From Balasore, the Committee received the same news. The committee was convinced about the efficiency of Watts who, they were sure, would be able shortly to procure a full restitution of what had been taken in Fort William and from the *aurungs*. To facilitate his works, the committee had already sent to Watts some *gomastahs*, whose works were to account for the money and goods that had been taken by Manikchand at Calcutta. Watts was further directed to obtain bills for the gentlemen at Dacca from Jagat Seth's house, amounting to one lakh of rupees. The members of the Dacca factory were thus directed to start their investment on the basis of small advances. For the functioning of the Lakhimpore factory, Watts was similarly directed to procure bills from Jagat Seth's house for fifty thousand rupees. At Lakhimpore, the committee had sent Verelst and Smith with a few more to "begin their purchases immediately."[75]

About the money and goods that Watts and the other officials of different factories had received, the Select Committee directed Watts to send down the treasure immediately to them in light boats with a military guard. The committee

73 Watts' letter to Select Committee, 28 March (S.C.R., 9 April, pp. 58-60).

74 Clive's letter to Pigot, 29 March (Hill, II, pp. 302-303).

75 Letter to Court, 10 April (F.W.I.H.C., II, pp. 219-220),

likewise directed all the other Chiefs of the lesser establishments to send up "all goods and money as expeditiously as possible to Fort William."[76]

After nearly fulfilling their desired objects about the French in Chandernagore as well as the restitution money from the Nawab, the English again started their old game of controlling the Nawab of Bengal completely according to their own interests. Thus Clive instructed Watts about their future policy towards Sirajuddaulah. "The Bent of our Politicks hitherto has been laughty and by submissive letters such as the occasion required to persuade him to abandon the French to us, we must in pursuit of that system now endeavour to convince (him) that what we have done is best both for him and us." He directed Watts, in the same letter, to represent before the Nawab about the might of the English and observed : "Our sole view is to stop the ambitious progress of the French, to effect which he must enter into a strict Alliance with us; That we shall always be ready to support him against his Enemies,......that we do not aim at any further possesssions than what our *Phirmaund* has given us, that we shall henceforwards act as Merchants, but shall always keep us a Force sufficient to support him against all his Enemies."[77]

Thus the above may quite plausibly be interpreted to mean that the main drive of Clive's policy was to expel the French from Bengal at least during this particular stage of English trade in the Bengal *subah*.

But Sirajuddaulah thought in a different way. He had no desire that the English should rule the roost without any rivals. At the same time, the Nawab was not quite sure about the faithfulness of the English; he was doubtful whether the whole British force would always be ready to obey him. So when the Nawab saw that the threat of an intended Afghan march to Bengal had blown over,[78] he began to deal with the English

76 S.C.R., 23 April, p. 66.

77 Quoted in Forrest, *Clive*, I, pp. 399-400.

78 A current and widely-believed report was that a considerable money-bribe to the Afghans had prevailed upon them to return to their own country.

in a more uninhibited manner. It was reported to Watts that the Nawab was again in active communication with Law and Bussy.[79] Betraying his soft corner for and sense of attachment to the French cause, the Nawab wrote to Clive: "If you want the French Factory it is well. Whatever they paid into the treasury, write to Mr. Watts to make good here, and it is very well; then you keep possession of the Factory. But if it be agreeable to you, it will be showing yourself a men of a great mind to give it up to them that they may carry on their trade as before."[80]

Law had taken shelter at the French factory at Kasimbazar with his small force under the protection of the Nawab and many French fugitives from Chandernagore had joined him. Bussy was reported to be at Cuttack where he had enlisted the support of the Marathas. From Cuttack, a march of some days would carry his forces to the banks of Hugli. The possibility of a combined French-Maratha attack created a critical situation for the English at Calcutta and its neighbourhood. Hence the Select Committee of Calcutta at once sent an agent to Cuttack to collect and transmit all news about the goings-on in the camps of the French or the Marathas or Mirza Sallee.[81] Therefore, it was decided to deploy informers at the strategic points so that the committee was kept constantly apprised about the developments. The committee gave top priority to "getting the best information" about Bussy's advance to Bengal.[82] Of course, the expenses for all this were to be borne by the English.

Though the Nawab protected Law and his small force at Kasimbazar, his vacillating conduct made him an unpredictable commodity. The Nawab did not help Law with money[83] but permitted him to attend his *darbar*, and sent to him a detachment of militia known by the name of

---

79 Gleig's *Clive*, p, 76.

80 Quoted in Forrest, *Clive*, I. p. 401.

81 Mirza Sallee was the renter of the province of Orissa from the Marathas.

82 S. C. R. , 23 April, p. 66.

83 Hill, *Three Frenchmen*, p. 96.

Talinga.[84] It became also known to Watts that "the French were erecting batteries, and digging a ditch round their Factory at Cossimbazar." Watts further came to know that the French refugees from Chandernagore, Dacca and Jugdea, all assembled together, numbered "150 Europeans and 100 Tellingees" Watts immediately applied to the Nawab to demolish the works of the French, as well as to deliver them one and all to him. But though the Nawab complied with a part of his demand by sending one hundred men to demolish the works, he did not concede the demand of turning out the French from Kasimbazar. What Watts was afraid of was that preparations might be afoot for a Nawab-French combination against the English. He wrote to Clive: "As the French are so strong here and I am apprehensive the Nabob may entertain them."[85] At the same time, Law reported to the Nawab that a fleet of 40 French ships had attacked Bombay. Watts also came to know of this. So it seemed to him that the Nawab had again begun showing favour to the French.

The Nawab was evidently filled with misgivings about the English strategy. In a letter he asked Clive that why the English were still waiting at Hugli when they had already captured Chandernagore. In reply to this, Clive exposed his fang. He urged the Nawab that the latter should permit him to attack the French at Kasimbazar. Such permission, Clive added, "could convince the English that he (the Nawab) bore the goodwill of an ally towards them" and that the Nawab would be expected to preserve his neutrality in such a case.[86] During this time the English had again taken up their old plea that the Nawab should consider the enemies of the English as his enemy.[87] The English sought to take cover under the plea that their demand was a part of the treaty which the Nawab had signed. The plea was, however, a

84 *Tarikh-i-Munsuri*, Edt. by H. Blochmann (*Journal of the Asiatic Society of Bengal*, Vol. XXXVI, Part I, 1867, p. 89. Also, *Riyaz*, p. 371, f.n.

85 Watts' Letter to Clive, 5 April (Hill, II, pp. 316-317),

86 Orme, *Indostan*, II, p. 146.

87 *Tarikh*, p. 89. Also, *Riyaz*, p. 671 f.n.

blatant lie. The Nawab was discreet enough to reject the plea. He realised that if he gave the English a free hand, their forces would certainly unleash murder and destruction among the French, which would create panic among all the people, as well as cause economic ruin of the *subah*. Though Clive had to return to Madras with his troops at that time yet he kept on watching out and marking time. At any rate he did not want to see Bengal at the mercy of the Nawab.[88] The Nawab, on his part, did not consider that there would be any breach of faith with the English by sheltering some of the French fugitives.[89] The English, on their part, thought that a war with the Nawab was inevitable and that only by show of strength they could browbeat him and secure their advantages. Thus wielding the big stick and pursuing all kinds of duplicity they accused the Nawab of breach of faith, which was their first salvoe. They discovered a few letters allegedly written by the Nawab to Bussy inviting him to come to Bengal.[90] These they used as the handle to support their allegations against the Nawab. The letters were, however, not of unimpeachable veracity. There was a strong case that these were all forged. In fact after the battle of Plassey, Clive informed the court that the letters were a part of the conspiracy to put the Nawab in the wrong.[91]

This consuming desire of expelling the French from Bengal led the English to believe that to gain their end the must start by waging a war a against the Nawab. In this

88 *Ib'd.*, p. 89.

89 Forrest, *Clive*, V. I, p. 405.

90 *Ibid.*, p. 90. Also, *Riyaz*, p. 371, f.n. Also, Forrest *Clive*, I, p. 406. W atts wrote to Clive on 5 April, 1757, that the former would obey Clive if he could get the copies of the Nawab's letters to the French--Hill, II, p. 317.

91 There is a great doubt about the discovery by the English of the Original letters writteen by the Nawab. Clive informed that he could obtain through Watts only the true copies of thes letters, which was a mischievious lie. On the other hand, Scrafton said that these letters were discovered only when the English had joined in the conspiracy to dethrone Sirajuddaulah-Mairtra, *Sirajuddaulah*, pp. 325-326.

atmosphere of mutual suspicion, the English adopted the offensive and hence Scrafton was directed to stay at Murshidabad, when he came to the capital to settle a problem connected with the Dacca factory. It was in this process that the Watts-Omichand-Scrafton combination was formed and it made every effort to gain the maximum benefits for the English and even, if possible, to form a party at the *darbar* against the Nawab. These developments took shape after the fall of Chandernagore Accordingly, Watts adopted plans to cultivate friendship with the leading men of Bengal in order to consolidate the strategic position of the English in Bengal politics. Therefore, Watts hinted to Clive that the latter should cultivate friendship with Nandkumar and wrote on 5 April : "If you think proper when he (Nandkumar) comes to you again, you may tell him the *Golaub que Foul* is fresh and flourishing. Omichand and I are of the opinion it is better not to let him smell it yet, but keep him in hopes...... we are endeavouring to get the *Phousdarry* of Hughly for him, in which if we succeed, I hope to reap for the Company some advantages."[92]

In the same letter, he similarly urged Clive to win over Jagat Seth as well. He requested Clive to write to Jagat Seth and desrire him to send his *gomastah* to Calcutta and depute another *gomastah*, named Baijnath, who might reside at Hugli "with the utmost security and safety". Though Jagat Seth, in some cases, did not act rightly for the cause of the English yet the latter had no complaints against him. It was felt that any misgiving in the Seth's mind about the credibility of the English should be forthwith removed and all snags in mutual relationship should be immediately rectified.[93] The fact was that after the fall of Calcutta Baijnath had purchased some goods of the Company from the plunders at half price. Watts wished to regain them and as such he wrote to Clive in the same letter : I think we may ask, though not demand, the difference between the price he bought

92 Watts' letter to Clive, 5 April (Hill, II, p, 316-317).

93 *Ibid.* (*Ibid.*, p. 318).

those goods at and their real value."[94] Watts believed that these types of transactions with the Seths would create an atmosphere favourable to the English.

That this Watts-Omichand-Scrafton combination was in dead earnest at Murshidabad, during these days, to form a party against the Nawab, is evident from Scrafton's letter to Walsh on 9 April. In this letter Scrafton urged that the English should proceed on some fixed plan and be prepared to take proper counter-measures in case of a rupture with the Nawab. He observed in his letter : "Give Mr. Watts a hint of this, the least encouragement, and he will set about froming a party in case of the worst. How glorious it would be for the Company to have a Nabob devoted to them."[95]

Thus when the Nawab busy in fulfilling the terms of the tre ty and had given orders to the Seths for the payment of money to Watts, which the Nawab's soldiers had carried away as loot "from Cossimbazar, Dacca and the *aurungs*",[96] Watts was fully engaged in his cunning diplomatic game of hatching plots against the Nawab and forming a part at the *darbar* in his favour. Additionally Watts continued to egg on Clive. On 11 April he wrot to Clive about the dilatory policy the Nawab in complying with the terms of the contract. Most of the ministers of the Nawab, Watts added, were the enemies of the English, who raised suspicion in the mind of the Nawab by constantly warning him that the English might attack him. Watts also reported that the ministers assured the Nawab about the increase of the French striking power on account of Bussy's march with a large army within the vicinity of Bengal. To strengthen their point about the French counterweight against the English they reported to the Nawab that the French had arrived at Pondichery with 17 ships of war, 3,000 soldiers and 4,000 *caffrees*. Rajaram, one of the Nowab's Officers, had reported to the Nawab from Midnapore that according to

94 Hill, II, p. 318

95 Scrafton's letter to Walsh 9 April (Hill, III, p. 342).

96 Letter from the Nawab to Clive, 10 April (C. C. C., p. 37).

his information forty French ships had advanced to attack Bombay and crush the English there. The Nawab believed these stories, which was an indication of the Nawab's partiality for the French. Without trying to hide his contempt Watts reported to Clive that Sirajuddaulah was always guided by "five or six of these low people." In such a situation Watts wanted to net as many defectors as possible. For instance, if Nandkumar could be made a supporter of the English interest, through his help the English might obtain more than 38 villages, "many of which lie at a distance from Caleutta." Watts wanted to know about Clive's ocinion in this matter ; and if the plan appeared feasible to Clive only then the Resident would act. In formulating all these plans, Watts was greatly indebted to Omichand for the latter's "superior understanding" and hence he always consulted Omichand "on all occasions". About his league with Omichand towards the fulfilment of a secret plan of conspiracy against the Nawab, Watts wrote to Clive : "Omichand and I have had many conversations on a subject I didnot know how to address you about. I opened myself to Scrafton and from him learn Omichand's and my endeavours for yours and the Major's service will not be disagreeable."[97] Watts' view of the situation led him to believe that the English should not take any hasty action but strike only at the point when the Resident's intrigues had fully matured.

Thus when Watts came to know about the proposed March of the English army to Murshidabad, he tried to dissuade Clive from under-taking this scheme as it would violate "our treaty with the Nabob, who is complying with his part of it." This action would throw the *subah* again in confusion and would prevent the "Company's getting an investment for another year, the consequences of which may be fatal to them." Thus Watts continued his intrigues against the Nawab and urged Clive that "nothing but an open and apparent breach by the Nabob in his contract ought to induce us to rekindle the war in this province."[98] In the same letter Watts infor-

97 Watts' letter to Clive, 11 April (Hill, II, pp. 322-323).

98 *Ibid.*, p. 323.

med Clive about the non-arrival of the English *gomastahs* from Calcutta, which he had urged as early as 10 March. For this unusual delay of their arrival at Murshidabad, "the Nabob blames us, "observed Watts, saying that "as soon as we have finished these accounts. he (the Nawab) will deliver over what was brought to his account from Calcutta." Along with this letter, Watts also enclosed a copy of an acquittance or clearance which Watson and Clive were to sign, but at the same time, he warned Clive not to affix his signature, "till you are advised, I have received everything that was taken." However, the Nawab was very eager for this acquittance. So Watts requested Clive to give him an authority to sign the acquittance on behalf of the Admiral and the Colonel, and finally observed in his letter: "As you may with greatest security depend on me on every occassion, I hope to be favoured with your confidence and advice."[99]

It was clear to Watts that this conspiracy against the Nawab could be successful only by expelling the French from his *darbar* and Watts continuously went on intriquing to this end at the Nawab's court. The Nawab was also apprehensive of the march of the British troops towards Murshidabad in pursuit of the French and and at last he was won over by Watts On 12 April, the Nawab promised before Watts to send Law the next day, "to settle the terms of his capitulation with the English." Thus Watts was in full hope that "everything would end well"[100] concerning the English aim of reducing the French in Bengal to cypher. Accordingly on 12 April, Law received summons from the Nawab to attend the *darbar* on the next day.[101] Watts' meeting the Nawab the same day, i.e. on 12 itself, according to the instruction of Watson told its own tale of the anti-French moves going on. Law began to suspect the intrigues of Watts and decided to meet the Nawab "early in the morning of 13, with five or six persons well armed."[102]

---

99 Hill, II, p. 324.

100 Clive's letter to Court, 16 April (F.W.I.H.C., II, p. 122-23 para 7).

101 Hill, *Three Frenchmen*, p. 98.

13 April was a day of great excitement at Murshidabad. Law proceeded with great caution. Finally he went to meet the Nawab. At about 5.00 p.m., after having waited for a long time, he became impatient and enquired from the Nawab's officials about his urgent summons to him. He came to know that as the Nawab had received numerous complaints from the English against the French, he had decided to summon both Law and Watts to settle matters in his presence, so that neither should fear the other. When the *darbar* hour started, Law noticed that Watts had already taken his seat in the hall with the *diwans* of the Nawab. In fact owing to Watts' intrigues the scale was heavily loaded aganist the French interests. Watts had already convinced the Nawab about the necessity of expelling the French. So when Law had taken his seat, a *diwan* of Nawab asked him if he had "anything particular to say to Mr. Watts." Law replied in the negative. There upon Watts, speaking as it were he was the alter ego of the Nawab, addressed Law in English: The question is, Sir, whether you will resolve to hand over your Factory to me and go down to Calcutta with all your people, you will as well treated and will obtain the same terms as the gentlemen of Chandernagore, this is the Nawab's wish."[103]

Law replied in a defiant tone that he would do nothing of the kind, but if he was forced to leave Kasimbazar, he would surrender the factory to the Nawab and "to no one else." At this watts became greatly excited and turning his face to the *diwan*, he apprised the latter about his conversation with Law. Then, on his part, the *diwan* asked Law to comply with the propsal of Watts as the Nawab was to maintain "a good understanding with the English." Watts then took the *diwan* inside and Law had great reason to suspect that they intended to make him prisoner. Watts then went to the Nawab, who was in another room, after sometime, some *jamadars*, the agent of the Seths and some English officials also asked Law to submit "entirely to what Mr. Watts demanded." Law

---

102 *Ibid.*

103 Law, *Memoire* (Hill, III, pp. 203-204).

firmly rejected the proposals and requested that he be allowed to see the Nawab. The officials prevented Law but the latter replied that as the Nawab had summoned him, he would not leave the place till he met the Nawab. Thereupon the *diwan* and the agent of the Seths went to the Nawab and apprised him of Law's wishes. The Nawab then permitted Law to meet him and instructed Watts to withdraw to some other room.

Law went alone before the Nawab. The Nawab desired that Law should accept Watts' proposals. "I do not wish to embroil the whole country for your sake," told Nawab to Law, observing further, "you are not strong enough to defend your self. you must give way. You ought to remember that when I had need of your assistance you always refused me."[104] Law had nothing much to say in reply and told the Nawab that he would be dishonoured, if he would accept Watts' proposals. Law then expressed his desire to go to Patna. Except the Nawab and Khwajah Wayid all others assembled there opposed his view and asked him to go to Midnapore or Cuttack instead. It was not difficult for Law to guess that this was a clever plan of Watts to swoop on the French if they would take that route. Hence Law again asked the Nawab for his permission to patna, The Nawab replied that Law could take the road which he liked. "May God conduct you" were the last parting words of Sirajuddaulah to Law. Law stood up and left for the factory in order to make preparations for their journey to Patna.[105] About this last meeting, the author of *Tarikhi-Mansuri* observes that Sirajuddaulah promised to call Law at the time of need, "hoping that he would be ready to come at his call.' But Law considered that such a future meeting

---

104 Law Observes in his *Memoire* that during his conversation with the Nawab, "I noticed that the Nawab kept his eyes cast down that it was as if against his will that he paid me such a compliment." Law, *Memoire* (Hill, III, p. 205).

105 Law, *Memoire* (Hill, III, p. 206). Also, Hill, *Three Frenchmen*. pp. 100-102.

had been rendered impossible. He left Kasimbazar at his free will.[106]

After obtaining the permission fron the Nawab, the French began to prepare to quit the factory at Kasimbazar during 14 and 15 April. But Watts, in the meanwhile, "tried to get the French" in his power, though the Nawab was determined "not to deliver them up" at the mercy of the English. Watts informed Walsh on 14 April that the French were not so numerous as he had thought before. They comprised only 70 Europeans, 80 Tellingees with about 50 country sepoys. He further reported that they had been directed by the Nawab to leave the *subah* of Bengal, though they would "keep their effects to pay their creditors." On a triumphant note he added that the Nawab had also promised to Watts that the Nawab would comply with his agreement and assist the English "with his whole force if the French should attempt to enter his kingdom again."[107]

If one could read the Nawab's mind at this stage one could perceive that though the Nawab directed the French to leave Kasimbazar, he was not well disposed towards the English as well. The repeated demands of Watts for expelling the French together with the arrogant tone of letters that he had received from the Colonel and the Admiral had given Sirajuddaulah sufficient cause for annoyance and apprehension. On 13 April, he threatened Watts not to go beyond limits in the presence of Jagat Seth, Manikchand, khwajah Wajid Abdul kasim, Ranjit Rai and Omichand. The humiliation which Watts thus suffered at the Nawab's hands made him observe in his letter to Walsh on the next day that he wished

106 *Tarikh*, p. 89. Muslim historians generally shared this view that Sirajuddaulah wanted the help of the French in case of need at the time of Law's departure, though this was not corroborated by other contemporary evidences. But on the basis of this, the later English authors supported this and even went to an extreme by observing that Sirajuddaulah helped Law with men and money at the time of his departure – Stewart, *History of Bengal*, p. 520. Also, Broome, *Bengal Army*, I, p. 119.

107 Watts' letter to Walsh, 14 April (Hill, II pp. 329-330).

to bring the matter to the notice of Walsh and the Colonel alone, and hoped that no public discussion might be made of it.[108] However, Watts forbade Walsh to take any action against the Nawab because the Resident wanted to get the French in his power by appeasing the Nawab. The tone of the Admiral Watson's letter about the Anglo-French conflict in Bengal also enraged the Nawab beyond limit. Thus after this incident of 13 April, the Nawab replied to Watson on the next day: "if you are not disposed to come to a rupture with me, you have my agreement under my hand and seal, when you write, look upon that, and write accordingly."[109]

Sirajuddaulah wanted to replenish his treasury with what was obtained from the capture of the French factory as well as from what-ever could be grabbed from the closure of the French trade and had already written to Clive on 29 March to pay into the treasury amounts and goocs equivalent to what the Nawab used to get from the French. He also hinted to Clive to repay the various debts of the French. In reply Clive wrote to the Nawab on 15 April and again on 20 April what the "conquerors are never answerable for the debts of the vanquished." However, the Colonel directed Watts to reach a settlement with the Nawab in regard to this matter.[110]

Law reviewed his force at Kasimbazar on 15 April. Leaving the charge of the French factory on Bugros[111], the French soldiers under Law left Murshidabad on the 16th of the month. On receipt of this news, Watts immediately sent two spies to try to sow the seeds of defection among the French soldiers.[112] But his efforts failed. The French arrived at Patna on 3 June, where they were cordially received by Ramnarain. The French were given by the Nawab's order, "a very suitable site," to build their barracks.[113] Contrarily

108 *Ibid.*

109 Nawab's letter to Watson, 14 April.

110 Letters from Clive to the Nawab, 15 April and 20 April C.C.C., p. 36 and 38).

111 Hill, *Three Frenchmen*, p. 103.

112 *Ibid.*, Also, Hill, II, p. 337.

113 Law, *Memoire* (Hill, II, p. 209).

Watts received a letter from the Nawab promising that the latter had given definite instruction to Ramnarain "to turn them out of his bounds."[114] Watts had already informed Clive on 16 April that the French had evacuated Murshidabad. Clive had also immediately decided to send a detachment of English troops in pursuit of the French.[115]

The report of this kind of harrying of the French by the English revived the indignation of the Nawab. He had already assured Clive that he had no intention to entertain the French and had got demolished their works as well. But quite evidently this promise could not satisfy Clive, who began to suspect "something" about the actual intention of the Nawab.[116] But the Nawab could not brook the fact that after the expulsion of the French from Kasimbazar, the English would try to pursue them. He was so exasperated that he immediately directed Watts to quit his presence and to appear no more at the *darbar*. He also gave Watts to understand that the letter should either retire to Calcutta or give an assurance that the "English should make no futher attempts to molest the French". Watts refused either and obtained permission to consult the Calcutta Council in the matter.[117] This humiliation of Watts at the *darbar* kindled the rage of Watson, who wrote a very strong note to the Nawab observing that while a single Frenchman remained in Bengal, the Admiral would never cease pursuing him.[118] This determination to expel the French was, in truth, complementary to the English strategy to intimidate the Nawab by a show of strength. Thus in the same letter, Watson charged the Nawab for the non-fulfilment of the treaty. "I find that what you wrote me in your letter dated the 1st of Rajib (22 March) is not yet complied with," observed Watson in his letter to the Nawab. "You therein assured me," Watson

114 Translation of a letter sent by the Nawab to Watts by Ranjit Rai, 15 April (C.C.C., p. 39).

115 Orme, *Indostan*, II, p. 147.

116 Clive's letter to Court, 16 April (F.W.I.H.C., II, p. 222).

117 Orme, *Indostan*, II, p. 147.

118 Forrest, *Clive*, I, p. 407.

continued in the same letter, "that you would fulfil all the Articles you had agreed to by the 15th of that Moon. Have you ever yet complied with them all?............How then can I place my confidence in what you write?"[119] Thus both Watson and Clive insisted upon their demand of expelling the French from Bengal as a part of the treaty, which was again a mischievous lie. On the contrary, it was rightly pointed out by Watts to Clive on 26 April that "our attacking the French I take it has nothing to do with our Articles of peace, neither is he (the Nawab) bound thereby to deliver them up."[120] Even Clive had admitted on 29 March that the Nawab had performed "almost every article of the treaty."

Watson's arrogant demand infuriated the Nawab, who declared, "They are always writing to me to deliver up the French; I will receive no more of their letters."[121] But the French expulsion from the Murshidabad *darbar* was already a settled fact and was destined to have very evil repercussions on the Nawab's fate. In the immediate aftermath of this the English gained much in their trade. The French factories in other parts of Bengal soon passed under the control of the English.

Clive nursed great doubts about the Nawab's motivations and had already decided to commence hostilities against him On 22 April, he wrote to Watts: "After the Nabob's last Message I cannot depend upon his friendship, and shall therefore get everything ready for a March." And on the next day, he wrote a threatening letter to the Nawab: "Your behaviour to our *vacqueel* has given me great uneasiness;...... but remeber that if you have given ear to my enemies and are resolved to break through the Articles of Agreement, you will become responsible for all the blood that shall be spilled, and all the msichief that shall be done."[122]

119 Watson's letter to the Nawab, 19 April (Hill, II, pp. 344-345).

120 Hill, II, p. 349.

121 *Ibid.*, p. 303.

122 Quoted in Forrest, *Clive,* I. p. 409.

By this time, the mutual suspicions between the Nawab and the English had greatly in creased and Clive thought a rupture not only unavoidable but also necessary. He persisted in his resolution of sending a detachment against the retreating French. However, when the news came to him about the discontent among the high officials of the Nawab at the *darbar*, he became discreetly quiet at least for the time being, and instructed Watts to cultivate friendship with the disgruntled offiicials of the Nawab.[123] Even then the Colonel was fully bent upon waging a war against the Nawab of Bengal on ground of non-fulfilment of the February-treaty on the part of the latter. But quite evidently his plan was to take full advantage of the Nawab's weakness. He openly hinted to Mohanlal about the "desolation of war", which "this rich and fair courtry was to feel." He cautioned Mohanlal "that where confidence is wanting there can be neither peace nore friendship."[124] There was thus no hiding of the spirit of belligerence in his words.

Watts was also not idle at Murshidabad. But he was unlike Clive in keeping his own counsel and proceeding very diplomatically. From the atmosphere of the Nawab's court, he could gather the information that everything was not well with the Nawab's officialdom. He informed Clive that Sirajuddaulah continued to be a bitter enemy of the English, and would certainly join with the French and attack the English "whenever he is disengaged from the apprehensions of the Pytans and the My Rajah."[125] Watts also give a hint of his plan of toppling the present Nawab and getting him replaced by another who was favourable to the English. "I am sensible", he observed in his letter to Clive, "how absolutely necessary it is to have a Nabob attached to our interest (which this man will never be), in order to keep the French from resettling in this province ." But in doing so, Watts

123 Orme, *Indostan*, II, p. 147.

124 Clive's letter to Mohanlal, 23 April (C.C.C., p. 40).

125 This is in reference to the possible invasion of Bengal by the Pathans and the rebellion of a *zamindar* in Bihar respectively.

was sensible of persevering with great caution, lest their desire might get divulged. He advised Clive "to temporize and pacify the Nabob for the present, and appear to give over all thoughts of war till the French are marched to a distance, till the Pytans are advanced nearer and till some schemes" were effected for execution. He advised Clive to "be ready to march at an hour's warning" with all his carriages, arms and weapons necessary for this undertaking.[126]

In the mean time the *darbar* of the Nawab had become a welter of intrigue. This gave Watts an opportunity to form a party at the *darbar* against Sirajuddaulah. The great Hindu bankers, the Seths, were aggrieved against the Nawab. Jagat Seth had already set the ball rolling against the Nawab by reaching an understanding with Yar Latif Khan, a divisional commander of the Nawab. Soon this party of the conspirators was joined by others who had their own axes to grind. Their common aim was to set up such a man on the *masnad* from whom they could derive the greatest benefit for themselves. It is reported that Yar Latif received a secret monetary allowance from the Seths. When their plans had made substantial headway, the conspirators opened communication with Watts for English support. Everything was done in utmost secrecy. As Watts' meeting with Yar Latif might create suspicion in the mind of the Nawab, the Resident sent Omichand to Yar Latif to ascertain the real intention of the conspirators and the modalities of their action. Omichand was thus to act as a courier or messenger. Apparently it was a humble part. But Omichand by temperament an arch conspirator, soon raised himself to the first rank of the anti-Sirajuddaulah conspiracy.[127] The mission of Omichand to warm up Watts became successful, as he, as well as the Seths, increased the fear of Watts that the Nawab would break his agreement with the English at the earliest opportunity. Thus Watts became convinced that war was inevitable and recommended to Clive to accept the proposals of Yar Latif Khan. The plan of Watts

126 Watts' letter to Clive, 23 April (Hill, II, p. 353),

127 Gleig's *Clive*, p. 80.

was to fall on the Nawab in conjuncture with Yar Latif, when the Nawab would move to Patna to suppress the Afghans. He then wrote to Clive: "Whenever the Nabob breaks with us he (Yar Latif) will join us as soon as possible with his whole force on condition of our making him Nabob." If the English would agree to do this, Yar Latif promised through Omichand that he would grant the Company, a large tract of land near Calcutta and "a sum of ready money sufficient to satisfy the navy, military and all the inhabitants of Calcutta. Yar Latif also requested Clive through Omichand, as Watts mentioned in his above letter, "You will write a soothing letter to the Nabob, which may entirely allay the apprehensions he has of us and induce him to march northward, which he will, the moment his fear of us cease." In concluding his letter, Watts cautioned Clive to preserve the strictest secrecy by observing: "All that we have to do is to lull him into security, and by that means induce him to march northward. You must be sensible what greater honour will accrue to you from this project and how much secrecy is necessary."[128]

On receiving this letter, Clive did not show much enthusiasm but reserved his comment on Yar Latif. He informed Watts that if the Nawab was determined to sacrifice the English, the English must preempt it by striking the first blow. Yet he wanted to be assured that Watts' arrangements were absolutely fool-proof. "You should enquire if Luttee (Yar Latif Khan) be a man of interest," wrote Clive in reply to Watts, observing further to "consider the honour of the nation and, if possible, avoid engaging us in any executions."[129]

The Nawab's own officials, for the benefit they expected to reap by eliminating Sirajuddaulah, confirmed Watts' fear that the Nawab would turn hostile to the English at any moment. So Watts' doubts about the Nawab's policies and steps deepened. He informed Clive on 26 April that the

---

128 Watts' letter to Clive, 23 April (Hill, II, p. 354).

129 Clive to Watts, 28 April (*Ibid.*, p. 366).

Nawab outwardly maintained his contract,[130] granted *parwana* to the English, whenever the Company asked "within the compass of his Agreement." He further observed in the same letter to Clive by hinting: "He (the Nawab) writes to you that your enemies are his and his yours, but this is only a private letter and not mentioned in the Agreement, on the contrary he says we shall not war in Bengal while he continues firm to his Agreement."[131] But all this, as Watts felt, was only the tip of the iceberg. He was afraid as he stated, that at a deeper level the Nawab meant evil to the English commercial and political interests in Bengal.

Therefore, Watts pleaded for the violation of the treaty: "There is no dependence on the Nabob, that he is secretly our enemy, and that we have almost positive assurances of the French being in his way, and have great reason to believe he will join them on the first occasion, which junction must be fatal to our affairs here; prudence certainly requires us to guard against such an accident."[132]

as a counterpoise to this danger, Watts informed Clive about the proposals of Mir Jafar, the Nawab's Commander-in -Chief which he (Watts) had received on 24 April and which seemed "more feasible" to him than the proposals of Yar Latif. Mir Jafar sent his agent, Petrus, privately to Watts and informed the latter that the Nawab was generally disliked by everybody for his shows of bad temper and ill-treatment towards almost everybody.[133] It was further reported that

130 The Nawab also informed Clive on 26 April that he had nearly complied with all articles of the February-treaty—Nawab to Clive, 26 April C.C.C., p. 42).

131 Watts' letter to Clive, 26 April (Hill, II, pp. 362-363).

132 *Ibid.*

133 It was the house of Jagat Seth where the persons who were opposed to Sirajuddaulah used to assemble secretly. They discussed their plans about the deposition of the Nawab. This secret assembly could not come to a definite conclusion for a long period of time, after the fall of Chandernagore. They at first proposed for a Hindu rule. But when it was not liked by some others, the name of Mir Jafar was

(contd....)

whenever Mir Jafar went to visit the Nawab, he (Mir Jafar) feared assassination, and, therefore, always kept his "forces in readiness." Mir Jafar further informed Watts by invoking his fear that the Nawab was only waiting for the recovery of Mohanlal, and for the arrival of some forces, that were expected from Patna in eight or nine days to attack the English. Therefore, Mir Jafar proposed before Watts that if the English would consent to his proposals, a number of first grade officials of the Nawab, such as Rai–Durlabh, Rahim Khan, Bahadur Ali Khan and others, were ready to join with the English forces in seizing the Nawab and setting up another person on the *masnad* according to the approval of the English. As such, Watts informed Clive in the same letter: "He (Mir Jafar) requested, you will wirte your proposals of what money, what land you want, or what treaties you will engage in."

On receipt of the reply from Clive Watts would meet Mir Jafar, sort out all "the particulars of his scheme, proposals and demands" and communicate everything to Clive immediately.[134] At the same time, Watts wrote to Clive about his personal opinion by observing "that Meer Jaffeir was by far the properest person to be elevated to that Rank,

---

proposed. But Mir Jafar at first turned down the proposal as he was hesitant about ending the house of Alivardi. Then the conspirators proposed the name of Yar Latif Khan, a divisionnl commander of Siraj's army, and hence his name was sent before Watts. Watts occepted it and recommended for Clive's approval. But Clive reserved his opinion. Meanwhile, Mir Jafar began to lose his position at the *darbar* and as such, he consented to replace Sirajuddaulah. Mir Jafar immediately obtained the full support of the conspirators, headed by the Seths and Rai-Durlabh. They now firmly believed that the concurrence of the English was essential to the completion of the wishes. Hence Mir Jafar sent his proposals to Watts. – Maitra, *Sirajuddaujah*, p. 67. Also, Roy, *Murshidabad Kahi*, pp. 66-67. Also, Mukhopadhyay, Rajiblochan, *Maharaj Krishnachandra Rayasya Charitam* (Cal. Reprint, 1355 B.S. i.e. 1948 A.D.), p. 33. Also, Mukhopadhyay, *Rai-Durlabh*, pp. 57-60.

134 Watts' letter to Clive, 26 April (S.C.R., 1 May, 1757, pp. 73-76). Also Hill, II, pp. 362-363.

as his abilities were greater, his reputation better, and his connections were more extensive than those of Laitty." At the same time, Watts hinted it to the Colonel that "if this change was to be accomplished by their forces, as he (Watts) much doubted, whether, after all, the Moors had spirit enough to attempt so extraordinary an Enterprize themselves, it would be right to form the outlines of a new Agreement of which the old one ought to be the basis, and to frame such additional Articles, as might effectually indemnify the Company for the risk they ran, and procure an ample satisfaction for the losses private persons had sustained in the devastation of Calcutta, of which no care had been taken in the former Treaty.[135]"

Watts wanted to defeat the Nawab by diplomacy and intrigues. Thus, in the same letter he advised Clive to tell the Nawab for the present: "It would appear that if we propose coming to rupture, our business is at present to amuse, lay aside all appearance of war while we concert of measures with the principal '*jumidars*', and that before we show our intentions of any act of hostility or motion of the forces northward, a necessary step is to be taken: is the withdrawing of the Company's goods and people from all the subordinates, as you must be sensible the neglect of that will throw them entirely at the Nabob's mercy." In this way Watts wished to conceal their hostile projects against the Nawab and, to ensure further precaution, he requested Clive to answer his letters in cypher.[136]

Watts was much impatient to know from Clive about the latter's reactions to Mir Jafar's proposals as he wanted to finalise an agreement with Mir Jafar without delay. His plan was to move along the lines suggested by Mir Jafar, and he wanted the Company to follow suit. So when Clive

135 Watts' *Memoirs*, pp. 76-77.

136 Hill, *Abstract*, p. 17 (S.C.R., 1 May), Also, Hill, II, p. 364 In the Committee of Enquiry Clive admitted in his evidence in 1772 that he corresponded with Watts in cyphers.--Extract from the First Report, 26 May, 1772 (Hill, III, p. 312). Also, Caraccioli III, p. 70.

sent Captain Grant with a few men, to recover the money and goods from Kasimbazar and other subordinate factories. Watts forbade this party to come up and asked them to return. In fact Mir Jafar had advised him that the English should not try to send any ammunition up, as all boats were strictly searched by the Nawab's soldiers. He similarly advised Watts to send no soldiers towards Kasimbazar but only peons. Watts again requested Clive to depend on him as well as on Mir Jafar. Hence, he observed in his letter to Clive, only two days after the proposals of Mir Jafar were sent, "Depend on it, I shall act for the best and you may be assured, I am under no apprehensions for myself and that will never suffer in my reputation. All I want is your favour and good name."

He thus again advised Clive to suspend his "resentment for a few days." Nothing should be done to arouse the Nawab's suspicion, he added. This attitude of the English was essential because the Nawab had heard about the retreat of of the Afghans from Delhi and his troubles with the *zamindar* of Bihar had come to an end. "Upon this the Nabob is very uppish", observed Watts and urged Clive to make an agreement with Mir Jafar as "there is none equal to him." At the moment, as Watts felt, the English had nothing to do but "it is our business to follow his (Mir Jafar's) advice." Watts again cautioned Clive to keep everything secret and "talk of nothing else but mercandise." To lull the Nawab about the actual designs of the English, Watts advised Clive to send a part of his army to Calcutta and "keep only a garrison in Chandernagore and appear to give over all thoughts of war and send your people no where but keep all quiet.[137]

Scrafton, who was at Murshidabad at this time to assist Watts in his business and whose works were also sanctioned by the Select Committee in its resolution on 28 April,[138] informed Clive from Kasimbazar about the rage of the Nawab

137 Watts' letter to Clive, 28 April (S.C.R., 1 May, pp. 77-78). Also, Hill, II, pp. 366-367.

138 Hill, *Abstract*, pp. 16-17.

against the English after receiving letters from Mathuramal and Nandkumar that the English were sending up men and ammunition towards Murshidabad. In his rage, the Nawab affronted Omichand, ordered Mir Jafar to resist the English and despatched orders to recall Law and "swore destruction" of the English. A messenger was sent to Watts ordering him that if the English would march "a foot beyond" their present camp, "war was inevitable." But "if you will put your troops into quarters" observed Scrafton, the Nawab would,, recall his army."[139]

The activities of Clive at his camp near Chandernagore were not liked by the members of the Select Committee at Calcutta. They became frightened owing to the threatening attitude of the Nawab. They were also displeased with Clive for his direct correspondence with Watts, Scrafton, as well as with Nawab himself. Hence, they directed Clive on 28 April that all letters concerning the Company's affairs must be replied to after the concurrence of the Select Committee and not by Clive on his own. They also expected Clive to return with all forces to Calcutta, as the large expenses for the troops in the camp made a huge drainage of the Company's wealth.[140] Though Clive replied that he was doing all thoes things for the benefit of the Company, ultimately he had to submit before the advice of the Select Committee. By the advice of Watts, he also agreed to send back a part of his troops to Calcutta.

At the end of April, the English boats carrying soldiers and ammunition had been stopped by Rai-Durlabh.[141] This made the Nawab furious with the English. The Nawab ordered Mir Jafar—the Commander of his army, to proceed to plassey and teach the arrogant English another good lesson. Mir Jafar had to start for Plassey with his army very reluctantly; however, he left his agent at Murshidabad, to carry on

139 Scrafton to Clive, 28 April (Hill, III, pp. 344-345). Also, Hill, *Abstract*, p. 17.

140 Forrest, Clive, I, p. 413. Also Gleig's *Clive*, p. 83.

141 C.C.C., p. 44.

correspondence with Watts.[142] But Watts was in a scup, since Mir Jafar's departure from Murshidabad was a set-back for the execution of their secret intrigue against Sirajud-daulah.

Clive could no longer remain at his camp near Chandernagore as he got urgent summons from the Select Committee of Calcutta, of which he was one of the members. He went to Calcutta and placed before the Select Committee Watts' letters of 26 and 28 April, as well as the 28 April letter from Scrafton. On 1 May the committee began thoroughly to discuss the matter. Mir Jafar, being a far more important person than Yar Latif Khan, the committee naturally gave him greater weight. Mir Jafar was the brother-in-law of the late Nawab Alivardi Khan and held both under him and Sirajuddaulah the office of paymaster general, which necessarily gave him great influence with the army. Moreover. he was the choice of the principal men like the Seths and Rai-Durlabh. After selecting Mir Jafar as their choice, the committee decided that as the present Nawab could not be relied on, his deposition from the *masnad* became inevitable for "the interest of the Company" on three grounds. In the first place, the dishonesty of the Nawab shown in the February-treaty and its aftermath convinced the Company that he was only waiting to gain time. Secondly, he intended to break the peace as shown by his intrigues with the French and thirdly, the Nawab was hated by everybody which convinced the English that "there will be a Revolution" against him, whether the English would interfere or not. The committee thus thought that it would be a mistake not to assist his probale successor.[143] Therefore, the committee agreed unanimously to assist Mir Jafar, if he would properly remunerate the English for the risk which they were preparing to undertake, "of entering

142 Orme, *Indostan*, II, p. 150. Also, Thornton, *British Empire* p. 51.

143 S.C.R., 1 May (Hill, *Abstract*, pp. 17-18). Also, First Report, 26 May, 1772 (Hill, III, p. 312).

into a fresh war with the Nabob."[144] So the committee made some demands from Mir Jafar. In the first place, he must confirm the *farman*, the privilege of a mint and all other grants made by Sirajuddaulah. Secondly, he must take adequate steps for the restitution of the losses suffered during the sack of Calcutta. Thirdly, the bounoaries of the Company must extend from Baranagore in the north and the lake in the east. Fourthly, the Company must have liberty to fortify and garrison the factory of Kasimbazar. Fifthly, there must be an offensive and defensive alliance with the new Nawab as well as the prohib tion of the French from "re-settling their settlements" on condition that the English would pay "the equivalent of their duties." Sixthly, the Moors would not be allowed to fortify any position within 20 miles of the river from Hugli to Hijli. Seventhly, that the revenues of a district might be made over to the Company for the maintenance of European and sepoy forces for the support of the Nawab. Eighthly, the new Nawab must effect restitution of the Company's total loss by the taking of Calcutta and the out-settlements. Among the sufferers the Blacks and Armenians were not included, i.e. their losses might not be made good. Ninthly, that wherever the English troops were called to the ass.stance of the government, the expenses must be borne out by the new Nawab; and lastly. that an English Resident was to reside at Murshidabad and be admitted at the *darbar*.[145] The committee then decided that Clive should transmit these terms to Watts and urge him to expedite the matter.[146]

On the next day, Clive wrote to Watts enclosing the proposals, thus informing him that everything had been settled with the committee. At the same time, he directed Watts that he might take the liberty, in consultation with Omichand, to add any other article, or drop any one which, in their opinion, might disgust Mir Jafar.[147] Thus fully backed by the

144 Letter to Court, 14 July, 1757 (F.W.I.H.C., II, pp. 225-226).

145 *Ibid.* Also, S,C.R., 1 May (Hill, *Abstract*, pp. 17-18). Also, Hill, II pp. 373-374.

146 *Ibid.*

147 Clive to Watts, 2 May (Hill, II, pp. 372-373.

committee, Clive began to play the double game, as his activities during this period would clearly testify. "The most of the articles of peace are complied with", he observed in his letter to Pigot, but "for my own part, I am persuaded there can be neither peace nor security while such a monster reigns."[148] While Clive imposed upon the credulity of the Nawab by telling him about the "perfect harmony and friendship which subsisted between them;" he sent by the same messenger, another letter for Watts, that observed, "The Nabob is a villain. and cannnot be trusted, he must be overset, or we must fall."[149] In his letter of 2 May, Clive wrote to Watts, "I have wrote the Nabob a soothing letter, this accompanies another of the same kind to Moon Lol (Mohanlal)."[150] With the aim of removing all suspicions from the Nawab's mind, Clive planned very cleverly. He informed Watts, "Tomorrow morning we decamp, part of our forces return to Calcutta and other will go into garrison here." He wrote to the Nawab to follow his example by recalling his army from Plassey.[151] But at the same time, he directed Watts to "enter upon business with Meer Jaffier as soon as you please. I am ready, and will engage to be at Niesaray in twelve hours after I receive your letter." In the same letter, he urged Watts to encourage Mir Jafar: "Tell Meer Jaffier to fear nothing, that I will join him with 5,000 men who never turned their backs, and that if he fails seizing him, we shall be strong enough to drive him out of the country; assure him that I will march night and day to his assistance, and stand by him, as long as I have a man left."[152]

On 5 May, Clive wrote to Watts about the arrival of Scrafton. He also recommended to him the insertion of an

---

148 Quoted in Beveridge, *A Comprehensive History*, I, pp. 724-725.

149 *Ibid.*, pp. 726-727.

150 In reply to his letter, Mohanlal wrote to Clive on 3 May that, the Nawbb was faithful to his agreement with the English-C.C.C. p. 46.

151 Scrafton, *History of Bengal*, p. 83.

152 Clive to Watts, 2 May (Hill, II, p. 373).

article in the treatey, which would mention about Omichand's compensation for his losses "from consideration of his services." Clive also dierected Watts and the gentlemen at Kasimbazar that if they thought safe to remain in the factory or with Mir Jafar, they might do so, otherwise the Colonel would provide for them retreat by way of Jangipore.[153] On 6 May, Watts informed Clive that he had consulted Omichand about their secret scheme with Mir Jafar in which the Hindu bankers like Jagat Seth were also involved. Omichand had no high opinion about the *Gentoos*[154] However, Watts professed that he would conclude nothing without taking Omihand into confidence. He soon hoped for a meeting with Mir Jafar when everything would be finalised.[155]

On 6 May, Watts received the resolutions of the Select Committee concerning their treaty with Mir Jafar. Watts also received various reports about the Nawab's intentions. He received a report from Khwajah Wajid that the Nawab wrote frequently to Bussy to come to Bengal for his aid and that for the benefit of Law the Nawab had executed a bill of exchange for ten thousand rupees.[156] The Colonel placed this letter of Watts before the Select Committee on 12 May, informing further that Khwajah Wajid had been disgraced by the Nawab.[157] Due to these developments at Murshidabad, Watts became inpatient to consult Mir Jafar about the proposals and fully sort them out with him. But as Mir Jafar was at Plassey, the Resident consulted the agent of Mir Jafar. They inserted positive sums in the articles concerning money transactions. After their meeting, the agent, Omar Beg, left for plassey on 10 May to apprise Mir Jafar of his discussions with Watts. Omar Beg returned to Murshidabad

153 Clive to Watts, 5 May (*Ibid.*, p. 377).

154 By *Gentoos* Watts meant the Hindu bankers like the Seths who had no good opinion about Omichand. From this day, Omichand began to despair, because there was no love lost between him and the Seths.

155 Watts to Clive, 6 May (Hill, II, p. 377).

156 Hill, II, p. 379.

157 S.C.R., 12 May (Hill, *Abstract*, p. 18).

on the 14th with assurances from Mir Jafar that all the articles had been agreed to. But Mir Jafar had also insisted that the confederacy should be kept secret from Omichand. Probably this had been suggested by the Seths, who might have apprehended that Omichand's influence with the English would interfere with their own.[158] As there was no personal meeting between Mir Jafar and Watts, Clive left greatly uneasy and wrote to Watts: "I know not how to refrain from shewing my resentment at the Nabob's bad faith in not withdrawing his army.[159]

On 14 May Watts sent to Clive the articles of the treaty for the final approval of the Select Committee, along with the information about Omichand. At this juncture Omichand realised that if the conspiracy succeeded, watts would be amply rewarded by Mir Jafar, whereas, he himself would reap no extra benefit other then the restitution common to all Hindu merchants of Calcutta. He, therefore, claimed a commission of five per cent in all the wealth and treasures to be obtained from the Nawab's treasury.[160] Watts now did not think that Omichand could merit such a favour or "has acted so disinterested a part as I once imagined" and as such, he ignored Omichand's claim of five per cent and did not mention it in the treaty. Meanwhile, Watts had come to know about some mischievous acts of Omichand. He informed Clive about this. One of the mischiefs was alleged to be as follows In the February-treaty, the Nawab, in consideration of the plunder of Calcutta, had agreed with Ranjit Rai and Omichand, to pay 20,000 gold *mohars*, which was to be distributed among the leading men of Calcutta. Besides, the Nawab had agreed tc pay two lakhs of rupees, of which one lakh was agreed to be paid to Ranjit Rai, Rs. 25,000 to Omichand and the rest Rs. 75,000 was to be disposed

158 Orme, *Indostan*, II, pp. 150-151. This imoosition of restraint perplexed Watts, for he had trusted Omichand fully. But now from this day they began to hate each other, though they cooperated in the conduct of the confederacy.

159 Clive to Watts, 13 May (Hill, II, p. 379).

160 Hill, II, p. 380.

of among those whom Omichand thought proper to favour. Quite naturally Ranjit Rai was very eager to get a share of 20,000 gold *mohars* as well as one lakh of rupees promised to him. But, in order to gain favour from the Nawab, Omichand had advised him to disgrace Ranjit Rai so that the latter would not get his share and the Nawab would save his money thereby. The Nawab had followed this advice and in consideration of Omichand's advice, issued *parwanas* and directed several *aurungs* to deliver up to Omichand his money, goods, and effects. To corroborate the fact, Watts had asked Omichand to apply to the Nawab for the promised money but Omichand had replied that as "it was a secret contract", it was not proper to mention it. However, Omichand had added that he would think of the means to get it.[161] Further, when watts had shown Omichand the articles of the treaty with Mir Jafar, Omichand did not approve them but insisted on his demand for five per cent on all the Nawab's treasury, which would amount of two crores of rupees, besides a quarter of the Nawab's wealth. He also told watts that Mir Jafar should oblige himself to take from the *zamindars* no more then they had paid in Murshid Quli Khan's time. To secure Rai-Durlabh to his side, Omichand proposed giving him a quarter part of whatever they could dupe Mir Jafar into parting with. "These and many other Articles,' Watts observed in his letter "in which his (Omichand's) own ambition, cunning, and avaricious views were the chief motives, he positively insisted on and would not be prevailed upon to recede from one Article.''[162]

It was felt that this obstinacy of Omichand would ruin the affairs of the English in Bengal and also forfeit their credibilitv with the people. Mir Jafar, likewise "expressed an utter distrust" of Omichand. As the delay in executing the treaty was dangerous, Watts had a meeting with petrus and Omar Beg, both of them Mir Jafar's agents If these articles were agreed upon, Watts suggested to Clive to "get

161 Watts to Clive, 14 May (Hill, II, pp. 380-382).

162 *Ibid.*

the Articles wrote on large thin paper in Cypher, the sheet to be divided into two columns." Watts wrote to Clive in the same letter: "On the first division the Agreement to be wrote in cypher which is to be signed by the Admiral, you, the Committee and Council, affirming in the name of God and our Saviour that you will abide by this Agreement. In the second division I shall write the Agreement in English and on the third it will be wrote in Persian. The two last I shall sign and seal when the Articles are agreed to."[163]

Furthermore Mir Jafar wanted to know from Watts about the operations of war. He thought it desirable for Clive to write a letter to the Nawab that according to the latter's desire, Clive had withdrawn his army. In this way, Watts wanted to dupe the Nawab and so he, in concluding his letter, observed to Clive "You therefore request him (the Nawab) either to comply with his promise of recalling his troops to the city or let you know his real sentiments that you may take proper measure accordingly."[164]

Contrary to the wish of Mir Jafar, Watts inserted an additionasl article guaranteeing reimbursement to Omichand amounting to Rs. 30 lakhs. This was extremely odious to Mir Jafar. His agent, Omar Beg, reached Clive's camp on 16 May and took up the matter with him.[165] Clive who also had no good opinion of Omichand, decided to dupe and deprive him.

During this time, Watts received a blank paper from Mir Jafar with his seal upon it in order to have the articles wrote on the paper "so that you may depend upon everything being fixed on his (Mir Jafar's) part," as Watts wrote to Clive. "Therefore, if you approve of them, I entreat you will send them me with the utmost haste, when I will finish everything in two hours' time."[166]

163 *Ibid.*

164 *Ibid.*

165 Forrest, *Clive*, I, p. 418.

166 Watts to Clive, 16 May (Hill, II, op. 382-383).

Clive went to Calcutta with the articles of agreement and on 17 May placed the document before the Select Committee for its approval. The following was the text of Watts' articles of agreement: "First, that Meer Jaffier will confirm all the grants made to the English by the present Nabob.

Second, that he will make an alliance with the English offensive and defensive against all enemies either country or European.

Third, wherever the French are in the provinces of Bengal, Bahar and Orixa to be delivered up with all their effects and factories and they never be permitted again to settle in either of the said provinces.

Fourth, on account of the Company's losses and expenses to be paid them one crore of rupees.

Fifth, on account of the losses of Europeans—30 lacs.

Sixth, on account of Gentoos——— 30 lacs.

Seventh, on account of Armenians—— 15 lacs.

Eighth, on account of Omichand—— 30 lacs.

Ninth, whatever ground there is within the the Calcutta ditch belonging to the *Zamindars* to be given up to the English and 600 yards without the ditch all round.

Tenth, a tract of land whose rents in The Mogul's Books amount to 100,000 rupees yearly to be bought at a reasonable rate from the *Zemindars* and the Nabob to assist us in the purchase. We paying the annual *Piscash* or revenue as usual to the Nabob, whatever profit may arise from this *zemindary* to go towards paying the English Military.

Eleventh, whenver the Nabob wants the assistance of our Army the Extraordinary expenses to be paid by him."[167]

The Select Committee then proceeded to examine the foregoing articles. To the first four and the 9th, 10th, and 11th, they made no objection but rather esteemed them highly

---

167 S.C.R. 17 May, pp. 97-99.

beneficial for the Company. Only in the fourth article the compensation for the losses of the European sufferers was left blank to be filled up by Mir Jafar himself.[168] The fifth, sixth and seventh were judged proper to be altered as the committee did not think the allowances proportionate to the real losses. Hence, in the fifth article, the compensation for European losses increased from 30 to 50 lakhs of rupees. In the sixth articles the sum of the losses of the Hindus was reduced from 30 to 20 lakhs of rupees. In the seventh article the compensation for the Armenians' losses was reduced form 15 to 7 lakhs. These sums, slicedoff from the shares of the Hindus and Armenians, were to be divided among the Europeans in such a manner as would apear most equitable to Watson, Pocock and the Select Committee. The eighth article in favour of Omichand, the committee thought, should be totally deleted 'as his behaviour rather merits disgrace and punishment." The committee also thought to insert three other articles in the treaty: "Twelfth, that the Moors do not fortify by the river side below Hughly. Thirteenth, that the whole of this agreement be fully complied with within one month from his being seated as Nabob at Muxadavad or any other city within the provinces of Bengal, Bahar and Orixa."

"Fourteenth, on the condition Jaffier Ally Cawan Bahadar solemnly ratifies and swears to fulfil the Above Articles, we the underwritten do for and in the behalf of Honourable East India Company declare, on the Holy Evangelists and before God, that we will assist Jaffier Ally Cawn Bahadar with our whole force to obtain the *subaship* of the provinces of Bengal, Bahar and Orixa, and further that we will assist him to the utmost against all his enemies whatever, whenever he calls upon us for that purpose provided when he becomes the Nabob, he fulfils the above Articles." On 17 May, these articles of agreement were signed by Watson, Drake, Junior. Clive, Killpatrick and Becher.[169]

At Murshidabad Watts was much impatient and nervy. He expected that within three days he would get the articles

168 Hill, II, p. 384.

169 S.C.R., 17 May, pp. 97-99. Also, Hill, II, pp. 383-385.

of agreement from Clive. His relation with Omichand had already entered into a wry patch. He wrote to Clive on 17 May that when the articles of agreement came back to his hand, he would find out the means of executing the project. He warned that if the English put their faith in Omichand "all affairs would have been overset" and all confidence would be lost. Omichend also hit back almost immediately. Contrary to the advice of Watts and Petrus, Omichand went to the Nawab on 16 May and told him that "he had a secret of great importance to communicate to him." The Nawab promised secrecy, on which Omichand informed him that the English had sent to messengers to Ganjam to put in touch with Bussy and that they had reached an understanding. The French, Omichand warned the Nawab, were coming to Bengal to join with the English. By this downright lie, Omichand gained the favour of the Nawab who granted him a *parwana* on the Burdwan Rajah for the payment of four lakhs of rupees to him. In concluding his letter to Clive Watts referred to this and stated, "this lye of his I am apprehensive will alarm the Nabob and prevent his withdrawing his army which will be very detrimental to our scheme."[170]

In reply to this, Clive wrote to Watts that "Omichand was the greatest villain upon earth, and that he now appears in the strongest light what he was always suspected to be, a villain in grain." Clive advised Watts to do nothing that might arouse Omichand's suspicion. Along with this letter, Clive enclosed two drafts of agreement, the one real and the other fictitious. In the fictitious treaty Clive formed a plan to deceive Omichand. Clive also warned Watts not to make any delay in the execution of the treaty. About Omichand, Clive further observed: "Flatter Omichand greatly, tell him the Admiral, committee and self are indefinitely obliged to him for the pains he has taken to aggrandize the Company's affairs, and that his name will be greater in England then ever it was in India."[171]

---

170 Watts to Clive, 17 May (Hill, II, p. 386).

171 Clive to Watts, 19 May (*Ibid.*, pp. 388-389).

But Clive had to take a great trouble and risk for deceiving Omichand through the fictitious treaty. In this ignoble transaction, he manipulated everything most craftily. After the meeting of the Select Committee, held on 17 May, Clive informed Drake on the following day that when he sent both the treaties before Watson for his signature, the latter refused to put his signature on the fictitious treaty. The real treaty was drawn out in white paper, while the fictitious document was written on red paper.[172] So Clive had to take the great risk of getting forged the signature of Watson. Later on Clive in his evidence told the Parliamentary Committee of Enquiry that when Watts had nearly completed the conspiracy, he acquainted Clive about the fresh trouble created by Omichand by demanding "a huge proportion of share from Sirajuddaulah's treasury", and threatened, if he (Watts) did not comply with that demand, "he would immediately acquaint Serajah Dowla with what was going on and Mr. Watts should be put to death. That when he received this advice, he thought art and policy warrantable in defeating the purposes of such a villain."[173] Sykes also gave the same evidence before the committee. Sykes stated that when he went to visit Watts, he found him under great anxiety; "that he (Watts) took him aside, and told him Omichand had been threatening to betray them to Surajah Dowla, and would have them all murdered that night, unless he would give some assurances that the sum promised him (by Watts) should be made good; that upon this visit Mr. Watts further said, that he was under the greatest anxiety how to counteract the design of Omichand."[174]

Clive further said in his evidence "that he never heard that Mr. Watts had made a promise to Omichund of any money directly or indirectly." As such when Watson refused to affix his signature, he directed Lushington to put Watson's name in the fictitious treaty, "whether the admiral has con-

172 Forrest, *Clive*, I, pp. 420-421.

173 Evidence of Lord Clive, First Report, 26 May, 1772 (Hill, III, pp. 315-316).

174 Evidence of Sykes before the Parliamentary Committee of Enqiry in 1772 (Quoted in Forrest, *Clive*, I, pp. 419-420).

sented or not." And this was accordingly done by Lushington. Clive also narrated that he "never made any secret of it; he thinks it warrantable in such a case, and would do it again hundred times."[175]

To judge the whole situation of events, no impartial historian would fail to record that Clive could not escape from the responsibility of this ignoble transaction. Undoubtedly he lowered down the dignity of the high office of Commander-in-Chief as well as blackened the name of the English nation. Clive's evidence before the Parliamentary Committee of Enquiry that he had to deceive Omichand because the latter threatened Watts that if Watts did not comply with his demand, he would divulge the whole plot to Sirajuddaulah, was also a mischievous lie. The threatening alleged language of Omichand was a piece of invention by Clive and his associates. It was a facesaving device on their part to justify their heinous transaction. The almost continuous correspondence of Clive with Watts during this period, which according to Clive himself was "too voluminous",[179] does not mention anywhere about this threatening language of Omichand.[177]

The regular treaty was sent to Watts for the final approval of Mir Jafar but after that some English notables had some after-thought and wanted to make a private treaty with him. The Englishmen in Bengal had grossly inflated ideas about the disposable wealth of the Nawabs of Bengal. This treaty was such as would make it clear to Mir Jafar that he would have to pay a very high price, both to the Company and to individuals, for British support. So a gratuity for the army and restitution for the losses in 1757 of the Company

175 Evidence of Clive, First Report, 26 May, 1772 (Hill, III, pp. 315-317). Also, Conaccioli, III, pp. 77-78.

716 Long, *Unpublished Records*, p. 140.

177 But a British author of later day tries to save Clive from his false statemen, though the author's statement does not prove to be very tenable. He observes: "Watts' correspondence with Clive has never been published, but the substance of it appears in Clive's evidence (First Report, 1772)."—Elphinstone, *The Rise*, p. 305 f.n.

as well as of private individuals were included. The Select Committee approved this idea, because they felt that it was they "who really set the whole machine in motion." Taking an oath of seciecy from the Bible, they instructed Watts to demand twelve lakhs of rupees on their behalf.[178] Clive conveyed it in a letter to Watts, that instead of trusting to Mir Jafar's generosity, "his private engagements should be obtained in writing to make them (the committee), a present of twelve lacs of rupees and a present of forty lacs to the army and navy, over and above what is stipulated in the agreement."[179] Watts latter took the credit for insisting that Mir Jafar should be tied down to precise figures, lest "a false delicacy might produce disputes."[180]

The Select Committee at Calcutta and Clive in particular now judged it proper to obtain a personal conference with Mir Jafar "to concert about a plan of military operations". To effect this without alarming the Nawab's suspicions, it was agreed to send Scrafton to try to arrange a private conference with him at Plassey on his way to Murshidabad. Therefore, Clive was directed by the committee to write a letter to the Nawab informing him that Scrafton had been sent to him "on an Affair of the utmost consequence", and hence the Nawab might direct Rai Durlabh and Mir Jafar not to detain the messenger to Plassey for "a Moment". When Scrafton arrived at the Capital, he would acquaint the Nawab about the proposals that the Marathas had made to the English. It was so arranged that *en route* to Murshidabad, Scrafton would meet Mir Jafar in the camp at Plassey,[181] where he would remain with Mir Jafar "till the Nabob's order comes and by that means may get a personal conference with Mir Jafar when a plan of operation might at once be determined on". This Clive observed in his letter to Watts about the proposals of the Marathas, which Scrafton was to lay before the Nawab:

---

178 Clive to Watts, 19 May (Quoted in Forrest, *Clive*, I, p. 427). Also, Hill, II, p. 388.

179 Quoted in Beveridge, A *Comprehensive History*, I. p. 731.

180 Watts' *Memoirs*, p. 87.

181 Letter to Court, 14 July, 1757 (F.W.I.H.C., II, p. 227).

"I desire that in this way you will be persuaded that there is not the least intent to take from you any part of the Reputation of conducting this Affair, Mr. Scrafton having orders to follow your instructions, the shortness of the time as well as many other considerations require that we bring this Affair to a speedy Conclusion."[182]

About May 10, a messenger came to Calcutta with a letter to the English governor purporting to come from the *Peshwa*, Balaji Rao. In this letter, the Marathas asked for British assistance against the Nawab of Bengal. Clive came to know about the Maratha letter. n his immediate reaction he suspected the messenger to be a spy of the Nawab, "to discover our sentiments and who possibly may have received some distant Hints of our Designs."[183] The Maratha letter was thus placed before the committee and the other members agreed with Clive. As the Marathas were no friend of the English, their plea was turned down diplomatically. Thus the committee and Clive determined to send the letter to the Nawab through Scrafton. "When I am persuaded," observed, Clive "the Nabob will be induced. to put more confidence in us by the important news we have communicated to him"[184] So the English posed themselves as the supporters and well-wishers of Sirajuddaulah.

Meanwhile, the Nawab was informed by his spies about the arrival of the Maratha messenger at Calcutta. So when he came to know that the letter was on the way, he became impatient to know the contents.[185] He sent a special guard to bring Scrafton speedily. The Nawab's guard saw Scrafton near the camp of Mir Jafar and forced him to proceed to Murshidabad.[186] Watts went with him to the *darbar* of the Nawab, where Scraftion delivered to the Nawab a letter from Clive, in which the latter again professed the English sincerity to the

182 Clive to Watts, 19 May (quoted in Forrest, *Clive*, I, p. 427).
183 Clive's letter to Drake, 11 May (quoted in Forrest *Clive*, I, p. 429).
184 Clive to Watts, 19 May (quoted in *Ibid.*, p. 430).
185 Scrafton, *History of Bengal*, p. 85.
186 Hill, *Abstract*, p. 20.

Nawab.[187] Scrafton then placed the Maratha letter before the Nawab, by which action the latter was deeply impressed. The Nawab promised before Scrafton that he would immediately order Mir Jafar to return to Murshidabad and as soon as Clive wrote to him that the English would use no treachery against the Nawab, "he would withdraw his army under Roydulub."[188]

Indeed, Sirajuddaulah had still some doubts about the English. Before the delivery of the Maratha letter, the tension between the Nawab and the English had reached its highest peak. After Watts had received the secret articles of agreement sent to him by Clive on 19 May, he had got various reports about the Nawab's ill-will against them, though most of them were not authentic. On 20 May, he informsd Clive that if the Nawab did not withdraw his army from Plassey[189], it might greatly jeopardise the interest of the English. He further informed Clive on 23 May, that Sujauddaulah-the Nawab of Oudh, had been requested by Sirajuddaulah to come to his assitance against the English. "Accordingly a considerable person is arrived" from him to settle the terms of agreement "with the Nawab of Bengal."[190] Quite evidently this was a false allegation founded upon no corroborative evidence. Watts again charged the Nawab for his negotiation with Bussy that if the latter would help the Nawab, he promised the former 20 lakhs of rupees.[191] Omichand informed Watts about this Bussy-episode, which Watts himself admitted sometimes later, that Omichand's lie about Bussy had served no purpose.[192] Watts also received reports from Khwajah Wajid that the Nawab had directed Law "to stay where he is and prepare

---

187 Clive wrote to the Nawab : "Notwithstanding all that the English suffered from you, I give you this last proof of my desire to live in peace with you". – Orme, *Indostan*, II, p. 156.

188 Scrafton to Clive, 25 May (quoted in Forrest, *Clive*, I, p. 430).

189 Watts to Clive, 20 May, S.C.R., May (Hill, *Abstract*, p. 20)

190 Watts to Clive, 23 May (Hill, II, p. 392).

191 *Ibid.*

192 Hill, *Abstract*, p. 20.

to return upon the first advice."[193] Watts also informed Clive about Mir Jafar's anxiety regarding the acceptance of his (the latter's) proposals.

Another hitch prevented the Nawab from reposing confidence in the English. While Clive was complaining that some of the money promised in the February-treaty had not been paid by the Nawab, the Nawab complained that Watts was not granting receipts for the Company's effects returned to him. The Nawab, as well as Mohanlal, in their separate letters to Clive, informed him to direct Watts to give discharge letters for what he had received.[194] In reply to this, Clive wrote to the Nawab: "Your Excellency cannot in reason desire us to give an acquittance for the whole when only part has been received." But the English wanted to win the diplomatic battle. As the zero hour approached they felt that their purpose would be foiled if they could not meet Mir Jafar and his associates personally. So Clive further observed in the same letter to the Nawab : "However, agreeable to your desire I will get an acquittance properly signed and sealed which shall be sent to Mr. Watts with orders to deliver it to Your Excellency as soon as these accounts are fully settled."[195]

Sirajuddaulah had already promised before Scrafton to direct Mir Jafar to return. But Scrafton wanted to return of the whole force from Plassey. So he had another interview with the Nawab and pointed out to him that the English could not rely on any of his professions as long as the greater portion of his army was encamped at Plassey. The Nawab was persuaded and on 27 May, he wrote to Clive that he had ordered the three commanders to return with their armies from Plassey and "they will accordingly speedily be with me."[196]

Mir Jafar returned to Murshidabad on 30 May and on the same day, Scrafton left for Calcutta accompanied by

193 Watts to Clive 23 May (Hill, II, p. 39).

194 Nawab's letter to Clive, 21 May, and Mohanlal's letter to Clive, 21 May (C.C.C., p. 48).

195 Clive's letter to the Nawab, 25 May C.C.C., p. 49).

196 Forrest, *Clive*, I, pp. 430-431.

Omichand. So Omichand could not have a meeting with Mir Jafar. Watts still thought his life and those of his associates insecure so long as Omichand remained at Murshidabad. Watts used every argument to convince Omichand that as he was a conspirator of equal rank, his remaining at Murshidabad would not be safe. Omichand was further informed that it would be difficult for a man of his age to escape on horseback at the moment of crisis. But Omichand refused to leave until he obtained the share of the Nawab's treasury. Scrafton assured him that after the deposition of Sirajuddaulah he (Omichand) would be appointed as the principal agent of the English at Murshidabad and that the emolument of the office would compensate all his losses. At last Omichand consented, and they started for Calcutta in *palkeen*. On their way, Scrafton found that Omichand had disappeared in the morning. He waited on the road till three in the afternoon on 31 May, when Omichand again joined him. During the escapade Omichand had a long interview with Rai-Durlabh at Plassey.[197] He came to know that he was going to get nothing. Omichand, therefore, questioned Scrafton with much sharpness and suspicion, but Scrafton again deceived him by telling that "Roydoolub could not know anything of that stipulation, since Mr. Watts had not got communicated the treaty...even to Mir Jafar himself." On 8 June they reached Calcutta. Omichand was received with every appearance of cordiality by the members of the Select Committee. They continued to treat him as their friend until the fall of Sirajuddaulah.[198]

After his return to Murshidabad, Mir Jafar had an audience with the Nawab but the latter received him with marked disfavour. Thus Mir Jafar smelt a rat and after his return from the Nawab directed all his officers "to keep their troops in readiness to defend his palace." In the same evening, on 31 May, Watts sent Omar Beg to the palace of Mir Jafar. Omar Beg was very much optimistic and told Watts that he would get the articles "drawn out and signed" within the same

197 *Ibid.*, pp. 431-432.
198 Elphinstone, *The Rise*, p. 310.

night or the day after. But Mir Jafar refused to affix his signature, due to his fear of offending Rai-Durlabh" who commands a large part of the army, if he concludes the matter without consulting him."[199]

Rai-Durlabh returned to Murshidabad on 2 June. Mir Jafar immediately sent Omar Beg to him with the articles. Most of the articles were agreed upon by the *diwan*, but he raised an objection to the money stipulated, informing Mir Jafar that there was a small sum in the treasury and if that would be plundered it would be too little to meet all the demands of the English. Therefore, Rai-Durlabh's proposal to Mir Jafar was of "giving the English half of what might come into his and Meer Jaffer's possession after the Nabob's death."

This proposal of Rai-Durlabh was a great damper to Watts. He informed Clive on 3 June in the same tune: "Our scheme with Meer Jaffeir is overset, and there is reason to believe that Omichand's four hours' visit to Roydulub at Plassey has been the cause of it." Watts firmly believed that their scheme with Mir Jafar had been totally overset by Omichand : "This proposal of Roydulub's is much the same as what was made me some time ago by Omichund; therefore if you'll strictly examine him I imagine you will find it a concerted scheme between him and Roydulub." In the midst of such developments Watts lost faith in his Indian allies. He felt totally disgusted in complying with a scheme with the Indian people who could not be trusted. On the scheme as it stood Watts believed that if Rai-Durlabh could obtain a commission on what he might get for the English, or "such a proportion of our part", it would be "greatly advantageous for the Company" to comply with. Mir Jafar, as Watts felt, was a tool in the hands of Rai-Durlabh. Therefore, if Clive would agree to part with a commission for Rai-Durlabh "all affairs may yet end well." Watts also saw that Mir Jafar did not have so many supporters "as he boasted of". Mir Jafar

199 Watts to Clive, 31 May, S.C.R., 3 June (Hill, *Abstract*, p. 21) Also, Hill, II, p. 396.

might soon be dismissed from the post of Commander-in-Chief, as Watts could read the situation, and then the English could expect no great assistance from him except that he would remain neutral in the event of a battle. If the English became successful, Mir Jafar and all the rest would reap the benefit; if it became otherwise, they would have no concern with the English at all. Therefore, Watts advised Clive in the same letter: "If you think you are strong enough, I am of opinion we had better depend on ourselves, and enter into no contract or have any connection with such a set of shuffling, lying, spiritless wretches."[200]

But in an unexpected manner Watts' apprehension of treachery on the part of the Indian conspirators was removed within a day. When he sent his proposal before Mir Jafar and Rai-Durlabh "either to give us half of what they might get, or to stand to the old agreement", they chose the latter. They also gave assurances to Watts that they would send back the contract properly signed to Watts the next day. If they abided by this arrangement, Watts thought, there would be no more delay in despatching it to Clive through Omar Beg.[201]

Clive was naturally impatient for not getting back the articles from Watts. He was afraid that Watts might have been duped by the conspirators. So he wrote to Watts about this unnecessary delay as he thought there should have been no delay after the removal of Omichand from Murshidabad. "Surely you are deceived by those you employ", wrote Clive to Watts, "or you have been deceiving me". Out of fear, Clive observed, "The affair is now publicly talked of, and if it does not take place within a short time after the receipt of this, I will set it aside, being determined not to undertake it in the Rains."[202] But Watts was not certainly sitting idle. He was as much keen about the execution of the treaty as Clive, for he fully knew the dangerous consequences if it leaked out. He informed Clive on the same day about the signature

200 Watts to Clive, 3 June (Hill, II, pp. 396-397).

201 Watts to Clive, 4 June (Hill, II, pp. 397, 398).

202 Clive to Watts, 5 June (Hill, II, p. 398).

of Mir Jafar on the treaty. But to make assurance doubly sure, Watts thought that Mir Jafar must take an oath to observe all the conditions of the treaty. Therefore, Watts thought it necessary to meet him secretly in the evening of 5 June.[203] But as this interview was attended with a great risk of discovery, the palace of Mir Jafar being under strict watch by the Nawab's spies, observance of complete secrecy was absolutely necessary. Petrus provided a *palkeen* for Watts[204] and in the afternoon of that day, the covered *palkeen*, as it generally carried women of distinction, went without interruption to Mir Jafar's palace, who with his son, Miran, received Watts in one of the apartments of his seraglio. Mir Jafar confessed before Watts that his own troops did not exceed 3000 horses but he expected that some other dissatisfied commanders might join with him on the day of battle. He further promised that if the Nawab tried to defend the city, Mir Jafar would attack his palace as soon as the English force would be in sight; but if the contest took place in the battlefield, "he would regulate his conduet" according to the situation. Furthermore, Mir Jafar "gave his full assent to the terms of the real treaty". Then placing the *Koran* on his own head and his hand on the head of his son, he swore with great solemnity that he would faithfully perform all he had promised.[205] It was also decided to entrust Omar Beg with the task of immediately proceeding to Calcutta with the treaty and all other relevant documents. Watts returned to his residence as he had come.[206]

The secret treaty, finally signed by Mir Jafar, contained twelve articles to be executed by the latter. But the proposed English treaty had contained thirteen articles related to Mir Jafar's part and one more, which was to be executed by the British. There was also a slight change of language. In the

203 Watts to Clive, 5 June (*Ibid*)

204 Forrest, *Clive*, I, p. 433.

205 Watts to Clive, 6 June (Hill, p. 399).

206 Orme, *Indostan*, II, pp. 160-161. Also, Broome, *Bengal Army*, I, pp. 129-130.

final treaty, Mir Jafar wrote in his own hand : "I swear by God, and by the Prophet of God, to abide by the terms of the Treaty, as long as I have life." The modified articles in the treaty were :

I "Whatever Articles were agreed upon in the time of peace with the Nabob Suraja Dowlat Monsoor-ul-Mulek Shah Kuly Khan Behauder, Hybut Jung, I agree to comply with.

II. The enemies of the English are my enemies, whether they be Indians or Europeans.

III. All the effects and factories belonging to the French, in the provinces of Bengal (the Paradise of Nations), Behar and Orissa, shall remain in the possession of the English, nor will I ever allow them any more to settle in the three provinces.

IV. In consideration of the losses which the English Company have sustained by the capture and plunder of Calcutta by the Nabob and the charges occasioned by the maintenance of the forces, I will give them one crore of rupees.

V. For the effects plundered from the English inhabitants of Calcutta, I agree to give them fifty lakhs of rupees.

VI. For the effects plundered from the *Gentoos*, Mussalmans, and other subjects of Calcutta, twenty lakhs of rupees shall be given.

VII. For the effects plundered from the Armenian inhabitants of Calcutta, I will give the sum of seven lakhs of rupees. The distribution of the sums allotted the natives, English inhabitants, *Gentoos*, and Mussalmans, shall be left to the Admiral, and Colonel Clive, and the rest to the Council, to be disposed of by them to whom they think proper.

VIII. Within the ditch, which surrounds the borders of Calcutta are tracts of land belonging to the several *zemindars*; besides this I will grant the English Compahy six hundred yards without the ditch.

IX All the land lying to the south of Calcutta, as far as Culpee, shall be under the *zemindarry* of the English Company and all the officers of those parts shall be under their jurisdiction. The revenues to be paid by them (the Company) in the same manner with other *zemindars*.

X. Whenever I demand the English assistance, I will be at the charge of the maintenance of them.

XI. I will not erect any new fortifications below the Hooghly near the River Ganges.

XII. As soon as I am established in the Government of the three Provinces the aforesaid sums shall be faithfully paid."[207]

So long as Clive did not receive the articles of agreement, he strongly believed that Watts had been duped by the conspirators, as he had already mentioned it in his letter. On the same day, Clive wrote another letter to Watts "to get the Articles back again", for Clive wou'd "not embark in any undertaking with such a sett of cowardly rascals."[208] But on 6 June, Watts informed Clive about the signature of Mir Jafar and that Mirza Omar Beg would set out with all the papers concerning the agreement on the next morning.[209]

Mir Jafar, even after his return from Plassey, continued to cultivate bad terms with Sirajuddaulah. The rivalry between the two rose to such a pitch that the Nawab dismissed Mir Jafar from the post of the Commander-in-Chief. This step of the Nawab was not the result of any knowledge or suspicion on the Nawab's part of the plot of Mir Jafar;[210] Sirajuddaulah's action was the expression of his already existing ill-feeling against Mir Jafar. This news, however, gave Clive much uneasiness and he immediately wrote to Watts that perhaps their scheme with Mir Jafar had been divulged, "I cannot help

207 Mir Jafar affixed his signature on the 15 *Ramzan*, i.e. on 5 June, 1757. Aitchison, *A Collection of Treaties*, etc. Vol. I, No. LXIII, pp. 185-186. Also, Watts, *Memoirs*, pp. 93-96. Also, Bolts' *Considerations*, pp. 5-6.

208 Clive to Watts, 5 June (Hill, pp. 398-399).

209 Watts' to Clive 6 June (*Ibid.*, p. 399).

210 Thornton, *Brtish Empire*, p. 52.

suspecting some discovery has been made by the Nabob, and that Roy Dulub is treacherous towards Meer Jaffier and us."[211]

Meanwhile the confederate of the conspirators was increasing gradually. Jagat Seth secured Yar Latif on the side of Mir Jafar. Rai-Durlabh, who had also become a strong supporter of the English, as per Watts' letter to Clive, confessed that Omichand had been insinuating that if the English "were once permitted to march this way" they "should not quit Muxadabad these three years." In a mood of anger, Watts further wrote to Clive about Omichand in the same letter: "In short no devices has that cunning serpent left unassayed to mar our affairs; because he has not had the management of them himself." In the same letter, Watts expressed his great faith in Mir Jafar's sincerity. He waited with impatience for Clive's permission to him to escape from Murshidabad on horseback before the hour of crisis.[212]

On the morning of 7 June, Watts sent Omar Beg to Clive with the articles of agreement. On the same day, he expected direction from Clive to proceed to join with the English soldiers, along with other members of the factory, as their remaining at Kasimbazar any more would be dangerous. So Watts again solicited for Clive's order to leave the capital immediately.[213]

On the next day, Watts impatiently wrote two letters to Clive. In the first letter, he again informed Clive about the departure of Omar Beg with the articles on the previous day, that a delay of two days had been occasioned owing to Omichand's visit to Rai-Durlabh at Plassey. He further stated that he had not been deceived, nor he had any intention "to deceive any man." "I hope you will now be convinced that you have been too hasty in your suspicions of me," wrote Watts to Clive. In the second letter of the same

211 Clive to Watts, 6 June (Hill, II, pp. 399-400).

212 Watts to Clive, 6 June (S.C.R., 11 June). Also, Hill, *Abstract*, p. 21.

213 Watts to Clive, 7 June (Hill, II, p. 400).

date, Watts again informed Clive that Omichand had been the cause of this delay in the transmission of the articles.[214]

It was indeed a coincidence that when Watts had completed his scheme with Mir Jafar, the Nawab's threatening messages to the latter increased daily. The dismissed Commander-in-Chief held consultation with some of his supporters on 8 June, either to take the field against the Nawab or to wait for the coming of the English force for assistance. On the other hand, Sirajuddaulah was ready to fall on Mir Jafar at any moment. "Whether we interfere or not," Watts observed in his letter to Clive "it appears affairs will be decided in a few days by the destruction of one of the parties."[215]

On 10 June, Clive informed Watson about the possibility of the arrival of Omar Beg in the evening. So the Colonel asked the Admiral to help him with sailors during the impending fight. On the next day, Omar Beg arrived at Calcutta and delivered the treaty.[216] Watts also did not think it safe to remain at Murshidabad any longer. He wrote two letters to Clive on 11 June informing him that he with his party of English gentlemen would escape on the next day evening "at the farthest". On the same day Siraj received a letter from Mathuramal that Mir Jafar had confederated with the English against him, but the Nawab did not believe it at that time.[217] Mir Jafar himself advised Watts to escape from Murshidabad immediately, "as the least delay now may ruin our affairs."[218] In another letter Watts informed Clive how Mir Jafar with his supporters were becoming ready for an armed struggle with the Nawab. In this event, Watts believed that the Nawab would "be deserted by most of his people". Watts again solicited from

---

214 Watts' two letters to Clive, 8 June (Hill, II, Nos. 428, 429, p. 401).

215 Watts' to Clive, 9 June (Hill, II, p. 403).

216 Forrest, *Clive*, I, p. 433.

217 Thornton, *British Empire*, p. 52, Also, Orme, *Indostan*, II, p. 165.

218 Watts to Clive, 11 June (Hill, II, p. 403).

Clive his permission to escape. If Watts could not get Clive's direction within 12 June he was determined to set out from Murshidabad on the 13th.[219] On 11 June, Clive instructed Watts to escape from Murshidabad immediately.[220] On 12 June, Watson's 150 sailors with all the English troops at Calcutta proceeded to Chandernagore to join with Clive's forces. On 13, this whole body of troops, under the command of Clive, resumed their march towards plassey.[221]

At Murshidabad, Watts was repeatedly warned by Mir Jafar not to remain at Murshidabad as the Nawab's artillery might start firing upon his (Mir Jafar's) palace. Upon this advice, Watts immediately left his house in the city in the evening of 13 June and went to the English factory at Kasimbazar. They were four in numbers Collet and Sykes, the second and third of the factory, and a surgeon, who were to make their escape with Watts. Most of the servants of the factory had been sent off earlier on various pretences.[222] Watts, Collet and Sykes then began to discuss the mode of their escape. Watts proposed to go to the camp of Mir Jafar and to join with him; Collet suggested their taking refuge with the Dutch: but Sykes differed in his opinion. A retreat to Mir Jafar would immediately bring to light their secret understanding with him and the Dutch seemed incapable of affording them any protection 'against so powerful an adversary"; it was then thought reasonable to buy horses so that by riding on horse back. they could at the earliest join Clive's army.[223] Watts then went to the Nawab to obtain his permission to leave the city, on the plea of a hunting expedition to Maidapur, which was a very usual practice with the English. Watts then came back again to the factory of Kasimbazar. He directed the servants to prepare a supper for them, saying

---

219 Watts to Clive, 11 June (*Ibid.*, p. 404).

220 Clive to Watts, 11 June (*Ibid.*).

221 Letter to Court, 14 July (F.W.I.H.C., II, p. 228).

223 Sykes' account of his escape, enclosed in a letter, dated 25 March, 1767 (Hill, II, pp. 408-409).

that they would return during the night. Mirza Shah Bazbeg—an Uzbeg Tartar who was faithful to Watts, also accompanied them. Thus the four Englishmen and the Tartar, armed with pistols, mounted their horses about an hour before the sunset.[224] Fortunately for them almost at the same time two messengers arrived from Clive, with a letter written on 11 June, permitting Watts to escape from Murshidabad. It was dark before they arrived at Daudpur. Here they saw some soldiers of the Nawab, but the darkness of the night favoured their escape. At midnight, they came to a village called Agradip, situated on the bank of the river, where they had a second misfortune. At the entrance of the village there was a party of the Nawab's soldiers. But even this time, they were lucky as the soldiers were drowsy and preparing to sleep. When Watts and his party went to the southern extremity of the village, they found two small boats on the bank of the rever. At this place they dismounted from their horses, leaving them under the care of the Tartar, and embarked the boats.[225] They rowed down the stream about eight miles, when they found a party of soldiers with some boats, dispatched to escort them from Clive's camp. They thus escaped safely out of reach of all dangers and on 14 June, at about three in the afternoon, Watts and his party joined Clive at Kalna.[226]

On 14 June Sirajuddaulah sent a messenger to Watts but to his great amazement, he heard the news of his nightly escape and that greatly alarmed him. He now believed Mir Jafar's confederacy with the English and as such the war seemed inevitable to him. But the Nawab had already disbanded half of his army, while the other half was also not satisfied.[227] But the Nawab, instead of taking strong action against Mir Jafar, tried to reconcile with him, with

---

224 Forrest, *Clive*, I, pp. 438-439.
225 *Ibid.*, p. 439.
226 Orme, *Indostan*, II, pp. 165-166.
227 Orme, *Indostan*, II, pp. 165-166.

a view to rendering infructuous Mir Jafar's union with the English. He summoned Mir Jafar to his palace but the latter refused to meet the Nawab.[228] Then on 15 June, the Nawab personally went to the palace of Mir Jafar. The oath of loyalty was administered and Mir Jafar promised to help the Nawab by touching the *Koran*.[229] The Nawab also showed his sincerity by restoring Mir Jafar to his former position as the Commander-in-Chief. Quite evidently this was a great blunder on the part of Sirajuddaulah. The Nawab had already erred before in abandoning the French, he now doubly erred in restoring Mir Jafar to his old position. But at the moment, on account of this apparent reconciliation, the Nawab felt secure. As such he wrote a strong note to Clive: "Almost everything in conformity to the treaty has been delivered back to Mr. Watts......... Notwithstanding this Mr. Watts and rest of the Council at Cossimbazar, going to the Gardens on the pretence of a party of pleasure, have retired from thence in the night, which appears to be done with a deceitful design and intention to break the treaty. For certainly without your orders and directions Mr. Watts would never have acted in this manner."[230]

Before the escape of Watts from Murshidabad, Clive had written a letter to the Nawab informing him of his intention of going to the capital, with a view to a peaceful settlement of the outstanding matters with the Nawab In that letter Clive wanted to place his grievances before the arbitration of important officials, like the Seths, Mohanlal, Mir Jafar, Rai-Durlabh, Mir Madan and the rest of the great men. But Clive now could not lull the Nawab into inactivity. The Nawab began to make preparation for a war against the English.

From Kalna, Clive also began to advance with his forces towards Plassey. On 16 June, the English soldiers

228 Thornton, *British Empire*, p. 52.

229 Orme, Indostan, II, pp. 167-168. Also, Beveridge, *Comprehensive History*, I, p. 732.

230 Nawab's letter to Clive, 15 June (C.C.C,, p. 53: Also, Hill, II, p. 411).

reached Patlee and on 17, they were at Katwa.[231] But Clive spent the next two or three days at Katwa in great anxiety, as there was no report from Mir Jafar. Meanwhile a messenger whom Watts had sent to Mir Jafar, when the English army were at Kalna, [232] returned on 20 June. The messenger reported that he had a meeting with Mir Jafar and his son Miran in their palace and then they were interrogating him, there appeared some persons from the Nawab. As soon as they entered, Miran threatened to cut off the head of the messenger as a spy and promised to do the same to the English, if they dared to cross the river. From this report the English at Katwa could not come to any definite conclusion about Mir Jafar.[233] Clive thus resolved to summon a council of war.[234] But in the evening of 20 two letters arrived from Mir Jafar, one written to Omar Beg who was than in the camp of the English, and the other to Clive. In this letter, Mir Jafar hinted to Clive that his tent would be either on the left or the right of the Nawab's army, from where he promised to send further and frequent information.[235] This intelligence made Clive decide to advance without any ado.

It is needless to mention here about the battle of Plassey or the events of the day of 23 June on which the fateful engagement took place. It would be sufficient to mention that the conspirators played their own game as already decided upon. During the entire course of the so-called battle Durlabhram and Mir Jafar's army did not fire a shot.[236] Still the victory seemed certain for the Nawab, but for the death of his trusted commander Mir Madan, after which the whole situation in the battlefield changed. Being perplexed Sirajuddaulah sought the advice of Mir Jafar and Rai-Durlabh.

---

231 Gleig's *Clive*, p. 90.

232 Orme, *Indostan*, II, p. 169.

233 *Ibid.*

234 Malleson, G.B., *Ru'ers of India* (*Lord Clive*), Oxford, 1895, p. 92.

235 Orme, *Indostan*, II, p. 169.

236 Hill, I, p. CCI.

Both of them advised the Nawab to stop the war for the present and opined that they should fight the English on the next day.[237] Meanwhile Mir Jafar wrote a letter to Clive which was received by the latter at about 5 p. m., asking him to make a great and sudden charge on the Nawab's army, so that the army would be frightened to retreat and then the conspirators would do their part. He further informed Clive that he, together with Rai- Durlabh and Yar Latif, would move from right to left to facilitate the English victory.[238]

The Nawab yielded to the persuasions of Mir Jafar and Durlabhram in an evil hour for the dynasty and for himself. He sent orders to Mohanlal to retire, whereupon the English troops advanced and took possession of the deserted tents of the Nawab.

Despondency now prevailed in the mind of the Nawab and he left the battlefield in the evening on an elephant. He made such a haste of his flight that "he was himself one of the first that carried the news of his defeat to the Capital."[239] At Murshidabad the Nawab, in utter haste, tried to collect men for his support, but could secure none. The unfortunate Nawab at last left Murshidabad in utter disgust, accompanied by his wife and some treasures. Law had already set out with his body of Frenchmen on receipt of an invitation from the Nawab and reached the vicinity of Rajmahal, when the news of the disaster at Plassey reached him and so he did not advance further.[240]

Plassey was neither a great battle, nor was it a fair fight. The battle proved to the hilt that the life of Siraj was a story of betrayal. Thus Malleson observes "It was only when treason had done her work, when treason had driven the Nuwab from the field, when treason had removed his army

---

237 *Seir*, II, p. 233.

238 Mir Jafar's letter to Clive, received on 23 June at 5.00 p. m. (Hill, II, p. 423).

239 Scrafton, *History of Bengal* p. 96.

240 Beveridge, *Comprehensive History*, I, p. 586.

from its commanding position, that Clive was able to advance without the certainty of being annihilated."[241]

This defeat of Sirajuddaulah was a very great political achievement for the English in Bengal. For achieving this objective, the contemporary English officials lavished high praise on Watts. Scrafton observed about Watts' "admirable assiduity", his "right judgement" and his "great firmness" in remaining in the *subah's* capital, which made the English victory possible.[242] Clive wrote to the Court of Directors that Watts' "services at the *Darbar* have been very great", in promoting "the ruin of the French" and "in negotiating the treaty with Jaffer Ally Cawn."[243]

241 Malleson, *Decisive Battles*, p. 68.

242 Scrafton, *History of Bengal*, p. 91.

243 Clive's letter to Court, 6 August, 1757 (Long *Unpublished Records*, p. 140).

4

SCRAFTON AND HASTINGS AT THE DARBAR OF MIR JAFAR

Luke Scrafton[1], who donned one of the important roles among the leading officials of the Company in the defeat of Sirajuddaulah, was appointed, unofficially by Clive's nomination after the battle of Plassey, the British Resident at the *darbar* of Murshidabad.[2] This was a mark of recognition for Scrafton's great services to the Company, along with his knowledge of persian. The aim was fully to utilise his valuable services as a negotiator and interpreter. After Sirajuddaulah's army had been routed and the Nawab had scampered out of his capital, for all practical purposes deposed from his *masnad*, Clive picked up Scrafton as the person suitable to control and stabilise the situation in favour of the Company after the victory at plassey.

In the morning of 24 June, Clive deputed Scrafton and Omar Beg to conduct Mir Jafar to Daudpur. When Mir Jafar saw Scrafton, he advanced with his son to meet him. But he received Scrafton with an "air of anxiety", as he was conscious of not actually joining with the English during the

---

1 Luke Scrafton arrived in Bengal on 25 September, 1746. In 1756 during the trouble with Sirajuddaulah, he was the third officer at Dacca. Mention has already been made about his intrigue against Sirajuddaulah, in collaboration with Watts.—Letter to Court, 8 April 1762 (F. W. I. H. C., III, Edt. by R. R. Sethi, Delhi, 1968), p. 575.

2 Proceedings of the Select Committee at Fort william in Bengal, 1758. Edt. by Firminger, W. K. (Cal, 1914), p. 1 f. n.

time of the battle according to his promises.[3] However, when Scrafton delivered the Colonel's letter written to him, Mir Jafar felt much relieved. In that letter, Clive congratulated Mir Jafar on the victory, which according to the writer "is yours, not mine". Clive also urged Mir Jafar to join with the English army with "utmost expedition" and take Scrafton into fullest confidence. Further the latter would congratulate Mir Jafar on behalf of Clive.[4]

Before Mir Jafar could enter Murshidabad, the frightened inhabitants of the city stood in "dreadful suspense" as they were afraid of massacre and plunder by the victorious army. So Clive tactfully sent in advance Watts and Walsh to Murshidabad to make the proclamation in favour of Mir Jafar Khan. This turned the fear of the people to astonishment. Within 26 June, tranquillity was restored in the city, though Mir Jafar continued to be doubtful and anxious. At last Watts and Walsh prevailed on him[5], after which Mir Jafar's doubts were removed to a great extent.

The victorious Clive entered Murshidabad on 29 June, escorted by a party of 200 Europeans and 300 sepoys. The beautiful city of Murshidabad with its magnificent buildings greatly charmed him. In after years he described the city as "extensive, populous and rich as the city of London, with this difference, that there are individuals in the first (i. e. in Murshidabad), possessing indefinitely greater property than any in the last city."[6] In the afternoon, Clive accompanied by Miran proceeded to the royal palace, where Mir Jafar and all the Rajahs had assembled to receive him. In the hall of audience, after mutual greetings, Clive invited Mir Jafar to sit on the *masnad*. but the latter hesitated. Clive then led him to the

---

3 Scrafton, *History of Bengal*, pp. 96–97. Also Orme *Indostan*, II. p. 178.

4 Clive's letter to Mir Jafar, 24 June, 1757 (C.C.C., p. 57).

5 Scrafton, *History of Bengal*, p. 98.

6 Evidence of Clive, First Report, 26 May, 1772 (Hill, III, p. 314).

masnad and placed him on it. He saluted him as the Nawab of Bengal and then presented him *nazar* of gold *mohars*.[7]

Before the arrival of Clive at Murshidabad, Watts and Walsh had tried to solve the question of the payment of the stipulated sums by Mir Jafar. But Durlabhram declared that "the whole amount of Siraj's treasury was not sufficient to meet the demand" of the English.[8] This declaration of Durlabhram and the mysterious silence of Mir Jafar aroused the English officers' suspicion. They began to believe that they had been duped.[9] Clive's arrival at Murshidabad on 29 June was thus substantially aimed at sorting out the tangle.

Before Clive's arrival Scrafton had not meddled in the above affair. After the arrival of Clive, however, Scrafton accompanied him to the house of Jagat Seth. This had been agreed upon by Mir Jafar as well. Watts, Miran and Rai-Durlabh also followed them. Omichand also joined the party, though he was not invited. He sat down at a distance, outside Jagat Seth's hall. Then the treaties, written in Persian and English, were read out and explained. Though Rai-Durlabh continued to insist that there was very little in the treasury, it was finally agreed that one-half of the money should be paid out immediately both in cash and kind; but the other half should be discharged within a period of three years. Rai-Durlabh was allowed the commission which omichand had thought to be his share. After the end of the conference Clive and Scrafton moved towards Omichand, when Clive said, "It is now time to undeceive Omichand." Thus Scrafton turned to him and said in the native language, "Omichand, the red paper is a trick, you are to have nothing." These words overpowered Omichand like a "blast

7 Clive's letter to the Select Committee, 30 June (Quoted in Forrest, *Clive*, II, p. 5. Clive wrote further to the committee that the courtiers followed his example and paid their usual homage to Mir Jafar — —Forrest, *Clive*, II. p. 5.

8 Orme, *Indostan*, II, p. 180.

9 Letter from Watts and Walsh to Clive, 26 June (Hill, II, p. 430).

of sulphur." He almost fainted, but one of his attendants caught him in his arms and carried him to his *palkeen*.[10]

Besides these arrangements with the Company, Mir Jafar had to distribute large sums of money to the English officials in order to purchase their alliance. It was Becher a member of the select Committee, who suggested that the members of the committee were entitled "to be considered". Thus Mir Jafar not only rewarded them with presents, but his generosity extended even to those who were not members of the Select Committee.[11] Along with others, Scrafton received a sum of two lakhs from the treasury of the Nawab.[12]

Rajah Durlabhram, or better known as Rai-Durlabh, who was appointed *diwan* of the new government, became a pillar of strength in the new regime. The financial settlement with Mir Jafar and the English was concluded by Durlabhram, and Clive soon became close to him. On 14 September, Clive left for Calcutta leaving Scrafton, Watts and Manningham at Murshidabad to transact the Company's affairs.[13] On that day, a detachment of English soldiers from Patna had arrived at Murshidabad and was stationed at the factory of Kasimbazar. Over and above this, after Clive had returned to Calcutta, in a letter to Mir Jafar he instructed him to follow the advice of Rai-Durlabh and the Seths in all matters.[14] Thus, Mir Jafar realised within a short time, that the *masnad* of Bengal was not altogether a bed of roses and that he was hemmed in from all sides. The Nawab also discovered that many of the *zamindars* were unwilling to recognise him as the Nawab of the *subah*.

---

10 Orme, *Indostan*, II, pp. 181–182. Orme states that after this incident, Omichand remained many years in "stupid melancholy" and began to show some symptoms of madness. But the accuracy of Orme's statement is doubtful. On 3 July, Scrafton wrote to Drake: "Omichand shams the sick, and swears he has lost faith in men." Forrest, *Clive*, II, pp, 7–8.

11 Thornton, *British Empire*, p. 55.

12 Evidence of Clive, First Report, 26 May, 1772 (Forrest, *Clive*, II. pp. 9–10 f.n.)–

13 Orme, *Indostan*, II. p. 196.

14 Clive's letter to Mir Jafar, 2 October (Mukhopadhyay, *Rai, Durlabh*, p. 88).

Intrigues and jealousies in those days were very common leading often to double-crossing. During the plassey episode Durlabhram was closely associated with Mir Jafar khan. He was also a fellow conspirator of equal rank. But very soon he began to think that Mir Jafar had not rewarded him according to his merit, while Mir Jafar thought Durlabhram "to craving". As an offshoot of this mutual distrust Clive entered into a secret agreement with Durlabhram to protect the latter's life. Mir Jafar also could feel that there was something happening behind his back. This widened the gulf between the Nawab and Durlabhram and the result was their mutual mistrust. Durlabhram, in order to offset any move against him, tried to strengthen his party at the *darbar* and in this he enlisted the sympathy of Scrafton.[15] The British Resident reported to Drake that Durlabhram had come round and become very close to the English It was evident that the *diwan* would go the whole hog in order to obtain favours from the English. He assisted Scrafton to buy a large tract of land at Behrampore and after appropriating the proceeds and commissions on many other scores he began *benami* money-lending to the *zamindars*.[16]

Mir Jafar felt very uneasy owing to the reports of Durlabhram's secret activities. It was Durlabhram who had raised Mir Jafar to the helm. This fear of Durlabhram haunted the mind of the Nawab so much that he thought that Durlabhram might repeat the old strategy of treachery to remove him from the *masnad* in collaboration with the English. Thus, Mir Jafar resolved that the power of the Hindus should be drastically cut down, which would go to minimise the influence also of the English later on. Mir Jafar's crisis was further aggravated by three rebellions against him: one at Midnapore headed by Rajah Ram Ram Singh, another at purnea under Hazyr Ali Khan and Achal Singh, while the third was at Patna under Rajah Ramnarain. These revolts, mostly headed by Hin-

15 Mukhopadhyay, *Rai Durlabh*, pp. 90–91.

16 Khan, Abdul Majid, *Transition in Bengal*, 1756–75 (Cambridge, 1968, pp, 22–23).

dus, were presumed to have been instigated by Durlabhram. The Nawab now decided to wield the big stick and determined to treat Durlabhram as a rebel.[17]

After concluding the affairs of Midnapore, the Nawab turned his attention to Purnea, where the rebels had confined the reigning prince and usurped his authority. Hazyr Ali had become the ruler of Purnea and appointed Achal Singh as his *diwan*.[18] The Nawab immediately directed his forces to advance to Purnea, but the soldiers refused to advance until they were paid in full their arrears of pay.[19] At this critical moment only the army under Khadem Husain Khan obeyed the Nawab and advanced to Purnea on 6 October to suppress the rebellion. So the Nawab requested Scrafton, for the services of 500 soldiers from Calcutta. When Scrafton informed Clive about this the latter directed Captain Grant to be ready with his soldiers. Mir Jafar also wrote to Clive presonally for quick military help.[20] Clive responded favourably and Captain Grant with 500 soldiers joined Khadem Husain. Clive informed the Nawab that Scrafton would keep him informed about the movement of the English troops.[21]

Clive directed Scrafton to be ready to act according to the wishes of the Nawab. He also conveyed to Scrafton his determination to assist the Nawab in suppressing the purnea rebellion. But Clive became apprehensive that, Law, who had arrived in Bengal with French ships, might try to add an edge to the old rivalry between Nawab Shujauddaulah and Mir Jafar. Scrafton, as directed by Clive, immediately took

---

17 On the basis of contemporary writings as well as official records it should be admitted that Durlabhram had some influence in two cases, apart from the rebellion under Rajah Ramnarain. Clive also hinted it to the Secret Committee—Clive's letter to the Secret Committee, 23 December, 1757 (F. W. I. H. C., II, pp. 257–259). Also Orme, *Indostan*, II, p. 186.

18 *Seir*, II, p. 249.

19 Orme , *Indostan*, II p. 269.

20 Mir Jafar's letter to Clive, Rd. 14 Oct. (C. C. C. pp. 75–76.

21 Clive to Mir, Jafar 19 Oct. (*Ibid*)., p. 77.

up the matter with Mir Jafar. As a result, the latter assured Clive that Law and his party would leave Bengal within a day or two.[22] When Scrafton informed Mir Jafar about the movement of the British force for the assistance of Khadem Husain, the Nawab became very glad. About the expenses of the British troops, he wrote rather unctuously to Clive : "I shall this day go to camp and only wait for your arrival to proceed. Mr. Scrafton had spoke to me about the expenses of your army; when you come we will settle it. Our interest is but one. I shall never do anything without first asking your advice."[23]

But still the atmosphere at Murshidabad remained tense. Mir Jafar became panicky when Clive informed him that the widow of the late Nawab Alivardi Khan had delivered letters to Ramnarain and Shujauddaulah' requesting them to remove Mir Jafar from the *masnad*.[24] This unnerved Mir Jafar; additionally he began to suspect Durlabhram the more.[25] But this was quite according to Clive's desire. He wanted to take the fullest advantage of the Nawab's fear. Scrafton, who had formed a secret alliance with Durlabhram, now appeared as a mediator. A reconciliation was effected between the Nawab and Durlabhram at the intervention of Scrafton on 17 October, when each swore " oblivion of former distrusts and future friendship."[26]

Scrafton soon found that it was not possible for him to put an end to the confusion that reigned everywhere in the capital.[27] The Nawab was obsessed with the fear of treachery.

---

22 From Mir Jafar to Clive Rd. 24 Oct. (*Ibid.*, p. 78).

23 Mir Jafar's letter to Clive, 4 November (*Ibid.*, p. 83).

24 Orme, *Indostan*, II, p, 270.

25 Durlabhram still had some connection with the widow of Alivardi.

26 Orme, *Indostan*, II, p. 270.

27 This mental agony of Scrafton was also due to Watts' absence from Murshidabad. The latter returned to Calcutta on 31 October. In the Select Committee held on 12 November, Watts was present as a member of the committee— —Hill, *Abstract*, p. 30.

He was also trying to go back upon the articles of treaty with the English. Rebellions were breaking out in all regions of the *subah* and a strong rumour was afloat that Ramnarain had leagued with Shujauddaulah. If this alignment was a fact Scrafton had nodoubt that Bengal would be lost to the English.On 7 November, in great panic Scrafton wrote to Clive, "if you do not set out, with or without troops, permit me to go to Calcutta." In reply to this, Clive wortc to Scrafton. "I shall march with my whole army. I have wrote to the Nawab and Ramnarain...Do not suffer yourself to be unquieted beyond reason at the situation of affairs; but consider them coolly, and give me daily accounts of what is passing. The march of the army is absolutely necessary as well as to support the Nawab against his enemis, as to see justice done ourselves."[28]

Before the Select Committee, Clive placed three letters from Scrafton. In his letter of 4 November, Scrafton informed the committee that Mir Jafar was not very willing to pay the remaining half of the money promised by him in the treaty. Therefore, he recommended seizure of the district of Burdwan, and securing the remainder of the debt from the Nawab. In his second letter of 6 November, Scrafton thought it necessary for the English troops to take the field and requested the committee to direct Captain Muir "to hold the garrison of Calcutta in readiness to march at a moment's notice." His third letter on 7 November enclosed one from Mir Jafar promising to pay the money for the English troops after the arrival of Clive at Murshidabad.[29]

Clive refused to advance with his troops for the assistance of the Nawab, unless the latter would pay him one lakh of rupees for the expenses of his army. When Mir Jafar came to know of it, he immediately advanced Rs. 50,000. The Nawab desired that Clive should arrive with haste, when they could amicably decide "the daily and other expenses" of the English army. "We must consult together before we proceed", observed Mir Jafar in his letter to Clive. The

28 Malcolm, John, The *Life of Robert Lord Clive*, Vol. II (London, 1836), p. 376,

29 S. C. R., 8 November (Hill, *Abstract*, p. 29.

Nawnb had also paid ten thousand rupees to Scrafton for the expenses of the English army sent to Purnea.[30] Scrafton acknowledged these acts of the Nawab and informed Clive that Rai-Durlabh had been directed to pay fifty thousand rupees to the English army. The Rajah desired Scrafton to take the money, but Scrafton was hesitant to receive it, unless the Colonel would direct him to receive.[31]

Clive wrote a letter to the Select Committee from the French Gardens on 17 November, which was placed before the committee on the next day. Clive reported that Scrafton's letter did not confirm the news of Shujauddaulah's march to join with Ramnarain. According to Clive's view, the Company's only difficulty at that time was to reconcile Ramnarain and other great men to the Nawab. Still the Colonel hoped that he could achieve this end at Murshidabad. In his view, if the foreign enemies could be kept out of the *subah*, there was a great chance of securing the remainder of the debt which the Nawab owed to the English.[32]

At Murshidabad, Scrafton's mediation between the Nawab and Durlabhram did not seem to have bridged the gulf between the two. It was further circulated by Miran that intrigues were going on at Delhi with a view to preventing the Imperial *Sanad* being given to Mir Jafar Khazn for his accession to the *masnad* and, instead, to placing Mirza Mehdi, an infant brother of Sirajuddaulah on the *masnad*. Rai-Durlabh once told Scrafton early in october, "in ten days you may expect to see Bengal in a flame."[33] Miran had strong reasons to suspect Rai-Durlabh's integrity and he told Scrafton about Rai-Durlabh's "evil intentions towards him." He accused Rai-Durlabh as the prime mover in all the hostile designs against the Nawab. After having raised a panic by these

30 Mir Jafar to Clive, Rd. 13 November (C. C. C. pp. 84–85).

31 Scrafton to Clive Rd. 15 November (*Ibid.*, p. 85).

32 C. S. R., 18 November (Hill, *Abstract*, p. 31).

33 Clive's letter to Secret Committee.

reports, Miran sent a band of ruffians during the night of 9 November to the house of the widow of the late Nawab Alivardi Khan, with whom the infant Mirza Mehdi resided. They murdered the child. But the two Begams in the *harem* were spared.[34]

All these incidents alarmed Rai-Durlabh so much that he did not move out of his house and pretended sickness. But Clive wanted to induce Rai-Durlabh for a final settlement on this issue and wrote to him : "I have many matters of great consequence to talk to you about. I set a great value on your friendship and desire you will firmly rely on mine."[35] But Rai-Durlabh still remained incommunicado at Murshidabad. Scrafton, however, undertook the initiative for a new reconciliation between Miran and Rai-Durlabh and visited Miran on 17 November, where the oath of frienndship and confidence was again renewed.[36] Now Rai-Durlabh sent a great portion of his troops to the camp to the Nawab. The Nawab receiving no reproaches from Scrafton thought that all resentments had been overcome and at last prepared to march with his army to join with the others at Rajmahal to quell Ramnarain's insurrection.[37]

But till the end of December 1757, the Company did not receive from Mir Jafar the stipulated sums promised in the agreement. Clive became very indignant and wrote to the Court of Directors that when he had left Murshidabad in September., the *diwan* Rai- Durlabh had promised him that the "first half-yearly payment of the Nabob's debt" was to be paid in November. One-half of it would be paid immediately in ready money and the rest "as the November revenues came in." Scrafton, staying at Murshidabad, had been instructed to oversee the arrangement; still there had been, as per Scrafton's reparts, unusual delays in payment.[38]

---

34 Orme, *Indostan*, II, p. 272.

35 Quoted in *Indian Historical Quarterly*, Vol. XVI, 1940, p. 25.

36 Orme, *Indostan*, II, p, 263.

37 *Ibid.*

Mir Jafar reposed almost a pathetic faith in the generosity of the English officials and hoped that they would relax their demands on account of the Company. But the officials remained dogged and firm, which he did not relish at all. Scrafton in his reports complained of the "passionate and haughty way" in which the Nawab treated him. Thus Clive posed to the Select Committee that if the Nawab continued to be reluctant to make over the lands he had promised in the treaty, the English might occupy them by force.[39] When Clive with his troops came to Murshidabad on his way to join the Nawab, he reassured Rai-Durlabh of English protection to the Nawab against his enemies. At Murshidabad Clive received repeated promises of expeditious settlement of everything But even after he had joined the Nawab and advanced up to Rajmahal things stood where they were. So Clive resolved to set his foot down and not to move further till these matters were settled. He directed Scrafton to warn Rai-Durlabh about the consequences of the loss of the English protection. This warning went home and Rai-Durlabh began to show some agility. The *diwan* immediately left Murshidabad and visited Clive at Rajmahal on 24 December. At a conference in which all of them were closetted with the Nawab it was agreed that the English dues would be immediately discharged by orders on the revenue-managers of various districts and that the promised grant of land to the Company was to be legally implemented without any further delay.[40] As regards the arrears of the stipulated sums to the English, the Nawab directed Durlabhram "to issue under the seals of the Nabobship and *Duanny* (*diwani*) the patents empowering the Company to take possession of the ceded lands south of Calcutta, with the authority of *Zemindarry*."[41] Reimbursement was also furnished for the expenses of the English army, and the "*Perwannah* for the granted lands passed in all its forms."[42] In addition to all

39 Dodwell, pp. 150-151.

40 Mukhopadhyay, *Rai-Durlabh*, p. 101.

41 Orme, *Indostan*, II, p. 276.

42 Forrest, *Clive*, II, p. 44.

this, the Nawab had to surrender the revenues of the districts of Burdwan, Nadia and Hugli to the English in adjustment of half of the stipulated sums. This arrangement was to continue until the treaty obligations had been discharged. Scrafton was put in charge of these districts.[43]

On 29 December, from his camp near Rajmahal, Watts wrote to the Select Committee that the original *parwana* for the lands had been forwarded to him under the care of Thomas Manusell[44] with directions to get some copies taken of it under the *Kazi's* seal at Murshidabad and then return the original to the committee. On 31 December, Scrafton acknowledged receipt of the original *parwana* for the lands.[45] On 29 December Clive and Watts also wrote to the committee from the camp, expressing their hope that Scrafton had already received seven lakhs of rupees, being the first instalment of payment by the Nawab of his debt.[46] Scrafton acknowledged the receipt of this amount.[47]

Clive and Watts, on their way to Purnea, wrote to the Select Committee on 8 January, that they had received from Mir Jafar the *parwana* in which direction was given "in the strongest term" to the Rajahs of Burdwan and Nadia and to the *faujdar* of Hugli and Hijli for the payment of the remainder of the Nawab's debt to the Company. The original *parwana*, they stated, would be sent to the committee "by the first safe conveyance", but they enclosed copies of it for the satisfaction of the committee. On the next day, they wrote to the committee that the original *parwana* had been sent to Scrafton. The latter was again asked to "get six copies of each" under the *kazi's* seal. Scrafton was further directed to send the originals to the committee by the "first safe conveyance."[48]

---

43 Scrafton, *Reflections*, p. 109.

44 Thomas Manusell was a Commissary to the army.

45 S.C.R., 4 January, 1758 (Hill, *Abstract*, p. 35).

46 P.S.C., 11 January, 1758, p. 3. Also, Hill, *Abstract*, p. 35.

47 Letter to Court, 10 January, 1758 (F.W.I.H.C., II, pp. 278-279).

48 P.S.C., 24 January, p, 5.

During this time, the Company's Calcutta mint started coining of both gold and silver *siccas*. Specimens of the Company's *siccas* were sent to the Murshidabad *darbar*. The "weight and standard" were examined and approved of by Jagat Seth. Yet when there arose some difficulties in regard to the circulation of the *siccas* throughout the *subah*, Scrafton intervened. Thanks to his intercession, the Company coins were ordered, by beat of drums through the streets of Murshidabad, to be accepted absolutely on par with the Murshidabad *siccas*. Thus the officials of the Company had great hopes that "the Company will reap very considerable advantages from their mint," and the private individuals at Calcutta would be greatly benefited thereby.[49]

New English settlements in different parts of Bengal began to come up at a quick rate during this period. Many Indian inhabitants also sought shelter under the English. All this was, on the one hand, due to Mir Jafar's weak administration and on the other, the ability and effectiveness of Scrafton to gain more advantages for the Company Verelst and Smith wanted the settlement of some Indian weavers in the neighbourhood of the Lakhimpore factory, under the protection of the English. But as the "bounds round their factory" were not sufficient to accommodate any great number they asked for the committee's consideration taking on rent the lands nearabout the factory of Lakhimpore.[50] The proposal was favourably considered by the committee as they thought that it would yield "great advantage" in future. Therefore, the Committee requested the factors to Kasimbazar to apply to the *darbar* for settlement on rent of the entire Lakhimpore *parganah*. Thus, Scrafton acted according to the direction of the committee and obtained a *parwana* "for the Company and their successors," for a tract of land against the annual payment of Rs. 1107 into the Nawab's treasury. The committee became very happy and directed the factors at Lakhimpore to make the best use of the

49 Letter to Court, 10 January (F.W,I.H.C., II, pp. 274-275).

50 *Ibid.*, p. 278

grant "for the advantage of our employers" and to encourage as great a number of weavers as they could, to reside within the bounds of the English Company. The manufactures of the weavers, under the "immediate inspection" of the Company, gave the Company the benefit of Rs. 10,000 annually from the Lakhimpore *zamindari* alone.[51]

For the further development of the factories of Lakhimpore and Dacca, Scrafton paid to these factories a part of the money which he had received as the balance of the first instalment of money from the Nawab. Scrafton retained the rest of it, except Rs. 50,000 which he advanced to Hastings and Sykes at their request for the use of the Kasimbazar factory.[52]

The committee also began to think about a fortified place near Murshidabad, which would not only improve the Company's relation with the timorous Nawab but also prevent the latter from undertaking any coersive measure against the Company. Accordingly, Manningham, who then resided at Murshidabad, was written to seek the grant of the Behrampore plain and to obtain the necessary *parwana* to build a new fortified factory there. In this affair also Scrafton lent an active hand and obtained a *sanad* in the month of March for four hundred *bighas* of land on Behrampore plain.[53]

Nawab Mir Jafar Khan became confirmed on the *masnad* of Bengal by an Imperial *Sanad* granted by the court of Delhi. To celebrate this the Emperor bestowed honour on Clive and Watts. Scrafton felt elated and informed the President of the committee at Calcutta of the Nawab's largesse. Mir Jafar's assuming *de jure* power was considered a "desirable circumstance" for the Company in Bengal. Henceforth the Nawab's authority in the *subah* would be fully established and the latter's orders and decrees would be honoured throughout the

51 Latter to Court, 31 December, 1758 (F.W.H.I.C.. II, p. 345),

52 *Ibid.*, p. 279.

53 But the Company could not build a factory immediately till the "Citadel at Calcutta is finished".—letter to Court, 10 January 1758 (F.W.I.H.C., II. p. 282).

domain. This would not only secure the English from any attack from the French but the former's influence at the *darbar* would also considerably increase.[54]

The combined advance of the armies of Mir Jafar and Clive disheartened the rebels in Purnea and led them to abandon their position. Within a short time, Achal Singh was taken prisoner and the whole district was assigned to Khadem Husain. The Nawab's surrender of the revenues of Burdwan, Nadia and Hugli had already greatly heartened the English and removed their mistrust of the Nawab, at least for the time being. Clive now announced his readiness to advance to Patna.[55] This greatly damped the spirit of the French who realised that there was no hope of fomenting discord between the English and the Nawab.

On 16 February, the Select Committee received a letter from Scrafton at Murshidabad informing them that the Resident had come to know from Rai-Durlabh's brother that in south India, Salabat Jang's brother had called the Marathas for his assistance and they had defeated Bussy in a battle and imprisoned him.[56] The fortune of the French in Bengal also underwent the same eclipse. After the fall of Sirajuddaulah, Courtin, the Chief of the French factory at Dacca, and his party escaped from Dacca and went to Rangpur, where Mir Quasim was the governor. The French party remained on the bank of the river Tista where they erected a strong mud fort. Mir Qasim, as directed by the Nawab, advanced against them early in 1758 and surrounded them from all sides. The French defended themselves bravely but the odds were against them. Finding no other alternative, Courtin wrote to Scrafton, the British Resident at Murshidabad, offering to surrender as prisoners of war.[57] At this juncture also Scrafton worked very tactfully. Anticipating the Select Committee's approval of his

54 Letter to Court, 23 January, 1758 (F.W.I.H.C . II, p. 307).

55 Broome, *Bengal Army*, I, p. 192.

56 P.S.C. 18 February, p. 8. Also, Hill, *Abstract*, pp. 36-37.

57 Scrafton's letter to the Select Committee, 18 February (Hill, *Abstract*, p. 37).

action, he requested the Nawab to send a *parwana* to Mir Qasim, directing him to cease hostilities. On 22 February, the Select Committee approved of Scrafton's action and accepted Courtin's offer of surrender.[58]

Meanwhile, the city of Murshidabad was in great consternation. A report was spread in the city about the death of Mir Jafar during his encounter with Ramnarain at Patna. There was no more news, but Scrafton was very particular to obtain constant intelligence. On enquiry, Scrafton came to know from the house of the Seths that they had received this news from Patna about a week earlier. The Resident could ascertain, the Nawab's intention to assassinate Ramnarain had been foiled and Ramnarain had returned to Patna without visiting Mir Jafar. There was no more news about the incident.[59] Scrafton informed the Select Committee on 14 February that a rumour was rife at Murshidabad about the murder of the Nawab by the forces of Sunder Singh. Scrafton requested the committee to send to him "with all expedition a company of sepoys" as to guard the house of the Resident.[60] On receipt of this the committee resolved to send 50 Europeans "to protect the treasure and preserve order in the city until the Government is settled."[61] Scrafton wrote another letter to the committee on 15 Ferbuary, which the latter received on 17, informing them that though no further intelligence had arrived from Patna yet Miran had collected forces and artillery at his garden house and hence the city was in great alarm.[62]

In consequence of these alarming letters from Scrafton, the committee immediately resolved to send Captain Gaupp, with a party of thirty Europeans and a company of sepoys to Murshidabad. As these reports, if confirmed, might create

58 P.S.C., 22 February, 1758, p. 12. Also, Hill, *Abstract*, p. 38.

59 P.,S.C, 18 February, p. 8.

60 Scrafton's letter to Select Committee, 14 February (P.S.C., 18 February, p. 8).

61 S. C. R., 18 February (Hill, *Abstract*, pp. 36–37).

62 P. S. C., 18 February, p. 8.

great confusion in the capital, resulting in further troubles against the government, which, in its turn, might put to risk the money in the possession of Scrafton, the committee resolved to write to the Resident to send all valuables immediately to Calcutta. The committee further directed Scrafton to send them reports "from time to time" concerning the armies of the Nawab and the Company.[63] About half an hour after sending the letter to Scrafton, the committee received another letter from the Resident dated 16 February, informing them that Miran had just sent him a message through an express messenger. Miran's report was that the Nawab had safely arrived at Patna on the 28th of the previous month. There had been no military action at Patna at all, and the report of the Nawab's murder was absolutely false. There had been only some disputes between the Nawab and Ramnarain. This false report about the Nawab's death, as Miran reported, had put a stop to all business at Murshidabad "for these two days." Miran expressed regret for having been the cause of so much unnecessary troubles and even apologised to Scrafton.[64] Upon the receipt of this letter from Scrafton, the committee countermanded their earlier decision of sending fifty Europeans to Murshidabad, but now ordered only thirty *topasses* to be sent to Scrafton "for the security of money he has with him."[65] For constant and quick relaying of news from Murshidabad, the committee also directed Scrafton to fix several stages of messengers between Murshidabad and Kalna. On their own part, the committee decided to fix other stages of messengers between Kalna and Calcutta.[66]

After the departure of Rai-Durlabh from Murshidabad for Patna, the seals of the Nawab were seldom used. This caused great trouble to the Company's officials since the absence of the seal almost stopped all official business. Scrafton's difficulty was the greatest. The deadlock compelled Scrafton

63 *Ibid.*; Also Hill, *Abstract*, pp. 37–38.

64 *Ibid.* p., 9.

65 *Ibid.*

66 Letter to Court, 2 March (F. W. I. C. H., II, p. 317).

personally to go to the country-house of the Nawab, where he persuaded the officer-in-charge to open the seal on 21 February. After this the Nawab's seals were affixed on the *parwana* concerning Behrampore and also on a permission to coin for the Company, *siccas* equivalent to Rs. 2,50,000 at the Dacca mint. Scrafton further informed the committee that as soon as he returned to Murshidabad from the Nawab's country-house, he would despatch all the money received on account of the Company and private sufferers.[67]

The English factors to Lakhimpore received bills from Scrafton amounting to £ 1,54,950. They had received the cash payment of £ 52,317 and written to Scrafton about the proposal of Rajakrishna for deferring the payment of the remainder due from him.[68] On 7 May, Scrafton despatched to the Select Committee the cash accounts for the months of February, March and April, the account for the antecedental six-monthly instalment of the Nawab, as well as the instalments of that were due. But the factors to Lakhimpore found great difficulty in collecting the amount of the bill from Rajakrishna. Scrafton was convinced that Rajakrishna had employed his revenues "to other purposes". Hence the Resident sent an agent to take charge of the defaulter's lands till the dues of the "Company be fully discharged". The committee believed that by this arrangement "no loss can happen there on to the Company.[69]"

In the month of May the news of the return of the troops from Patna, after the Nawab's reconcilliation with Rajah Ramnarain, reached Murshidabad. When the armie of Rai-Durlabh and Clive reached near the capital, Miran, who had been left in charge of the government at Murshidabad, immediately took refuge in *Moti-jhil* out of fear. Subse-

67 P. S. C., 24 February, p. 16. Also, S. C. R. 24 February (Hill, *Abstract*, p. 38).

68 Consultation, 1 May, 1758 (B. M. P., III, pp. 21-22)

69 B. M. P. , III, p. 24.

70 Orme, *Indostan*, II, p. 353.

quently, however, he summoned all his troops and announced his intention to advance in order to welcome back his father.[70] This created terror in the city, and on the arrival of Clive, he found that the markets were closed, even the Seths had suspended their business and "the populace in a state of tumult and trepidation.[71]" On enquiry, Clive found that Miran had begun to suspect a league between him (Clive) and Rai-Durlabh to do away with his (Miran's) life. Clive immediately wrote to Mir Jafar, complaining about Miran in the "sharpest terms" saying that the Colonel would no longer remain in Bengal, "sacrificing zeal to distrust". But before the Nawab's reply reached Clive, Scrafton had convinced Miran "of the meanness of his suspicions" and had got him to ask for Clive's pardon in the most polite manner. Mir Jafar was still at Rajmahal. But when all this news reached him, he cut short his hunting near Rajmahal and rushed to the capital. He arrived there on 30 May, but could not meet Clive as the latter had already left for Calcutta on the 24th of the same month.[72]

At this time the Company felt great difficulty for want of *kanungos* at Burdwan owing to which the Company's affairs almost came to a standstill in that district. The committee thereupon wrote to Scrafton to send some *kanungos* to Calcutta.[73] The committee also decided to write to Colonel Forde directing him to support Scrafton "in all his dealings with the Nawab and the *darbar* officers.[74]"

On 21 June, Scrafton, wrote a letter to the Select Committee which the latter received on 24, requesting them to relieve him from the post of the Resident. He, at the same time, requested them to deliver his charge of the Company's affairs at Murshidabad to Warren Hastings.[75]

---

71 Broome, *Bengal Army*, I, p. 201.

72 Orme, *Indostan*, II, p. 353.

73 S. C. R., 29 May (Hill, *Abstract*, pp. 42–43). Also, P. S. C., 29 May, p. 32.

74 Hill, *Abstract*, pp. 42–43.

75 B. M. P., III, p. 32.

In the month of June, there were some changes in the composition of the Calcutta Council. On 20 June, Captain John Samson arrived at Calcutta with orders from the Court of Directors dated 3 August and 11 November 1757, by which the government of the Company was to be put on rotation upon Watts, Manningham, Becher and Holwell successively. But the Calcutta Council felt that this would create "many inconveniences at that juncture and as well as be prejudical to the Company's affairs in Bengal." Hence, they recommended a deviation from the above orders for many weighty reasons. In their consultation of 26 June they unanimously requested Colonel Clive to become the President of the Company's affairs in Bengal.[76] Clive accepted the offer and became the President of Fort William in Bengal "till a preson is appointed from Europe."[77]

The report of Nawab Shujauddaulah's movement towards Bengal bewildered Scrafton, who wrote to the committee on 24 June that according to his reports the Nawab of Oudh had reached Ghazipur. The local Rajahs had invited him and he was moving ahead to cross the river Karmanasa and march farther east. Thus, at Murshidabad, Miran was getting ready to march towards Rajmahal with his forces to repel the invasion of the Nawab.[78] The Calcutta Council became greatly alarmed and directed Scrafton to send "timely advice" about Shujauddaulah's movements, as well as Miran's activities.[79] But when the authentic information reached him, Scrafton wrote in reply on 9 July that the cloud of fear had dissipated as Shujauddaulah had returned from Benaras to his capital at Lucknow. His intended march had been undertaken only to oblige Rajah Balwant Singh of Benaras to pay

---

76 Letter to Court, 26 August, 1758 (F. W. I. H. C., II. p. 319).

77 F. W. I. H. C., II, p. 323.

78 P. S. C. 4 July, p. 37. Also S. C. R., 4 July (Hill, *Abstract*, pp. 44–45).

79 *Ibid.*

his revenues. As such at Murshidabad Miran gave up the idea of marching to Rajmahal.[80]

Scrafton suffered from a high mental tension, when various alarming reports about the intrigues of Marathas and the French, as well as Delhi and Deccan politics reached him. In a state of perplexity he could not decide his course of action. and, therefore, solicited advice from Calcutta. He wrote three letters to Calcutta, one on 12 and two on 13 July, requesting their urgent direction in that state of apprehension and uncertainty. It was reported that Sheobhat, under the pretence of a *sanad* from Rai-Durlabh, had established himself in the government of Cuttack and accordingly, the Nawab directed Muslihu-u-din Muhammad Khan to seize the reins of government from Sheobhat. Though outwardly all seemed well in the Nawab's court, the troops were clamorous for their arrears of pay. It was also reported by Scrafton that Muhammad Baqar Khan had arrived from Delhi with the news that Nizam Ali, after defeating Balaji Rao, had marched against Bussy but had failed to quell him completely. As reported, after that incident Bussy had started marching towards Bombay carrying great treasure and with a force consisting of more than 700 Europeans and 12,000 sepoys. It was further reported that Law had advanced to Delhi, after remaining sometime with Balwant Singh. The affairs of Delhi had also entirely changed and the distant *subahs* as far as Lahore and Kashmir were paying revenues regularly to the Emperor as in former times. But as bengal had been a defaulter, the *wazir* of the Emperor was angry with Mir Jafar, and sent a very threatening letter to him. As per Scrafton's report, on receipt of this letter the Nawab had immediately offered to pay 20 lakhs in gold *mohars*. Scrafton had further intimated that Bakhat Khan, whose father was a *buxy* to the *wazir* had brought a letter from the latter, which was believed to contain "some very extraordinary proposal" to Clive. Scrafton also expressed his apprehension that at the *darbar* of the Nawab, there were some intrigues

80 p. S. C., 13 July, p. 39.

going on between the Nawab and the French, as indicated by the arrival of a messenger with letters for the Nawab from Pondichery. Miran had also sent two messengers to Deccan. The messenger from Pondichery, as Scrafton reported, was an Arab in a *tellingee* dress, who had come with the news of the French plan to besiege Madras and sent a detachment of French troops consisting of 5000 sepoys towards Cuttack. Thus Scrafton sought the Committee's advice whether he would privately secure the Arab before he could meet the Nawab or shadow the Arab to observe his motions.[81]

After receiving these letters from Scrafton, the Calcutta Council seriously considered all these developments and informed Scrafton that they would approve of his securing the Arab and his party, provided he was well assured about the French intrigue, but not at the cost of creating misunderstanding with the Nawab, "which must be altogether avoided." The committee also directed Scrafton to examine the authenticity of all reports before sending them to Calcuttra. The committee believed that in the existing situation of uncertainty a harmony with the Nawab was absolutely necessary as the Nawab was yet to pay large part of the money according to the treaty-terms to the Company. The committee directed Watts to proceed to Murshidabad and to try his utmost to promote harmony with the Nawab and also to obtain the "discharge of the payment" from him. Watts was further directed to find out the truth of the reports contained in Scrafton's letters.[82]

At the Nawab's *darbar*, there were a number of complaints against the misuse of the trade by the English merchants, resulting in the loss of revenues to the government. This was brought to the notice of Scrafton by the Nawab's *munshi*. In this connection the Resident communicated with P. R. Peakes and his council at Dacca in the month of July, prcatically approving of their opposition to a native merchant who had received *parwanas* from the Nawab's *diwan* to

81 P. S. C. 17 July, pp. 40–41.

82 *Ibid.*, p. 41.

trade in Rasulpur and Hydrapore. There was another complaint against an English *gomastah* at Chilmaree who had given protection to a number of merchants, resulting in a loss to the government of Rs. 70,000. Scrafton himself thought that most of these complaints were baseless and he wanted Peakes to "prevent the encroachments of your black servants."[83]

Scrafton was empowered to receive revenues of the districts of Burdwan, Nadia and Hugli as *quid pro quo* for the Nawab's defaults in payment of the promised sum in the treaty. But the Resident faced immense difficulties in collecting the revenues of Nadia and Burdwan. About the Rajah of Nadia, Scrafton informed the Calcutta Council that the Rajah was most unwilling to pay the revenues of his district. So Scrafton recommended that the Rajah should be threatened with the loss of his caste and other corporal punishments, so that the Company might get its dues from him. He further suggested that either Rai-Durlabh would pay the balance out of the treasury or to pay nine lakhs for the ensuing year, on account of the Nadia Rajah's defaults. The Resident believed that the main cause of the outstanding dues was the Rajah's extravagance. Scrafton suggested that a trusty person should be sent to Nadia to collect the revenues and to deprive the Rajah "of all power" in his district.[84] On 21 July, Scrafton again wrote to the Calcutta Council acquainting them that finding no other way of collecting revenues from Nadia, he had sent one Lahori Mal, on the recommendation of Nandkumar, to Nadia who would act as a *tahsildar* of the district. The said Lahori Mal had been sent to Nadia with a party of twenty sepoys. Scrafton had also given him a *khelat* in the name of the Company and requested for its confirmation.[85]

In pursuit of some stern actions against the Rajah of Nadia, Scrafton recommended the arrest of Sibchandra—the

83 Vansittart, Henry, *A Narrative of the Transactions in Bengal*, Firt Indian Reprint, Calcutta, 1976), pp. 9-10.

84 Long, *Unpublished Records*, p. 195.

85 Consultations, 24 July (B. M. P. III, p. 38).

son of the Rajah, at Calcutta. When this came to be known to the Rajah's son, he personally appeared before Scrafton and produced the accounts of revenues of his district according to which the gross receipts did not exceed more than six lakhs. But Scrafton did not believe this and wrote to Calcutta that "as father and son are both villains, I give no credit to their accounts."[86] As a last resort, the Resident became more severe with the Rajah of Nadia and requested the Calcutta Council to allow the Rajah only Rs. 10,000 annually or whatever the Company might "think proper for his expenses." It was further suggested to keep the Rajah's son at Calcutta "as security for the father's good behaviour."[87]

But about the collection of revenues from Burdwan, Scrafton was less severe to the local Rajah; still he recommended to intimidate him as well. He wrote to the Calcutta Council that the Rajah of Burdwan had promised to pay the revenues after the *puniyah* ceremony, when he would fix a date of his payment. "When this is settled" observed Scrafton, "permit me to recommend it to your Honour, etc., to order the revenue to be paid in Calcutta" and if the Rajah failed to make payment on the fixed date, the Company's troops should advance to his district to intimidate him. He further observed that these districts should be kept in the possession of the Company for two years and the Nawab should not be allowed to interfere in any but *faujdari* affairs till the Company's sums were paid.[88]

Scrafton then informed the Calcutta Council that the Nawab's second sixth-monthly instalment to the Company, amounting to nearly ten lakhs of rupees was still due. Within it the outstanding dues of revenues from Burdwan and Nadia districts alone constituted Rs. 5,78,000. Still

86 *Ibid.*

87 Long, *Unpublished Records*, p. 195.

88 Firminger, *Fifth Report*, p. 124 f. n.

the Resident hoped that the greater part of 10 lakhs would be collected within ten days.[89]

Scrafton wrote a letter to the Calcutta Council on 2 August acknowledging the receipt of five gold *mohars* minted by the Company, which had been examined and the standard had been approved of by the government. But he informed that the Nawab had issued *parwanas* for the redress of the complaints of Malda *gomastahs*. In the same letter he further informed the committee that the Burdwan accounts had been procured, but he reveived Rs. 11,000 less than the account given by the *gomastah*.[90]

The practice of borrowing money in advance was prevalent among the *zamindars*. The Englishmen began to explore the possibility of advancing such loans after the plassey period. Clive disapproved of such loans to the *zamindars* and ordered that the interest on any loans made by the Europeans should be limited to 12 per cent only. In spite of this, Scrafton advanced loans of Rs. 50,000 to the *zamindar* of Rajshahi and got back Rs. 90,000.[91]

In the political field at Murshidabad, Scrafton did not feel at home at least for sometime during the period. Moreover, the hot and humid monsoon weather did not suit him. On 23 July, the Resident made a personal complaint

89 Scrafton reported to the Calcutta Council the names of persons from whom nearly ten lakhs of rupees was due in respect of the Nawab's second sixth-monthly instalment;

Dotchand Paul of Burdwan		......	Rs. 1,00,000
Ditto	Ditto	......	Rs. 50,000
Still due		......	Rs. 2,43,000
Nadia		......	Rs. 1,85,000
		Total	Rs. 5,78,000
Royeshoy		......	Rs. 1,25,000
Mahmud Ali		......	Rs. 60,000
Dudhiram		......	Rs. 30,000
Rahmat and Mritunjay		......	Rs. 2,00,000

—Long, *Unpublished Records*, p. 195, f.n.

90 Consultations, 10 August (B.M.P., III, p. 38)

91 S. C. R. , 31 December, 1766.

before Clive that the latter, and more particularly Watts, had deprived him "of all influence in the city". He also did not feel happy at the trend of *darbar* politics which placed his friend Rai-Durlabh "in great personal danger". When this rivalry between the Nawab and Rai-Durlabh reached its highest pitch in July, NandKumar came forward to support the cause of the former, which was not known to Scrafton. Nandkumar informed Clive that if he was vested with sufficient authority, he could find out the ways and means of realising the amount due from the *zamindars*.[92]. Thus Clive unhesitatingly employed him as proposed, because the Company was immediately in need of money. To secure his own position Nandkumar, as an agent of the Company, offered help to the Nawab in the removal of Rai-Durlabh. This was welcomed by the Nawab immediately. Thus on 24 July, Rajah Rajballabh was appointed *diwan* of Miran (in a way that of the second Nawab) and on 26 of that month, Rai-Durlabh was ordered to deliver the entire accounts to Rajballabh.[93] Two days, after when Scrafton came to know about this, he wrote to Clive in anguish: "Nuncomar is an intriguing rascal: the elevation of Raja Bullub by his agency greatly affects our influence here. Our enemies gain grounds daily, Roy Dullub is gravely menaced.[94]"

The humiliation of Rai-Durlabh so strongly hurt Scrafton's feelings that he further wrote to Clive that "unless we openly protect him (Rai-Durlabh), be assured he is very short lived". To divert the Nawab from this "torrid atmosphere" of his *darbar*, Clive, at Scrafton's suggestion, invited Mir Jafar, to pay a visit to Calcutta, which the Nawab accepted. On 6 August, Mir Jafar, with immense pomp, went down the river and was received by Watts with all possible

92 Forrest, *Clive* II, p. 62.

93 Orme, *Indostan*, II, p. 357.

94 Quoted in Forrest, *Clive*, II, p. 61.

honour.[95] Scrafton became very happy at the departure of Mir Jafar from Murshidabad. On 22 August, he wrote to Hastings: "Thank God, His Excellency is at last gone. He has led me to a hell of a life here by the constant attendence I have been obliged to pay to him .... I believe he is gone away well satisfied.[96]"

This departure of Mir Jafar was, however, accompanied by a new series of intrigues against Rai-Durlabh. Two days after his departure, Miran directed a body of troops, who were clamouring for their pay, to "go and demand it of Roydoolub". They surrounded the house of Rai-Durlabh and so the latter, to save himself from disgrace gathered a considerable number of his own troops. Meanwhile, Scrafton intervened and arrived with a body of troops at Rai-Durlabh's house before any bloodshed could take place and prevailed on both sides to remain quiet.[97] Scrafton immediately informed Watts about the incident as the latter was then with the Nawab at Mankar *en route* to Calcutta. The Nawab pretended to know nothing about the incident and authorised Watts to bring away Rai-Durlabh to Calcutta. Watts immediately arrived at Murshidabad and, with the help of Scrafton, he put Rai-Durlabh with a few attendants into his boat [98] Thus Scrafton protected the life of Rai-Durlabh, but blamed Watts for this unhappy event.[99]

Scrafton did not remain at Murshidabad any longer after this incident. Moreover, he had laboured under a very bad

---

95 Broome, *Bengal Army*, I, p. 208. The visit of the Nawab was celebrated with great festivities; as described by Scrafton: "Indeed, we have been so much taken up in balls, musick, and visits to do honour to the Nobab, and poor me the eternal interpreter, that all publick affairs have been totally neglected"—Dodwell, p. 159.

96 Quoted in Dodwell, p. 159.

97 Scrafton, *Reflections*, p. 116.

98 Orme, *Indostan*, II, p. 358.

99 Scrafton blamed Watts for the appointment of Nandkumar as the Company's agent. Nandkumar's double-dealing was responsible for the downfall of Rai-Durlabh; he (Scrafton) murmured in protest—Feiling, *Hastings*, p. 33.

state of health. In the month of September he requested permission from the Select Committee to go to Madras for a "change of air" and it was accordingly consented to.[100]

After the departure of Scrafton from Murshidabad, Warren Hastings succeeded him as the Resident at the Nawab's *darbar*.[101] At that time Hastings was a civil official of 25 years of age only. But after coming to India he had become conversant in Indian languages as well as in the habits and manners of the people. As such he was the choice for this responsible post by both Clive and Watts. His stay in the interiors of Bengal had helped him again a broad idea of the court politics during the rule of Sirajuddaulah. He had also shaped well as an assistant to Scrafton during a brief spell of temporary Presidentship by Watts.[102] By this new appointment at Murshida-

---

100 Letter to Court, 29 December, 1759 (F.W.I.H.C., II, p. 450). Clive had great regard for Scrafton; he wrote to George Pocock, the Governor of Madras : "Mr. Luke Scrafton is a young fellow of great worth and honour. Much I fear he is too far gone to be recovered by the coast air,...For God's sake return him to me in good health and condition."—quoted in Malcolm, *Clive* II, pp. 174-175.

101 Hastings succeeded Scrafton as Resident at the *darbar* in August, 1758, but his formal appointment was on 14 November, 1759. Firminger, *Fifth Report*, p, 169 f.n.

102 Warren Hastings was born in December, 1732. He was a good scholar. At the age of fourteen he gained the first place in the examination for the King's Scholarship. His friend, Elijah Impey was placed fourth. Hastings sailed for India in January, 1750 and eached Calcutta in October. After remaining three years at Calcutta he was sent to the factory at Kasimbazar in October 1753, where Watts was incharge. Watts soon recognised his abilities and deputed him to organise an *aurung* of raw-silk at some little distance from Kasimbazar. In 1756 he was imprisoned by Sirajuddaulah. At the end of 1757, he was appointed second in the Kasimbazar factory. He took trouble to study the languages of the country. He became fluent in Bengali, acquired a good knowledge in Urdu and a useful knowledge in Persian. He himself said : "I never acquired a perfect knowledge of Persian, and what I did know was acquired from official practice."—letter to Court, 20 August 1757 (F.W.I.H.C., II, p. 245). Also, Malleson, *Hastings*, pp. 34-35. Also, Beveridge, *Hastings in Lower Bengal*, pp. 209-210. Also, Moon, Penderel, *Warren Hastings and British Indian* (London, 1947), pp. 7-21). William Watts was the President of Fort William and Governor of the Company for four days from 22 June to 26 June 1758,

bad Hastings' works were doubled, for he was not altogether relieved from his duties at Kasimbazar factory. In the factory works, Francis Sykes—the third, gave him only nominal help.[103] At Murshidabad, John Hackett was stationed as an assistant "at the particular request" of Hastings.[104]

Thus Hastings emerged from the obscurity of an expert Warehouse keeper at Kasimbazar and soon became prominent in his new role at Murshidabad.[105] He wanted to cultivate acquaintance with the Nawab as well as the principal persons and officials at the *darbar*. So on 12 August, 1758, he wrote to Clive that he (Hastings) came to know about his new appointment from Watts "in the room of Mr. Scrafton" and had taken charge of his new office. Previously he had been introduced by Watts "to the Nabob and the principal persons of the city'', but to drive the advantage home he solicited Clive to give him letters of introduction, which he could submit before the Nawab and Miran. Similar letters, he thought, might be necessary for the Seths as well as Rai-Durlabh, after, of course, the latter returned from Calcutta. As the Nawab was also at Calcutta at that time, Hastings further wrote to Clive in the same letter to inform the Nawab about the new Resident, who had been posted at Murshidabad at the recommendation of the Colonel. He stated that his success at Murshidabad would "entirely depend upon such an introduction." At the end of the letter, Hastings expressed his deep gratitude to Clive ; "As I look upon myself to be indebted principally to you for my being allotted to this office, of whatsoever advantage it may prove to me with respect to my own private

---

103 Feiling, *Hastings*, p. 26.

104 Letter to Court, 29 December, 1759 F,W.I.H.C., II. p. 452).

105 In the month of December 1758, Hastings wrote to Creswick; "I have already informed you of my appointment as second in Council at the factory of Cossimbazar....In the beginning of last August produced another change in my situation. I have since that time resided at the station in the quality of agent for the Company's transactions with Government, which, if not mos profitable is one of the most creditable employs in the service.''--Beveridge, H., *Warren Hastings in Lower Bengal (Calcutta Review*, vol. LXV, 1877), pp. 213-214.

interest, I think it incumbent on me to make my sincere acknowledgements to you for your favourable intentions herein, which I cannot do better than by a constant attention to the business intrusted to my charge, and my earnest endeavours to promote the interest of the Company as far as my capacity will enable me, in which I hope, I shall have the good fortune to meet with your approbation."[106]

Clive acknowledged the receipt of this letter and assured Hastings about his assistance " to increase your influence at the *Darbar*." Clive had already talked to Umid Roy—the new *naib-diwan*, about the appointment of Hastings. In the above letter to Hastings he enclosed letters of introduction to the *naib-diwan*, to Miran and to the Seths. But the personal safety of Rai-Durlabh's family still haunted Clive's mind. Rai-Durlabh was personally safe at Calcutta under English protection, but he had left his wife and daughter at Murshidabad to the mercy of Miran. So Clive wrote to Hastings in the same letter that in case Rai-Durlabh's family needed a guard of sepoys to escort them down to Calcutta, the Resident should assist them with such facilities. As the Company was in great want of money, Clive did not forget to write to Hastings to expedite the collection of money from the Nawab's treasury : "the remainder of the last sixth."[107] Hastings in reply professed that he would supply an escort of sepoys for the safe passage of Rai-Durlabh's family from Murshidabad, as desired by Clive. But in this endeavour, Hastings was afraid of "some very bad consequences". Miran had posted spies in every passage leading to Rai-Durlabh's house "and one upon each of his boats" to prevent the exit of his kith and kin. Miran had, however, assured Hastings that he had no other intention than detaining Rashbehari—the brother of Rai-Durlabh, till the *khalsa* accounts were settled with Umid Roy. In regard to this Hastings took Rashbehari into confidence. Still it was

106 Hastings' letter to Clive, 12 August, 1758 (quoted in Gleig, G.R., *Memoirs of the Life of the Right Hon. Warren Hastings*, vol. I, London, 1841, pp. 54-56).

107 Clive to Hastings, 20 August, Gleig, *Hastings*, vol. I, p. 59).

realised that the removal of Rai-Durlabh's family with their treasures was "not so easy to be effected." Hastings urged Clive for further direction about this matter. About the realisation of the remainder of the instalment from the Nawab, Hastings stated that as most of the principal men had gone to Calcutta with the Nawab, he faced "a great obstruction" in his business. Nothing could possibly be done, the Resident stated, "till their return."[108]

Meanwhile, Clive receivsd a report about some tumult at Murshidabad, over the confinement of the son of one Rajah. Hastings assured Clive that the report was baseless, but added that Rajballabh was "a very troublesome person". Clive took up with Hastings the matter concerning safe removal of the family of Rai-Durlabh. Both of them agreed that the matter was fraught with great risk, especially if a guard were sent to escort Rai-Durlabh's family. The Colonel, however, made it clear that he never intended that Hastings should use force, "but only furnish them (Rai-Durlabh's family) with a party of sepoys" to escort them down to Calcutta. "You are not acquainted with the connexion between Roy Doolub and the English", observed Clive in his letter to Hastings on 31 August, "that they (the English) are bound not only to protect him, but his family also; you may remonstrate with decency, as often as opportunity offers, that it is unjust to keep the mother and daughter away from the father". Thus, he advised Hastings, "I would have you to act on all occasions so as to avoid coming to extremities, and will convince the *Durbar* that we always have it in our power to make ourselves respected". About the collection of money, Clive advised him to be "a little severe." "It is the nature of these people to do nothing through inclination",[109] observed Clive to Hastings.

Mir Jafar arrived at Calcutta on 1 September. Pressed by Clive he at last permitted the removal of Rai-Durlabh's family from Murshidabad. When the permission reached

108 Hastings' letter to Clive, 24 August *Ibid.*, pp. 59-60).

109 Clive's letter to Hastings, 31 August (*Ibid.*, p. 61).

Murshidabad, Hastings immediately intimated this to Clive: "The Nabob has given his permission for the removal of Roy Doolub's family to Calcutta". This wrote the Resident to Clive on 7 September. Finally on 12 September, the members of Rai-Durlabh's family started for Calcutta, escorted by a guard of English soldiers.[110]

Hastings soon realised that his new appointment was a bed of thorns. He came to know about Nandkumar's appointment to collect the revenues of Burdwan and Nadia besides Hugli. As Hastings felt, this was an interference with his powers and he became much aggrieved. On 25 August Scrafton also informed him from Calcutta: "I am much vexed when I write you that Nun Comar is appointed collector of the revenues of Burdwan, Nadiya and Hugli by the committee. This takes Burdwan and Nadiya out of your power: You will have nothing more to do than to collect for the other balances." Scrafton, in fact' was jealous of Nand Kumar, as the latter was supported by Watts. He informed Hastings in the same letter, "whenever you have any public complaint against him (NandKumar) don't fail to represent it to the Council."[111]

Very much annoyed, Hastings wrote to Clive on 7 September that he would use "all possible means for collecting the remainder of the last sixtn", but there was a wide difference between securing the payments due in respect of a large amount and that of collecting several small balances remaining outstanding from the "old accounts". Hastings did not have long to wait to act on Scrafton's advice. In the same letter, he informed Clive that he had received a letter, two days before, from the Rajah of Burdwan in which the latter had informed the Resident that Nandkumar had sent peons to the Rajah directing him to pay the revenues of Burdwan to him (Nandkumar) at Hugli, "and to repair immediately to Calcutta

110 Orme, *Indostan*, II, p. 359. Also Mukhopadhyay, *Raj-Durlabh*, p. 125.

111 Scrafton's letter to Hastings, 25 August (Quoted in Beveridge, *Hastings in Lower Bengal*, p. 217).

in order to settle the monthly payments of his *tuncaws* for the present year."[112] Hastings then proceeded to express his surprise that Nandkumar's proceedings were sanctioned by the committee. He informed Clive that he had forbidden the Burdwan Rajah to obey Nandkumar's orders. Hastings, at the same time, assured the Rajah of Burdwan that the business entrusted to his (Hastings') charge could not be transacted without his knowledge. Yet Hastings confessed to Clive : "I will not pretend to be ignorant that I have sometime since heard that he (Nandkumar) was appointed Collector of the Burdwan and Nuddea *tuncaws*."[113] Nandkumar also informed Hastings that the former had received the *khelat* from Clive "for that purpose". But the grievance of Hastings was that the committee did not take him into confidence about Nandkumar's appointment.

Hastings drew Clive's attention to the defects of the Burdwan revenue accounts, the revenues being already six and a half months in arrears. The Burdwan Rajah informed Hastings that the exorbitant demands of Nandkumar had prevented him from paying any part of his *kist* and that if he was obliged to go to Calcutta for a fresh *kistbundee* with Nandkumar, it might occasion the 'loss of at "least a month more." To overcome this delay Hastings sent a copy of the *kistbundee* which he had settled with the Burdwan Rajah, and if it would meet the approval of Clive, as it would save "a great expense" and "unnecessary loss of time," it might be accepted in order to expedite the payment of revenues. Along with this copy, Hastings also transmitted to Clive the *kistbundee* by which the Burdwan revenues were in the past paid annually to the Murshidabad government.[114]

Clive promptly replied to the letter of Hastings. On 10 September, the Colonel informed the Resident that the former

---

112 Hastings' letter to Clive, 7 September (Beveridge, *Hastings in Lower Bengal*, p. 218).

113 Hastings' letter to Clive, 7 September (Gleig, *Hastings*, I, pp. 62-63).

114 *Ibid.* (Gleig, *Hastings*, I, pp. 63-64).

had been surprised for the "ignorance" of the latter, the fact being that Nandkumar had been appointed collector of the revenues of Burdwan, Nadia and Hugli for a period of two years and that the money collected was to be paid at Hugli. This arrangement had been made before Hastings' appointment as Resident at Murshidabad. For the collection of money at Hugli, Clive wrote to Hastings : "One reason for desiring to have the money paid at Hughley in preference to Muxadavad was to avoid giving the Nabob and the great men about him umbrage in seing such large sums coming into the public treasury; and then sent out again for the use of the English." Clive also consulted Watts at Calcutta about this matter. Watts assured the Colonel that he had intimated all the above to Hastings. In this situation the Resident was to collect only three and a half lakhs of rupees—the remainder of the last sixth of the instalment of payments by the Nawab, and "to carry on the *Durbar* affairs." His area of operation was thus drastically reduced. If Scrafton had not informed Hastings about his business which he should have done at the time of the take-over, Clive believed that Scrafton "was wanting in the duties of his office," when he delivered charges to Hastings. Clive did not inform this matter earlier to Hastings because he thought that the latter "was fully acquainted with" his business. Clive further informed Hastings, that it was not for his misconduct or incapacity that a part of the duties of a Resident had been withdrawn from him, "for no one will be more ready to support your character and welfare than myself." Thus Clive desired Hastings to write to the Burdwan Rajah to comply with Nandkumar's directions about the Rajah's proposed coming to Calcutta. The *khelat* was given to Nandkumar in full council, Clive reassured Hastings, without the least thought of "lessening your credit or authority at the *Durbar*."[115]

In reply, Hastings informed Clive that he was not ignorant about Nandkumar's appointment to collect the revenues of

---

115 Clive's letter to Hastings, 10 September (Gleig, *Hastings*, I, pp. 64-65). Also, Beveridge, *Hastings in Lower Bengal*, p. 218,

Burdwan and Nadia, but neither Watts nor Scrafton had ever given him information that collection of "such parts of their revenues as were included in their accounts of the last sixth" was to be withdrawn from Hastings. He added that Scrafton had clearly stated in his letter to the committee that the balance of the revenues of Burdwan and Nadia would be collected by the Resident at the *darbar*. Therefore, it was surely no unreasonable thing in me to imagine that whenever these revenues were taken out of my hands," observed Hastings to Clive, "I should be previously ordered to resign them." Hastings further stated that as per Scrafton's specific instruction to him "I was to collect the remainder of the last sixth which amounted to eleven lacs of rupees, and wait the orders of the Board with regard to the Burdwan and Nuddea *Tuncaws* for the year." And it was in full consonance with Scrafton's instructions that Hastings had "acted all along". There was a balance of nearly four lakhs due from Burdwan and Hastings thought it his business to settle the matter, that he could add the balances of the previous year with the present and could "settle the payments of the whole together," which method had been adopted by Scrafton in regard to Nadia revenues. And as Hastings noticed that since the current year's Burdwan revenues were already five months overdue, it was his duty to finish the *kistbundee* "more expeditiously and more for the advantage of the Company". Hastings thought that his arrangement would add "some degree of merit" to himself but to his dismay he saw that it was disapproved by the authority. Thus, as desired by Clive, Hastings wrote to the Burdwan Rajah that the new Resident had "no longer any business in the collection of his revenues" and for further particulars, he was to obey Nandkumar's order. The same order Hastings also sent to Nadia but the Nadia Rajah, "without waiting for any advices' from Hastings sent Rs. 83,000 of the Nadia revenues to Hugli.[116]

Hastings wrote in the same letter of Clive that he was at a loss to decide how to proceed with the collection of the

116 Hastings' letter to Clive, 14 September (Gleig, *Hastings*, I, pp. 66-68).

remaining balances of the Hugli accounts, as he became "apprehensive of meeting with a fresh mortification," in case he took the matter up "with any of the *Zemindars* of Nuncomar's jurisdiction." Therefore, Hastings required Clive's further clarification. Hastings was aware that his objection on "any measures" might be disapproved by the council. So he prepared himself to apply to "the small part of the business" that still remained in his hand. Hastings then wanted to clarify the stand of his previous letter that "the transferring of the Burdwan and Nuddea affairs to Hughley proceeded in the least from any ill opinion prevailing at Calcutta "of his conduct or capacity". So he wrote to Clive in the same letter : "It was universally believed that I was appointed at Moraudbaug principally for the collection of those revenues. But I must beg leave to declare that the confidence which I place in the promises which you have made me, and suffer me to add the expressions which I am told you have done me the honour to make use of in my favour, are sufficient to prevent my entertaining the least thought that you intended me any slight or prejudice on this occasion."[117]

Hastings developed a sharp animus against Nandkumar, though the party to blame was the Calcutta Council and Clive, but certainly not Nandkumar.[118] The subsequent offshoot of this hatred and anger was not at all pleasant and as Walsh truly observed, "thus was sown the seed which afterwards assumed prodigious magnitude and bore bitter fruits."[119]

In the same letter to Clive on 14 September, Hastings made a complaint against Nandkumar that the latter had sent peons on Mahisadal *gomastah* for an account of Rs. 86,388, the balance of Mahisadal account, that had already been paid to Hastings at Moradbagh. Still Nandkumar insisted on the *gomastah* of Mahisadal to pay that amount to him as it

117 *Ibid.*

118 Beveridge, *Hastings in Lower Bengal*, p. 219.

119 Walsh, *Murshidabad*, p. 221. Also, Roy, B.K., *Maharaja Nanda Kumar*, p. 28.

belonged to Hugli accounts. Thus, Hastings became indignant and informed Clive that this proceeding was surely a contempt of his authority. It was an encroachment on his jurisdiction as the Resident. Hastings blurted out fury while concluding his letter to Clive : "It was never your intention, in placing me at Moraudbaug, that I should only hold the business for Nuncomar, till he was properly settled and at leisure to take it out of my hands."[120]

Greatly perturbed by this unpleasant affair about the revenue collection, Hastings had another dose of tension and alarm from something that happened at Murshidabad. After giving a preliminary report of the incident on 15 September, Hastings wrote another letter to Clive in which he narrated the incident as told by the Nawab himself. On the night of 13 September, the Nawab had gone to the palace of Miran and after a short stay, returned in his *palkeen* to the Imambara, where he was surrounded by sepoys in the most disorderly manner. It was the day of the *Muharram* festival and the Nawab had ordered Khwajah Wajid to place proper guards inside and outside the Imambara. The arrangement having been made thus, Mir Jafar entertained no suspicion of danger. But one of the Nawab's spies informed the Nawab that Khwajah Wajid had instigated his people to create disturbances when the Nawab arrived there. Hastings believed that the tumult was a part of a conspiracy to do away with the Nawab's life.[121] But there had been a timely discovery and the insurrection had been put down. Khwajah Wajid and his supporters had been forced to disperse from that place by the intervention of the Nawab's "own people". After enquiry, on the next day, the Nawab came to know the whole affair. Rai-Durlabh had sent Khwajah Wajid a bill of exchange for two lakhs of rupees to be paid to Mir Ali, who would distribute it among the soldiers, after which under the pretence of demanding the arrears of their pay

120 Hastings' letter to Clive, 14 September (Gleig, *Hastings*, I, p. 68).

121 Hastings' letter to Clive, 15 September (Gleig, *Hastings*, I, p. 69).

the soldiers, as instigated by Wajid, might surround the Nawab and kill him. Upon this discovery, the Nawab had dismissed Khwajah Wajid from service and had directed him to leave the city forthwith. Hastings also observed in his letter that the Nawab "is greatly exasperated against Roy Doolub, whom he looks upon as the author of all this confusicn."[122]

Hastings after a personal enquiry came to know from Brindaban, one of Rai-Durlabh's brothers that the "troops then assembled were at his devotion" Thus, Hastings also began to believe in the suspicions generated against Rai-Durlabh Meanwhile the Nawab had informed Hastings that he had obtained a letter written by Rai-Durlabh to Khwajah Wajid, containing the names of Watts and Scrafton, as approvers of Rai-Durlabh's project to murder the Nawab. And in this endeavour, as alleged, Clive had also given his approval through Watts and Scrafton.[123] Hastings then asked the Nawab to give him a copy of the letter but the Nawab refused without consulting Watts and Scrafton. The Nawab asked Hastings to write to them to come to Murshidabad. But since these officials did not come Mir Jafar delivered a copy of Rai-Durlabh's letter to Hastings informing the latter that the letter had been obtained by Miran from Khwajah Wajid by a promise of reconciliation.[124]

Clive treated the story with great pinches of salt. He informed Hastings on 6 October, "You have not yet been long enough at the *Durbar* to make yourself acquainted with the dark designs of the Mussulmans. The moment I perused your letter I could perceive a design in the Nabob and those about him against Roy Doolub, and you may be assured what is alleged against him and his letters to Coja Huddee is a forgery from begining to end."

Clive believed that Rai-Durlabh was "not such a fool" to commit anything in writing. His cautious attitude before

---

122 Gleig, *Hastings*, I pp. 70-71.

123 Orme, *Indostan*, pp. 360-361.

124 Beveridge, *Hasting in Lower Bengal* p. 65.

the battle of plassey was a convincing proof of it. Besides, Rai-Durlabh very well knew the English attachment to Mir Jafar and so he would never dare to intrigue against the Nawab. "The Moors in general are villains enough to undertake anything which may benefit themselves at another's expense," Clive wrote to Hastings in undisguised anger.[125] Clive became convinced that the Nawab wanted to instigate him against Rai-Durlabh expecting that the ex-*diwan* might be turned out of Calcutta and the Nawab would then plunder all his wealth. The Nawab's rather too quick permission for khwajah wajid's departure without examining him, added to Clive's suspicion.[126] "I cannot avoid entertaining the strongest resentment against the Nabob", wrote Clive to Hastings, because the Nawab had dared to accuse him of entering into such a heinous plot. In concluding his letter to Hastings, Clive resentfully stated: "After the treatment he (Mir Jafar) received at Calcutta, he must have known that the English are endued with sentiments of honour and conscience, which the Moors are utter strangers to; and I must desire you will infrom him that if he give ear to such things as these, there will soon be an end to all confidence and friendship between us."[127]

After this incident at Murshidabad, Hastings thought it opportune to pursue his vendetta against Nandkumar. In a letter to Clive in November, Hastings wrote about the Nawab's great dissatis faction about the appointment of Nandkumar. As Hastings stated, the Nawab had told Hastings that the latter "would be wanting in his duty if he did not acquaint Clive with the Nabob's sentiments." The Nawab was surprised "at our attacnment to such a man", that he deserved as little from the Company as from the Nawab. In conclusion, Hastings ironically added, "I own it is no very agreeable office to me to say any thing that may turn to prejudice of another person."

125 Clive's letter to Hastings, 6 October (Gleig, *Hastings*, I, pp. 71-72).

126 Scrafton's *Reflections*, p. 117.

127 Clive's letter to Hastings, 6 October (Gleing, *Hastings, I*, p 72).

Again in the draft of a letter dated 20 November, he wrote: "I cannot omit to inform your Honour that every time I have visited the Nabob, he has continually expressed the greatest dissatisfaction with Nandkumar's appointment."[128] In his letter to Scrafton also he spouted venom against Nandkumar: Jagat Chand, Nandkumar's son-in-law, tells everybody here that a strong party was formed against Nandkumar in order to exclude him the *tuncaw* concerns, but that he got the better of them all by advising the Colonel to send Mr. Lushington into Burdwan as collector there. A strange story."[129]

But Clive was a strong supporter of Nandkumar, and replied to Hastings on 28 November: "I cannot think Nandkumar deserving of the Nabob's resentment without it be for his known attachment to the English, of which I am fully assured. The Burdwan revenues are little or nothing behindhand, the *tuncaws* in the other lands he has nothing to do with, the true cause of the Nabob's hatred to Nandkumar proceeds from his not joining with Omar Beg in Roy Doolab's ruin and overthrow" Clive further informed Hastings in the same letter that the Nawab had offered a title and *jagir* to Nandkumar, if the latter could bring the affair of Rai-Durlabh's letter in favour of the Nawab. Hence Clive scornfully remarked, "you may lay it down as a maxim that the Mulsamans will never be influenced by kind treatment to do us justice." He advised Hastings that in the existing situation the interests of the Company should get the highest priority.[130]

About the collection of several outstanding dues of the Company's revenues, Hastings began to make several complaints from the end of September. These letters were placed before the Calcutta Council on 2 October. In his letter of 25 September, Hastings complained that during the Nawab's late visit to Calcutta most of the principal men had accompanied him, owing to which the collection in Rajshahi and other *zamindaries* had been greatly delayed. The balances

---

128 Beveridge, *Hastings in Lower Bengal*, p. 219.

129 *Ibid.*, p. 220.

130 Clive's letter to Hastings, 28 November (Beveridge, *Hastings in Lower Bengal*, p. 220). Also, Gleig, *Hastings*, I, p. 77.

remaining in the last sixth amounted to Rs. 10,76,512–4–9, even though the revenues of three districts had been transferred under the charge of Nandkumar. But Hastings had already received from Nadia Rs. 38,556–2—3, which brought the outstanding dues from that district to Rs. 1,16,436–12–9. The balance due from Burdwan was Rs. 3,60,642-1-9. The *zamindars* of Tamluk, Mahisadal and Gumgar pretended that the balance of their revenues had been already collected by Nandkumar. The remainder of Tamluk and Gumgar revenues supposed to be transferred to Nandkumar was Rs. 31,666–7–6. The balance of Nadia and Burdwan was Rs. 4,77,078–14–6, including Rs. 2000 which was due from Nandkumar. In all, Rs. 5,10.745—6 was due. Hastings wanted himself to be put in charge of collection of this amount instead of Nandkumar, of course, by the premission of the Calcutta Council. Hastinge also wanted to know if any of the remaining revenues was to be transferred to Nandkumar's charce. Scrafton informed Hastings that Raj Durlabh should be responsible for the amount of Rs. 84,258-15 due from Mithuchad and Mritunjay, which, Scrafton desired, might be deducted from Raj-Durlabh's commission. Hastings further informed that Umid Roy had sent him an account of revenues to the government from the Company's lands amounting to Rs. 1,98,423–1–0. But Hastings stated that there was a due also from the government to the Company, an amount of Rs. 83,705, which had been paid by the Burdwan *vakil* to Kunjabehari, brother of Rai-Durlabh and the former *Rai-Rayan*, though it properly belonged to the Company's share of revenues. This sum together with Rs. 5,448—15 was the balance of the Fatiganjpur revenues for which the *Rai-Rayan* was responsible, the total amount thus being Rs. 89,153—15. The *Rai-Rayan* desired that from this amount, the Company's dues might be deducted and the balance of Rs. 1,09,269–2 might be paid into the government treasury. If these suggestions of Hastings were approved of by the council, the Resident desired for their green signal so that he could credit the balance of the Fatiganjpur account in the Company's book.[131]

---

131 Hastings' letter to the Select Committee, 25 September (B.M.P., III, p. 53).

In examining the revenue papers, Hastings discovered a great anomaly in the Company's present title of lands, held in and around Calcutta and granted to them by the new treaty with the Nawab. So, on 27 September, he addressed a letter to Clive informing him that those lands were held only by virtue of the Nawab's *parwana*, but no *sanad* had yet been granted for them, nor they had been entered in the *kanungo's* books as the *zamindari* of the Company. The Nawab's *parwana* might have sufficient validity during his life time but might have no force with his successors if they chose to dispute it. Hastings hoped that there might not be any difficulty in obtaining a *sanad* for the *zamindari* of the Company's lands, but only if the steps were immediately taken. If deferred, the steps might be looked upon as a new demand. Hastings thus suggested to Clive "to make such enquiry into this affair", as the latter would judge proper After intimating all this the Resident awaited further direction.[132]

The Governor and Council at Calcutta after receiving this letter from Hastings resolved to give serious attention to the points raised. But for the present they desired Hastings to exercise "his own discretion as to the best and speediest method" of removing the defects of the title of the Company's lands. Thus, on 14 October, the committee appointed Kasinath to act under Hastings "to settle the yearly revenues to be paid to the Nabob and other affairs relative to the lands." He was directed to "set out immediately after the *Dassarah*.[133] Kasinath carried with him all the necessary papers with instruction that "in case he should have occasion to apply to the *Darbar*", he should lend Hastings, who would move in the matter, "all the assistance in his power."[134]

The Fort William authorities tried to add, by means of bribes, provision of another item to the treaty in order to reduce the scope of obligation upon the Company. The

132 Hastings' letter to Clive, 27 September (B. M. P., III, p. 53). Also, Gleig, *Hatsings*, I, pp. 73-74.

133 S. C. R., 14 October (B. M. P.. III, pp. 54-55).

134 S.C.R., 16 October (B. M. P., III, pp.54-55).

Ninth Article related to the land lying "to the south of Calcutta as far as Culpee", which had been made the *zamindari* of the English Company. Thus, on 14 October, they instructed Hastings: "Though our treaty with the Nabob expresses from Calcutta southward to Culpee, yet the above mentioned limits to the north and north-east may nevertheless be explained to be within the bounds prescribed by the said treaty as being within the *purganah* of Calcutta. Our meaning is not that you should insist on this in behalf of the Hon'ble Company as what they have a right to, but if the Nabob can be made sensible, it will be no loss to him, as we shall pay him the usual rents; and if he is willing to yield it upto the Hon'ble Company, it will be a very advantageous acquisition. To effect this you are to try every method to gain those to your interests that have influence at the *Durbar*, and if presents are found necessary to win them to you, we permit you to go as a year's revenues of the said lands."[135]

Hastings negotiated with the Nawab for two months for the desired *sanad* of the Company's land. On 20 November, he informed Clive that according to the direction of the Calcutta Council, he had paid one lakh of rupees to the Nawab "on account of the Calcutta lands." But the Nawab desired another lakh, which was also paid to him "to keep upon the best terms with the Nabob." Besides this, Mir Jafar requested Hastings to advance two lakhs on loan to him "which he would repay with the customary interest." Hastings did not commit himself to Mir Jafar on this point, but he solicited Clive's advice that "in case the Nabob should again mention" about the loans, he should be advised about what reply he was to give. According to Hastings' opinion the Nawab might be favoured with loans from the Company as "the Nabob's wants are to all appearance very pressing." Hastings had the greatest pleasure of informing Clive that "the greatest difficulties in the settlement of the Company's lands" had been happily resolved. "The lands without the line" observed Hastings, "extending as for as Baugenbazar (Bankibazar), are allowed to the Company". There remained

135 *Ibid.*, 14 October.

only obtaining a *parwana* for the possession of Anurpur and "to settle the accounts of Ballia Bussendree." The Nawab had agreed as far as the former was concerned and the latter would be taken up and settled in a few days. The Nawab had directed his officer, the *Rai-Rayan*, to deliver unto Hastings a draft of Anrupur settlement with an account of the revenues. When all these points were satisfactorily settled, Hastings hoped that the *sanad* would also be drawn out and executed without any further delay. The other points relating to the artitrary taxes imposed on the *zamindars* were left to be adjusted with the Nawab after the grant of the *sanad*.[136]

Clive and the Calcutta Council had much appreciation for Hastings for his discovery of the discrepancy in the title of the lands and his having satisfactorily solved the problem. But the idea of lending money to Mir Jafar, they did not look with favour. So Clive replied to Hastings on 29 November; "I cannot think that he is in that distress for want of money which you represent. To my certain knowledge he is in possession of gold to the amount of several lacs of rupees, and if you were to hint to him whenever he pleads poverty, that you are not ignorant of his hidden resources, I believe it might put an end to the disagreeable topic of borrowing money.[137] But in an over-all view of the situation he had nothing but praise for Hastings. Thus, Clive wrote to Hastings: "I am very sensible of the pains you have taken, and shall not fail acquainting the Company by the first opportunity, how much you have contributed to bring that important matter to so happy an issue."[138]

On 1 December, Hastings informed the Calcutta Council that *zamindari* of the lands north of Calcutta as far as Bankibazar had been settled and adjusted with the *sanad*

---

136 Hastings' letter to Clive, 20 November (Gleig, *Hastings*, I, pp. 74-76).

137 Clive's letter to Hastings, 28 November (Gleig, *Hastings*, I pp. 76-77).

138 Gleig, *Hastings*, I p. 78.

after much difficulty.[139] "But notwithstanding this intelligence we shall not esteem it secure", observed the Calcutta Council in their letter to the Court of Directors, "till the *sunnud* has passed the forms and is sealed. When we receive the grant properly authenticated we shall acquaint Your Honours of the advantages we expect will accrue to the Company from the possession of those lands." They further informed the Directors that they had always applied to the Nawab for the *parganah* of Anurpur, a tract of land north-east of Calcutta "in order to square the Companies boundaries." But about the grant of Anurpur *parganah* to the Company, the Calcutta Council received a letter from Hastings dated 6 December, acquainting the council that when the Resident pressed the Nawab to confirm and grant the *sanad* that would include the Anurpur *parganah* a well, the Nawab reacted to it unfavourably and angrily. In a fit of rage Mir Jafar declared that the lands obtained by the Company "greatly exceeded his agreement." He said that he promised to grant the Company a tract of land, the revenues of which would amount to one lakh of rupees, but "if it was otherwise expressed in the treaty, it was owing to the treachery of Roydoolab who had deceived him in it." Thus, the Nawab expressed his unwillingness to include Anurpur to the Company's zamindari. Instead of this be offered to give them the *waddadari* of that *parganah*. But then the Nawab cooled down, thanks to the intervention of Rajballabh. He came round and directed his *Rai-Rayan*, the officer entrusted with such work, to draw up the *sanad* which, Hastings hoped, would be finalised within two or three days. Hastings intimated that in order to expedite the passing of the *sanad*, the Nawab was at last forced to forego his objections about the Anurpur *parganah*, which was thus going to be included in the Company's *zamindari*.[140]

So everything was settled in favour of the Company and within a period of six months of his rule, Mir Jafar,

139 Frankland was directed to take possession of the same in the Company's name.

140 Letter to Court, 31 December (F.W.I.H.C., II, pp. 341-342).

for all practical purposes, was reduced to a mere figurehead. In this process the objection of Clive not to advance loans to Mir Jafar was also waived. The Calcutta Council stated in their letter to the court that the Nawab was greatly in want of money, "large arreas being due to his troops" as well as the Nawab's probable confirmation of the *sanad* for the lands, induced the members of the council to lend him the sum, "reserving to ourselves the rent and revenues of the lands of the company are to have the *zemindarry* of, as security for the payment."[141]

Towards the end of the year 1758, it became a general practice among the Company's servants to carry on illicit private trade throughout the *subah*, to the great detriment of the merchants of Bengal, though this practice was strictly forbidden by the Company's authorities. Thus, in a letter, without date, but probably written at the end of 1758, Hastings informed Clive about the complaints of the Nawab against one John Clarke, who had taken possession of two or three *ganjas* at Bakharganj. He used the name of the Company and carried on illicit trade, interferring with the *zamindars* and the officials of the government in the collection of the revenues and customs. As Hastings had no authority to deal with such a man, as well as did not know on what accounts or orders this person resided at Bakharganj, he thought it proper to inform Clive "with the complaints alleged against him", that Clive might take such action as he deemed fit.[142].

141 *Ibid*, p. 348. Also, Long, *Unpublised Records*, p. 208. At the end of December, Hastings worte to Creswick: "A very strong and noble fortification has been creating in Calcutta, the outworks of which will be finished, I hope, in another twelve months. I forget whether I informed you that one of the articles of the treaty with the Nabob was that the Company should possess a large tract of land to to the southward of Calcutta, paying the customary rents to the king's treasury: This acquisition, I hope, will be confirmed in a few days by a patent granted to the Company in the king's name, this having been the subject of the negociations of the *Darbar* for the two months past."-Beveridgs, *Hastings in Lower Bengal*, p. 214.

142 Beveridge, *Hastings in Lower Bengal*, p. 222.

Thus, as the English power began to rise behind the scene, the English officials and merchants carried on their trade in Bengal in a very aggressive arbitrary way. Mir Jafar had already complained about this as early as just one month after his accession to the *masnad*, as was seen in Scrafton's complaints to Peakes, the Chief of Dacca, on 21 July. The illegal individualistic trade went on increasing and it reached such monstrous proportions that Hastings was forced to write similar complaints to W. B. Sumner, Chief of the Dacca factory, in December '58 and January '59. The Resident as well as the Nawab became much concerned about such illegal trade which meant serious loss both to the Nawab and to the Company. On 12 December, Hastings wrote to Sumner that Chevalier, an English merchant at Dacca, was reported to be carrying on trade of salt to Chilmaree in Rangpur district, to which he was not entitled. The said merchant had tken *muchelkas* from all other traders of salt, not to sell any salt until the salt of that English merchant "be all disposed of."[143]

But this unprivileged trade of Chevalier continued as before, in spite of the protest of the Nawab as well as the complaint of Hastings. Thus, the Resident had to write another strong note to Sumner that Chevalier had "acted in a very violent and arbitrary manner" at Chilmaree and Kurigram[144], by oppressing the merchants of those place, and had not allowed other merchants to buy or sell salt and tobacco without his permission. Thus, Hastings desired from Sumner to make "the strictest enquiry" and to take effectual care to prevent such complaints. The same English merchant, Chevalier, wrote a letter to Attaullah, the *waddadar* of the *parganah* of Baharband, which Hastings forwarded to Sumner for his perusal. In this the said merchant arrogantly wrote : "You write, that if I belong to the English, I must have the English *sunnud*, and desire a copy of it to be sent you. In answer,

143 Hastings, letter to W. B. Sumner, 12 December (Vansittart, *Narrative*, I, pp. 10-11.

144 Both these places are in Rangpur District, now in Bangladesh.

I ask, who are you, that I should sent you a copy of the *sunnud*? If you want to be informed who I am, and who sent me send a man to the Chief, who will answer you. If the people of your *Pergunah* are guilty of any insolence to mine; I shall chastise them handsomely for it. Forbid your people that they enter into no quarrels with mine; if they do without reason, they shall be punished.[145]

As it appeared, Attaullah-the *waddadar*, had immediately put up a complaint before the Nawab. The Nawab had handed over a copy of it to Hastings. The latter after an English translation, sent it to Sumner asking him what autho rity Chevalier had to act in that way : "That the magistrates the public officers of the government, have undoubted right to see the Company's *dustuck*, having no other way to distinguish between the agents of the Company and others usurping the English name; nor the Company any means besides to secure their own privileges." In the footnotes of the same letter, Hastings remarked that the sending of such a letter by Chevalier was "only an aggravation." Therefore, the Resident insisted upon Sumner either to put a stop to such complaints or to recall Chevalier, who nad not "behaved in so moderate or prudent a manner as he ought."[146]

But in the month of January 1759, Hastings came to know from a complaint of one Mohammad Husain to the Nawab that Sumner himself carried on a large-scale personal trade without paying any duties. So Hastings wrote to Sumner on 30 January: "You have begun to carry on a large trade in salt and betel-nut and refuse to pay the duties on those articles, which has likewise encouraged others to do the same in your name. Hastings further informed Sumner that the English had no right to carry on such trade: "We have not, I believe any right to trade in salt and betel-nut, at least it was never (that I know of) stipulated in our favour with the Nabob; and with respect to the salt trade, I myself know, that

145 Vansittart, *Narrative*, I, p. 12.

146 *Ibid.*, p. 11.

none of the company's servants, not the Colonel himself, has ever engaged in it without the Nabob's *perwanah.*"[147]

Since the *sanad* of the Company's lands, which Hastings had hoped to obtain within a few days, did not reach Calcutta even in the month of January, the Calcutta Council resolved to write to Manningham not to advance two lakhs of rupees to the Nawab. Hastings was directed to explain to the Nawab that the Company was to pay the "King's rent only". If any difficulties were created by the revenue Chief, *Rai-Rayan*, he might be satisfied with reasonable presents. The council at the same time directed that Kasinath be sent to calcutta immediately.[148] After some days the Calcutta Council again resolved to write to Manningham and Hastings to acquaint the Nawab that it was the Company's "firm resolution" to pay nothing beyond the king's rents as agreed upon in the 9th article of the treaty. The Company had wanted the lands only on the ground that the profits from the lands would enable them to maintain a force for the Nawab's defence. In view of this the council failed to account for the hesitant attitude of the Nawab in complying with the treaty.[149] The council wanted to remind the Nawab that the *siccas* (the instalments paid by the Nawab to the Company) paid in the first half, were largely in bad rupees, a loss which the Company would not tolerate.[150] In this way at last Mir Jafar was forced to bend down and Hastings obtained the requisite *sanad* for the Company.[151] The Company also, through Manningham, advanced a loan of two lakhs of rupees to the Nawab in the month of January, 1759.[152]

Early in 1759, the political situation in Bengal to began take a new shape on account of the changed atmosphere at Delhi.

147 Hastings' letter to Sumner, 30 January, 1759 (Vansittart, *Narrative*, I, p. 10).

148 S. C. R., 2 January, 1759 (Hill, *Abstract* p. 47).

149 S.C.R. 15 January (B.M.P., III, p. 6)

150 *Ibid.* (Hill, *Abstract*, p. 47).

151 Firminger, *Fifth Report*, p. 216, f.n.

152 Long, *Unpublished Records*, p. 287.

Alamgir II, the Mughal Emperor, and his family became virtual prisoners in the hands of the *wazir* Ghazi-ud-din. The Emperor's son, Ali Gauhar, who was the crown prince or *Shahzadah*, became a fugitive from Delhi, wandering for support and remained for some months under the protection of the Rohillas. He was informed of the distracted state of the *subah* of Bengal and hence began to advance with a band of adventurers towards the region. When the *Shahzadah* arrived at Benaras, the Seths informed Mir Jafar about the *Shahzadah*'s movements. On 31 January, Hastings informed Clive that one of the Seths had carried a letter for the Nawab on the previous night with the information of the *Shahzadah*'s arrival at Benaras. The Seths expressed their intention of going on a pilgrimage to Parasnath about the middle or end of the month of February. They would take with them their whole family and treasures. Only Kewadas would remain behind at Murshidabad as care-taker of their house. Hastings began to doubt the seths, motives. The whole thing seemed to him "deeper than a mere pilgrimage" and it became more so to him "as I believe the two Brothers were never known before to leave their House, both at the same time."[153] On the next day Hastings informed Clive that a guard of 2,000 sepoys with four heavy Afghan arms, called *jazails*, had been arranged for the protection of the Seths on the way.[154]

In the beginning of February, the *Shahzadah* began his march towards the frontier of Bihar. Hastings informed Clive on 7 February that the *Shahzadah* had already completed three days' march from Benares. The *Shazadah* had also invited Law to join him with one thousand troops. The prince had at that time 3000 soldiers with him and was recruiting more along his march. Meanwhile, Shujauddaulah, the Nawab of oudh, intended to imprison him but could not do so because the *Shahzadah* had already gained a leeway on his march towards Bihar. The Prince dispatched a letter to Ramnarain, the deputy Governor of Patna under Mir Jafar,

153 Hastings' letter to Clive, 31 January, 1759 (Forrest, *Clive*, II, p. 126.

154 Forrest, *Clive*, II, p. 126.

seeking to meet him and make him an ally. But the Rajah declined to meet him until he got permisson from Mir Jafar. Mir Jafar directed Ramnarain to remain at Patna and promised to come to his assistance. In the meantime, Miran informed Hastings that his father intended to encamp at Bomenia [155], till Clive with his forces joined him.[156] At the same time Miran urged Hastings to represent the matter to the Colonel and ensure his (Clive's) "taking the Field immediately" to assist the Nawab, as the delay might cause "ill consequences" and as the *Shahzadah* had already arrived near Patna. [157] On the next day, Hastings informed Clive that the Nawab had asked the Seths to reach an adjustment with the Prince "at any cost of money."[158]

Clive acted with promptness. He wrote to Hastings on 10 February that he would write to the Nawab immediately. Clive added that upon receipt of this letter Hastings should wait upon the Nawab and assure him about Clive's constant attachment to the Nawab's cause. The Nawab should be particularly assured that he could depend upon the English nation which would support him "to the utmost" and that the English would "prove an overmatch for all his enemies." In his letter to the Nawab Clive enjoined upon him not to come to "any terms" with the *Shahzadah*. "On Monday, the last of this month, I shall take the field, and will have everything in readiness to march to your assistance if necessary. Rest assured that the English are your staunch and firm friends, and that they never desert a cause in which they have once taken a part."[159]

Six days later Clive wrote again to Hastings informing him that he had written to the Nawab upon hearing from the Resident that the Nawab had authorised the Seths

155 Bomenia is a little way to the north of Murshidabad, across the river.

156 S.C.R., 10 February (B.M.P., III, p. 8).

157 Forrest, *Clive*, II, p. 126.

158 S.C.R., 10 February (Hill, *Abstract*, p. 45).

159 Forrest, *Clive*, II, p. 127.

to buy off the *Shahzadah* and had warned him that this measure would inevitably ruin him. Clive wrote to the Nawab that he had got the information: "Your Excellency is going to offer a sum of money" to the *Shahzadah*. This action, he warned, would induce both Shujauddaulah and the Marathas to come to Bengal to drain the Nawab's money, "till you have none left in your treasury." The Colonel again urged the Nawab to "rely on the fidelity of the English."[160]

On his march to Bengal, *Shahzadah* had, in the mean time, made common cause with Shujauddaulah. The combination appeared formidable and there were letters too from the *Shahzadah* to Clive. The Colonel directed Hastings to reply in consultation with the Nawab and in such a style and to such a purport as might convince these adventurists that "it will not be prudent in them to venture into these provinces."[161] Meanwhile Hastings informed Clive that the *Shahzadah* with Muhammad Quli Khan was advancing with great rapidity and had sent an advance body of horse to assist the Seths. To meet this danger, Hastings requested Clive to save the *Subah* of Bengal by sending up "a light party of Europeans."[162]

On such a report from Hastings, Clive started for Murshidabad and reached Kasimbazar on 8 March. Hastings went up and received Clive on the way. During his short stay, Clive assured the Nawab that all the English troops "would fight for him to the last man" and he "complied with the Nabob's solicitation to ride on the same elephant with him."[163]

About the Seths' intended pilgrimage at Parasnath, that had aroused Clive's suspicion as well, the Colonel wrote a letter to them on 31 January, but they did not reply to it. But when the Seths heard about the news of Clive's advance, they began to behave more discreetly. Hastings

160 *Ibid.*
161 Clive's letter to Hastings, 19 February (Dodwell, p. 162).
162 S.C.R., 8 March (Hill, *Abstract*, p. 50).
163 Forrest, *Clive*, II, p. 129.

wrote to Clive on 16 February that on that day he had taken leave of the Seths at their first encampment and the Seths had "behaved with unusual civility to him." As a matter of fact Hastings visited the Seths three days before he wrote the above letter. The Seths informed the Resident that they realised that they should not have left Murshidabad at such a critical time, but as they had so long prepared for the intended pilgrimage and had sent the greatest part of their treasure before the news of the troubles first arrived, their journey could not be postponed. But they would surely return within a month and a half from Patna and as Parasnath lies partly on the way, they would offer their devotion there also. The Seths further informed Hastings that they had written a letter to Delhi for an order granting Clive a *jagir* and had met with success. "I am not sure" wrote Hastings to Clive "that I clearly understood him in this last particular." Clive received this letter on 19 February and on 20, he received a leteer from the Seths as well: "We are going to a place of devotion with all our family in a day or two, accompanied by some of the Nabob's forces. By the favour of God, we hope to return in six weeks."[164]

Although upon the advice of Clive, the Nawab gave up his idea of buying off the *Shahzadah*, he did not venture personally to march towards Patna. He recalled Mir Qasim Khan-his son-in-law, from Rangpur and planned to send immediately under his command 5,000 horse and 5,000 *barkandases*. At the same time, the Nawab requested Clive to march immediately and promised to join Clive in ten or twelve days. But Clive advised Hastings to encourage the Nawab to take the field himself without loss of time.[165]

Mir Jafar was staying at Sadiqbagh[166], two miles from the city, where Clive had an audience with the Nawab. In their discussions about the military operations they deci-

164 *Ibid.*, pp. 140-141.

165 Malcolm, *Clive*, I, p. 398.

166 Mir Jafar's letter to Clive, 17 March (Calendar of Persian Correspondence, Vol. I, Reprint, Delhi, 1970, p. 8, No. 107.

ded to buttress Ramnarain both materially and morally. Hence Mir Qasim Khan was directed to proceed to Patna with the utmost haste. Miran with his forces was to wait at Rajmahal till Clive joined him. All these arrangements caused some delay in sending the army to Patna. Meanwhile the *Shahzadah* arrived at Fulwari—seven miles West of Patna. Ramnarain wanted to decoy and amuse the enemy for some time, till the arrival of the Bengal army. The Rajah kept up a show of submission, but when he was informed of the near approach of the Bengal army, he turned out the *Shahzadah's* agent, and sent a message to the latter that he acknowledged no master but the Nawab of Bengal.[167] The *Shahzadah* was provoked and ordered the start of fighting for the capture of Patna. The skirmishes went on till 5 April, when the news of the arrival of the Bengal army reached the *Shahzadah's* camp. The *Shahzadah* was frightened. He ordered lifting of the siege on Patna and withdraw in haste.

On 8 April Clive, accompanied by Miran, made his entry into Patna and pursued the *Shahzadah's* army up to the river Karmanasa. The *Shahzadah*, deserted by his followers, took to a wandering life with a handful of men. The Nawab, who was in a state of constant apprehension, was overjoyed at the news of this success. In his deep sense of gratitude he wanted to settle the question of a *jagir* for Clive without delay. Hastings wrote to Clive on 24 April : "He (the Nawab) expresses the most grateful sense of the services which you have performed for him, and declared to me his resolution to use every means in his power to procure an order from the Court for your *jagir*, being ashamed that you should do so much for him without the prospect of reaping any advantage to yourself by it."[168]

At the close of June, when Clive was approaching Murshidabad on his return from Patna, Hastings could not attend the *darbar* for some days owing to the illness and subsequent

167 *Seir*, II, p. 307.

168 Hastings' letter to Clive, 24 June (Forrest, *Clive*, II, p. 142).

death of his wife at the end June or beginning of July. In a letter on 4 July, he informed Clive : "You have, I doubt not, heard of the misfortune which has fallen me in the loss of my wife. For this cause, I cannot immediately, attend to the Nabob, but Mr. Sykes will wait on him in my stead to-morrow, in order to lay before him the subject of your letter, and I shall endorse this application by a letter to the Nabob, which will, I hope, prove as effectual as if I spoke to him in person about it."[169]

Thus the Nawab had to discuss with Sykes, the acting Resident on behalf of Hastings, about Clive's *jagir*. The Nawab told Sykes that he wanted to create Clive an *Omarah* of the empire. For this the Nawab wanted to bestow a *jagir* to Clive in the province of Bihar but "found it would be attended with inconvenience to the officers of his government."[170] Thus, the Nawab authorised the Seths to settle this issue. The clever Seths overcame the difficulties and recommended that Clive should be given the quit-rent arising from the lands ceded to the Company in the vicinity of Calcutta. This was accordingly done. The reward was great, but, according to the Nawab, inadequate to the services he had received from the Colonel.[171] Soon after receiving the *parwana* assigning quit-rent, Clive proceeded to Calcutta. After translating the *parwana*, Hastings sent it to the Calcutta Council. In December, the Court of Directors were apprised of this grant and a copy of the *parwana* was forwarded to them.[172]

---

169 Hastings' letter to Clive, 4 July (Beveridge, *Hastings in Lower Bengal*, p. 215).

170 Forrest, *Clive*, II, p. 142.

171 The Nawab in company with Jagat Seth and some other persons met the Colonel two miles north of the city. After some conversation the Nawab retired, but Jagat Seth, in the presence of some witnesses, presented the *jagir* to Clive, on behalf of the Nawab (Forrest, *Clive*, II, p. 143.) In fact the *jagir* so called was the quit-rent, by which instead of paying their revenues to the Nawab, the Company was henceforth to make the payment to Clive who now held the (Company's) lands as his demesne.

172 *Ibid.*, p. 144.

The English Company was in great need of money during this time. Clive applied to the Seths for a loan on the Company's account. But the Seths replied that the "Government has made such large draft upon them lately, it is out of their power to comply with his request." So to redress the low state of the English treasury, Clive wrote to Hastings to demand the payment of two lakhs of rupees lent to the Nawab. Hastings replied that the "Nabob was incapable of paying any ready money" but had offered to satisfy the English by granting a new revenue on Burdwan and Krishnagar.[173]

Clive was now virtually the Nawab of Bengal and Hastings who acted under his advice, became a dictator to Mir Jafar. Mir Jafar, the nominal Nawab, was a miserable creature in the midst of political troubles. The Company's supporters subjected Mir Jafar to continual insults. The foreign policy of the Nawab also was now controlled by the Company. The treasury of the Nawab had nearly been exhausted. The maintenance of large bodies of useless troops aggravated his distress. Devoid of energy and a slave of habit, Mir Jafar proved himself incapable of remedying the situation. The conduct of his son also alarmed him because he sometimes thought that Miran's ambition might clash with that of the English. Clive, had on many occasions, warned the Nawab about the character of his son and the persons by whom the Prince was surrounded. On 21 September, Clive wrote a letter to Hastings giving his opinion on Miran: "Meer Juffier's days of folly are without number, and he had, long before this, slept with his ancestors, if the dread of our power and resentment had not been his only security. Sooner or later, I am persuaded, that worthless yount dog (Miran) will attempt his father's overthrow. How often have I advised the old fool (Mir Jafar) against putting too much power into the hands of his nearest relations. Tell him from me, that Rajah Bullub is an aspiring, ambitious villain; and, if he does not get him removed from his son's

---

173 Long, *Unpublished Records*, p. 462.

presence, he will push him to some violent and unnatural revolution."[174]

But the Nawab could not follow Clive's advice. He also could not reduce the troops of his son, nor cease to retain him in his station. Thus the power of Miran gradually increased and as a consequence the relation of Mir Jafar with the English became gradually strained. The government of Mir Jafar was a personal and autocratic government. The Nawab did not know the Company and felt no obligation to it; it was Clive to whom he expressed his gratitude. In view of this Mir Jafar was alarmed at the news of the near prospect of Clive's departure for England. The news also upset the first civil servants: Holwell, Amyatt, Sykes and Hastings. Hastings wrote a long letter to Clive and requested him to postpone his departure for the time being: "I own with great concern I learnt that your resolution is fixed to return this session to Europe.........yet, permit me sir, upon this occasion to lay before you such consequences as from my little experience of the *Durbar* affairs, I apprehend may attend your absence."[175]

Hastings believed that though Mir Jafar was attached to the English, the people around him, particularly the Seths, who were the great sufferers for the rise of the English power, would gladly use every possible means to alienate the Nawab's affections from the English. It was thus that he wrote to the Colonel: "At present, the personal obligations which he confessedly lies under to you are sufficient to intimidate them from any open attempts against us; but as your absence will encourage these people to throw off the mask and the Nabob is but of an irresolute and unsettled temper, I don't think it possible that he can hold out against the united influence of so many evil counsellors, as will be perpetually instilling into his mind the necessity of reducing

174 Clive's letter to Hastings, 21 September Malcolm, *Clive* II, pp. 103-140 f.n.).

175 Hastings' letter to Clive, 17 August (Macolm, *Clive*, II, pp. 106-107).

the English power."[176] Hastings also stated that there was nobody to succeed Clive "with the same influence". If Clive would depart for England, the French might attack Bengal: "If the French attempt anything against Bengal before your departure, I think I can answer for the Nabob's readiness to assist you against them; but that he will exert himself as zealously in our favour when you are gone, I greatly doubt."[177] Thus on the pressing request of Hastings, Clive postponed his voyage back to England, atleast for the time being. An added consideration was provided by the news of an impending invasion of the Dutch.

The fear of a possible Dutch attack had also been hanging fire for sometime. Soon after Clive's return to Calcutta from his expedition against the *Shahzadah* the news of this new danger had come. The earliest news about the Dutch expedition against Bengal reached Calcutta from Madras in the month of July. Herbert, the English Resident at Batavia, conveyed this news to Madras[178], but Clive at first refused to believe it, because earlier the Dutch had congratulated Clive for the downfall of Sirajuddaulah.[179] Still on 21 July, Clive sent a letter to Mir Jafar through Hastings. Hastings replied to Clive on the 25th about his discussion with the Nawab: "I waited on the Nabob last night with your letter and acquainted him with the Armament set on Foot at Batavia with your Advice to him on that Head. He replied that Cuttac (Cuttack) was not properly under his jurisdiction, but that he will take effectual care to guard the passes of Midnapoor (beyond which country his Authority did not extend) in case the Dutch should attempt to come by that Quarter; and that he would give orders to Ameerbeg to follow such Directions as he should receive from you in order to obstruct their Entrance by way of Ingallee."[180]

---

176 *Ibid.*, p. 107.

177 *Ibid.*, p. 109.

178 Dodwell, p. 168.

179 Malcolm, *Clive*, II, p. 69-70.

180 Hastings' letter to Clive, 25 July (Forrest, *Clive*, II, p. 146).

The Nawab told Hastings that the coming of the Dutch "was very probable", as they had applied to him sometime ago, for a *dastack* to bring a quantity of saltpetre from the *subah* of oudh, to replenish the deficiency of their investment at Patna, when Mir Jafar had refused them to pass through Bengal. But after this, the Dutch had obtained Shujauddaulah's consent for the establishment of a factory in oudh. They had sent the Nawab of Oudh a considerable *nazranah* in money, broad cloth and other commodities. From this conversation with Mir Jafar, Hastings could not understand exactly what the Dutch design was but it seemed to him that there was no passage through Shujauddaulah's territory except by the Ganges. "It can hardly be practicable for them to carry on any trade from there without opening a way thro' Bengal", observed Hastings in the same letter to Clive, "which has been positively denied them by the Nabob, unless they have thoughts of Effecting it by Force."[181]

On 4 August, Hastings informed Clive: "I told the Nabob of the News of the Armament sent from Batavia, he declared to me that he would send to the Dutch and acquaint them that if they brought any armed forces into his country he would look upon them as Enemies, and treat them accordingly."[182]

At last a single Dutch ship arrived in the Ganges on 21 August. On 2 October, Bisdom received news about the arrival of the rest of the ships at Piply.[183] On 3 October, the Calcutta Council received a letter from Madras stating that "the Dutch force of 500 Europeans and 1,000 Malays is evidently intended for Bengal." Soon after this seven Dutch ships appeared at the mouth of river Hugli. Mir Jafar was then at Calcutta on a visit to Clive. The English believed that the Nawab himself had invited the Dutch.

181 *Ibid.*, pp. 146-147.

182 Hastings' letter to Clive, 4 August (Forrest *Clive*, II, p. 147). Also, Malcolm, *Clive*, II, p. 90.

183 Dodwell, p. 168.

But on the news of their arrival, the Nawab declared that he would go at once to the down of Hugli and to "drive them out of the province."[184]

Mir Jafar arrived at Hugli but behaved with the Dutch officials most cordially. "How different his Real sentiments are from this Declaration", wrote Hastings to Clive on 12 November, that the first appointed interview of the Nawab with the Dutch was fixed on 11 November but deferred "for fear of disobliging them". In the evening of 12 November, the formal interview was held with great grandeur The persons who formed the procession consisted of Vernett, the Chief of the Dutch, with four of the members of his council, four officers, two *diwans* and the *vakil* preceded by one hundred soldiers, one hundred and eight sepoys and a number of *barkandases* and peons following in the rear. The Nawab, seated on a chair, received them very graciously while "Shibu Babu" stood behind him and acquainted the Nawab with the name of each who approached. They showed their respect to the Nawab, while the latter told them to "carry on their business" as in former days and promised his favour and protection. The Nawab then asked the Dutch officials to meet him at a secret session the next morning. So Hastings came to the conclusion that the Nawab was treacherous to the English and informed Clive: "Everyday's transactions confirm me more and more in the opinion that the Nabob is acting a treacherous part with you."[185]

Clive was not surprised by Hastings' letter'. He had also begun to suspect that the Nawab had invited the Dutch troops in Bengal as a counter-measure against the English supremacy in the *subah*. Clive made up his mind to take up "the strongest measures" and counteract the Nawab's evil designs against the English. Clive discovered another strong proof of Mir Jafar's errant behaviour in the effusive way in which

184 Forrest, *Clive*, II, p. 153.

185 Hastings' letter to Clive, 12 November (Forrest, *Clive*, II, p. 153).

he had recently treated Khwajah Wajid.[186] With a thorough knowledge of Mir Jafar's character, Clive addressed him a letter in such a style that the Nawab would be cowed down by its perusal. Hastings informed Clive about his conversation with the Nawab at Murshidabad. The Nawab seemed "extremely disturbed in mind" during the conversation He changed colours upon the receipt of Clive's letter and "declared himself innocent," of any deceitful intention against the English. Hastings informed Clive that the Nawab "offered to give every proof that you could require of his friendship and sincerity".[187]

A few days latter, Hastings informed Clive that the Nawab seemed "as zealous in the cause as he was before" for the interest of the English. He would not do "any further cuase for complaining, at least, in this affair " The Nawab desired Hastings to settle his misunderstanding with Clive, and the Resident now believed that the Nawab had become sincere after the receipt of the letter from Clive. Miran also wrote Hastings on the same subject and declared his earnestness to join Clive against the Dutch.[188] About the Nawab, Hastings wrote to Clive: "The firemness which have :shown, and your resentment of the Nabob's cold behaviour, you have had every effect that could be wished for." Hastings further informed in the same letter that the Nawab "really" wanted encouragement from Clive, because "whenever you forsake him, his ruin will be inevitable."[189]

The Dutch began to engage themselves in enlisting soldiers at Chinsurah, Kasimbazar and Patna. Having captured seven English ships, the Dutch tore down the English flag and burnt the houses of the Company's tenants at Falta and Raipur.[190] Apparently with strong displeasure the Nawab

---

186 Khwajah Wajid was employed by the Dutch at that time.

187 Hastings' letter to Clive, 18 November (Malcolm, *Clive*, II, pp. 92-93).

188 Malcolm, *Clive*, II, p. 93.

189 Hastings' letter to Clive, 21 November (*Ibid.*, p. 94).

190 Forrest, *Clive*, II, p. 155.

declared in the presence of Hastings, that he would immediately put a stop to their activities and send instructions to Ramnarain, to surround the Dutch factory at Patna and to molest them severely. In his eagerness to show his attachment to the English, the Nawab even issued *Parwanas* to Amir Beg Khan to put an entire stop to the Dutch trade at Hugli [191]

The information of the landing of the Dutch troops and their activities of creating terror within the *subah* prompted Clive to attack them and he directed Colonel Forde to march against them. Early in the morning of 25 November, fighting started on the plains of Bedara[192] and the Dutch were completely defeated. They made their submission before the English and prayed for terms for peace. A few of the Nawab's troops cooperated in this attack upon the Dutch, but Miran did not arrive at Hugli till the Dutch had been finally destroyed.[193] He advanced with a large army with full determination to destroy the Dutch at Chinsurah and to drive them out of the *subah*, "for breaking their engagement to his father" Hastings informed the Calcutta Council that the Dutch factory at Kalkapur had been surrounded by Miran's army, and the same thing would be done at Patna.[194] Miran then advanced to Ghareti, where the Dutch expressed a desire to settle matters and sought for the terms of peace.[195]

After the settlement with the Dutch, Clive wanted to proceed to England for the recovery of his health, but before he could proceed another danger erupted. The arrival of the Dutch armament in Bengal again stirred the *Shahzadah* to invade Bengal and he was joined by most of his allies.

---

191 Roy, A.C., *The Career of Mir Jafar Khan* (Calcutta, 1953, p. 189).

192 Midway between Chandernagore and Chinsurah.

193 Malcolm, *Clive*, II, p. 95. Even after their defeat at Bedara, the Dutch continued their intrigues against the Nawab. Thus Hastings instructed the Nawab to send Mir Qasim against them. In January 1760, Mir Qasim completely defeated the Dutch—Roy *Mir Jafar*, p. 195.

194. Letter to Court, 29 December (F.W.I.H.C., II, p. 462.

195 *Ibid.*, p. 463.

Soon after the treaty with the Dutch, Major Caillaud was appointed to command the English troops in Bengal and directed to proceed to Murshidabad with his force. After sometime Clive, accompanied by Forde, set out for Murshidabad to make arrangements to meet the fresh danger from the *Shahzadah*. But at Murshidabad there occurred a trouble between Mir Jafar and his ambitious son, Miran. On 26 December, Hastings informed Clive that the Nawab considered the demands of Miran "most unreasonable". "He (Miran) insists upon his taking the Field, to stay four years at Patna, to be allowed 12000 Horse with an immense Artillery etc to be regularly supplied with Money from the Revenues of Bengal for their maintenance, a proposal, the Nabob has positively refused to consent to. I fancy the Nabob is averse to an expedition to the Northward from no other reason than his son's obstinate resolution to have the command of it. If he could find means to get over that obstacle, I believe he would be glad to go himself, but this I fear he wants spirit to effect."[196]

Clive reached Murshidabad on 6 January, 1760, and introduced Caillaud to the Nawab. The Colonel overruled Mir Jafar's objections to the expedition, arranging that Miran should only accompany his troops under the command of Caillaud. On 18 January 1760, Caillaud began his march to Patna joined by Miran at the head of a large force. Thereafter Clive returned to Calcutta. Hastings wrote to Clive on 19 January : "It will not give you much surprise, after such repeated Instances of the Nabob's irresolute fickle Temper, to hear that the plan which the Nabob agreed upon with you for the operations of the campaign is entirelyover sett. Cassim allee Cawn remains behind, and the Chuta Nabob under pretence of having met with a lucky Minute exacted from his Father his consent that he should take the Field, which Advantage he made immediate Use of, & marched out to Saddoc baug, where he received his Dismission from the old Nabob the Day before yesterday."[197]

---

196 Hastings' letter to Clive, 26 December (Forrest, *Clive*, II, pp. 166-167).

197 Hastings' letter to Clive, 19 January (*Ibid.*, p. 167).

Evidently Clive did not feel perturbed after this intelligence.

On his return to Calcutta Clive began his preparation foi his voyage to England. Thus Hastings worte to Clive: "The Nabob asked me if I thought you could be persuaded to put off your design of returning to Europe; of which I gave him but little Hope."[198]

On 21 February, 1760, Clive sailed for England. About his dealing with Hastings, Forrest observes that Clive's "censure was at times conveyed in language too forcible, but he was liberal in praise when it was due."[199] Evidently such probation stood Hastings in good stead later on when he rose to the helm of affairs in India.

Yet when Clive returned to England, the whole political atmosphere of Bengal looked dark. The fear of political destabilisation loomed large. Hastings predicted the crisis and it came true in a startlingly quick manner. The *Shahzadah*, now donning the imperial title of Shah Alam II, was proclaimed as Emperor and was recognised by Ahmad shah Abdali. The Emperor with his forces soon advanced to attack Bihar, in league with the Nawab of oudh. Some Bengal *zamindars* and officers, whom Mir Jafar had insulted, joined them. Maratha raiders also entered into Bengal and prevented the collection of revenues. Almost every second Indian politician was supposed to be behind these invaders. Rai-Durlabh was suspected of inviting the Marathas; Nandkumar was supposed to be in league with Shah Alam. Yet the Murshidabad rulers seemed to be indifferent; the Nawab and Miran poured out money, as Hastings wrote, "on idle schemes of luxury". Caillaud reported that the Nawab's soldiers were starving. Bihar was half-lost and it was rumoured that Ramnarain might go over to Shah Alam and Shujauddaulah in self-defence. A year of war combined with the English merchants' illicit trade had drained the revenues of Bengal. The councillors whom Clive left in power were totally inefficient and incapable. Holwell—the

198 Eorrest, *Clive*, II, p. 168.

199 *Ibid.*

acting Governor, pending Vansittart's arrival, was narrow-minded and prejudiced.

The change from Clive to Holwell was painful to Hastings. In dealing with Clive, Hastings had to deal a master-mind, a man with a breadth of view, "who comprehended at a glance all the points of a case." Clive had given Hastings the largest power and did not interfere with the details of his action, "recognising always the soundness of the aims he put before himself." Both Clive and Hastings made it a cardinal point of their policy to make Mir Jafar the figure-head, until on his death, the whole management of the *subah* of Bengal would devolve on the English. But Holwell and his councillors were by nature incapable of following these ideas. Their only aim was "to use Mir Jafar as a golden sack into which they could dip their hands at pleasure."[200]

Holwell's temporary Governorship gave Mir Jafar an opportunity to raise his so far repressed objection to the English merchants' enjoying untaxed the internal trade of Bengal. Thus the Nawab issued a *parwana* to the council and not to the Governor prohibiting them to trade in salt and betel-nut. Holwell refused to reply to this as it seemed an irregular communication. But he wrote to Hastings asking "on what pretence we are prohibited trading in the two articles of salt and betel-nut?"[201] Hastings explanied the situation and replied to Holwell that the Nawab had issued this *parwana* to the council at the desire of Clive.[202] He reminded Holwell that when the Nawab had discussed this subject with Clive, to exclude the Company from trading in salt and betel-nut, Hastings had pleaded strongly against this arrangement. The reasons alleged in favour of the Nawab's claims, as Hastings wrote to Holwell, were "that these articles were farmed and

200 Malleson, *Hastings*, p. 42.

201 Holwell wrote to Hastings that "if he (the Nawab) pleases to address me on those subjects, I will reply to him" – Vansittart, *Narrative*, I, p. 12.

202 Clive, before his departure, went to Murshidabad to pay a courtesy call on Mir Jafar.

that the English were prohibited from trading in these articles before the Revolution." Hastings continued in his letter on a very critical note: "the same rule will lay the Company under the same restrictions in regard to grain, sugar and almost every branch of their trade." For the honour of the English nation, Hastings replied in regret as well as anger: "I think we hvae been at the expense of so much blood and treasure to little purpose if we are to be bound by precedents drawn from the abject state in wihch we remained before the battle of Plassey." About salt trade, Hastings concluded: "I believe we have for a long time past indirectly given up our rights to the salt trade by sending that up the country with the *Bux-bunder's rowanas*[203], which method had constantly been practised by such of the Company's servants as have had any concern in the trade......But the Company's servants (particularly the gentlemen at Dacca) have traded in betel-nut ever since the Revolution.........whether the Company's title to a free trade in salt ought to be insisted upon, as it has been long discusced, and as it will cause so great a loss to the *Buxbunder*'s revenues, I will not presume to determine."[204]

Quite evidently the allegations of the Nawab about free trade did not cut any ice with the Company. The passes for free-trade originally intended for the Company were extended to the Company's servants and the latter used them for their own internal private trade. Thus the English agents fattened the purses both of their masters and themselves. The European adventurers bought forged passes, hired agents who used the Company's uniforms and decorated their boats with the British flag. Thus it was of no wonder that Hastings saw "no boat without one (the British flag) between Calcutta and Patna."[205] Thus Mir Jafar's protests were ignored and by 1760 these passes were considered a right, instead of a favour.

---

203 Customs-Collectors' permits.

204 Hastings' letter to Holwell, 19 February (Dodwell, p. 237).

205 Spear, Percival, *Master of Bengal*: *Clive, and his India* (London 1975), p. 114.

Taking advantage of the political situation in Bengal and the news of Shah Alam's advance with Shujauddaulah; the Marathas under their leader Sheobhat made frequent incursions into Bengal from the early part of 1760. Already during the *Shahzadah*'s first invasion, Sheobhat had made an incursion into Cuttack early in April 1759. Behind this earlier Maratha incursion there did hang a tale. This invasion of Sheobhat was supposed to be at the Nawab's invitation. Hastings, on his part, had informed Clive about this. The Colonel, believing the report of the Nawab's invitation to be true, wrote a most severe letter to Mir Jafar and warned him that by doing so he would bring on his head the "curses of his subjects."[206] Hastings tried to find out the Nawab's secret connections with Sheobhat and sent a *vakil* to the Nawab. The Nawab informed the *vakil* that the coming of the Marathas was true, but he assured the *vakil* that there was no danger from them as they were coming to assist him. Hastings informed Clive about his talk with the Nawab on this affair: "This he repeated to me, when I waited on him at Rajmahal, and added that he had sent to forbid the proceedings (of the Marathas) having no longer occasion for their services."[207] After some days, the Nawab complained to Hastings about the treachery of Rai-Durlabh, who was alleged to have supplied Sheobhat with 25 lakhs of rupees.[208] A serious charge like this against Rai-Durlabh gave Hastings great surprise. He wrote to Clive that the Nawab's discourses were rather too contradictory to be believed. The Nawab first told the Resident that "Sheobhat was coming in consequence of his own invitation." Then he said that he had ordered the Maratha leader not to enter Bengal, evidently after the English had come to know about this move. Hastings thus stated that he could not understand why the Nawab tried to make a scape-goat of Rai-Durlabh: "much less

206 Scrafton's letter to Hastings, 21 April, 1759 (S.C.R., 2 May).

207 Hastings' letter to Clive, 27 April, 1759 (Roy, *Mir Jafar*, pp. 157-158).

208 S.C.R., 10 May, 1759.

could I conceive how Rai-Durlabh could have any hand in it." Hastings informed Clive in the same letter: "I was informed that Mirza Saleh had proposed to the Nabob to send for the Marathas, but whether he approved of the scheme or declined it, I was not told."[209] In another paragraph of the same letter, Hastings wrote, "the Nabob upon the receipt of fresh advices confirming the news of the Marathas' approach towards Cuttack, determined immediately to march back (from Rajmahal) to the city."[210] From the above correspondence, though there was no direct responsiblity of the Nawab for this Maratha expedition, there was reason to belive that the Nawab had tried to ensure Maratha help to ward off the fiirst invasion of *Shahzadah*, and that when the English came to know about it the Nawab pretended his usual innocence.

However, when Sheobhat threatened Bengal again there was hardly any move to arrest Sheobhat's advance till the beginning of January, 1760. The Maratha Chief, at the head of 3,000 horses and a small infantry, advanced as far as Midnapore and demanded *chauth*. The Nawab became restive and it was suggested to him that the army should be immediately dispatched to Burdwan. Accordingly Mir Jafar sent a force under the command of Mir Qasim, but the latter could not effectively stop the Maratha advance from Midnapore. The Nawab became fidgety and repeatedly requested the English for help as the invaders might advance up to Murshidabad. This anxiety of the Nawab regarding Sheobhat was regarded by Holwell as a false scare. He wrote to Hastings. "It is true he (Sheobhat) has possessed himself of Midnapore, but as yet there appears not the least foundation for his supposed advance to the city."[211] Holwell thought that in case Sheobhat tried to advance to Murshidabad, the English troops would join Mir Qasim and would also place Rai-Durlabh under

---

209 *Ibid.*

210 *Ibid.*

211 Holwell's letter to Hastings, 22 February, 1760 (Holwell, J.Z., *India, Tracts*, London, 1764 pp. 25-26).

arrest in order to stop the Maratha advance. Though Holwell did not believe in Rai-Durlabh's complicity in this case, he directed Caillaud "to keep a watchful eye over him. (Rai-Durlabh) at this juncture."[212]

Hastings informed Holwell that the Nawab had sent a *harkara* (courier) with a letter to Sheobhat and that the *harkara* had seen Rashbehari, Rai-Durlabh's brother, in the camp of Sheobhat. Holwell replied that no such *harkara* came to the camp of Sheobhat. Holwell himself had also received a news from Balasore regarding Rashbehari and of Rai-Durlabh's sending money to Sheobhat, but on the "strictest enquiry" Holwell did not find any truth in the report. Holwell knew that Rashbehari was "dangerously ill" and had never been out of Calcutta after November. Still, on 7 March Holwell brought Rashbehari before him and came to know the "falsity of the intelligence". Therefore, he wrote to Hastings, "let the Nabob judge of the rest, and let him be satisfied, that who will be with Subut, neither, Roy Doolub nor Rajaram shall have it in their power to injure him." The Nawab wrote to Holwell asking him "to put Roy Doolub in fetters." But Holwell could not inflict such a disgrace "without being guilty of a breach of the sacred laws of protection granted to him, unless a proved violation on his side justifies it". If there were sufficient grounds, only then Holwell would not only put Rai-Durlabh "in irons" but put him up directly to the Nawab. It had also been hinted to Holwell that a present of four lakhs of rupees was ready for him if he would deliver Rai-Durlabh before the Nawab. But Holwell informed Hastings that he "would not be guilty of such an action" even "for four crores of rupees."[213]

Holwell received a letter from Hastings on 11 March informing him about the intended march of the Nawab with his forces to Sakrigali, the pass where Shah Alam was to be checked. In reply to this, Holwell stated that he had kept 200 European troops under Captain Spear in readiness to join

212 Holwell, *Tracts*, p. 23.
213 Holwell's letter to Hastings, 8 March (Holwell, *Tracts*, pp

with the Nawab after his first call. But Holwell did not receive any news from Mir Jafar about Shah Alam's advance towards the passes. In the mean time, Mir Qasim Khan had converged his forces with Spear's at Burdwan. If Holwell got the demand of more troops from the Nawab, he informed Hastings, he would send Captain York wirh three to four thousand Europeans, field artillery and sepoys, directly to Khirpai. Holwell sought further news from Hastings.[214]

On 21 March, Holwell again informed Hastings that the monthly expenses of the expedition under Spear would not be less than Rs. 50,000. Therefore he advised Hastings to press the Nawab for money "as the state of our treasury is very low". Hastings should also insist on an immediate remittance, to enable the Governor to support the expedition; otherwise the Governor would be forced to recall his troops to garrison. Meanwhile, Watts had informed Holwell on 18 March that the Nawab had directed Mir Qasim to march against Sheobhat and to prevent his advance to Birbhum. So, Holwell informed Hastings that the Nawab's "irresolution and supineness, I much fear, would prove his destruction at last, in spite of our utmost endeavours to save him." Holwell also informed Hastings in the same letter that the former had come to know from a trusty person that Mir Jafar had agreed to surrender and apply to Shah Alam for mercy: "That on advices reaching him that the Morattors intended to enter the country by way of Patna, he has sent his son and the Major to oppose them; that it never was his intention to oppose His Majesty's arms, to whom he was an old professed slave; but by the evil counsels of Rajahram Narain, his son Mhiran and the Major, had acted contrary to his intentions and orders; and that if the Prince desired it, he was ready to surrender himself to his pleasure." But enclosing this petition of Mir Jafar to Shah Alam, Holwell remarked that if these were the tricks of the Nawab, "it is time we should look to the Company and ourselves."[215]

214 *Ibid.*, 15 March, pp. 31-32.

215 *Ibid.*, 21 March, pp. 32-33.

An English army under the command of Macklean began to march from Cuttack on 23 March towards Midnapore. Caillaud and Spear's troops had meanwhile, exhausted the military stores and there were difficulties in the despatch of reinforcement under Captain Fischer. Holwell had received a news from Spear that Shah Alam was within two or three day's march of the Nawab's army. So Holwell informed Hastings that he had given positive orders to Fischer to rush at full speed to join Spear, "with the utmost expedition."[216]

In reply to Holwell's letter, Hastings wrote in favour of Mir Jafar. He stated that the Nawab was innocent in the matter of his alleged correspondence with Shah Alam and that the Nawab's *munshi* had declared that the letter had been forged.[217] But this argument of Hastings, did not appear convincing to Holwell. Holwell had managed to get this letter of Mir Jafar from Shah Alam. And as the *munshi* was aware of it, and, before he "gave it a perusal", was "well prepared against a surprise," and thus pronounced it a forgery. The letter "contained the very dictates of the heart" of the Nawab but, according to Holwell, "for want of more sufficient proof", the English should not proceed further about the letter."[218]

Hastings again pleaded in favour of the Nawab by informing Holwell that the Nawab was in great expense for "our troops in his pay". But Holwell was convinced that if the English troops, who constantly attended the Nawab, were reduced, the action would lay the foundation of Nawab's independence. Holwell wrote to the Nawab on 22 April, about the payment to the English troops and the "necessity for his disbanding his rabble of *Burcundasses*, and the greatest part of his useless cavalry."[219]

During the month of May, Holwell repeatedly pressed Hastings for money for the very "low ebb of the Company's

216 *Ibid.*, 1 April, pp. 38-39.

217 Holwell, *Tracts*, p. 50.

218 Holwell's letter to Hastings, 20 April (Holwell, *Tracts*, pp. 50-51).

219 *Ibid.*, 25 April, pp. 53-54.

treasury'". The financial stringency had brought all investments at the *arungs* completely at a stand. But the Company did not receive "a Rupee" for the expenses of the troops under the command of Spears and Fischer. Therefore, Holwell pressed Hastings for obtaining from the Nawab "at least one lack of rupees on this account." After having repeatedly experienced the Nawab's running into arrears, the English adopted a "very worst system of politics", a kind of political blackmail, "by insisting on an advance before our troops leave the garrison." Holwell stated that the Company would suffer great distress in furure "without this precaution". Holwell further demanded from Hastings the re-payment of two lakhs of rupees from the Nawab "in the most urgent terms," but if the Nawab could not advance that amount, "a fresh *Tunka* on the Kistnagur country must absolutely be insisted on". Holwell "had the greatest reason to complain "about the Nawab's behaviour, in obstructing the collection of revenues in Burdwan and Krishnagar districts, and if the Nawab did not immediately order his people to withdraw from those districts, "I will, without any ceremony, drive them out''. In the same letter to Hastings, Holwell informed him that when Holwell had applied to the Seths for a loan of ten or fifteen lakhs of rupees, they had refused to lend under various pretences. "However, I doubt not" wrote Holwell, "but an occasion may offer, for manifesting a proper resentment to that house for this refusal."[220]

But Holwell's above complaints about the collection of revenues from Burdwan and Nadia were all false. Two years earlier, Scrafton, the then Resident, had already stated, how the English had collected money from these districts with severity and also collected much more than the government.[221] As a matter of fact the English regularly collected very large amounts from the districts of Burdwan, Nadia and Hugli and often resorted to excesses, so much so that the Nawab became anxious for the deteriorating condition of these districts. Thus.

220 *Ibid.*, 6 May, pp. 56-58.

221 B.M.P., III, p. 36.

in the beginning of the summer of 1760, the Nawab wanted the restoration of the revenues of thesc districts to him. He offered a security of jewels in lieu of them, to discharge the balance of 20 lakhs of rupees.[222] The English had to agree to his proposal.

Holwell's letters to Hastings were a clear proof of his prejudice against the Nawab. In the month of May, the acting Governor concocted a violent scheme. As he posed: had not Mir Jafar betrayed the cause of the English to the Dutch? had he not been bargaining with Shah Alam behind the back of the English ? So what he proposed was a virtual annexation of the *subah* by getting rid of Mir Jafar. Though still a subordinate with no voice in policy, Hastings did not support the scheme of Holwell. He was still in two minds. In June, Hastings wrote to Caillaud, "Let the Nabob be ever so bad, we are bound if not in justice, in honour and policy to support him through these troubles....Neither his tyranny nor rapaciousness are to be vindicated, tho' I cannot think him in his nature cruel, but where are we to meet with a better man?" He refused to believe that Shah Alam had any plan of conquest. At the most his was an expedition of plunder. In the same letter, Hastings continued, "but should the Nabob's behaviour ever drive us to such fatal extremities, as we have the means in our hands, why should we not take possession of the government for ourselves?"[223]

But in the month of June, Holwell informed Hastings about one of the allegedly barbarous acts of Mir Jafar. He wrote to Hastings that the Nawab had cruelly eliminated the Begams of Alivardi's family. He had sent a *jamadar* with one hundred horse with order to Jessarat Khan to murder the Begams. But when Jessarat Khan refused to act, the Nawab directed the messenger to carry out his order. The person carried the ladies out at night in a boat about two miles above Dacca, "tied weights to their legs and threw them over board." The ladies struggled hard for their lives but they were pounded

224 Vansittart's *Narrative*, I, p. 37.

223 Feiling, *Hastings*, pp. 34-35.

on their heads with *lathies* after which they had their watery graves.[224] Holwell concluded that these were the acts of the monstrous Nawab whom the English "are supporting and fighting for.[225]

Hasting's impression about Mir Jafar also underwent a change when he heard about the above dastardly crim.[226] An entire catalogue of murders committed at Mir Jafar's behest was in the air. If it was true, Hastings informed Holwell, nothing could excuse our supporting such a tyrant. He wrote to Caillaud, "God forgive me for attempting to vindicate him from the charges of cruelty and barbarity."[227] Meanwhile news reached Murshidabad in the first week of July of the death of Miran on 3 July by a lightning. Probably, as many believed, the English had done away with him, as Miran was resentful of the increasing influence and power of the English in the Nawab's *darbar*. Hastings immediately wrote two letters on 12 July about the death of Miran, one to Holwell and another to the Select Committee. In reply to his letter, Holwell wrote to Hastings that "the sudden death of the young Nabob is very striking". If Rajballabh would meet with a similar fate, he added, "the country would have had a double benefit."[228]

Miran's death immediately brought the serious question of succession before the Nawab. But the Prince's death was a

224 The members of Alivardi's family who were drowned in the river included Ghasiti Begam, Amina Begam, Murad-ud-Daulah, Lutfun-nisa Begam, an infant daughter of Sirajuddaulah and about seventy women of inferior status. What happened to the widow of Alivardi was uncertain, as it was reported that she escaped the fate of the rest of her family—Vansittart, H., *Original Papers Relative to the Disturbances in Bengal*. Vol. I (Lond., 1765), pp. 62-63.

225 Holwell's letter to Hastings, 13 June (Holwell, *Tracts*, p. 60).

226 It was rumoured at Murshidabad that the ladies of Alivardi's family were murdered at the instruction of Mir Jafar. There were some investigations. The final outcome, however, did not assjgn with certainty Mir of Jafar's hand in the murder. Malleson,*Hastings*, p. 43, f.n.

227 Feiling, *Hastings*, p. 36.

228 Holwell, *Tracts*, pp. 86-87. Also, Mukhopadhyay, S.C., *Diwani in Bengal*, 1765 (Varanasi, 1980), p. 5.

great relief to the English. To use the language of Clive, Miran was so unworthy "as to make it most unsafe trusting him with the succession.[229] Whatever might have been the motive of the English on the question. it became evident that Mir Jafar could not remain a silent spectator. The Nawab wrote to Holwell in July, wishing Miran's son to succeed him.[230] But Holwell was in favour of Mir Qasim. So the Nawab wrote a letter to Holwell, which the latter received on 10 July: "The letter you wrote me concerning Meer Mahomed Cossim Allee Cawn, I have received. You acquaint me, he is a noble, good and brave man. Mr. Hastings has also spoken me to the same purpose and has desired me, to let him succeed my son. This rejoiced me much, because I was sensible he is highly deserving of my favour and friendship. I have no friends dearer to me then himself and family, and should be very glad, if it was in my power to give it him; but the Colonel has wrote me a letter[231], a copy whereof I have enclosed for your perusal, and you will then be able to judge, what motive has induced me to prefer the Chuta Nabob's son."[232]

The death of Miran came as a great shock to Mir Jafar. For a few weeks together he could not attend the *darbar* to transact business and as a result disorder and confusion prevailed in the state administration. Some repacious councillors took this opportunity to amass wealth through extortion, sensing that the government would not last long. Confusion became worse confounded due to a military uprising at Murshidabad. The Nawab was not in a position to pay off the arrears of salary to his troops at Patna, nor was he able to pay a large number of indisciplined soldiers in his palace,

229 Malleson, *Hasting*, p. 44.

230 C.P.C. I, p. 18 No. 277.

231 This was a letter from Caillaud recommending the succession of the infant grandson of Mir Jafar, under the guardianship of Rajballabh.

232 Mir Jafar's letter to Holwell, Rd. 10 July (Vansittart, *Narrative*, I, p. 32).

who refused to be further satisfied with empty promises and demanded immediate payment of their salary. Hastings informed about this chaotic situation at Murshidabad to the Select Committee at Calcutta. On 14 and 15 July, the troops surrounded the palace, insulted the treasurer and other officers, "whom they pulled out of their *pallanquins*, and treated with other indignities." On 16, they assembled in a large body, closed the doors of the palace and allowed none to enter. As their number began to increase, they used abusive languages to the Nawab, "threatening him with death", if their demands were not fulfilled. This scene lasted for two days, when Mir Qasim Khan intervened and put a stop to the soldiers' recalcitrance. the Nawab promised to pay the full arrears, for which Mir Qasim became the security. Mir Qasim paid to the soldiers, from his own treasury, three lakhs of rupees. This satisfied the soldiers, who retired from the palace for the time being. But Hastings still had great doubt that the danger was over. Asad Zama Khan, the Rajah of Birbhum, was waiting with a considerable force. "and tho' no open Hostilities have been committed by him," observed Hastings, "it is no longer doubted, but his design is to revolt from the present government."[233] After this incident, Hastings thought about going to Calcutta for transacting some important business and accordingly informed the Select Committee in his letter of 25 July.[234]

The new Governor Vansittart arrived from Madras replacing Holwell, and on Holwell's representation of a Memorial, Vansittart shared the same view as put forward before him by the outgoing Governor.[235] Vansittart noticed the unsettled condition of Bengal and seriously thought in terms of a change. After the death of Miran, Hastings also felt the necessity to clean the augean stables, an important part of which was to

233 Hastings' letter to the Select Committee, 18 July (S.C.R., 28 July, p. 60). Also, Vansittart, *Narrative*, I, pp. 30-31.

234 Hastings' letter to the Select Committee, 25 July (Hill, *Abstract*, p. 65).

235 *Original Papers*, pp. 8-18.

throw out Mir Jafar. In the overthrow of Mir Jafar and installation of Mir Qasim, the Resident played an important role. Though Hastings did not initiate this movement, he fully approved of it. He believed that this change would be beneficial for the *subah* of Bengal as well as the Company. Vansittart was also convinced of Mir Qasim's ability to tide over the situation. After his arrival, the Governor wrote to Mir Qasim about his "good character" as he had come to know from Holwell and Hastings.[236]

At this period, Holwell received letters from Mir Qasim in which requests were made for English help to Mir Qasim for the latter's succession to the *diwani*. Holwell duly communicated these letters to the Governor. The matter was fully debated in the Committee.[237] Vansittart narrated his view about the condition of Bengal under the rule of Mir Jafar. It was stated that under Mir Jafar the soldiers had become unruly and had surrounded the palace more than once. Owing to the weakness of the government and the general dissatisfaction of the people, the *zamindars* were withholding their revenues. The Nawab had so little time and capacity for attending to business, that what little was collected in the treasury, was appropriated by his favourites for their own profit. 'The Nawab, thro' an habitual indolence, was quite incapable of managing his government in such critical circumstances." As there was no legitimate successor after the death of Miran, Vansittart declared that "the whole province seemed to turn their eyes on Meer Cossim.........esteemed a capable man in business."[238]

Thus the Select Committee decided to obtain permission from Mir Jafar to get Mir Qaism at Calcutta apparently to be introduced to the new Governor. The Governor provided a

---

236 Vansittart's letter to Mir Qasim, 8 August C.P.C., I, p. 20, No. 307).

237 As Caillaud was in favour of the infant son of Miran under the guardianship of Rajballabh, this debate became inevitable – Holwell, *Tracts*, pp. 88-80.

238 Vansittart, *Narrative*, I, pp. 13-16.

good incentive for Mir Qasims' visit by informing the Nawab that there should be consultations regarding the next campaign against Shah Alam, as well as regarding the accounts of money. Thus, Mir Jafar was duped. Yet he much reluctantly permitted Mir Qasim to go to Calcutta for transacting all the above state business. Mir Qasim arrived at Calcutta on 20 September,[239] and the scheme was that he should be declared as the successor of Mir Jafar and that he should enjoy the same power that was lately enjoyed by Miran. The ball would be set rolling immediately after the Calcutta deliberations.

Mir Qasim, a man of great shrewdness and abilitiy, after his arrival at Calcutta, read the characters of the English officials "as an open book". He realised immediately that they were thirsting for money. So he persuaded them not only to facilitate his succession but to make him the *de facto* ruler. Accordingly, on 27 September, Mir Qasim entered into a secret treaty with the Special Committee of the executives of the Calcutta Council, by which it was decided to bestow to the Company the districts of Burdwan, Midnapore and Chittagong.[240] Besides, there were other conditions not committed in paper, but it was decided that as soon as Mir Qasim would seat on the *mansad*, he would lavishly pay Vansittart, Holwell, Sumner, MacGuire, Caillaud Culling Smith and Captain York.[241]

With the mission of persuading the old Nawab, Vansittart and Caillaud proceeded from Calcutta with 200 Europeans and a battalion of sepoys. Hastings met the governor's party at Chinsurah on 4 October. Travelling by easy stages, the troops reached Kasimbazar on 14 October when Hastings was immediately sent to persuade the Nawab to meet Vansittart

---

239 Holwell, *Tracts*, p. 89.

240 *Original Papers*, pp. 38-39.

241 Malleson, *Hastings*, pp. 45-46. In this transaction there is no proof that Hastings received money from Mir Qasim. But one modern writer has expressed doubt that as Vansittart's ally and the Company's Resident at Murshidabad, Hastings must have received presents—Marshall, P.J., *East India Fortunes* (Oxford, 1976), pp.169-170.

the next morning.[242] Accordingly the Nawab met the governor on 15 October and the English paid their return visit on the 16th. But these two days were passed "only in general conversation". On 18, the Nawab came to Moradbagh to talk on business. There the English officials prepared three letters addressed to the Nawab, informing him about their mission. The Nawab seemed much affected by the perusal of the letters and tried to put an end of the conference. But the English prevailed on him to be present at a dinner at Moradbagh and continuously prodded him for his reply. The Nawab confessed his inability to struggle against so many difficulties but desired time to consult with his friends. The Nawab then shut himself up in the palace. Almost immediately Caillaud launched an action with his troops, in company with Mir Qasim, and entered into the courtyard of the palace. The Colonel then sent the governor's letter to the Nawab for reply, but the Nawab tried to resist. Meanwhile, Hastings and Lushington passed on several messages to the Nawab. But still the affairs remained in a state of suspense for two hours, when at last the old Nawab's resistance totally collapsed. He sent a message to Mir Qasim that he was ready to seed his seal and "all the ensigns of dignity," provided Mir Qasim took the whole change of the government. Mir Qasim was further requested to save his life and honour, and to give him an allowance sufficient for the maintenance of the old Nawab. When Mir Qasim agreed to all these conditions, he was proclaimed as the Nawab of Bengal. After this, the old Nawab did not want to remain at Murshidabad "even for one night" and submitted to that end before the Colonel. The old Nawab, furnished with a strong escort of Europeans, went to Calcutta to live under English protection.[243]

After the deposition of Mir Jafar, Hastings did not attend the *darbar* of Mir Qasim as the Resident of the

242 Feiling, *Hastings*, p. 37.

243 Vansittart and Caillaud's letter to the Select Committee, 21 October (Vansittart, *Narrative*, I, pp. 50-54). Also, Lushington's letter to Clive, 3 December, 1760 (Malcolm, *Clive*, II, pp. 267-268, f,n.).

Company. In his letter to Vansittart, Mir Qasim lavished praises on Hastings and requested the Governor to send him to his *darbar*.[244] In another letter which the Nawab wrote in January, 1761, he again requested the governor to send Hastings to him. In the same letter, Mir Qasim agreed with Vansittart, about the necessity of suppressing the Rajah of Birbhum, for which, he had sent five hundred horses and five hundred soldiers to Birbhum.[245]

Hastings continued officially as the Resident at the *darbar* till February, 1761[246] though he did not actually attend on the Nawab in that capacity. In February, 1761 Hastings was appointed to act as the Governor's assistant and in August of the same year, he became one of the members of the Calcutta Council.[247]

244 Mir Qasim's letter to the Governor, 12 December C.P.C.,I., p. 42, No. 688).

245 *Ibid.*, 7 January, 1761, p. 48, No. 774.

246 Beveridge, *Hastings in Lower Bengal*, p. 211.

247 Feilling, *Hastings*, p. 39. Sumner, Playdell and MacGuire were succeeded by Cartier, Johnstone, Hay and Hastings. Soon Cartier, Johnstone and Hay began to oppose the policy of Mir Qasim and so forçed the latter for revolt – Malleson, *Hastings*, p. 49.

5

THE NON-RESIDENCY INTERREGNUM: THE RISE AND FALL OF MIR QASIM

By a letter from the Company to the Court of Directors on 16 January, 1761, Warren Hastings services as the Resident at the *darbar* of Murshidabad were terminated from the month of February. This was done mainly because of the pressure from the Governor who wanted Hastings' assistance "in carrying on the continual correspondence" at Calcutta. Hastings was, therefore, appointed a member of the executive council at Calcutta and the business of the *darbar* was entrusted to the Chief of the Kasimbazar factory "without taking up too much of his time."[1] Therefore, no man was appointed at Murshidabad with the Resident's separate powers and functions.

Mir Qasim was unlike Mir Jafar, inasmuch as he tried to infuse an efficient administration and thereby established the independence and dignity of the Nawab. Very soon, after his accession, he made the irksome realisation that the battle of plassey had bound the Nawab, hand and foot, to the English alliance. This alliance also meant the transference to Calcutta of the nerve-centre of power and authority over Bengal. As a matter of fact every transaction after Plassey strengthened the

1 Letter to Court, 16 January, 1761 (F.W.I.H.C., III, p. 304).

predominance of the English. Mir Jafar, as already seen, was reduced to a simple tool in the hands of the English and the circumstance of every successive occasion forced him to be more submissive. This pitiable position of the Nawab of Bengal was totally unbearable to an ambitious and aggressive man like Mir Qasim. His soul revolted against this beggarly existence.[2]

The little care that the English had for the Nawab was reflected in their rampant illicit inland trade in Bengal. Somewhat checked during the time of Clive, after the latter's departure it began to be carried on in the most extensive and nonchalant manner owing to the weakness of his successors. "Men set no limits to their efforts to enrich themselves." The privileges of the Company's trade thus, not only covered their private enterprises under the Company's name but even their servants and dependents claimed an exemption from internal duties on the same plea. As a result, the Nawab's revenue was adversely affected and his authority insulted.[3] Mir Qasim realised that only if the Nawab and his officials possessed full unrestricted powers, any abuse of this privilege could be easily checked.

Vansittart—the Governor, lacked the qualities of Clive. In his council, all the members except Hastings, were against him. So they opposed him almost on all issues and as the Governor was the upholder of the power of the Nawab, they opposed every move of the Nawab also. Ellis—the Chief of the English factory at Patna, and Batson at Dacca, aligned themselves with the interests of this faction of Vansittart's Council. Whenever the Nawab's offiicials interfered with their illicit internal trade, these two English officers used their forces, seized the Nawab's officials and made them prisoners with the intention of getting them punished by the council of Calcutta. This gave them an opportunity to throw the blame directly upon the Nawab and indirectly upon Vansittart.[4]

---

2 Malleson, *Decisive Battles*, p. 128.

3 Gleig's *Clive*, p. 186.

4 *Seir*, II, pp. 445-446.

Mir Qasim was bent on establishing his independence—an object neither surprising nor reprehensible. To free himself from the clutches of the English at the first step, the Nawab transferred his capital from Murshidabad to Mungher. Mir Turab Ali Khan—the uncle of the Nawab, was appointed the deputy-*nazim* at Murshidabad, while the Nawab carried with him "all his effects, requisites, elephants, horses and treasury" to Mungher.[5] The fortifications of the fort of Mungher were strengthened, and then the Nawab marched on to Patna to meet Emperor Shah Alam II. To his great satisfaction, the Nawab found that his interest was not injured by Carnac—the English commandar, in league with the Emperor, as was suspected. Mir Qasim then strengthened the administration of Bhiar by taking into his own hands its direct administration.[6]

Vansittart's Council was a sharply divided body; as already pointed out, a majority of the members were opposed to him. Similarly, they did not like the growing independence of the Nawab on the one hand, and, on the other, they refused to tolerate any encroachment upon their ill-gotten gains from the Nawab's officials. So, within two months of Mir Qasim's accession to the *masnad*, the members began vehemently to oppose the new Nawab's government. Amyatt, one of the members of Vansittart's Council, entered a minute on the proceeding of the Select Committee on 8 January 1761, expressing strong resentment against the elevation of Mir Qasim and entirely disapproving the dethronement of Mir Jafar.[7]

In November 1761 Hastings was deputed to settle matters with Mir Qasim as the council had reason to believe "that some busy persons had been attempting to foment jealousies bet-

---

5. *Riyaz*, p. 385.
6. During this time, Rajah Ramnarain was dismissed from the post of deputy-Governor of Bihar. He was imprisoned afterwards.
7. Firminger, *Fifth Report*, p. 125.

ween them and the Nabob."[8] Colonel Coote, the English commander, also suspected jealousy on the part of the Nawab and requested the Calcutta Council to send Hastings for a satisfactory rapprochement with the Nawab; the fact that lay behind Hastings' choice was that he enjoyed the confidence of both the Colonel and the Nawab.[9] Hastings was thus directed to meet the Nawab at Mungher. But before Hastings could actually start, a cold war had already developed between the Nawab and Ellis—the English Chief at Patna, that complicated the matters more seriously.

Ellis brought certain complaints before the Nawab about the ill—behaviour of the Nawab's officials at Purnea. But, the Nawab on the other hand received reports from Mir Sher Ali Khan, the *naib* of Purnea, about the acts of oppressions committed by George Gray, the Chief of the English factory at Malda, who had seized and imprisoned the *peshkar* of Hiraman—the *zamindar* of Tajpur. The said Malda Chief had also sent sepoys and Europeans for purchasing grain as well as had erected new factories everywhere in Purnea. Mir Qasim informed Ellis about all these acts of floating of authority and oppressions, enclosing also a copy of the letter written by Sher Ali to Gray. But Ellis informed the Nawab that he had repeatedly represented before the Nawab the complaints which had been made to Ellis against the *zamindars* of Purnea. The English Chief of Patna further complained that the insolence of the *zamindars* and the Nawab's officers exceeded all bounds, resulting in the stoppage and ruin of the Company's business everywhere. Hence, as Ellis informed the Nawab, a person in the district of Mungher, for his seizing some salt-petre belonging to the Company, had been imprisoned by him and had been sent to Calcutta for trial.[10] Ellis also claimed that the Company's officials had the liberty of

8. Auber, Peter, *Rise and Progress of the British Power in India* Vol. I (London, 1837), p. 84.
9. Long, *Unpublished Records*, p. 370.
10. Ellis's answer to Mir Qasim, 4 January, 1762 (*Original Papers*, I, pp. 137-138).

trading everywhere in Bengal, and accordingly, he desired from the Nawab, a *parwana* upon Sher Ali "to forbid his officers to stop any goods of the *Gomastahs* in Purnea."[11]

When the Nawab heard that the man in question was an official collector of the Nawab, who had been carried off from Mungher, he became greatly enraged. He immediately wrote to Ellis that if that person had committed any fault, it would have been proper to inform the Nawab about it. "Since my servants are subjected to such insults, my writing can be of no use," observed the Nawab in his letter to Ellis. The Nawab felt that these types of harassment and aggression on the part of the English would seriously undermine the weight and authority of his government.[12]

An incident occurred at this time that inflamed the passions of the Nawab against Ellis still more. Ellis sent some forces to Mungher fort on the presumption that some English deserters had taken shelter in it. On the news of the arrival of the force from Patna, the *naib* of Mungher fastened all the gates of the fort and did not allow the English soldiers to search the fort. Thus, the Nawab observed in his letter to the Governer: "I am ignorant what provocation has induced that gentleman to send sepoys to attack the Fort of Mongher." The Nawab pointedly referred to the "sacred obligations" of the treaty, which the English seemed to be bent upon violating. "Why you, gentlemen, in defiance of the treaty. should thus commit hostilities against my forts, and my servants?", the Nawab asked the Governor in a bitter mood. The Nawab also informed the Governor that he had taken measures for his defence and had "stationed men in the Forts."[13]

In reply to this letter, the Governor informed the Nawab, that before sending the force to Mungher, Ellis applied to Rajah Raj ballabh—the *naib* of Patna, and obtained a letter from him to Shujan Singh—the *kelladar* of Mungher, for undertaking such action. But the *kelladar* did not allow the

11. *Original Papers*, I, p. 138.
12. *Ibid.*, pp. 138-139.
13. Nawab's letter to the Governor, Consultation, 22 Februray (*Original Papers*, I, pp. 147-148).

English sergeant to enter into the fort for the search for the deserters. Moreover the *Kelladar* had quarreled with the English "for a trifling affair." Hence, the Governor wished the Nawab to issue a *parwana* to the saide *Kelladar* directing him to allow the English to search for the deserted soldiers and that the *kelladar* should be punished, in case such soldiers were found in the fort."[14]

Mir Qasim could not swallow such intolerable arrogance and in a rage he wrote to the Governor: "Whatever you write is proper; yet from my first accession to the government, I have perceived that many English gentlemen were ill-affected to me, and that the country was not in my own hands." Then the Nawab narrated the behaviour of the English officials: "From the factory of Calcutta to Cossimbuzar, Patna and Dacca, all the English Chiefs and their *gomastahs*, officers and agents in every district of the Government act as collectors, renters, *zemindars*, and *taalucdars*, and setting up the Company's colours allow no power to my officers. And besides this, the *gomastahs* and other servants in every district, in every *gunge*, *pergunna* and village, carry on a trade in oil, fish, straw, bamboos, rice, paddy, betelnut and other things; and every man, with the Company's *dustuck* in his hand, regards himself as not less than the Company." Still the Nawab believed and had assured himself that the Governor would not listen to what slanderers might inform him about the Nawab's proceedings. He further thought that whenever he would write to the Governor about "the oppression of the *gomastahs*," the Governor would punish them. But now from the letters which the Nawab received form the Governor, it became evident that whatever the Nawab wrote was considered unfounded and unreliable at the Governor's end, and whatever the English gentlemen wrote was accepted as gospel truth. So the Nawab declared in the same letter: "Mr. Ellis commits open acts of hostility against me, raises calumnies against me, corresponds with my enemies, and instead of a single letter sends two hundred sepoys; and all that he has written to you is utterly false."

14. *Original Papers*, I, p. 151.

The Nawab further assured the Governor that he had made a strict enquiry and come to know "that there is not an English deserter in the Fort of Mungheer." The Nawab wrote to the Governor "to send some persons from Calcutta" for enquiry and to bring the slanderer to shame. The Nawab strongly resisted and asserted that he would "upon no account permit the fort to be searched."[15]

This mutual jealousy and rivalry between the Nawab and the English was quickly rising to the boiling point and, as things stood, might bring at any time, an open hostility. Vansittart, the Governor, judged it prudent to remove this misunderstanding in good time before there was any serious crisis. The most effectual remedy, the Governor judged, would be to send a person in whom the Nawab had confidence. This mission would assure the Nawab that his suspicions of the English were groundless, give him the salutary advice to forget what had passed between him and Ellis and, finally try to bring about a reconciliation with the Nawab. With these views, Vansittart proposed before the council to implement the long-awaited mission of Hastings on a deputation to the Nawab.[16] The council agreed to this proposal of the Governor and they briefed Hastings about his conduct at the *darbar* of the Nawab: "We wish for nothing more, than to preserve the present tranquillity of the country, to avoid all disputes, and to conform to the terms of the treaty subsisting between him and the Company. We think proper to depute you, in whom the Nabob has great confidence, to make him those assurances on our behalf." Hastings was told that there were persons creating misunderstanding and distrust on both sides and so the Nawab might be assured that the English would severely punish such persons as were under their authority. Similarly the Nawab should also do the same on his part. Then the council

15. Nawab's letter to the Governor, 26 March (*Original Papers*, I, pp. 151-153).

16. Vansittart, *Narrative*, I, pp. 156-157.

instructed Hastings, on 15 March 1762 to proceed without any further delay.[17]

But Hastings could not proceed immediately. On the next council day Amyatt brought in a motion that an additional instruction should be added to Hastings' brief, which was "to endeavor to recover the promised twenty lakhs of rupees" from Mir Qasim, but the money "instead of being distributed amongst the members of the Board", that was assented to by Mir Qasim at the time of his accession, "should be brought to the credit of the Company". To this motion of Amyatt, Johnstone and Hay lent their hearty support.[18] But Vansittart refused to concur.[19] Nevertheless, it was agreed to by the majority of the members and was accordingly added to the instructions of Hastings: "And we further direct you, to apply to the Nabob for the twenty lacks of rupees, the amount of the bond he gave at the time the treaty was made with him, to the members of the Select Committee then present in Calcutta; to which sum, notwithstanding they returned the bond, we conceive the Company have a title. You will therefore use your best endeavors to recover the same as soon as possible, as the tranquillity of the country, by the success of our arms, has undoubtedly enabled him to discharge the above obligation."[20]

Hastings set out on his mission from Calcutta on 9 April. and reached Patna on 2 May, with a view to meeting Ellis at first, and ascertaining from him the cause of his conflict with the Nawab. But Ellis was in his country-house, some fifteen miles away from the English factory. Hastings awaited him for five days at Patna but being disappointed, proceeded to Sarseram, where the Nawab then encamped. Hastings delivered to him the substance of the commission. The Nawab listened to the suggestions of Hastings and then pointed it out to the

17. Copy of the Governor and Council's intstructions to Hastings, 15 March, 1762 (Vansittart, *Narrative*, I, p. 157).

18. Vansittart, *Narrative*, I, pp. 157-158.

19. Auber, *Rise*, I, p. 84.

20. Vansittart, *Narrative*, I, p. 163.

latter that it was Ellis who was creating misunderstanding between him and the English.[21] But the Nawab refused to pay twenty lakhs of rupees, and afterwards, he gave Hastings a reply in writing: "That you gentlemen, should unreasonably demand twenty lacks of me, surprises me greatly. This is a behaviour unbecoming men of dignity, in whom it is doubtless improper, after having refused a thing, to repent of it, and demand of it in the name of their masters. It is true, I formerly offered to give such a sum to Mr. Vansittart, and some other gentlemen; but they positively refused to accept it." About the feasibility of such a demand of the English, the Nawab raised the question of difficulty and observed: "Now most of the gentlemen, to whom I made this offer, have left the country; and as to the one or two who still remain here, I do not think that they will demand it of me." About the mischievous men, creating misunderstanding between him and the English, the Nawab declared that there were none with him who dared to speak against the Company, but on the side of the Company, there was at least one, who spoke ill against the Nawab: "The acts of violence committed by Mr. Ellis before my face; the insults on my people, and the disturbances raised in the country; my authority rendered contemptible to all Indostan; and the obstructions thrown in the way of every business of the government, in the province of Bihar. All these have I fully represented in my letters to Mr. Vansittart from the beginning till now, nor shall I dwell on such a subject afresh; because I am well persuaded, that Mr. Vansittart and the gentlemen of the council will make a strict enquiry into this affair."[22]

Hastings himself noticed that the condition of the *subah* of Bengal had deteriorated much owing to the oppressions committed by the English *gomastahs* and their agents; most preposterously every *gomastah* had become a judge and everyone's house, a *cutchery*. Thus, on 25 April, Hastings complained to Vansittart about the "oppressions committed under

21. *Ibid.*, pp. 165-166.

22. *Ibid.*, pp. 166-168.

the sanction of the English name" and how the Nawab's subjects were unable to resist them. This evil was not confined to the dependents of the English alone, but was "practiced, by people falsely assuming the habits of our seepoys, or calling themselves our *gomastahs*."[23]

Hastings also realised that the Nawab's letter addressed to the council, pointed out Ellis as his arch-enemy. So Hastings prevailed upon the Nawab that he should defer sending it to Calcutta, till he (Hastings) could get a reply from Ellis about his grievances against the Nawab. Hastings then wrote a letter to Ellis but his answer could not satisfy him. So Hastings observed in his letter to Vansittart that he was at a loss how to deal with Ellis. The behaviour of Ellis was so imprudent "that a proper representation of it, cannot fail to draw upon him the severest resentment of the Company."[24]

Vansittart then wrote a letter to Mir Qasim informing the Nawab that Hastings had been sent concerning the affairs of Mungher. Hastings had been instructed to search the fort and direct Ellis to recall his troops. Similarly, the order had already been issued "for the chastisement of such of the Company's *gumashtahs*" as injured the business of the government. Thus Vansittart requested Mir Qasim to do the same on his part and to issue the same order "to his *faujdars*, *zamindars* and *daroghahs* of the *chaukis*." The Governor further desired that if the *zamindars* made any complaint against "the Company's *gumashtahs*," the former might be informed of the whole affair.[25]

In reply to his letter, Mir Qasim informed Vansittart that though the former continued to be firm about his treaty obligations with the English and resolved to preserve the duties of friendship, yet Ellis invented slanders and passed

23. Hastings letter to Vansittart, 25 April (Vansittart, *Narrative* I, p. 169).

24. *Ibid.*, 13 May, 1762, pp. 174-175.

25. Vansittart's letter to Mir Qasim, 16 May '62 (C.P.C., I, p. 163, No. 1530).

them on to the Governor. Hence Mir Qasim observed in his letter to Vansittart: "It grieves me, that you should pay such regard to what he writes, conclude everything that I write to be false, and still tell me to let the fort be searched; and treat this affair, which is the greatest mark of indignity and distrust, as a trifle." The Nawab became surprised that the Governor still could not discover the designing and malicious persons between him and the English.[26]

Hastings realised the awkward as well as disgraceful situation to which the Nawab of Bengal had been driven to. This gravely injured his rights on the *subah*, eroding his (the Nawab's) authority, and if it was not prevented in time, it might culminate in an open rupture. So he cautioned the Governor about this danger and informed him: "The world judging only from facts, sees the Nabob's authority publickly insulted, his officers imprisoned, seapoys sent against his forts; and is told, that the chief of the English in these parts disavows the Nabob's right to the *subaship*. The obvious end of such symptoms is an open rupture." These acts of undermining the authority of the Nawab's government, Hastings observed, might encourage the Nawab's enemies to revolt. Shujaud-daulah had been informed that the English had commenced hostilities with the Nawab and such a false report might be fatal both for the Nawab and the English.[27]

In reply to Hastings' letter, Vansittart informed him that the Nawab's reply to the representations of the Calcutta Council, was "exactly uniform with all his former declarations", and this uniformity was a strong proof that the Nawab spoke "with a good conscience." However, Vansittart entirely approved of Hastings' mission to square up matters between the Nawab and Ellis. Vansittart wrote to Hastings that

26. Mir Qasim's letter to Vansittart, 24 May (Vansittart, *Narrative*, II, pp. 150-151).

27. Hastings' letter to the Governor, 26 May (*Original Papers*, I, pp. 180-181).

if Ellis did accept the "good offices" of Hastings, the latter might fully represent the matter before the council.[28]

In the month of June, the Nawab returned from his camp to Mungher and informed the Governor that he could not bear the disgrace about the concocted account of the concealed Europeans in the fort of Mungher. Thus the Nawab stated in his letter "that punishment ought to be inflicted on those who wish to foment ill-feeling between the Governor and him."[29]

Hastings also had arrived with the Nawab at Mungher, where he was told by the Nawab that Ellis had declared his disapproval of the Nawab's accession on the *masnad*. Ellis expected a change in the government after the arrival of the next ship of the Company. So Hastings tried to satisfy the Nawab about the impossibility of any such thing. However, Hastings did not think that this matter was invented by the Nawab or the people about him.[30] Even the Governor conceded the right which the Nawab had claimed and wrote to Hastings: "It is a natural right which the Nabob has, in common with all other governments, to prevent by force, if fair means fail, any injury being done to his subjects by any other persons."[31]

Hastings found the rapprochement with the Nawab an impossible task, owing mainly to Ellis's obstinacy and intransigence. He had used every method to settle the differences between the two, but these had proved ineffectual. As Hastings' mission could not bear fruit, he took his leave of the Nawab at Mungher and returned to Calcutta.

Though Hastings' mission of reconciliation between Mir Qasim and Ellis failed, yet he drew the attention of the Governor to certain abuses connected with trade, that were rampant and unchecked and practised under the authority of the British name. The Company long enjoyed the privilege

28. Governor's letter to Hastings, 26 May (Vansittart, *Narrative*, II, p. 175).

29. Nawab's letter to the Governor, 5 June (C.P.C.,I., p. 164, No. 1539).

30. Vansittart, *Narrative*, II, p. 178.

31. Vansittart's letter to Hastings, 27 June (Vansittart, *Narrative*, II, p. 190).

of their trade clear of customs duty, but this privilege was confined to goods imported or exported by sea. The internal trade of the *subah* was in the hands of the Bengal merchants. The government had the exclusive right in dealing with some articles that had traditionally been the sources of the government revenues. All other articles were subjected to duties levied at various stations, so that goods could not be removed without making some payments to the State. But, as already noted, the influence acquired by the English, after Plassey, encouraged the servants of the Company to enter on their private account into the internal trade.[32] As a consequence when the Nawab tried to assert his right over the internal trade of the *subah*, he was shocked to learn that his officers who tried to realise duties on the goods from the English traders were seized, manhandled and confined in their factories by the English officials. One such officer of the Nawab was Mirza Muhammad, who was seized at Dacca and sent to Calcutta for trial; others had been seized by Ellis at Patna and had also been sent to Calcutta. Thus the Nawab thought that the only way to save the honour of his government was to lay hands on the intransigent English mercantile agents, and to keep them in confinement as a punishment. The Nawab sent orders, accordingly, to all directions.[33]

Thus the English were again on great alarm for what they called encroachments upon their trade privileges by the Nawab's officials. With a view to coming to an agreement on the vexed subject of inland trade, Vansittart proposed, in October, 1762, to visit the Nawab.

Vansittart left Murshidabad on 12 November, accompanied by Hastings, and arrived at Mungher on the 30th of the same month. They were received by the Nawab with "usual

---

32. Thornton, *British Empire*, p. 91.

33. *Seir*, II, p. 499. At this time, Rajah Nobet Roy-the deputy Governor of Patna, was replaced by Mir Mehdi Khan, as the former was found unfiit to contest with such an incensed enemy as Ellis.

marks of respect and friendship" but the Nawab's constant topic of discussion with them was about the ill-treatment that he had received from Ellis. Vansittart then told the Nawab to forget all such disputes and also to make fresh regulations to "prevent any dispute in future."[34] But the Nawab went on complaining about the illicit private trade by the English in salt, betel-nut and tobacco, the privileges of which had been usurped by the English *gomastahs*. The Nawab strongly stressed that the English had no right to carry on these trades according to the *farman*. But the persistent acts of transgression by the English and their men had created disorder in his government. Thus, the Nawab insisted that he would confine the English private trade in the same manner as it had been before the days of Mir Jafar. Although by and large Vansittart shared the same opinion, he requested the Nawab that the English should be allowed to continue their inland trade "in the articles produced in the country" and to carry it on "upon the same footing with other merchants."[35] The Nawab consented to this proposal reluctantly, but declared that if after this settlement, and more disputes should arise, he would have no remedy left but to lay all trade entirely open and to give an order to all merchants to carry on their trade duty-free.[36]

After making these arrangements with the Nawab, Vansittart and Hastings left Mungher on 9 January 1763, and arrived at Kasimbazar on the 14th. But on their way they received an answer from the council to their letters which Vansittart and Hastings had written earlier on 15 December. The council became highly incensed for the arrangement made

---

34. Vansittart, *Narrative*, II, p. 211.

35. It was decided that the English merchants were to pay 9 per cent duties on salt, whereas an ordinary Bengal merchant carrying salt to Patna would have to pay 30 to 40 per cent. In case of disputes, the *faujdars* and officers of justice were to decide them and report their proceedings to the Nawab–Vansittart's and Hastings' letter to the Council, 15 December 1762 (Vansittart, *Narrative*, II, p. 216).

36. Vansittart, *Narrative*, II, pp. 211-212.

by the Governor with the Nawab, which would limit the inland trade of the English for all future years. They were not ready to give up their ill-gotten gains but wanted a reversal of the entire arrangement agreed to Vansittart, for which they wanted to leave Hastings at the *darbar* of the Nawab at Mungher for negotiations, until the complete satisfaction of the Vansittart's opponents. They also demanded a full discussion at Calcutta on the settlement arrived at with Vansittart. They also wanted the Governor to hold discussions with Ellis for that purpose.[37]

It had been agreed between the Nawab and the Governor that after the latter's arrival at Calcutta, the regulations should be sent from the council to different factories and then the Nawab would direct the same to his officers. But the Nawab did not wait any longer for the council's approval and sent copies of Vansittart's letter to his officers in all parts of the *subah* with order for their observance. He further directed that all English *gomastahs*, who would refuse to comply with them, should be turned out. When copies of these letters were delivered by the Nawab's officer to the Chief of the English factory at Dacca, the latter immediately forwarded the copies to the council at Calcutta with the remark that the regulations would bring about great loss to the English merchants, especially in their private trade. The English Chief at Dacca further remarked that the regulations were an encroachment upon the English privileges. These remarks served effectually to add fuel to the already inflamed minds of the opposition lobby in the council and they immediately called Major Carnac, another English commander, to Calcutta in order to hear his views. Vansittart could not suspect, until his arrival at Calcutta, that he would meet a very violent opposition for his settement with the Nawab. It was Amyatt—a member of the council, who informed the Governor that orders had already been sent for the members of the council to come down to

37. Council's letter to the Governor and Hastings, 27 December, 1762, (Vansittart, *Narrative*, II, pp. 231-232).

calcutta from their subordinate settlements with a view to their participating in the deliberation.[38]

On 17 January, 1763, Major Carnac took an active part in the deliberations of the Calcutta Council. Carnac was, according to Vansittart, "the author and director of the resolution". The council came to the conclusion that the Governor was in no way authorised to conclude terms with the Nawab except by the concurrence of the council: "That the regulations proposed by him, are dishonorable to us as Englishmen, and tend to the ruin of all public and private trade; that the President's issuing out regulations independently of the Council, is an absolute breack(h) of their privileges; and that, therefore, directions should be sent to Dacca, to suspend paying any regard to the regulations and orders, which the Nabob has sent to their factory."[39]

On 1 February 1763, Vansittart registered a note of dissent in this consultation in which he pointed out a distinction between the trade in articles imported and exported by shipping and the private inland trade of the *subah*. For the former trade of export and import by shipping, the Company had obtained the *farman* but the latter of private inland trade, of which salt, betel-nut and tobacco were the chief itemes of merchandise, the English had carried it on, on the basis of the *dastack* of the native government and hence, a duty on them must be paid. This duty varied from place to place according to the disposition and authority of the Nawab's collectors. Thus for bringing about uniformity of those duties, he as the governor had been deputed to settle the matter with the Nawab, Vansittart further stated. There can be no solid plan where nothing is fiixed, Vansittart pointed out. Therefore, as he submitted, his settlement with the Nawab was "the most comfortable to the Company's intentions and as such as honourable."[40]

38. Vansittart, *Narrative*, II, pp. 237-239. The indignant councillors were summoned from the subordinate factories, except the Chiefs of Patna and Chittagong for their long distance from Calcutta.

39. *Ibid.*, pp. 250-251.

40. The Governor's Minute in Consultation, 1 February, 1763 (Vansittart, *Narrative*, II pp. 252-254).

The Calcutta Council received fresh complaints from the Patna and Dacca factories. From the former the intelligence came that some bullocks loaded with the Company's salt-petre were stopped by the Nawab's officers in one of the *chowkies* and from the latter, great obstructions were put up against their private trade at Sreerampore. On the other hand, the council also received, a number of representations from Saiyyad Muhammad Khan—the deputy at Murshidabad, about the violence of the English *gomastahs*. On the first, it was resolved by the council to carry on all trade as before, and in case of obstruction from the government officers, oppose it by force;while upon the latter, it was resolved that if any representation came from the side of the government against the English *gomastahs* it should be ignored so that "it was taken no further notice of."[41] Thus it became clear that those who wished for a rupture with the Nawab, became the judges of the unfortunate situations in which the English and their men had taken the law in their own hands.

The relation between the Nawab and the English was becoming more and more embittered every day. When Vansittrat had visited the Nawab at Mungher, the former had given the promise that in regard to the trade down by the English the "business would be carried on in a proper manner." But after his return to Calcutta, the English, bent upon cowing down the Nawab's administration, sent forces to carry on their business as aggressively as before. They chastised the Nawab's officers when the latter resisted. For three years, the Nawab had not got "a single rupee" from the English and their *gomastahs*. They levied fines and penalties on the Nawab's officers, and if any one of them tried to resist it, the English lodged complaint against him before the Nawab.[42]

In reply to the Nawab's letter, the Calcutta Council drafted two letters. The first was written on 7 March, infor-

---

41. Vansittart, *Narrative,* II pp. 272-273.
42. Nawab's letter to Governor, 5 March, 1763. (*Original Papers,* II, pp. 110-111).

ming the Nawab that the *farman* and other public orders fully entitled the English to carry on their trade, foreign as well as inland, in the *subah* of Bengal. Although the aforesaid grants permitted the English to trade duty free, yet they were willing to pay 2½ per cent duty on the articles of inland trade. Then the council informed the Nawab that "the copies of the *farmans, hasb-ul-hukms* and treaties, together with regulations for collecting the aforesaid duty on salt and guiding the conduct of the Company's *gumashtahs* and of the officers of the *Sarkar*, will be sent to His Excellency by Mr. Amyatt and Hay, who have been deputed by the Council to explain to His Excellency the justice of those rights and privileges." The council further informed the Nawab that his agreement concluded with the Governor cannot be enforced as the council did not approve of it.[43] In their second letter, the council again complained to the Nawab that, notwithstanding their privileges, Nobet Roy (or Nobit Roy or Naubat Rai, the *naib* of Patna under Mir Qasim) demanded duties upon opium and disputed the Company's rights. Therefore, they insisted that the Nawab should send an immediate order to his officer, not to molest the Company's *gomastahs*, failing which, it would be deemed that the intention of the Nawab was to go in for an open rupture with the English.[44]

The Nawab then informed the Governor that the disorder had been set afoot by the English themselves—a situation not known to any Government in the past till the time of Murshid Quli Khan. The English sent sepoys, and seized the government officers, reducing the Nawab to a helpless spectator. Mir Qasim was firm to save his honour by all means. He wrote to Vansittart: "My reputation and honour is dearer to me than life."[45]

---

43. Council's letter to Mir Qasim 7 March (C.P.C., I. pp. 197-198, no. 1702). Also Vansittart, *Narrative*, III pp.349-351.

44. Ibid., 10 March (C.P.C., I,P. 199, no. 1705 .

45. Mir Qasim's letter to Vansittart, 15 march (*Original Papers.*, II, pp, 119-122).

In reply to Mir Qasim's letter, Vansittart informed him that he was ready to recall the English sepoys provided the Nawab would direct his officers not to obstruct the Company's business. With regard to salt-petre the Nawab received Rs. 16,000 annually from the English, which they also used to pay to Mir Jafar. Vansittart further requested the Nawab to discuss all matters in friendly terms with Amyatt as that might in a peaceful manner put an end to all these disturbances.[46]

Meanwhile, the Calcutta council had received intelligence that the Nawab had abolished all duties for two years within the *subah* of Bengal, to avoid disputes with the English. The opposition group in Vansittart's council immediately, i.e. on 22 March, took up this matter for discussion and strongly disapproved of the Nawab's move. Johnstone entered a minute in the consultation and called for the opinion of all the members. The council put off sending of the embassy of Amyatt and Hay for some days. The majority of the members that included Johnstone, Watts, Marriott, Hay, Cartier, Biller, Batson and Amyatt, were of opinion that the Nawab's abolition of duties on all goods for all merchants, was "highly detrimental to the Company's trade" as it would be very "destructive to the Company's royal privileges and rights."[47] But Vansittart and Hastings did not vote in support of the resolution of the council and entered their caveat by saying that the Nawab of every *subah* had "a right to do anything for the relief of the merchants trading under his protection."[48] But as the majority of the members of Calcutta Council were against the declaration of the Nawab, they carried the day, Vansittart had to write a letter to Mir Qasim, according to the direction of his council on 24 March, that the English had shown their earnet desire for peace with the Nawab. For this reason, they proposed sending Amyatt

46. C.P.C., I, P. 200, no. 1709.

47. *Original Papers*, II, pp. 124-130.

48. *Ibid.*, p. 131.

and Hay to negotiate a new treaty with him. That Ellis had used force against the Nawab's men was an act which the council approved,[49] since the Nawab had refused to answer letters in which clarifications had been sought from him. Still, the English were ready to support him; but if the Nawab would oppose the Company's people the council would look upon "such conduct as an open declaration of war."[50]

On 28 March, the Calcutta Council instructed Amyatt and Hay to discuss and settle with the Nawab the following demands: In the first place, the trade in the factory, as well the inland trade, carried on by the English *gomastahs* had met with the "greatest interruptions in all parts of the country" from the officers of the Nawab's government. Thus, it was the mission of the embassy to prevent such disputes in future. Secondly, the embassy was to acquaint the Nawab that his last settlement with the Governor had been disapproved by the council and thus he would have to issue orders to all his officers that the trade of the English would go on as usual. Thirdly, the embassy would have to prove by the *farman hasb-ul-hukms*, and treaties, that the English had right of a free trade, foreign and inland, throughout the *subah*. Fourthly, the embassy would convince the Nawab about the English rights and privileges, and the Company's desire for allowing him a duty on salt. Fifthly, the article of salt would be circulated equally with other articles by means of a *dastack* and be liable to no further interruption. Sixthly, to set right the future conduct of both sides of settling of disputes between the Nawab and the English some rules must be framed and observed by either side in future. Seventhly, the embassy would have to acquaint the Nawab about the nature of the Company's administration and the powers of the council as

49. When this resolution of the Nawab of making his *subah* duty-free was known to Ellis, he became furious and applied to Calcutta for waging war. This was accepted by the majority, except Vansittart and Hastings. The Governor and Hastings persuaded the members to try once more for a settlement—Malleson *Hastings*, p. 75.

50. Vansittart's letter to Mir Qasim, 24 March (Vansittart, *Narrative*, III, p, 367). Also, C.P. C., I, p. 200, No. 1709.

well as the President. The Nawab's pretension of ignorance could not be an excuse for his or his officers' actions that were detrimental to the Company's affairs. Eighthly, the Nawab's ill-founded suspicions must be removed and he must be convinced that the English were ready to support him, provided he did not attempt to infringe the Company's rights and privileges. Ninthly, with respect to the regulations for trade, the council thought it "the most proper method to have our rights acknowledged and the proposals agreed to by some public writing, under the Nabob's own hand and seal." Tenthly, the council thought it "absolutely necessary", both for the interest of the Nawab and the Company, to have an English gentleman stationed for his service as the Resident at his *darbar*. So the council had appointed Thomas Amphlett[51] to accompany the embassy on this deputation and that Amphlett would remain with the Nawab that all future transactions between him and the English would be carried on by this Resident hereafter. If the embassy could not fulfil all their negotiations, the unfinished task would be taken up and negotiated with the Nawab by Amphlett. Eleventhly, the embassy would insist on the Nawab for the dismissal of Muhammad Ali, the collector of Dacca, for his ill-disposition towards the English. Twelfthly, the embassy must apply to the Nawab for the proper *jagir sanads* of the three districts, so as to confirm the Company's rights on them. Thirteenthly, the embassy should demand before the Nawab, the payment of the sum of money, which Muhammad Reza Khan had disbursed from the revenues of Chittagong, on account of the Tippara expedition. Fourteenthly, the embassy must insist on the Nawab that his *sanad* containing the exemption of duties of all kinds of trade for a period of two years must be revoked and collection of duties must go on as before. It was strongly felt that a *sanad* like the above had "a design to prejudice the Company's trading business." And finally, the embassy

51. Thomas Amphlett—a relation of Clive, was a civil servant in Bengal. He was an engineer and was employed in the works of Fort William.

would carry with them, for the Nawab's perusal and reference, the copies of the minute entered by Johnstone and Hay.[52]

After given these instructions to Amyatt and Hay, the members of council thought it necessary to delay the march of their deputation for some days, as a fresh news reached Calcutta about an attack made by the Nawab's troops on a party of sepoys who had been directed to seize the Nawab's office at Gaya. Thus it was decided on 1 April that Amyatt and Hay should proceed to Kasimbazar and wait there for the Nawab's answer. If the Nawab would refuse to receive the deputation, it would amount to a declaration of a rupture with the English.[53] So the Calcutta Council informed the Nawab that though the latter was hostile against the English, the English had no intention "of bringing about a change in the government" and the deputation of Amyatt and Hay should be regarded "as the strongest mark of the Council's friendship for him." The sting in the tail, however, was the warning that the Nawab's refusal to receive them would mount to "a declaration of war on his side."[54]

Now the Nawab of Bengal had to deal not with a Clive. but with a Vansittart. He could not understand how settlement with the Governor could be unsettled by his subordinates. So Mir Qasim wrote to Vansittart about the strange attitude of the English, that while he was in Bihar, the English sent troops into Bengal. About not replying to Ellis's letters, the Nawab said that Ellis did not act in a straight-forward manner. From the acts of the Governor, it appeared to the Nawab that the Governor was not willing to help him, but wanted "to set up another Nawab." The Nawab believed that for mercantile affairs, the Nawab had relinquished everything, and there remained nothing for Amyatt to negotiate.[55]

52. Instructions to Amyatt and Hay, 28 March (Vansittart, *Narrative*, III. pp. 399-403).

53. Letter to Court, 18 April (F.W.I.H.C., III, p. 489).

54. Council's letter to Mir Qasim, 1 April (C.P.C., I, p. 204, No. 1721).

55. Mir Qasim's letter to Vansittarat, 2 April (C.P.C., I, p. 205. No. 1724).

Still the much awaited deputation of Amyatt and Hay did not stop, and on 4 April, they left Calcutta for Kasimbazar. Meanwhile Mir Qasim wrote to Vansittart that he had no objection to Amyatt's coming to Mungher, provided the English troops that were dispatched by every road, were recalled. If the Governor would refuse to recall the troops and was bent on the dishonour of the Nawab, Mir Qasim had no remedy. "It is every man's duty to take care of his honour,"[56] observed the Nawab in his letter to the Governer expressing his utter surprise that the latter did not see the faults of the Company's people when they were engaged most flagrantly in seizing and even beating up the government officers. It seemed to him that the English were preparing for war. Yet the Nawab had no objection to receiving Amyatt and Hay if they were accompanied by only one or two companies of sepoys.[57]

Meanwhile Amyatt was impatient for the non-arrival of any reply from the Nawab about his proposed visit to Mungher. However, the Nawab wrote to him on 21 April that he would be glad to meet Amyatt as he (the Nawab) had heard that Amyatt was a man of "many good qualities." But the Nawab expressed his surprise that while he received friendly letters from the deputationist, the fact was that the English had sent troops along every way with warlike implements. If Amyatt had the desire for peace, the Nawab insisted, "he would send the troops back."[58] The Nawab wrote a similar letter to Hay, adding that "no friend ever went to visit a friend with great guns and small arms."[59]

Vansittart became surprised over this baseless news emanating from Mir Qasim and informed him that the English did not send troops to Mungher ; only a company or two had gone with Amyatt and Hay to attend them on the road.[60] Amyatt

56. C.P.C., I, p. 207, No. 1730.

57. *Ibid.*

58. *Ibid* , p. 209, No. 1738.

59. *Idid.*, pp. 209-210., No. 1739.

60. Vansittart's letter to Mir Qasim, 23 April (C.P.C., I, p. 210, No. 1742).

also replied in the same vein to the Nawab saying that he was accompanied only by half of the attendants as were with the Governor during his last visit to the Nawab. Furthermora, Amyatt professed friendship and added that the Company's people were not responsible for the disturbance in the *subah* but trouble was always generated by "the officers of the *Sarkar*."[61]

Meanwhile, during their stay at Kasimbazar, Amyatt and Hay came to know about the arrest of the Seth brothers—Mahtab Rai and Swarup Chand by Taki Khan-the Commander of the Nawab. These arrests were effected by the Commander during the night of 21 April and the imprisoned were confined at *Hirajhil* by the Nawab's soldiers. Amyatt immediately informed Vansittart about the incident. The Oovernor became surprised for this act of the Nawab and informed the latter that this step was "extremely improper." The seths "were never thus disgraced in the time of any former *Nazims*."[62]

Mir Qasim himself had ordered the arrest of the seths from their houses at Murshidabad. They were detained for a few days at *Hirajhil*, after which they were carried to Mungher. Amyatt firmly believed that such a punitive treatment to the seths by the Nawab was due to his prepossession about the seths' close alliance with the English. So Amyatt represented before the Nawab that the seths never interfered in the business of the government, neither were they in alliance with the English. Amyatt demanded their release from Mungher.[63] But when the Nawab did not release the seth brothers, the Calcutta Council directed Amyatt and Hay to represent this matter personally before the Nawab, when they would arrive at Mungher.[64]

---

61. Amyatt's letter to Mir Qasim, 23 April (*Ibid.*, pp. 210-211, No. 1743).
62. Long, *Unpublished Records*, p. 464.
63. Amyatt's letter to Mir Qasim, 28 April (C.P.C.I., p. 212, No. 1752).
64. When he arrived at Mungher, Amyatt represented before the Nawab about the release of the Seths, but the Nawab replied that he meant them no harm and insisted on their residing with the Nawab according to the custom of the *darbar*. Letter to Court, 29 September (F.W.I.H.C. III, p. 517).

On 29 April, Mir Qasim again informed Vansittart that he had no objection to receiving Amyatt and Hay, provided they would come just as the Governor had previously come.[65] On the next day the Nawab again wrote a letter to the Oovernor complaining once again about Ellis's conduct. As the Nawab pointed out, the said gentleman professed that he had been authorised by the council to seize the *amils* of the *nizamat* with out giving notice to the *naib*. Thus while on the one hand, the Nawab's officers were tortured, on the other, Amyatt and Hay were dispatched to negotiate a new treaty. The Nawab failed to understand the real design of the English. He wondered 'how the English will observe the new treaty since they have not abided by the old."[66]

On 4 May, the Nawab informed Amyatt that he had sent Mir Abdullah and Chulam Husain to meet him and accompany him to Mungher. But at the same time, the Nawab felt that Amphlett's coming to Mungher as a Resident would not bear any tangible fruit since the Company bent upon transacting their business by means of sepoys.[67]

On 12 May, Amyatt and Hay arrived at Mungher. On 15, they had a meeting with the Nawab when the deputationists apprised him about the resolution of the council. It seemed to the English gentlemen that the Nawab was "somewhat convinced" about their intention.[68] The deputationists tried to discuss each item separately but soon found it difficult. Hence, the Nawab asked Amyatt to set everything down in writing. So on 23 May, Amyatt delivered to the Nawab a Persian translation of the list of demands. He submitted the following list of demands : In the first place, the Nawab must set matters right because he had not changed the treaty

65. Mir Qasim's letter to Vansittart, 29 April (C.P.C., I, p. 212, No. 1754).

66. *Ibid.*, 30 April (*Ibid.*, No. 1756).

67. Mir Qasim's letter to Amyatt, 4 May (*Ibid.*, pp. 214-215, Nos. 1762 and 1763).

68. Letter from Amyatt and Hay to the Calcutta Council, 18 May (Vansittart, *Narrative*, III, pp. 441-442).

he had made with the governor, neither issued *parwanas*, accordingly, to his officers. Secondly, that reparation be made for the losses sustained by the English, both before and after the said treaty was concluded. Thirdly that the *sanad* for the remission of all duties for the space of two years be immediately cancelled as it would deprive the English of the advantages of their *farman*. Fourthly, that an English Resident would always reside at his *darbar* to transact the business between the government and the Company. Sixthly, that the *jagiri sanad* be granted to the Company for the districts of Burdwan, MiPnapore and Chittagong. Seventhly, that the money coined in the Company's mint should be declared legal tender and the English would be allowed to coin three lakhs of rupees annually in each of the mints of Dacca and Patna. Eighthly, that the money spent by Reza Khan in the expedition of Tippara out of the revenues of Chittagong, would be reimbursed. Ninthly, that before the departure of Amyatt and Hay from Mungher, an exemplary punishment should be inflicted on Lal Singh who had massacred a number of English sepoys, and declared that he would cut every one of the English sepoys to pieces wherever they were found. Tenthly, that the seths be released and be permitted to go wherever they pleased. And lastly, that the Nawab should give an explicit answer to the above demands and with all convenient expedition issue orders accordingly.[69]

Along with these demands, Amyatt and Hay informed the Nawab that their intention was to establish peace and tranquillity in the *subah*. They also submitted that for the Nawab's service, it was necessary for a body of English troops to remain at Patna. The Calcutta Council might also Consent to their removal to Mungher, if proper cantonments were made for their accommodation. They also desired of the Nawab to direct Mehdi Ali Khan to adopt a conciliatory attitude towards the English, so that Ellis might also adopt the same course.[70]

69. C.P.C., I. pp. 218-219, No. 1778 A. Also, Vansittart, *Narrative*, III, p. 445-448.

70. Amyatt's letter to the Nawab, 23 May (C.P.C., I, pp. 271-278) No. 1778).

Nawab Mir Qasim did not answer immediately to the list of demands submitted by Amyatt. Rather the Nawab and Amyatt got involed in charges and counter-charges about the cause of disturbances in Bengal and each accused the other. On 25 May, Mir Qasim wrote two letters to Amyatt. In the first he informed Amyatt that he had come to know from Mehdi Khan that Eills was daily creating disturbances. Thus, the Nawab desired that the English troops stationed at Patna should either be recalled to Calcutta or sent to Mungher or to remain there only till they were wanted.[71] In his second letter, Mir Qasim observed to Amyatt that Mehdi Khan complained repeatedly that if a reinforcement was not speedily sent to him, he would relinquish his post. The Nawab believed most earnestly that if the English troops were not removed from Patna, "there is bound to be war between them." At the same time the Nawab requested Amyatt to send a reliable and competent person to Mungher to build cantonments for the English troops.[72] In reply to these letters, Amyatt wrote to Mir Qasim that English were not the aggressors. In most cases, the charges against the English were absurd. Amyatt also informed the Nawab that he was not authorised to remove the troops to Mungher.[73]

On 26 May, the Nawab delivered a copy of his reply to the Company's demands to Amyett and Hay with the observation: "As I have nothing to do with the customs or duties on any kinds of goods from any merchants whatever, and have wholly exempted them for two years to come, ye may engage in whatever trade ye please, nor will anyone meddle or interfere therein."[74] The Nawab then answered each article of Amyatt's demand. He rejected all the demands of the embassy.[75]

The Nawab's curt and negative reply to the Company's demands greatly surprised Amyatt and Hay. They noticed

71. Mir Qasim's letter to Amyatt, 25 May *Ibid.*, p. 219, No. 1781).
72. *Ibid.*, pp. 219-220, No. 1782.
73. Amyatt's letter to Mir Qasim, 25 May (*Ibid.*, p. 220, No. 1783).
74. Vansittart, *Narrative*, III, p. 448.
75. *Ibid.*, pp. 448-451.

that the Nawab did not comply with a single demand of the Company. They realised the failure of their mission and waited for the permission from the Nawab to start for Calcutta.[76]

While Amyatt and Hay were preparing for their departure from Mungher, a sudden and fresh dispute arose with the Nawab that forced them to stay at Mungher for a few days more. Some boats laden with arms for the English troops at Patna, when passing by Mungher, were stopped by the Nawab's officials. Amyatt and Hay demanded their release, but the Nawab, suspecting the English design as a fresh proof of affront to him and an excuse for larger hostilities against him, refused to part with them unless all English forces were removed from Patna. The activities of Ellis went directly against any move towards placing confidence in the sincerity of the English. Thus as an alternative, to test the sincerity of the English, the Nawab demanded the removal of Ellis and, in his stead, the placement of any one among Amyatt, MacGuire or Hastings at Patna. The Nawab's only aim was to counteract the mischievous designs of Ellis with the larger aim of preserving the peace with the English. The Nawab also informed Amyatt that "Ellis was resolved to attack the city of Patna."[77]

Amyatt and Hay still continued their efforts about the release of the English boats but without success. In their letters to the Calcutta Cuuncil dated 29 and 31 of May, they informed the latter that in spite of their "repeated remonstrances" before the Nawab for the release of the boats, the Nawab did not show the least confidence in their promises and declared that unless the detachment from Patna be removed, either to Mungher or Calcutta, he would take no step for a reconciliation. It seemed to the deputationists that the Nawab wanted to gain time[78], so as to fall on the English at a suitable opportunity.

76. Amyatt and Hay's letter to Mir Qasim, 26 May (C.P.C., I, p. 221, No. 1785).

77. Vansittart, *Narrative*, III, pp. 443-444.

78. *Ibid.*, pp. 451-452.

Thus the hostile attitude on both sides became acute and there seemed no chance for a compromise, as both the Nawab and the Company began to accuse each other, almost with no holds barred. Vansittart became surprised to see that the Nawab did not comply with a single demand of the English. The Nawab's stopping the English boats laden with arms and his seizing two thousand *maunds* of salt-petre, were regarded by Vansittart as open acts of hostility. Thus, the Governor wrote to the Nawab on 8 June that if the latter would refuse to release the boats, all hopes of peace and friendship would come to an end.[79] Due to the stern attitude of the Nawab, Amyatt also was convinced that the Nawab wanted war, and so he again requested the Nawab on 9 June, for allowing him to depart from Mungher.[80]

Mir Qasim became firm in his attitude and wanted to know from Amyatt "the meaning of the Governor's sending arms to Ellis." However, the Nawab still believed that this cold war might be put to an end by the discreet intervention of Amyatt.[81]

The critical situation of affairs induced the English in Calcutta to hold a consultation on 9 June. It was resolved "not to consent to the removal of the troops from Patna," whether the Nawab would comply with their demands or not, and in case of his refusal to release the boats with arms, Amyatt and Hay were instructed to return to Calcutta immediately "without taking leave of the Nabob". On their quitting Mungher, it was resolved by the council, they should advise

79. C.P.C., I, p. 223. No. 1797.

80. *Ibid.*, No. 1798.

81. *Ibid.*, p. 224, No. 1799. Nandlal Chatterjee in his book "*Mir Qasim—Nawab of Bengal*" points out that "the stubborn and unbending attitude which he (the Nawab) maintained was ill calculated to conciliate anyone" (p 209), and again that the negotiation of Amyatt came to a standstill as the Nawab's attitude was 'definitely hostile" (p. 216). But he does not point out the unbending attitude of the English against the ruler, that made war inevitable. Evidently Chatterjee's book is not impartial. He does not see the faults of the English.

the council as well as the Englishmen at Patna about the proper way of their security, in case the Nawab happened to "send troops to attack them."[82]

On 13 June, the Nawab again urged Amyatt about the expeditious removal of troops from Patna. He declared that Ellis was his avowed enemy, who was "creating disturbances for past two years". The Nawab again declared his intention of releasing the seized English boats provided Ellis was removed from Patna.[83] In reply to his letter, Amyatt wrote to the Nawab on 17 June that the Governor and council would not consent either to remove the troops from Patna, or to replace Ellis. So he requested the Nawab to permit him to return, and as such, a passport might be issued to him. Amyatt further hoped that the Nawab would not detain any one in his party as a hostage. But if the Nawab would insist, Hay might remain at Mungher.[84]

From the letters of Amyatt and Hay, the Calcutta Council reached the conclusion that there was the strongest reason to suspect that these disputes with the Nawab might end in a rupture. So the council formed an immediate plan for the deployment of forces, in case the war did actually break out. Accordingly, in the consultation of 18 June, the council resolved to plan the operation of their army in such a way that it "would best tend to the security of the Company's lands and the protection of the investment." Captain Knox was, therefore, directed to proceed with his troops, and detachments of 200 of the Company's troops and 300 sepoys were posted at Krishnagar and Kasimbazar. The troops would march in a line, "so as to be able to support each other, and the whole to act under the orders of Major Adams."[85]

On 22 June, Mir Qasim at last released the English boats with their muskets, but still Amyatt and Hay stuck to their old point that the English troops at Patna would not be removed. At the same time, the news reached the Nawab that Ellis was

82.. Letter to Court, 29 September (F.W. I.H.C., III, p. 518).

83. C.P.C., I, pp. 224-225, No. 1803.

84. *Ibid*,, p. 225, No. 1804.

85. Letter to Court. 29 September, (F.W.I.H.C,, III, p. 519).

bent upon a design to launch an attack on the fort of Patna and was preparing ladders and platforms for that purpose.[86] Ellis was further instigated by Amyatt when the latter informed him on 22 June, that two days before that Amyatt and Hay had been actually made prisoners, surrounded by a body of horse, but subsequently the Nawab had "promised to dismiss us the day after to-morrow,"[87]

Finally, the Nawab allowed Amyatt and his seven companions to quit Mungher on 23 June, detaining only Hay as hostage.[88] No sooner Ellis heard about the escape of Amyatt from Mungher, he immediately made a sudden attack on the fort of Patna and this rashness of Ellis precipitated the war. Ellis captured Patna easily. But the Nawab's troops, who had fled on the first surprise attack, returned, and regained the town almost as easily as they had lost it. The English soldiers then retired to their factory but soon found their position untenable. For reasons of security they hastend up towards Chhapra. The Nawab's commander pursued and attacked them and they were obliged to surrender. The captives were then carried off to the fort of Mungher.[89]

Up to 25 June, Mir Qasim was averse to war. He had explained his position and his desire for peace several times, before Amyatt and Hay. But the English did not comply with any of his requests. As gestures of goodwill Mir Qasim had releaseed the English boats stopped at Mungher and allowed Amyatt to return to calcutta. But when the Nawab learnt on 25 June that Ellis had attacked the city of Patna, his patience gave way and he was forced to order his army in the field. Thereupon, the Nawab sent a party of troops in

86. *Ibid.*, pp. 485-486

87. Amyatt's letter to Ellis, 22 June (Vansittart, *Narrative*, III, p. 389 f.n.).

88. Hay was detained at Mungher for the safety of Khwajah Petrus at Calcutta. Thus the council immediately imprisoned Petrus for the security of Hay, Letter to Court, 29 Sept. (F.W.I.H.C., III, p. 520).

89, Beveridge, *Comprehensive History*, I, p. 860.

swift boats to stop the boats of Amyatt and his companions to calcutta. The Nawab's soldiers overtook the English officials near Murshidabad. The commander summoned Amyatt to land or to surrender. On Amyatt's refusal there was fighting and at last the Nawab's troops became victorious. Amyatt and most his followers were killed on 3 July and a few others were carried as prisoners to Mungher.[90] Only sergeant with two sepoys escaped to calcutta to tell there the horrible tale.[91]

On 4 July the calcutta council received news about the armed conflict at Patna and Amyatt's escape from Mungher. The situation of affairs was thus "too urgent to admit of any delay" and in the consultation of that day it was unanimously resolve, except Vansittart and Hastings who remained neutral, that the former Nawab Mir Jafar should be restored to the government. To form a new treaty with him and for preventing any further disturbances in the *subah*, a committee was appointed to draw up a plan of articles with Mir Jafar khan.[92]

A report had already got current at calcutta about the murder of Amyatt, but it was finally confirmed on 7 July by a letter from Johanstone at Burdwan.[93] The hit back was now inevitable. The calcutta council issued a proclamation on the same day declaring war against Mir Qasim and restoration of Mir Jafar as the Nawab of Bengal, Bihar and orissa. It was broadcast all over that since Mir Qasim had committed inhuman acts of violence and oppression in the *subah*, all persons should join with Mir Jafar khan and thus restore the stable and peaceful political climate. It was declared in general terms to assist Mir Jafar in defeating the design of Mir Qasim.[94] On the same day, Mir Qasim wrote a

90. Letter to Court, 29 September (F.W.I.H.C., III, p. 522), Thomas Amphlett-the proposed Resident at the *darbar*, with 19 other civilians were killed in this struggle.

91. Malleson, *Hastings*, pp. 77-78.

92. Letter to Court, 29 September (F.W.I.H.C., III, pp. 521-522),

93. *Ibid.*

94. C.P.C., I, p. 228, No. 1814.

letter to Vansittart observing that Ellis had attacked the fort of Patna "like night robber,, and plundered the city for hours togetherr, but they were defeated and captured.[95]

Major Adams continued his march to Mungher, while Mir Qasim decided to fall on the English prisoners. He directed Somru, the German adventurer who was his adviser, to slaughter the prisoner, and Somru killed most of the prisoners, somewere "cut to pieces."[96] Among contemporary English men Vansittart was fair enough to admit that the onus for the escalation of the conflict lay with the English whose belligerent actions provoked the Nawab. Vansittart admitted: That we were the first aggressors, by the assault of the city of Patna will not be disputed." The Governor's impartiality forced him to say further: "Let any impartial person now put himself in the place of Meer cossim, and say whether he could have regarded this assault on the city af Patna, in any other light than as an act of treachery, and the strongest argument, that all the pacific declarations and preferred treaties, were only artifices to make him a dupe to our designs, and the instrument of his own ruin.[97]

---

95. *Ibid.*, pp. 227-228, No. 1813.

96. Among others, Ellis, Hay and Lushington were killed, Dodwell, p. 248.

97. Vansittart, *Narrative*, III, pp. 522-524.

6

ROLE OF THE RESIDENTS FROM THE RESTORATION OF MIR JAFAR TO THE GRANT OF DIWANI

Even after their declaration of war against Mir Qasim, the English could not venture to take up the responsibility of governing the *subah* of Bengal. Thus, they decided to restore Mir Jafar on the *masnad.* On his part Mir Jafar did not seem to remember his miserable performance as a ruler during the last three years that he held his office. He readily agreed to purchase a disgraceful honour for him as also for his successors when the Calcutta Council made the offer to him. He acquiesced to the new treaty concluded between him and the Company, by which his powers were further curtailed. The English had gained a bitter experience from Mir Qasim's government, which resulted in the fifth article being included in the treaty : "that whatever he (the Nawab) shall think proper to fix his court, he shall agree to a body of our forces being always cantoned near his person, for the security thereof and protection of his government, and that a Company's servant shall reside at his court to transact any affair between

---

1. Extract of a consulation of the 6th July, 1763 (*Original Papers,* II, pp. 277–280). Also, Vansittart, *Narrative,* III, pp. 498-500.

the Company and the government."[1] Thus, the English. Resident came back with a bang aided by the English militia. The draft treaty contained thirteen articles and it was entrusted to the care of Major Adams, Carnac, Batson and Cartier forming a deputation, to acquaint Mir Jafar with the resolution of the Calcutta Council. Mir Jafar read the article before putting his final singnature ; and he objected to some of them, namely articles 2nd, 4th and 7th.[2] As the Company was then at war with Mir Qasim they thought it advisable to accommodate the Nawab's wishes as far as possible : "better not to insist upon ' and formed a new agreement, on which Mir Jafar finally affixed his signature on 10 July 1763. The treaty also contained thirteen articles, among which the seventh article conclusively ensured the presence of a British Resident at his *darbar*. The Nawab agreed : "Wherever I shall fix my court, either at Moorshidabad or elsewhere, I will advise the Governor and Council; and whatever number of English forces I may have occasion for, in the management of my affairs, I will demand them, and they shall be allowed to me ; and an English gentleman shall reside with me, to transact all affairs between me and the Company and a person shall also reside on my part at Calcutta, to negotiate with the Governor and Council."[3]

Thus, in his restoration in July 1763, Mir Jafar did not obtain all the powers of the Nawab which his predecessor had enjoyed. The number of his troops was limited and he was not permitted to remove his *darbar* to any other place without the consent of the council. In this treaty ample provision was made for the interest of private traders and Mir Qasim's edict-abolishing all duties on trade-was declared null and void. Thus, Mir Jafar's restoration in July 1763, signalled a new political victory for the English, inasmuch as the latter "might remain the only merchants in Bengal,"[4] and be the *defacto* rulers of the *subah*.

2. Vansittart, *Narrative*, III, pp. 508-509.
3. *Ibid.*, p. 511.
4. Verelst, Harry, *A View of the Rise, Progress and Present State of the English Government in Bengal* (London, 1772), p. 49.

But the appointment of a Resident at Mir Jafar's *darbar* was much delayed after the ball had been actually set rolling. It was after four months of his restoration that the Governor informed the Nawab about the appointment of Watts to that post "in order to carry on the business of the Company." It was further enjoined upon the Nawab to pay due weight to the representations of Watts at the *darbar*.[5] Still after this appointment of Watts, he did not turn up at Murshidabad and take charge of his office for four another months, which is evident from the Governor's letters to the Nawab as well as to Irez Khan, theNawab's *naib* at Murshidabad, on 13 March 1764. In the letter to the Nawab the Governor again informed Mir Jafar about the appointment of Watts to reside at his court who would start from Calcutta the next day to meet the Nawab.[6] The Governor also directed Irez Khan fully to meet the new Resident's wants.

Watts, at last proceeded to Murshidabad after eight months from the date of restoration of Mir Jafar. The allowances of the Resident for his expenses as well as the number of staff of his office were fixed during this time. The Resident was allowed Rs. 1,000 for his own expenses as well as for maintaining his private servants, whether he remained with the Nawab or attended on him from his fixed residence.[8] Watts reached *Moti-jhil* on 26 March, and on the next day informed the Governor that Irez Khan had accorded a grand reception to him. Watts also solicited the council's further instructions about the demands to be put upon the Nawab, as it seemed

---

5. Governor's letter to Mir Jafar, 17 November, 1763 (C.P.C., I, p. 253, No. 1944),

6. C.P.C., I, p. 290, No. 2105.

7. *Ibid.*, p. 289, 2104. But Watts did not reside at the *darbar* of the Nawab after Plassey.

8. Long. *Unpublished Records*, pp. 537-538. The office of the Resident consisted of one *vakil* two *munshies*, four *chobdars*, two *jamadars*, twenty peons, ten *musalchees*, twelve bearers, two *chowry* bearers and such a number of *ferashis* and *lashkars* as he might employ for his assistance.

uncertain to him whether the Nawab would pay a visit to Calcutta soon.[9] The council wanted from the Nawab the necessary fund for the restitution of the losses of the English merchants during the troubles with Mir Qasim, which would form a very considerable sum. So the council instructed Watts to give "his assistance in these points." They wrote to Watts that pending the Nawab's visit to Calcutta Watts might make necessary enquiries and let the Council know the state to the Nawab's exchequer in view of the fact that the English demands would be tailored accordingly. Watts was further instructed to proceed immediately to his station at the *darbar* from *Moti-jhil* and to return to Calcutta accompanying the Nawab according to mutual suitability.[10]

But Watts could not proceed farther from *Moti-jhil* and as such the Governor again directed Irez Khan on 12 April to provide Watts with two or three elephants to carry his luggage, since the Resident was on a visit to the Nawab on public business.[11]

Still Watts could not meet the Nawab and he returned to Calcutta where he reached as late as the middle of May, on account of the obstruction on the road. So the Calcutta Council resolved to write to Major Carnac, the army Commander about Watts' return from Murshidabad and further desired him to persuade the Nawab to come down to Calcutta at the earliest because the council had "many material points to settle" with him. On 29 May, the council also informed the Nawab about the return of Watts to Calcutta. It was also felt that as Major Carnac "must frequently be away" from the Nawab for the regulation and management of his army, it was necessary that "some person of rank" must always attend on Nawab Mir Jafar Khan. The Nawab's administration must be transacted with the advice of the Resident and hence the council directed Batson to reside with

9. Proceedings of the Committee appointed for the administration of Bengal, 1763-64 (B.M.P., III, pp. 11-12).

10. *Ibid*

11. C. P.C. p. 298, No. 2158.

the Nawob at Patna.[12] So long as the Nawab was at the latter place for the conduct of war. The council hoped that the Nawab would transact the affairs of Patna in consultation with Batson on all occasions.[13]

Due to Mir Jafar's absence from Murshidabad, his government soon fell a prey aggressions committed by the English *gomastahs*. Gray, the Resident at Malda, wrote to the Governor in January 1764 about "the villainous practices used by the Calcutta *gomashtas* in carrying on their business." The mishief was not confined to any particular place, as is evident from a complaint from Senior-the Chief of Kasimbazar, who wrote to the Governor on the following March : "It would amaze you the number of complaints that daily come before me of the extravagencies committed by our agents and *gomasthas* all over the country."[14] The Calcutta Council received complaints from many places and similar complaints were also received from Middleton who stated that "Jekyll has used most violent and unwarrantable measures by seizing a *Pikar*". The Calcutta Council expressed its inability to punish the offenders and, therefore, the council resolved that all the Europeans should return to Calcutta by 30 November next "and that after that time no European shall be permitted to go up the country under any pretence whatsoever."[15]

Mir Jafar's negotiations with Shujauddaulah, the Nawab of Oudh, during the war with Mir Qasim. beeame known to the English authotities in Calcutta. The confabulations between the two alarmed them. So they directed Major Carnac to maintain a proper check upon the Nawab "while the war continued". Baston was also directed to acquaint the Calcutta Council with every transaction at Patna. But

12. At the time, Mir Jafar had gone to Patna on the plea of personal supervision of war against Mir Qasim.

13. C.P.C., I, p. 315, Oo. 2269.

14. Verelst, *View*, p. 49.

15. Long, *Unpublished Records*, pp. 538-539. *Paikar* or *pikar* was the middle-man or broker in the trade at that time.

Mir Jafar, instead of depending upon the English support, started fresh negotiations with the Nawab of Oudh.[16] This did not escape the watchful eyes of Batson, who asked the Nawab to show his latest correspondence. The Nawab expressed his inability and gave an evasive reply. This raised a suspicion in the mind of Batson, which was further strengthened by the arrival of Shitab Rai, at the time *diwan* of Bihar appointed by Shah Alam II, with whom the Nawab kept his conversation secret. When Batson wanted to know the details of his conversation with Shitab Rai, the Nawab expressed his great dissatisfaction and replied that Shitab Rai come to him just as a friend to offer him advice regarding future proceedings. The Patna Resident become exceedingly suspicious and acquainted the council about what he called the Nawab's double dealings.[17] This almost forced the council to decide that Mir Jafar must be removed from Patna, which would not only prevent the Nawab's continuing his negotiations with Shujauddaulah but also reduce the heavy burden of the Company to keep so large a force in the field for a long time.[18] Besides these considerations, the council wanted expeditiously to settle the discharge of the treaty monies payable by the Nawab. Hence, they directed Batson to prevail upon the Nawab to come down to Calcutta.

The old Nawab after being acquainted with the request of the council, clearly understood their real intentions. He expressed his reluctance to follow the advice and tried to impress upon the Resident that his absence from Patna "may be attended with dangerous consequences" as the enemy was cantoned within 80 miles.[19] But under increasing pressure the Nawab had to fall in with the wishes of the council and set out for Calcutta on 27 July, accompanied by Nandkumar. On the eve of his departure from Patna, the English Resident

16. Batson's letter to the Council, 9 June (Bengal Secret consultations, 21 June, 1764).

17. *Ibid.*, 13 July (B.S.C., 24 July, 1764).

18. B.S.C., 24 July, 1764.

19. *Ibid.*

waited on him and assured him of the Company's intentions to support him against all odds. The Nawab seemed to be pleased and after a journey of about a month, reached Calcutta on 3 September, where he was received with befitting courtesy by the English officials.[20]

Mir Jafar went to Calcutta in the hope of meeting Clive. It was already known at Calcutta that Clive had been appointed as the Governor of Fort William for the second time.[21] The Nawab remained at Calcutta for four months but during this period he had to face constant trouble in settling the much vexed problems relating to the treaty money. The Calcutta Council began to press him for money through Middleton. Being disgusted the Nawab replied through Middleton that at the time of his departure from Calcutta in July 1763, the Calcutta Council demanded of him at Chitpur Garden ten lakhs of rupees on account of the losses to the merchants of Bengal and Bihar caused by Mir Qasim's plunder. Mir Jafar then did not consent to it "in consideration of the largeness of the sum" in the hope that some abatement would be made in due course of time. But after his return ftom Patna, in September 1764, he was told to pay forty lakhs of rupees. And in November of the same year, the English raised the amount to forth-eight lakhs of rupees. As the old Nawab was unable to pay so huge an amount, he requested the English authorities at Calcutta to wait for the arrival of Clive, who would settle the amount as well as the terms of payment.[22]

After this reply, Middleton informed the council that the old Nawob had removed all his effects along with his family into boats, intending to leave Calcutta immediately.[23] But the Nawab was not permitted to leave Calcutta. The Nawab was rather seriously ill at the time. The Calcutta

20. *Ibid.*, 4 Sep:ember, 1764.

21. Letter from Court, 1 June, 1764 (F.W.I.H.C., IV, p. 52).

22. Nawab's letter to the Board, Rd. 10 November, 1764 (B.M.P., III, p. 21). Also, C.P.C., I, pp. 350-351, No. 2455.

23. Secret Department, 10 November, 1764 (B.M.P., III, p. 21).

Council did not pay any attention to his illness and pressed him to discharge in full his treaty obligations. But when the old Nawab began to languish for a few weeks, he was at last allowed, on 9 December, to return to Murshidabad.[24]

Accordingly, the Nawab set out for Murshidabad on 14 December[25] and Middleton was appointed Resident at the *darbar* of the Nawab.[26] Agreeable to his new appointment Middleton proceeded to Murshidabad after receiving instruction from the Calcutta Council. He was instructed to press the Nawab for "the regular payments of his assignments towards defraying the expenses of the war, and his balances of the restitution." The Resident was further instructed to "procure and transmit" to Calcutta "an exact state of the Nawab's revenues and of the expenses of his government." He was also advised to keep a close vigil upon and send an account of the number of the Nawab's troops and on the whole try to promote harmony and understanding between the Nawab and the English Company.[27]

After the Nawab's return to Murshidabad, when he was still seriously ill, the Calcutta Council continued a long Correspondence with the former about Muhammad Reza Khan—the *naib* of Dacca. Muhammab Reza Rhan was detained at Murshidabad for six months for his non-payment of the Dacca revenues to the treasury. The victimised officers solicited English help to the matter with Nawab, which was readily agreed to by the Company. Middleton was instructed to protect Reza Khan[28] from the hands of the Nawab. Encouraged by this support, Khan had a long conversation with the Nawab who directed Reza Khan to pay Rs. 27,60,000. But Khan represented before the Governor that as the country had been "ruined by famine" and he had been detained at Murshidabad for a period of six months, the affairs at Dacca

24. B.S.C., 6 December, 1764.

25. Letter to Court, 6 February, 1765 (F.W.I.H.C., IV, p. 295).

26. *Ibid.*, 26 November, 1764 (F.W.I.H.C., IV, p. 274).

27. *Ibid.*, 6 February, 1765 (F.W.I.H.C., IV, p. 295).

28. C.P.C., I, p. 363, No. 2496.

had been in a state of confusion. The Nawab became displeased with Khan, and had no trust in his submission. Thus, Khan who had reasons to hope for English patronage, waited for the arrival of Middleton at Moradbagh.[29]

On the representation of the Khan, Spencer the Governor of the Company, requested the Nawab to consider Khan's case sympathetically. It was stated that the officer was "attached to the Nawab's family and to the English also." The Governor believed that Reza Khan would behave with the Nawab "as a dutiful servant" and as such should "be shown all reasonable favours". The Governoı also wrote to Middleton on the subject of Khan.[30] So, Middleton-the newly appointed Resident, after his arrival at Murshidabad, got Khan released from his disgrace and showed his "greatest kindness to him. One day, the Resident called both Reza Khah and Nandkumar at his residence at Moradbagh for the adjustment of Khan's affairs. In their presence it was settled that Khan would have to pay Rs. 26,30,000 on account of the present year and Rs. 1,30,000 at the arrears of the previous year. But Nandkumar of his own proposed that if two or three lakhs of rupees remained due at the end of the current year, the arreas might be paid along with the revenues of the next year. But Reza Khan again represented to the Governor his inability to pay "so large a sum", unless he was given two or three months' time in the next year. Reza Khan again made meek submissions and hoped for protection from the Governor.[31]

In reply to the Governor's request, the Nawab informed him that Reza Khan had paid only Rs. 3,82.000 and was in arrears of a large amount of money "owing to his carelessness and inattention to the collection of the revenues." Still the Nawab had kept him at ease in his own house and Middleton must not have failed to notice that the Nawab's every act with Reza was much softer than what he deserved.[32] The Governor, however, again pleaded his support for Reza Khan, calling

29. *Ibid.*, 363, No. 2523.
30. *Ibid.*, p. 370, No. 2525.
31. *Ibid.*, p. 372, No. 2534.
32. C.P.C., I, p. 373, No. 2536.

him "a well-wisher of the *sarkar*." From the report of Middleton, the governor became satisfied with Reza Khan's *bona fides*; he felt that Reza Khan's service at Dacca might prove greatly beneficial to the Nawab.[33]

At Murshidabad Mir Jafar's illness persisted and it became worse day by day. This serious illness of the Nawab was immediately reported by Middleton to the Secret Committee on 29 Janurry, 1765.[34] The members of the committee earnestly hoped for his recovery, not for their sympathy with him, but because according to them the Nawab's death would go to complicate the matters: "such an event in the present juncture of affairs would occasion much confusion through the provinces."[35] The Resident further informed the committee that the Nawab had given khelat to Najmuddaulah, step-brother to the deceased Miran, to act in his place by declaring him his successor, in case of his death.[36] The old Nawab also wrote a letter to the Governor about the nomination of his son Najmuddaulah as his successor. The almost incurably ill Nawab furthre requested the Governor to protect and take care of his son and the rest of his family.[37]

The News of Mir Jafar's serious illness as well as his nomination of Najmuddaulah as his successor reached Calcutta on 31 January through a letter from Middleton. The Resident also sounded a note of warning that the Nawab's death was likely to be followed by disturbances in the capital. Spencer, the Governor, immediately took various measures to ensure the interests of the Company in case of any commotion or fracas. Evidently he did not want to take any risk at the time of the change-over. Captain Grant was directed to stay at Murshidabad with Middleton and take command of the Company's

33. *Ibid.*, p. 374, No. 2541.

34. Secret Department Records, 4 February, 1765, p. 74.

35. F.W.I.H.C., IV. pp. 296-97.

36. S.D.R., 4 February, 1765, p. 74.

37. Mir Jafar's letter to the Governor, Rd. 7 February, 1765 (C. P.C., I, p. 377, No. 2549). This was the letter of Mir Jafar, as he died on 5 February, 1765.

sepoys. Middleton, if he so desired, was authorised to detain any officer or troops that would pass through Murshidabad. The Resident was also to keep a close watch over the developments at the capital and should wait for instruction should the Nawab breathe his last. He was also authorised to take any measure at his own discretion, but to be cautious as to cause no bitterness, should Mir Jafar recover from illness.[38]

On the morning of 5 February, shortly before his death the dying Nawab requested Middleton to be present near him, but before the Resident could reach the place, the old Nawab was reported dead at about noon on 5 February, 1765. The death of Mir Jafar was immediately reported by Middleton on the same day to Calcutta.[39] Najmuddaulah immediately desired Middleton to be present during the time of his installation ceremony. Najmuddaulah was still in his boyhood and hence politically immature. Middleton, accompanied by George Grey, Captain Stables, S. Droze and other gentlemen, hastened to comfort the sons of Mir Jafar. All of them advised Najmuddaulah, as the heir to the *masnad*, "to administer consolation to others." The young Nawab sat on the *masnad*, accordingly.[40] The Resident, on behalf of the Company, offered *nazar* to Nawab Najmuddaulah,[41] as did the Seths and other principal citizens of Murshidabad.

At the *darbar* Najmuddaulah expressed his grief for the death of his father. In his inaugural speech, the young Nawab addressed the Resident that "whatever engagements his father had entered into with the Governor and Council, he would strictly adhere to, and that he hoped the Company would supply the place of his father to him." He also expressed his hope in Nandkumar and wished to retain him in the post of the *diwan*. Najmuddaulah was then pro-

---

38. Spender's letters to Middleton, 31 January and 1 February, 1765 (*Transition*, p. 70).

39. Middleton's letter to the Secret Committee, 5 February, 1765.

40. Nandkumar's letter to the Governor, Rd. 7 February (C.P.C., I, p. 378, No. 2552).

41. Middleton's letter to the Secret Committee, 5 February, 1765.

claimed as the Nawab throughout the city with usual ceremony. After the young Nawab's accession, Middleton saw perfect tranquillity in the city.[42]

Najmuddaulah not only expressed his full support to the English Company before Middleton, but on the same day, he gave a written statement addressed to the English authorities at Calcutta about his deep sense of attachment to them. He stressed that his eyes were fixed on the friendship with the English.[43] Governor Spencer also sent condolences to him for the death of his father and assured his friendship. But as the Goverenor and his council had some second thoughts, it was further intimated to the Nawab that the Calcutta authorities were considering measures beneficial to the welfare of the Nawab and the good of the country. The Governor also assured Najmuddaulah that the decision of the council about him would be intimated in due course.[44]

Spencer and his council wanted Najmuddaulah to be a ploy in their hands. They wanted to make the Nawab understand "that he receives and must hold the government by the influence and authority of the Company."[45] Hence they immediately recalled Johnstone from Burdwan to help in their decision to make the new Nawab supinely dependent on them. At the same time, the Calcutta Council, evidently to put up a show of good intentions, wrote to Middleton: "That we are much concerned on the event and shall pay proper respect to the memory of the deceased by firing Minute guns in the evening of this day, and that it is as yet our intent to support the family of Meer Jaffier. But as many arrangements will be necessary which...............cannot be immediately determined on."

The council further intimated the Resident that the officers of the late government would in the mean time normally carry on the business and, when the council would deter-

42. *Ibid.*

43. S.D.R., 8 February, 1765.

44. C.P.C., I, p. 397, No. 2554.

45. Letter to Court, 8 Feb., 1765 (F.W.I.H.C., IV, p. 312).

mine fully about the measure adopted, a Committee of the Board would be appointed to place Mir Jafar's successor on the *masnad* "in a proper and public manner", so that "the whole country may see that he receives his government from the Company." This committee would have the power "to see the said several arrangements carried into Execution."[46] The council had not yet decided what the new relations with the Nawab should be, but they were determined on big changes.

A week after Najmuddaulah's succession to the *masnad* the Calcutta council reinforced by the arrival of Johnstone from Burdwan and Major Hector Munro from up-country, took up the question of succession. The installing of the new Nawab was a golden opportunity for receiving presents, as also a highly agreeable chance for the Company's servants to feather their own nests. But pending the Company's decision, Middleton was further instructed on 8 February, to discourage any application for *sanad* for the Nawab from any quarter and although such *sanads* could not be of much weight without the Company's assistance, as Shah Alam II was already living under English protection, "Yet they might in improper hands be sufficiently so to embarrass our affairs and that it is, our intention if they should appear necessary to have them procured through our influence alone."[47]

On 12 February, the Calcutta Council started their discussion on the question of succession and the majority was of the opinion that the *masnad* should be enjoyed by a scion of the family of Mir Jafar. There were two candidates—Najmuddaulah and Mir Saidu, Miran's minor son. Between these two, the council decided in favour of Najmuddaulah. But as Burdett who was in favour of Mir Saidu, did not agree with the majority, the case could not be decided on that day. The supporters of Najmuddaulah argued that the latter had already received *nazars* from the British Resident at the *darbar* as well as from

46. S.D.R., 8 February, 1765.
47. *Ibid.*
48. *Ibid.*, 12 February, 1766.

the principal citizens of Murshidabad and that "his accession has already been everywhere circulated in the usual form throughout the provinces." But Burdett argued that Miran's son was the right successor, whereas Najmuddaulah was born of Mir Jafar's concubine. "Our Resident having paid his *nazar* on the occasion", argued Burdett, should not be considered as a sufficient reason for Najmuddaulah's confirmation.[48]

The adjourned council met again on 14 February, took up the questions of succession, appointment of new ministers under English control and collection of revenues in the *subah* of Bengal. They confirmed Najmuddaulah as the successor of Mir Jafar but did not repose the whole charge of administration on him, nor upon Nandkumar but recommended Mohammad Reza Khan—the then *naib* of Dacca, to be appointed as *naib subah*, "who shall have immediately under the Nabob the Chief Management of all affairs."[49] Thus, the choice of appointing the ministers of the Nawab's choice was also curbed and restricted.

The President of the calcutta council had already written a letter to Najmuddaulah on 14 February about the council's determination of nominating and supporting him on the *masnad* of Bengal. They also appointed a deputation of four English gentlemen, who would proceed to Murshidabad to see the Nawab seated in "proper terms and dignity" with the support of the company.[50] In the secret proceedings of 20 February. the Calcutta council directed the members of the deputation to proceed to Murshidabad to get the treaty with Najmuddaulah duly executed.[51] The Calcutta council also enclosed a copy of the terms of a grant of twelve and a half lakhs of rupees promised by Mir Jafar to Tinker-- so long unfulfilled--which should remain with the Resident, who might press the Nawab for its payment. The council worte separate letters to senior

49. C.P.C., I, p. 381, No. 2563.
50. S.D.R., 14 February, 1765.
51. *Ibid.*, 20 February, 1765.

and Middleton informing them about their appointment as members of this deputation, and referred them to the instructions carried by Johnstone and Leycester proceeding to join them.[52]

When Najmuddaulah agreed to all the terms of the treaty he was publicly reinvested by the members of the deputation as the Nawab of the Bengal *subah* in an open *darbar*, on the 10th day of Ramzan, corresponding to 3 March at about 2 o' clock in the afternoon. He presented various reward and titles to the members of the deputation each with a robe of honour, consisting of a *sarpech* set with jewels, a sword, a male elephant and a title.[53] The members of the deputation also extracted huge amounts of the money from Najmuddaulah Reza khan, Jagat seth and others. Verelst.- an English official at Chittagong, who later on became the Governor of the Company, reacted sharply when he heard about this type of ignoble transactions. He wrote to Middleton: "Some rumours have spread abroad that a present is intended to the council on the new accession. I hope, there is no truth in it. I should be sorry there was a thought, at so critical a time, of any such thing; for it must entail, on every one concerned, the world's severest censure.,,[54] However, the Resident did not feel ashamed for such ignoble extractions and worte in reply to Verelst "I have been told that the Nabob intends a present to all the board...... If such a thing be offered, I cannot, my friend, see the least impropriety in accepting of it; custom and conduct of one of our wrothiest men, justifies it, ... The present Nabob receives his government from our hands, as his father did. If anything of this kind was to be offered in consider-

52. Johnstone and Leycester were the members of the Calcutta Council, while Senior was the Chief of the English factory at Kasimbazar, and Middleton-the British Resident at Murshidabad.

53. Najmuddaulah's letter to the Governor, Rd. 6 March, 1765 (C.P.C., I, p. 390), No. 2599.

54. Verelst's letter to Middleton, 7 March, 1765 (Verelst, *View*, p. 51, f.n.).

ation of services to be done, or any kind of bargain made before hand, it would be highly improper to take it, but when it is given for what we think right, I do not, for my own part see the least harm in it."[55]

Meanwhile Clive, now Baron Clive of Plassey, reached Calcutta on the morning of 3 May, 1765. He had already been appointed President and Governor of the Fort William in Bengal and Commander-inchief of all the company's forces.[56] Besides clive, the court of Directors "thought proper to appoint a committee on this occasion", consisting of sumner and Sykes, who accompanied Clive to Calcutta, as well as Carnac and Verelst, who were in India at that time, to form the select Committee "with full powers to pursue" the course of action according to their judgment.[57] Clive, after being assured of the select committee's support and co-operation, surveyed the whole situation in two days. He criticised the policy of Spencer's government and called the first meeting of his council on 5 May, where most of the members present gave vent to their rage. Johnstone and Leycester challenged the extraordinary powers of the new Select Committee but Clive faced them by taking the firmest stand that the committee was the sole judge of their own power. Clive also declared that the whole transaction of Najmuddaulah's accession by Sepencer's government was a violation of the policy. Contrary to the positive orders from the court, the members of the deputation had, as if, put up the crown of Bengal for sale and. appropriated the money in their pockets. The members had with undue haste concluded this transaction which clearly proved that they were fully aware of its illegality. When Clive learnt how the individual pockets had been filled, he eagerly looked for some ways to compel them to "disgorge their illgotten gains,"[58] In such an atmosphere, with his pedestal shaking, Najmuddaulah was very eager to meet Clive. But Middleton—the Murshidabad

55. Quoted in Verelst, *View*, p. 51, f.n.
56. Letter from Court, 9 May, 1764 (F.W.I.H.C., IV, p. 43).
57. *Ibid.*, 1 June, 1764 (F.W.I.H.C., IV, p. 55).
58. Gleig's *Clive*, pp. 209-210.

Resident, urged the Nawab not to go to Calcutta "without the approbation of the gentlemen of the council."[59] The Nawab, however, refused to listen and wanted to go to Calcutta right then. The Nawab actually started from Murshidabad on 8 May. On his way, at Mankar, he received a letter from Clive promising "support and protection". Clive sent Sykes to receive Najmuddaulah and himself waited upon the Nawab.[60]

At Calcutta, Najmuddaulah complained about the extraction of money from him without his knowledge, and this Clive could not ignore. An enquiry into the matter was taken up. It continued for some days from the first week of June to the 21st of that month. It was proved that Johnstone, Senior, Middleton and Leycester—the members of the deputation, had received presents from the Nawab. Middleton—the Resident had received a present of Rs. 1,12,500 from the treasury of the Nawab through one Santiram Singh.[61] Spencer and the members of his council: Playdell, Burdett and Gray, had received money from the Nawab as well as from Jagat Seth.[62] Spencer, as well as Johnstone, Senior, Leycester and Middleton received presents from Reza Khan also.[63]

On 7 June, the question of receiving presents was taken up for discussion. Johnstone, Burdett, Leycester and Playdell confessed that they had received gifts, but they strongly justified it. On the other hand all the four members of the Select Committee—Clive, Sykes Verelst and Sumner were opposed to their acceptance. Clive as the President of the Select Committee stated "that no presents whatever ought to have been accepted after the receipt of the covenants, except in manner

59. *Transition*, p. 92.

60. Walsh, *Murshidabad*, p. 162.

61. S.C.R., Vol. 10, pp. 34-36.

62. *Ibid.*

63. S.C.R., 8 June 1765 pp. 50-51 (*Vide*, Mukhopadhyay *Diwani in Bengal*, Appendix-C, p. 187). Also, Reza Khan's second Narrative (S.C.R. 1765, Vol. 10, p. 37).

specified therein."[64] Thus Clive tried to carry out the order of the Court of Directors to get a refund of the presents, thus extracted, to the Company. Upon this, Johnstone immediately resigned from service and refused to acknowledge the authority of the Select Committee. The Select Committee thus issued notice to Middleton—the British Resident at Murshidabad, to refund the money to the Company. Others were notified through their attornies in India.[95] But, later on, the case instituted by the Company to refund the money, was withdrawn, evidently for political reasons.[66]

About the young Nawab, Clive formed a poor opinion. He found Reza Khan a man of ability but Clive was unwilling to put unlimited powers in the hands of Reza Khan alone. Thus, the Select Committee, keeping in view the youth and inexperience of the Nawab, thought it necessary to divert the administration in the hands of capable persons, who could form a bulwork for the government, as well as look after the Company's interests. It was, therefore, decided that Reza Khan be advised "to relinquish the title of *naib subah* for the safety of the present government and future tranquillity of the country". It was also deemed necessary to associate Reza Khan with Rai-Durlabh and Jagat Seth in the administration of the government, so that each might enjoy an equal share of power and authority. The three ministers, with equal authority, would regulate the affairs of the state. As per details, the Nawab's treasury would have three keys, one with each of the ministers, so that one could not draw any amount without the knowledge of the others. The British Resident at

64. Bengal Consultations, 7 June, 1765 (quoted in Auber, *Rise*, I, p. 134).

65. *Transition*, p. 96, f.n.

66. *Ibid*, General Carnac—a member of the Select Committee, received a present of Rs. 80,000 from Rajah Balwant Singh. The General received another present of Rs. 2,00,000 from Shah Alam. But when the covenants were sent afterwards to him, he refused to sign. As Carnac was not aware of the covenants, Clive supported him in respect of receiving presents. Beveridge, *A Comprehensive History*, I, pp. 378–379.

Murshidabad, would have to be maintained at the expense of the Nawab to keep a check on the accounts of the Nawab's government. The ministers would be required, each month, to submit thier accounts to the Resident, and thus be directly responsible for their work to the latter.[67] With these resolutions of the Select Committee, Najmuddaulah's stay at Calcutta came to an end, and the poor Nawab, shorn of all his powers, started for Murshidabad in great disappointment.

On 25 June, Clive left Calcutta for up -country to conclude a new settlement with Shah Alam II and Shujauddaulah. On his way, he halted at *Moti jhil* in order to meet the Nawab of Bengal and to suggest to him some important changes in his government. About the affairs at Murshidabad which had fallen in great disarray, he wrote to Sykes on 29 June: "I fear the military as well as the civil are so far gone in luxury and debauchery, that it will require the utmost exertion of an united committee to save the Company from destruction. However, let us always appeal to the rectitude of our intentions and we shall be enabled to complete the arduous undertaking with great satisfaction and honour to ourselves."[68]

When Clive met the Nawab and his ministers, he was surprised to notice the submissive and abject attitude of Reza Khan, whose powers, though "distinct and separate" were greatly encroached upon by Rai-Durlabh. The latter had already by his cunning moves substantially succeeded in upsetting the balance of power in the court politics and assumed dispensing powers in regard to the duties of all officers. The entire collection of revenues also was practically now in his hands. "This is certainly subversive," Clive observed in his letter to the Select Committee, "of our intentions as it has a tendency to increase the power of Roy Dullub and diminish that of Mahomed Reza Khan." As a solution to this problem, Clive wrote to the committee for "an early

---

67. S.C.R., Vol. 20, 21 June, 1765. Also, Clive's letter to Court, 30 September, 1765 (F.W.I.H.C., IV pp. 338-339).

68. Quoted in alcolm, *Clive*, II, p. 331.

appointment of a proper person to reside at the city" as "the best means of preserving tranquillity". Clive had a great confidence in Sykes and so he proposed that Sykes should be sent to Murshidabad, to remain there for a fortnight, to prevent any disunion among the three ministers of the Nawab. Middleton—the Resident, was to be given to understand that Sykes' visit to the city would not be prejudicial to his honour and interest.[69]

Though Clive wrote to the committee about Sykes' short visit for a "fortnight" to Murshidabad, yet his real intention was to replace Middleton.[70] Clive and the committee had come to form a poor opinion of Middleton for his having extracted presents from the young Nawab. To Clive, Sykes, was a man of integrity.[71] But the replacement of Middleton was not immediately done. The Select Committee decided to appoint Sykes only to reside for a few weeks at the *darbar*, without any injury to the importance of the existing Resident, in order to" support the present established system of administration."[72] The committee also enlightened Sykes about the nature of the system followed at Murshidabad, which had already been

69. Clive's letter to the Select Committee, 3 July (SCR., 7 July 1765, pp. 100-101).

70. Letter to Court, 30 September (F.W.I.H.C., IV, p. 361). Leycester and Gray strongly supported Middleton to be continued as the Resident. But when Middleton came to know of this resolution of the Committee, which was also hinted to him by Clive, when the latter was at Murshidabad, the Resident thought that the appointment of Sykes "must lessen the weight and influence" of his station; he solicited for the Chiefship of Patna that was vacant after the death of Billers. This was accordingly granted. Letter to Court, 30 September 1765 F.W.I.H.C., IV, p. 354).

71. "I need only add, that Sykes, for whom we intend the Residentship, is a gentleman whose flexible integrity, and long experience in the country politics, we have reason to expect the most exact performance of every duty in such a important station." Clive's letter to Court, 30 September (F.W.I.H.C., IV, p. 339).

72. S.C.R., 7 July, 1756, p. 98.

weakened and dishonoured by Rai-Durlabh. Therefore, Sykes was directed to proceed to Murshidabad and "to keep the most watchful eye" over Rai-Durlabh, to put a check upon his aspiring nature. The committee expressed its confidence in the zeal and competence of Sykes and hoped that his prudence would sufficiently guide him to act in the right manner in the affairs of Murshidabad.[73] The committee, also, at the same time, directed Middleton to arrange for the deputation of Sykes to the *darbar*, telling him once again that Sykes' visit would not be derogatory to his influence or prestige at Murshidabad. He was thus directed to assist Sykes in all matters, when the latter would arrive there, to transact the most important business in the immediate as well as the prospective interests of the Company.[74]

Clive soon convinced the Nawab about the latter's incapacity to transact the business of the *subah* even for a day without the English help and advice. Thus, on 9 July, the Nawab and his ministers affixed their signatures in triplicate on the regulations of the *subah* of Bengal and thus gave a final shape to the arrangements of 21 June. It wss also agreed that the payments to the soldiers would pass through Reza Khan's hand within certain stipulated sums. These stipulated sums, which included stipends for the Begams, Miran's sons and the Nawab's brothers, would be finally adjusted and passed by Sykes,[75] on behalf of the Company. After completing these projects at Murshidabad, Clive made preparations for his journey to up-country, to obtain *diwani* for the Company from Shah Alam. On his way to Benares, Clive wrote to Sykes from Bhagalpur to lay hands on Gray who was guilty of carrying on illicit private trade with the Rajah of Dinajpur. He also informed Sykes that Rai-Durlabh and Reza Khan were collecting "numberless proofs of this kind" and hence Sykes' presence at Murshidabad was very essential.[76]

Sykes arrivrd at Kasimbazar on 22 July, to restore the balance of power between Reza Khan and Rai-Durlabh on the

73. S.C.R., 7 July, 1765.
74. Select Committee's letter to Middleton, 9 July.
75. S.C.R., Vol. 10, pp. 121-122.
76. Quoted in Forrest, *Clive*, II, p. 280.

one hand, and induce Najmuddaulah to agree to the terms of the new arrangements according to Clive's suggestions, on the other. Sykes had a secret understanding with Clive to reduce, if possible, the Nawab's stipend to forty lakhs. But though the Nawab had meekly yielded before Clive, he was not so tame before Sykes.[77] So Sykes' negotiations at Murshidabad took a long time to be finalised. From Kasimbazar Sykes came to Murshidabad on 23 July. He immediately informed the Select Committee about Clive's suggestions to him, "to get the Nawab to throw the management of affairs entirely into the hands of the Ministers", which would *ipso facto* transfer the actual power into the hands of the Company. This arrangement would enable the Company to meet the expenses for the army, to remit the annual stipend to the Emperor and also to cover the Nawab's household charges. Sykes assured the committee that he would try his utmost to make the Nawab accept an annual stipend of fifty lakhs. He further informed them that he would immediately calculate the Nawab's actual expenses in order "to judge what stipend will be most suitable to his rank and Dignity."[78]

The Company at this time in great financial distress, demanded from the Nawab through Sykes, an immediate payment of six lakhs of rupees, an accout of the restitution money of the late Nawab. But Najmuddaulah denied the responsibility for paying the amount saying that he did not know that such "a large sum is ready in the public treasury."[79] However Sykes represented to him, in concert with Lal Singh, the *khazanchi*, the deplorable condition of the Company's treasury. The Nawab somehow procured a bill of the same amount from the Seths and the bill was duly forwarded to Calcutta.[80]

The main business of Sykes at Murshidabad was to complete the arrangements with the Nawab, which was done at

77. *Transition*, pp. 100-101.
78. Sykes' letter to the Select Committee, 24 July (S.C.R., 10 August, 1765).
79. C.P.C., I, pp. 411-412, No. 2660.
80. Lal Singh's letter to the Committee. Rd. 25 July (C.P.C., I, p. 423, No. 2685).

the end of July. After a mature consideration, the Nawab agreed to accept a stipend of Rs. 53,86,131–9 annually. Sykes thought it a reasonable stipend, as the huge expense of Nawab's household obliged him to raise the money.[81] It was on the one hand, a great Sacrifice on the part of the Nawab, and on the other, a glorious opportunity for the English to obtain the *diwani*, which Sykes thought, would easily be procured by Clive. "In the course of settling this business with the Nawab" Sykes stated in his letter to the Select Committee, "I have had the greatest attention to every part of his family to prevent their receiving any ill-treatment or bad usage from him." The charge of the disbursement of this money would rest upon the three ministers, who would effect monthly payment to the members of the royal family and the payments to the Nawab's sepoys, horses, servants, etc., would rest upon them as well. There now remained nothing to be done, but the execution of the Company's arrangements with Emperor Shah Alam II, which was Clive's responsibility. About the balance of power, Rai-Durlabh soon realised his errors and did not cause any further trouble. "There is at present the greatest harmony" observed Sykes in his letter, "and cordialit subsisting between the Nabob and his Ministers", as also "between the ministers themselves".[82] Thus, the Select Committee at Calcutta became fully satisfied with Sykes' arrangements and agreed to write to Clive on 10 August: "That Mr. Sykes has concluded with the Nabob the important business recommended by His Lordship which we request may be confirmed and sanctified by a *snnnud* from the king and that he continues at the *Durbar* only to have the obligation executed in form reserving however the full ratifications to His Lordship and the Committee."[83]

Clive always kept Sykes informed about the developments of his mission. On his way to Allahabad, he halted at Benares,

81. Sykes' letter to Sumner, 28 July (Bolts, *Considerations*, p. 135).
82. Sykes' letter to the Select Committee, 28 July (S.C.R., 10 August, 1765).
83. S.C.R., 10 August, 1765.

where Clive met with Shujauddaulah, on 2 August. Clive extended his support to Shujauddaulah, the Nawab-Wazir, and after this successful negotiation, Clive wrote a letter to Sykes expressing satisfaction for the latter's arrival at Murshidabad. Clive had great faith in Sykes' ability and so he wrote to Sykes from Benares on 3 August, instructing him to reduce the army of the young Nawab, which would go to reduce the allowances of the Nawab as well. After these directions, Clive further instructed Sykes to try to soothe the mind of Najmuddaulah, Reza khan, Rai-Durlabh and the Seths, so that everyone was ready to toe the line in accordance with the plan that the English had decided upon.[84]

During Clive's absence from Bengal the Select Committee at Calcutta and Sykes at Murshidabad fulfilled the desired object of Clive about the inland trade of Bengal, which, in this way, became the monopoly of the English merchants. Clive himfelf, had promised that "he would not engage in any kind of trade himself, but leave all commercial advantages to the servants, to be divided amongst themselves,"[85] But the Directors had already disapproved this plan by forbidding the renewal of this trade.[86] Thus, as it was interpreted, Clive had betrayed the confidence of the Directors and "entered into the partnership" with some Englishmen for the purpose of dealing in salt, betel-nuts and tobacco.[87] This partnership soon became, for all practical purposes another Company of East India Company's leading servants in Bengal. The consequence was that the Indian traders were deprived completely of trading in these articles. To give this idea a legal status the select Committee at Calcutta resolved on 10 August, "that the whole trade shall be carried on by an exclusive Company, formed for that purpose and consisting of all those who may be deemed justly entitled to a share." It was further resolved that these articles of common consumption would be "purcha-

84. Forrest, *Clive*, II, p. 281-282.

85. Bolts, *Considerations*, p. 165.

86. B.M.P., III, p. 300.

87. Bolts, *Considerations*, p. 166.

sed by this established Company", and that "application shall be made to the Nabob to issue the like prohibition to all his officers and subjects of the Districts where any Quantity of either of these Articles is manufactured or produced." In the ninth article it was also resolved that as some difficulties might arise in securing the produce at Dacca and Chittagong districts an application might be made to the Nawab "for *perwannahs* on the several *zamindars* of these districts, as well as those of Houghly, strictly ordering and requiring them to contract for all the salt that can be made on their lands with the English alone, and forbidding the sale to any other person or persons whatsoever."[88] Sumner acquainted the committee that he had communicated the intention in the 3rd and 9the articles to Sykes and advised him to apply to the Nawab for the necessary *parwanas*.

Accordingly, sykes pressed the Nawab to implement this resolution forthwith and the puppet Nawab very obediently sent a circular to different officers about the monopoly of the Company over these three important articles of inland trade, i.e. salt, betel-nut and tobacco. The Select Committee had also taken obligatory bonds from the Chiefs and landlords promissing that they would not "dispose of a single grain of salt...made within the dependencies of their territories to any person excepting the English gentlemen, called the English Society of Merchants"[89]

The Select Committee at Calcutta gave its full consent to Sykes for the loan of two lakhs of rupees that had been obtained by the Resident from the merchants of Murshidabad. The Committee also consented to the obtaining of an amount of fifteen or sixteen thousand rupees from Najmudaulah, which was a token of the latter's respect for the Company. About Sykes' plans to conduct the salt trade, the committee observed "We shall compare them with those communicated by the other Members of the Committee and after digesting the whole acquaint you with the result". About this trade in salt, the committee further observed in the same letter : "We are to

88. B.M.P., III, pp. 23-24.

89. Bolts, *Considerations*, p. 178.

infrom you that...consequence of advices received from Lord Clive since your absence positive orders have been issued for recalling all free Merchants by the 21st of October next. Advertisements to that effect not only posted up in Calcutta but circulated to all the subordinate settlements."[90]

Thus, after Sykes had finished all the tasks allotted to him at Murshidabad, the Select Committee sounded Clive about sykes' return to Calcutta.[91] But meanwhile Sykes had taken great strides for the benefit of the Company. On 14 August, Sykes sent to Calcutta the draft of a new treaty, which would bring into force the grant of the *diwani.* Sykes also informed the committee in his letter of 17 August about his proposal to Najmuddaulah "to dismiss the useless rabble" and to accept in its place 1000 or 1500 of the sepoys of the Company, whereby the latter might save Rs. 18 lakhs. The Nawab readily agreed to the proposal with the conviction that it would reduce a heavy load upon him and promote his ease, as well as augment the interest of the Company[92] whose blessings he needed the most. On the finalisation of these arrangements with the Nawab, the Select Committee conveyed to Sykes their full approval of his policy for dismissing the Nawab's "useless cavalry and sepoys" and making the Nawab agree to depend on the Company's forces "for the support of his dignity." They also likewise approved Sykes' proposal for ragulating the business of the *faujdars* of the *subah,* They further advised Sykes to keep a watchful eye "over the conduct of the ministers."[93]

Clive successfully concluded the treaty of Allahabad with the Mughal Emperor by which the Company obtained the *diwani* of the *subah* of Bengal. On 20 August, he wrote a letter to Sykes about his arrangements with the Emperor,

---

90. Select Committee's letter to Sykes, 10 August (S.C.R., Vol. 10, pp. 139-140).

91. Select Committee's letter to Clive, 10 August (*Ibid.,* pp. 124-125).

92. Select Committee Proceedings, 7 September, 1765.

93. Select Committee's letter to Sykes, 7 September (S.C,P., 7 September, 1765).

to which, he attached the greatest value. Clive depended much on Sykes, his strongest supporter in the Select Committee. He was most valuable to Clive after Sumner's defection. Clive, despite much controversy[94], installed Sykes in the post of the Resident at the *darbar*, where the latter permanently replaced Middleton on 21 August, 1765.[95]

Clive returned to Murshidabad from up-country to acquaint the Nawab with the recent arrangements made with Shah Alam II. But soon he realised that much enemity had grown between the Nawab and Reza Khan over the control of larger public funds of the *nizamat*. In the mean time Sykes even induced the Nawab, for a further reduction of 18 lakhs in the latter's stipend and agree to the control of Reza Khan over the Nawab's expenses. Quite naturally the Nawab's heart was not there in the agreement ; what irked him the most was the increasing power of the Khan. The Select Commtttee had also approved Sykes' arrangements—the reduction of the Nawab's stipend. Clive understood the cause of dissatisfaction of the Nawab and as such, at Clive's intervention, the Nawab's stipend was not reduced, though Clive induced him to disband his rabble army.[96]

From Murshidabad Clive reached Calcutta on 6 September. On the next day, he laid before the committee a copy of the treaty of peace signed at Allahabad concluded at once with Najmuddaulah and Shujauddaulah, together with the translation of the *sanad* obtained from the Emperor for the *diwani* of the *subah* of Bengal. The grant of *diwani* to the Company necessitated a new arrangement with Najmuddaulah. On 30 September. Najmuddaulah confirmed his acceptance of an annual stipend of Rs. 53,86,131-9 from the Company which had already been arranged by Skyes on behalf of the

94. Sykes was ignorant of the country language. He gained diplomatic experience, when he was the third at Kasimbazar factory. Clive wanted his support and, as such, Sykes was appointed both as the Resident and on Senior's departure for England, as Chief of Kasimbazar. *Transition*, pp. 107-108.

95. *Transition*, p. 107. Also, Mukhopadhyay, *Diwani in Bengal*, p. 133.

96. Wheeler, *Early Records*, p. 334.

Company. By the 8th article of the treaty, Najmuddaulah accepted a Resident at his *darbar* : "Wherever I am, I consent that an English gentleman shall reside with me to transact all affairs between me and the Company, and that a person of high rank shall also reside, on my part, at Calcutta to negotiate with the Governor and Council."[97] The details of the *nizamat* expenses of the *subah* of Bengal were agreed upon between Najmuddaulah and the English Company represented by Clive, Sumner, Carnac, Verelst and Skyes. Hence, the post of the Resident at the *darbar* after the grant of *diwani* was an employment of consequence. Sykes' views and principles were perfactly in harmony with Clive's plan of administration.[98] Naturally the rapport between the two was great.

Sykes was acting as the watchdog of Murshidabad administration. He was also determined to enhance his own position and to reap material advantage for himself under the mask of active efforts to maximise the profits of the Company. Within a short time Sykes realised that the Bihar administration was very slack. Middleton-his predecessor at Murshidabad, had been appointed as the Chief of the English factory at Patna, but did not enjoy Clive's confidence. Middleton also struck a bad patch with the junior officers working under him. While Dhiraj Narain's incapacity was well known, there continued the struggle for power between him and his more powerful *peshkar*, Shitab Rai. Rajah Dhiraj Narain was the *naib diwan* at Patna under the English Chief. He was succeded in the post by Shitab Rai. When Clive came to Patna for suppressing the attempted mutiny by the European officers, Shitab Rai told him about the anomalies in the Patna accounts and requested him for an enquiry by Reza Khan.[99] Now, after the grant of the *diwani*, Clive found it convenient to act accordingly. So Clive asked for an enquiry about the Bihar revenues which was to be conducted by Sykes with the assistance of Reza Khan. But in the

---

97. Quoted in Walsh, *Murshidabad*, p. 165.

98. Caraccioli, III, pp. 402-403.

99. *Seir*, III, pp. 17-21.

month of October, Sykes went to Calcutta and during his absence from Murshidabad, Reza Khan arranged the Bengal papers ready for despatch to Calcutta. As it is on record, Reza Khan was "looking over all the papers concerning the province of Bihar", awaiting for the arrival of Sykes, when everything was to be done according to Clive's pleasure.[100]

Clive also informed Reza Khan to work in concert with Sykes so that a favourable order could be got from the Select Committee. He had issued orders to all the Chiefs of the subordinate factories to return the Company's people to Calcutta within 21 October. If they refused to return to Calcutta whithin the date specified, they would be left completely at the mercy of the country government In such a case Reza Khan might take any measure for sending them to Calcutta. Clive hoped that with, advice of Sykes the Khan might be able "to carry on the business of the government in a proper manner,"[101] i.e. according to Clive's wishes and behests. At the same time, Clive sent a list of the names of the "Company's servants and free merchants "who remained in the muffasal" of Bengal to Reza Khan.[102] In reply and towards the execution of Clive's order, Reza Khan wrote to Clive that "whosoever acts contrary thereto will be sent for and the Governor will be informed thereof." The Khan also professed to do this work in concert with Sykes for the management of the business of the Company.[103]

It also came to the notice of the Select Committee that the Armenians and their agents also had begun to interrupt and enter competitively in the Company's investment at difficult places. So the Select Committee urged Sykes to "take every possible measure to prevent their holding any intercourse with those places, where we provide our investment,

100. Reza Khan's letter to Clive, Rd. 8 October (C.P.C., I, pp. 433-434, No. 2720).

101. Clive's letter to Reza Chan, 8 October (C.P.C., I, pp. 434-435), No. 2722),

102. Long, *Unpublished Records*, p. 546.

103. Reza Khan's letter to Clive, 24 October (C.P.C., I, p. 437, No. 2729).

which may tend the prejudice of the Company." It was thus hoped that Sykes would exert his influence to "see those orders strictly executed."[104]

At the end of October, 1765, Sykes took up the work of streamlining the Company's economy in Bihar by cutting down the useless expenses of the *nizamat*. One of his measures that he proposed to effect economy in the administration was the removal of Ihteramuddoulah[105] and Dhiraj Narain[106] from the posts of *naib* and *diwan*, respectively, of ground of incompetence. But Reza Khan as well as Rai-Durlabh did not want their dismissal before any alternative arrangement was made. The Select Committee also, in its letter to Sykes on 25 October, did not approve of his idea and recommended their continuance in view of the dignity of their station and the local leverage that they enjoyed.[107] Sykes reacted angrily against the committee's views and on 31 October brought complaints of fraud and villainy against the above officers before Clive. He sent a statement of the Bihar revenues and informed Clive that "after a scrutiny into several years' accounts I find very little has been really brought to the credit of the *Nizamut*". The expense incurred for the collection of revenues during the time of Rajah Ramnarain as well as of the *naib* in office, Ihteramuddaulah, was shown to be Rs.21,53,934-2-10, which was a staggering figure. But after a proper scrutiny, with the help of Reza Khan, Sykes had lowered down the expenses to Rs. 7,50,920 though still it seemed to him "great and heavy".[108] The Resident accepted the need to retain Ihteramuddaulah and Dhiraj Narain as "our connections" with Mir Jafar and Ramnarain "made it necessary to give them our countenance" and accepted the idea of retaining the offices of the two incumbents, with the setting up of three more offices ; but

104. Long, *Unpublished Records*, p. 557.

105. The brother of Mir Jafar Khan.

106. The brother of Ramnarain.

107. *Transition*, p. III.

108. Sykes' letter to Clive, 31 October (S.C.R., 5 November, 1765).

he did this reluctantly, declaring that this new set of people would be found to be incapable of managing the affairs of that province. But despite all deterrents and opposition Sykes was determined to effect a total change, though by degrees and without causing any disturbance all over the country.[109] The account of *jagirs* and charity lands compiled to the very high figure of Rs. 20,18,714-10 must have been misapproriated by fraudulent means by those "who had the management of affairs," and the Company deprived of it on that account. Thus Sykes wanted a thorough reformation and recommended to Clive that "an entire reformation wants to be made sooner or latter, which if you should not have it done now, I would recommend its taking place in April next, when the *punea* is made, and the value of each *purgunnah* is fixed, or as soon as you think it will be most consistent with the plan of government you are desirous of supporting. A regular and a proper mode once fixed on, and men of activity, steadiness and integrity employed in the management of the collections, who will pay proper attention to the Frontier Provinces, I am cofident that the province of Bahar will then yield very little short of one crore of Rupees."[110] Sykes, on his part, also informed Clive in the same letter that the *jagirs* and charity lands stood at the old rate "at what they paid many years ago" and they would now certainly produce "double the amount" ; and the surplus amounts must be "brought to the credit of the Company." Shitab Rai "as king's *dewan*" managed the department of the *Khalsa*, wherein he not only received the revenues but duties arising to the government, and as it was felt, this considerable amount "ought to be added to this account". Sykes not only wrote about it to Ihteramuddaulah but also to the Patna *mutasuddies*, who, however, declined to furnish the Resident with any accounts of the same, referring Sykes to Shitab Rai for them.[111] Sykes noticed that gross abuses prevailed everywhere and hence

109. *Ibid*.

110. *Ibid*.

111. *Ibid*.

he strongly felt the need for some regulations binding upon the *chowkies* all over the country. Accordingly, Sykes directed Reza Khan to write to the *faujdars* and *zamindars* of the different parts for an exact account of all the *chowkies* now kept up and suggested that "a few considerable ones might be established in the most convenient parts of the country."

Sykes made no bones to bring to Clive's notice the rampant corruption and abuse of power almost everywhere. He observed : "Fraud and villany appears to have been carried to so great a height in every Department that I am no longer surprised that the Nabobs of late have been so much distressed in their Government ; a total change by degree must be made." Sykes realised that for a thorough reformation, he would "have to struggle with every difficulty" because in this endeavour, he would be resisted by the powerful vested interests : the ministers, *mutsuddies*, *kanungos* and their dependents ; yet with Clive's support, he did not doubt that he would be able to accomplish the optimum expectations of the Governor.[112]

In the month of November, Sykes sent an account of the revenues to Clive and the Select Committee. The account concluded with the *faujdars*, *zamindars* etc. showed that the receipts for 1765 amounted to Rs. 1,29,29,016-10-2. This was a steep increase and there was history behind it. On Sykes' arrival at Murshidabad he had found that the revenues arising from the different Provinces and *Parganahs* of Bengal were not finally with the different officers of the government. He had also found that Reza khan's assessments were lower than what they had produced in the days of Alivardi , Sirajuddaulah and Mir jafar. So Sykes had revised them with the hope that if properly managed"we may reasonably expect an encrease with the least oppression to the farmers or tanants. "[113] For the "welfare of the Nabob and our Employers" Sykes was determined "to put a stop to the Scandalous practices." Sykes informed Clive that

112. *Ibid.*

113. Sykes' letter to Clive and the Select Committee, 17 November, (S.C.R., 22 November, 1765).

he would try his utmost to collect the full amount of Rs. 1,50, 04,887-2-5 of which he hoped to collect fifty lakhs within 11 February next, which would also include the December payments. About the disbursement of money, Sykes informed Clive in the same letter that he had supplied to the factories of Kasimbazar and Dacca, "the former with three lacks of *sicca* rupees and the latter with one of Arcots" and he promised to send to Calcutta six lakhs of rupees.[114]

One week after this letter, Sykes enclosed to Clive and the Select Committee, an account of the receipts and disbursements from the day of *punyiah* up to 61 October, in order to acquaint the committee about "a perfect idea of the state of affairs." He forwarded "a regular and monthly treasury account", so that an effectual stop to the existing scandalous practices might be made. The balance of Rs. 4,39,508-14-6 brought to the credit of Bengal, which had been concealed from the time of Mir Qasim. Sykes obliged the officer who dealt with it to make good the amount. The Resident was strongly apprehensive that he would find many such incidents and hence requested for a thorough enquiry.[115] Sykes further informed the committee that with the assistance of the ministers he had made arrangement of the *chowkies* and "supported for the collection of the proper duties and customs arising from the trade and merchandize of the country." Arrangements had been made to station eight to ten sepoys at every principal *chowki* to ensure receipt of "the just and lawful duties" of the government. The Resident also suggested for the abolition of innumerable non-functioning *chowkies* but to retain only some of the principal *chowkies* belonging to the *zamindars* to facilitate smooth collections in future.[116]

Thus, Sykes took up implementation of his plan for the collection of the Bihar revenues. Accordingly Dhiraj Narain was advised to pay an annual allowance to Ihteramuddaulah and not to permit the latter "to return to his station at Patna

114. *Ibīd.*
115. Sykes' letter to Clive and Committee, 25 November (S.C.R., 29 November, 1765).
116. *Ibid.*

or interfere any further in the affairs of that province on account of his incapacity." Thus, Shitab Rai became the head of the revenue collectors of that province. The revenues fixed for the ensuing session for Bihar amuonted to Rs.1,10,903-11-15, exclusive of charges, and a statements to this end had sent to Dhiraj Narain and Shitab Rai for their confirmation. They were directed to draw out the *Kistbundee* and to proceed immediately in making the collections. They were also required to keep the ministers regularly informed about their progress and to obtain the Resident's advice whenever necessary. To obtain an accurate and exact account of their "heavy expenses," Sykes entirely depended on Dhiraj Narain, Shitab Rai and the English Chief of Patna, "to form a true judgment of the value of that province."[117]

At this time, some troubles cropped up in the *parganahs* of Bhagalpur, Kolgong, Chugh and Pirgah over the collection of revenues. These were due to the incapability of Mirza Daud[118] who had been appointed the collector of revenues of those *parganahs* in April 1765. The said Mirza did not even frame any set of regulations for the collection of revenues. When Reza Khan asked him to deposit the revenues of those *parganahs*, Mirza "refused to give a single *dam* more than what was settled" previously. To solve this impasse Reza Khan, with the advice of Sykes, appointed Mir Waris Ali in place of Mirza Daud. Waris Ali agreed to collect "a large sum" in comparison to what had been settled in the previous years.[119] In reply to his letter, Clive approved of the removal of Mirza Daud from the *faujdari* of Bhagalpur for his fault of not paying the rent regularly. But at the same time Clive informed the Khan to send someone to receive the balance due from Damodar Singh, another important collector of revenue. Clive further informed Reza that as Rajah Shitab Rai had been indisposed for sometime, one Sadu Ram had been appointed to act in his place. Murlidhar, another

117. S.C.R., 20 December, *1765*.

118. Mirza Daud was the son-in-law of Miran.

119. Reza Khan's letter to Clive Rd. 12. November, 1765. (C.P.C., I, p. 445, No. 2745).

man, would set out for Patna immediately to assist Sadu Ram as well as Rajah Dhiraj Narain. Clive hoped that these men would carry out the business at Patna with success till Shitab Rai's recovery. With regard to different appointments, Clive asked the Khan to do everything in concert with Sykes.[120]

In the month of December 1765, the Resident informed Reza Khan that the latter as well as Rai-Durlabh had been granted by the Governor jagirs in the province of Bihar consisting of "some rich and opulent districts", the revenues of which would amount to four lakhs of rupees annually. Accordingly, the officers under Rajah Dhiraj Narain were asked to decide about some selected districts agreeably to the papers of the *band-o-bast* in the province of Bihar. There were reports that these two men were profiting themelves to a staggering sum from the jagirs that they already enjoyed. About one month earlier, however, the *amils*, with Sykes' knowledge, had gone to the *jagirs* of the Khan as well as Rai-Durlabh, "yet no account of the alleged great profits" had been received. But in this regard also the Khan assured Clive that everything would be settled with the knowledge of the latter and Sykes.[121]

In the begining of 1766, Clive and the Select Committee showered high praises on Sykes. Under his direction, the ministers worked with unanimity. "They as well as the people in general express great satisfaction at the orders we lately issued and enforced for recalling to the Presidency all free merchants and other Europeans", observed Clive to the court, who "by acts of oppression and violence.............. totally prevented the ordinary course of justice and given great interruption to the business of the administration."[122] Only one day after, Clive again wrote to the court commending the zeal of Sykes in the service of the Company. The Resident

120. Clive's letter to Reza Khan, 19 November (*Ibid*., p. 447, No. 2752).

121. Reza Khan's letter to Clive, Rd. 30 December (C.P.C., I, p. 455, No. 2764).

122. Clive's letter to Court, 31 January, 1766 (F.W.I.H.C., IV, pp. 382-383).

seemed to Clive a man of great moral integrity, and Clive was fully convinced that "a change in the morals and principles of this settlement is absolutely necessary."[123] But in this estimate Clive failed to see that the morals of Resident as well as those of his ardent supporters were not so high as he thought these to be and as he had intimated in his letter to the Court of Directors.

Under the changed circumstances, the Nawab of Bengal became indifferent to the modes of carrying on the inland trade by the English merchants. On the other hand, the Court of Directors in London repeatedly prohibited the monopoly of trade on salt, betel-nut and tobacco, which had become the rule with the English merchants of Bihar and Bengal. The Court of Directors directed that he who would violate this order "stands guilty of a breach of his covenant with us."[124] But still, directly against the letter and spirit of this order, the profitable trade in the above articles continued among the Company's officials. Sykes himself was fully involved in tobacco trade with the help of Reza Khan. Later on, the Resident used this system not only for his own profit, but for his friends and other business partners.[125] Mean time, Sykes had already entered, right from October 1765, into a profitable timber trade in Purnea. In this private commercial pursuit, the Resident had to compete with Richard Barwell, the then commercial Resident at Malda. Barwell had already established a monopoly of timber trade in Purnea. In November 1765, Sykes sent his *gomastah* to purchase timber in Purnea but when refused, the Resident made a complaint before the Select Committee against Barwell's agent. The case was considered by the committee, and on 19 February 1766 it was decided that since the Europeans were involved in making profits, the trade should be entrusted to the ministers of Murshidabad. This, in fact, enabled Sykes, with his influence over the ministers, to establish his personal monpoly over most of these articles. Barwell was already under

123. *Ibid.*, 1 February (*Ibid.*, p. 398).

124. Letter from Court, 19 February, 1766 (*Ibid.*, pp. 146-147).

125. *Transition*, p. 118.

pressure from the Seleet Committee to send his three European agents to Calcutta. In the next stage, Barwell related this matter to his father: "At this time Kishen Kinker, Mr. Sykes' *Gomastah* was in Purnea; and soon after proceeded up for the purchase of wood. Being disappointed by my having pre-engaged the proper people, he wrote, as is evident, to his master, and his master to Souchetroy (Suchet Rai) the *Diwan* or *Amil* of Purnea and Souchetroy to the Resident at the *Darbar*, a very pretty force, and which I confess makes my blood boil not a little."[126]

Thus, Sykes used Reza Khan for his neat manoeuvre to oust Barwell from the timber trade. Through all such private trade Sykes amassed, during the time of Najmuddaulah, twelve to thirteen lakhs of rupees. Sykes also carried on trade in saltpetre, wood and silk in Murshidabad and in other districts. Thus, after *diwani*, Sykes was more affluent than many of the servants of the Company. The Resident, later on, confessed before Hastings and gave a subtle justification of his conduct: "Towards the Company I have ever been attentive nor would one six pence I enjoy ever come into the Company's treasury, it was this whether it would go into a blackman's pocket or into my own."[127]

Clive came to Murshidabad in April 1766 and met with Sykes. His mission of coming to the capital was to celebrate the *puniyah* ceremony or the annual *darbar* for the adjustment of the *zamindari* accounts. On 6 April, the two Jagat Seth brothers placed before them a claim of fifty to sixty lakhs of rupees. Clive was of opinion that their claim to the tune of twenty-one lakhs, a sum which they had lent to Mir Jafar and the English army, was "just and reasonable." However, it was decided that the Company and the Nawab should equally share the payments to the Seths in discharge of the above debt within a period of ten years.[128]

126 *Bengal past and Present*, Vol. IX, p. 80.

127. Quoted in Sinha, N.K., *The Economic History of Bengal*, Vol. I (Calcutta, 3rd Edn., 1965), p. 224.

128 S.C.R., 14 April, 1766.

Punyiah was celebrated every year in the *Moti-jhil* palace which was adjacent to Murshidabad. Clive entered the *Moti-jhil* with Sykes, where the first *puniyah* of the Company was celebrated on 29 April, 1766. The forms proper to this ceremony were rigidly observed. On the occasion, the young *Nawab Nazim* Najmuddaulah sat on the *masnad*, with Clive as *diwan* on his right side. All the Rajahs and *zamindars* remained standing with the account of their respective revenues. The English officials received *nazars* from the assembled *zamindars*. Clive, Carnac and Sykes accepted for themselves and for the Company, the usual present of *Khelat* and an elephant to each.[129]

At the time of the *puniyah*, the collection of revenues from Bengal and Bihar was considerably more than that collected in the preceding years. The Select Committee with great satisfaction informed the Court of Directors that the net estimate of collections for the year 1765–66, including the ceded districts, amounted to Rs. 1,61,00.708 , which was an increase of Rs. 11,33,978 over the collection of the previous year, and this was due to the reduction of charges "without levying any additional tax on the *zamindars*." The revenues from Bihar also amounted to Rs. 61,86,276, which showed a surplus in net revenues amountiug to Rs.5,62,261. This increase in revenue was due to the abilities of Reza Khan, who had acted on the spot under Sykes' direction to regulate the revenue collections of Bengal.[130] The collections and balances of the land assessment of Bengal, covered under the *diwani* portion, excluding the ceded and *zamindari* districts of the Company, also considerably increased over the collections of the previous years.[131] The credit of the Resident considerably went up. Clive and the Select Committee lavished praises on Sykes and acknowledged his "assiduity".

129. Majumdar, P.C., *The Musnud of Murshidabad* (Calcutta, 1905), p. 188.

130. Letter to Court, 8 Sept., 1766 (F.W.I.H.C., IV,p. 436).

131. Majumdar, *Musnud*, Appen. 14, p. 304.

When the *puniyah* ceremony was over, Clive after a short stay at *Moti-jhil*, went to the garden of Sadiqbagh. Najmud-daulah, with accompanied by Reza Khan went there and remained with Clive up to 11 P.M. When the Nawab complained of a sudden illness. The Nawab had taken some ice water and after returning to his palace, he became sick and died almost immediately.[132] It was on 8 May that the young Nawab, still in his teens, breathed his last. There arose a suspicion in the minds of the people about the cause of Najmuddaulah's death. Verelst informed Sykes that the peoble had begun to doubt Clive's integrity. Sykes told this before a Parliamentary Committee about the rumour afloat at Murshidabad.[133] People also began to doubt Reza Khan's complicity in a plot to get the Nawab removed from the world.

After the death of Najmuddaulah, the English Residents at Murshidabad took up in a more vigorous manner than before various measures for the administration of revenue in the Bengal *subah*.

---

132. *Seir*, III, p. 13.
133. Third Report, 1773, p. 325.

7

BRITISH RESIDENTS–THE ADMINISTRATORS OF REVENUES

The grant of *diwani* to the English Company was unhesitatingly approved by the Court of Directors. In giving their approval the Court of Directors observed that when "the barrier of the Country Government was entirely broke down" and when the inhabitants of Bengal knew not "whom to obey at such crisis, we cannot hesitate to approve your obtaining the *Dewani* for the Company."[1] The court while expressing its cognizance of the duties of the office of the *diwan*, referred to the sad experience about the revenue collection of the ceded land of Burdwan and remarked that an Englishman had been found unfit "to conduct the collection of the revenues" Therefore, it recommended to the Calcutta Council to "entirly approve of your preserving the ancient from of Government."[2]

The office of the *diwan*, as the court understood through their voluminous correspondence, was to superintend the collection and disposal of revenues. This office, though vested in the Company, the court observed, "should officially be executed by our Resident at the *Durbar*, under the control of

1. Letter from Court, 17 May, 1766 (Long, *Unpublished Records*, pp. 617-620).
2. *Ibid*.

the Governor and Select Committee". During the time of the annual *puniyah*, the government should settle with each *zamindar* his monthly payments for the ensuing year. The court thus directed that this annual account "must be strictly kept up, and if deficient, the Company must trace what particular Province, Rajah or *Zemindar* had fallen short in his monthly payments, or if it is necessary to extend the power further."[3]

The court also observed in the same letter that the office of the Resident carried with it very great responsibility and that the "Resident at the *Durbar* being constantly on the spot, cannot be long stranger to any abuses in the Government, and is always armed with power to remedy them." Then the court clarified the duties of the Resident who would "stand between the Administration and the encroachments always to be apprehended from the Agents of the Company's Servents which must first be known to him, and we rely on his fidelity to the Company, to check all such encroachments, and to prevent the oppression of the Natives."[4] Francis Sykes, who was already the Resident at the *darbar*, continued to hold the restructured office. His residence was fixed at Maidapur in the suburbs of Mursidabad.[5]

Early in 1767, the Select Committee at Calcutta made it clear in their letter to the Court of Directors about the functions of the office of the *diwani*, its relation to the Nawab as well as to the Emperor and the mode of collecting revenues by the Indian ministers. The committee claimed that because of their obtalnining the *diwani*, "security to property, freedom to the trade and protection to the persons of the natural inhabitants are insured." They further thought that the "present circumstances be regarded as the spring which concealed under the shadow of the Nabob's name, did everything" "without offering violence to the original constitution." The Nawab was envisaged as an effective safety-valve. To

3. *Ibid.*
4. *Ibid.*
5. Firminger, *Fifth Roport*,p. 169, f.n.

avoid the jealousy of the inhabitants as well as of other Europeans, "the Nabob holds in his hands as he always did the whole civil administration, the distribution of Justice, the disposal of offices and all those sovereign rights which constitute the essence of his dignity."[6]

About the functions of the office of the *diwan,* the Select Committee apprised the court that the Resident at the *darbar* acted as "collector of the king's Revenue under the Inspection and control of the Select Committee" The Resident, in conjunction with Reza Khan, "superintends the whole collections, receives the monthly payments from the *Zemindars,* disburses the stated Revenues appropriated to the king and the Nabob, inquires into the causes of deficiencies, redresses Injuries sustained or committed by the officers of the Revenue and transmits the accounts of his office, the invoices of Treasure,and a monthly account of the Treasury with every other occurance (occurrence) of Importance to the President and Select Committee" Similarly, the collection of Bihar revenues was placed under the immediate direction of the Chief of Patna. He acted jointly with Shitab Rai and was subordinate to the Resident at the *darbar* to "whom he makes his consignments of Treasure and transmits monthly accounts of his office which the Resident forwards to us". The committee had also left it to the option of the Resident, "the particular mode of carrying on business" at his own discretion.[7]

To avoid confusion and delay in transacting the affairs, the powers and functions of the council and the Select Committee had been clearly demarcated. As the importance of administering revenues seemed great, it became the responsibility of the Select Committee "to support with all their Influence the authority of the Resident at the *Durbar,* and to see their orders for restraining the pernicious Interposition of your servants in the affairs of the government, rigorously enforced". The committee also intimated to the court about the

6. Letter to Court, 24 January 1767 (F.W.I.H.C., Vol. V. Edt. by N.K. Sinha, Delhi, 1949, p. 277)

7. *Ibid.*

"collection of the Royal Revenue" that had already been assigned to the management of Reza Khan, "under the immediate inspection of the Resident at the *Darbar*." As such, they prayed for some "stated salaries to the ministers" "for the maintenance and support of their dignity".[8] Thus, Reza Khan, as a servant of the Company, became *naib-diwan,* in which post he fully co-operated with Sykes with much zeal for public good, and hence received strong recommendation from Clive.[9]

Clive, at the time of his departure for England cautioned Harry Verelst—the succeeding President and Governor of Fort William in Bengal, by observing that "the people of this country have little or no idea of a divided power; they imagine all authority is vested in one man;" therefore, following the maxim—do in Rome as the Romans do, the importance and dignity of the President must be restored, "upon whose character and conduct much of the prosperity of the Company's affairs in Bengal must ever depend."[10]

After *diwani*, the public business of the Resident increased considerably and hence, at its meeting held on 11 February—in which Sykes was also present by virtue of his being a member—the Select Committee directed the Resident "to transmit in future to the Committee all accounts relative to the revenues". Hence, in compliance with the above order, Sykes placed before the committee, the treasury accounts for the months of December and January. The committee also resolved to direct the Resident to ascertain from the ministers the number of *parwanas* actually in force and how

8. (*Ibid.*, pp. 279-280.

9. Clive lavishly praised Reza Khan at the time of his departure for England. He observed before the Select Committee held on 6 January, 1767 that the "diligence, disinterestedness and abilities" of Reza Khan exceed those of any other Musalman I have yet seen".- B.M.P., III, p. 8.

10. Clive's letter to Harry Verelst, 23 January (Select Committee Records, 11 February, 1767, Vol. 13, p. 117).

many had become time-barred, without which it would be difficult to prevent impositions.'[11]

The indisposition of Reza Khan for sometime as well as the absence of Sykes from Murshidabad, "left the *Zemindars* at liberty to act in what manner they pleased". Sykes discovered that the *zamindars'* dues amounted to nearly forty lakhs of rupees. Still the Resident hoped that after "a close attention to business" he would be able to settle matters with the *zamindars* without causing any material loss to the Company. This, he could achieve before he started for Dacca. During Sykes' absence from Murshidabad, the scrutiny of the *zamindars'* outstanding balances devolved upon Reza Khan, "whose people", Sykes thought, "perhaps may appear to be guilty". In such circumstances "making a proper discovery", might not be possible until Sykes' return.[12] About the arrears of payment to the sepoys during the time of Mir Jafar Khan, the Resident observed in the same letter that this affair had been settled by Clive and the committee in the previous October at the sum of Rs. 5,00,000. But on Reza Khan's authority, the Resident was given to understand that the "claimants might be satisfied with less." Rajah Durlabhram had also frequently applied to Sykes, for payment of the arrears of pay to the troops which were under his command during the time of Mir Jafar. This also amounted to Rs. 50,000. But the Resident was rather surprised that in the settlement made by Clive this amount of Durlabhram's demand had not been included though his claim was "equally valid". Sykes also informed the Governor, that Clive, in consultation with Reza Khan, had reduced the payment of the Nawab's troops, in the settlement arrived at in November, from 19 to 16 lakhs. Sykes could not understand the logic on which this reduction had been effected. The Resident was not in favour of reduction and was of opinion "that the present sum cannot be lessened without lessening in a great

11. S.C.R., 12 February, 1767, Vol. 12, pp. 88-90.

12. Sykes' letter to Verelst, 6 March (S.C.R., 10 March, 1767. Vol. 12, pp. 113-116).

degree the dingity" of the Nawab, which the Company professed to maintain.[13]

When Sykes began to examine the accounts of revenues, he found that the *zamindars* of several districts, almost in an endemic manner, did not pay their stipulated dues. Sykes, came to know that the balance of revenues due, upto 7 March, was Rs. 25.87,000. Out of this sum, Rs. 7,55,956 was due from the district of Dinajpur, when the net realisable revenue of this district was Rs. 15,31,089-1. As the deficit of Dinajpur revenues was more than seven lakhs of rupees, Sykes issued an order to Rajah Baij Nath—the *zamindar* of Dinajpur, and his *peshkar* "to repair to Murshidabad with their accounts."[14] But when the *zamindar* did not turn up in time, an *amil* was sent from Murshidabad to direct the *zamindar* to clear the arrears and not to make defaults in future. It was said that the *amil*, who was sent from Murshidabad, collected money but embezzled a part of it at Dinajpur. But Reza Khan strongly refuted the charge against the *amil*, Eventually another letter was issued to the *zamindar* and his *peshkar* to repair to Murshidabad "in order that whatever frauds had been committed or sums embezzled, might be brought to light." When the two arrived at Murshidabad, Sykes went through the accounts for four days and found much slipshodness. The *zamindar* pleaded that he had not yet been able to collect all the revenues. He prayed that he be permitted to return. He promised to devote himself to collections and adjustments of the accounts and satisfactorily finalise everything definitely at the time of the nezt *puniyah*, when he would, without fail, bring all his accounts for inspection.[15] After a month of his return from Murshidabad, the *zamindar* of Dinajpur sent his *vakil* to the Governor with a representation by which he begged the

13. *Ibid*.

14. Reza Khan's letter to the Governor, Rd. 10 March, 1767, C.P.C. II, Supplementary, Delhi, 1970, pp. 44-45, No. 159).

15. *Ibid*., Rd., 21 March *Ibid*. p. 52. No. 186).

Governor's protection and also ensured that he would in good time sort out and remove all the deficiencies of his accounts.[16]

The accounts of Dacca revenues were also till then unsettled. though a statement of the annual sums received from Dacca had been sent to Clive. As such, Sykes personally went to Dacca to examine all accounts. The responsibility of auditing the Dacca accounts was invested in Rajah Maha Singh, who was also directed "to retrench several unnecessary expenses". Accordingly, the Rajah reduced the expenses to seventy or eighty thousand rupees. The Rajah was further directed to furnish Sykes with a full account of his revenues, as well as the *band-o-bast* and to find out the possible sources of increased revenues. The Rajah had already reduced the annual expenses on boats from three to one lakh. As Rajah Maha Singh was a zealous supporter of the Company, he was directed to provide Sykes with the relevant papers, on the basis of which the rents and *nazars* could be increased.[17] In the middle of April, Sykes returned to Murshidabad, with all his auditing of accounts completed up to the end of March.[18]

After his return from Dacca, Sykes reported to the Governor about his revenue settlement at Dacca, the amount settled being Rs. 25,81,438-4-13. This sum, the Resident had collected "without any severity" to the inhabitants. Sykes had carefully studied the system of taxation during the times of Alivardi as well as those of Mir Qasim Khan and found that while it was rated at Rs. 30 lakhs during the time of the former, it was slightly more during the time of the latter. The expenses for collecting revenues during the time of the Nawab had been reduced. As such though the amount of settlement seemed lower than that of the Nawab yet actually the Company obtained a net increase of Rs. 8,53,709-15-17.

16. Letter from Rajah Baij Nath to the Governor 16 April (*Ibid.*, p. 93, No. 321).

17. Letter from Reza Khan to the Governor, Rd. 17 March *Ib....*, pp. 48-49, No. 178).

18. Letter from Durlabhram Rd. 15 April (*Ibid.*, p. 91, No. 313).

The Resident had also "put an entire stop" to the unnecessary expenses for constructing boats annually for the use of the Emperor, thus axing down the expenses to Rs. 50,000. Sykes also recommended that "the business of the revenue should rest wholly with Maha Singh" for his "unquestionable capacity". He remarked that the general regulations and the reduction of improper expenses in the district of Dacca, had long been neglected due mainly to Clive's inattention. The Resident believed that there were some points to be settled for the "better security of the inhabitants" and to prevent their suffering from the oppression of the *zamindars* but he left these affairs to be concluded by the President. He was confident that durihg the time of *puniyah* "all the balances will have been collected" from Dacca, except from some few inconsiderable ones..[19]

During the time of *puniyah* in 1767, President Verelst came to Murshidabad, personally to attend the important function. He had left Cartier as the *ad hoc* in charge of the Select Committee. Verelst, in conjunction with Sykes, framed regulations for adjustment of revenues with the several *zamindars, taluqdars* and collectors. After making the necessary arrangements the President, jointly with Sykes, addressed a letter to Cartier and the Select Committee, observing that the revenues of over-rated districts had been struck off, "a practice which could answer no other purpose than giving you an idea of heavy ballances remaining uncollected, without the least prospect of receiving any part of them." Their object in this mission was an "equitable estimation of the rents, equally attending to the rights of the government and the welfare of the subjects". They claimed that though the amount of the outgoing year's statement exceeded one crore and sixty one lakhs, the present statement was less, amounting to only one crore fifty-nine lakhs. Yet there had been an upward rise in the collections. Whereas the previous year's collections amounted to only Rs. 1,43,15,310-9-13, the present year's collections would gain by an actual increase of sixteen

19. Sykes, letter to the Committee, 15 April (S. C. R., 18 April, 1767, pp. 164-168).

lakhs of rupees. The existing anomalies from overrating of land had been removed. About overrating Sykes observed that overrating was "A circumstance we had not an opportunity of being thoroughly acquainted with till now."[20] Thus, they aimed at rationalisation and streamlining of both fixing and collection of revenues.

They also claimed that the charge for the collection of revenues had been reduced to "above two lacks of rupees" which left the *zamindars* and collectors with "not the least plea for extortion or oppression." At the same, time they had also taken steps "to promote the cultivation of the lands, encourage trade, and afford every protection to the industrious *ryots.*" Among other instances of neglect, the Nawab's ministers had pointed out the instance of Mirza Kasim-the *faujdar* of Hugli, whose "conduct had been so atrocious and his behaviour so insolent," that he had refused to give any explanation of the account of the revenues due from him So, Sykes and the ministers were obliged to dismiss him. from his employment.[21] The regulation of *chowkies* in different parts of the *subah*, as made in the previous year, was fully enforced.

The French as well as Dutch Companies made constant complaints to the English authorities at Calcutta about the "interruption and oppression" to which their trading was subjected. Regarding their grievances, the President and Sykes came to the conclusion "that this country does not afford a sufficient quantity of goods to answer the demands of each Company." To satisfy their demands, "we must either yield them up a part of our investment, or use our endeavours to increase the annual produce of each manufacture". The English gentlemen recommended the latter method and accordingly directed all the *zamindars* to encourage cultivation. As a further proof of their desire to be conciliatory towards the French and the Dutch, they directed the ministers to abolish some of the minor duties levied on the French and the Dutch Companies.

20. Verelst and Sykes' letter to Cartier and the Select Committee, 28 June S.C.R., 6 July, 1767, pp. 220-230).

21. *Ibid.*, also, Long, *Unpublished Records*, p. 695.

About the Company's relation with Orissa, Verelst and Sykes had several conferences with Udipuri Gossain, the Maratha *vakil* appointed by the Martha *Peshwa*, Janoli, regarding the cession of Cuttack to the English. The Maratha *vakil* had demanded an annual payment of sixteen lakhs of rupees, the sum promised to him by Clive. But Verelst and Sykes promised to pay him an annual sum of thirteen lakhs of rupees, on condition that one-half of the first year's rent would be paid to him on the immediate cession of Cuttack and the other half would be paid when the Company would get full possession over it, "provided that Janojee shall be fully empowered by his superiors to conclude the treay and make the proposed cession." On this proposal, the Maratha *vakil* declared that he had "no authority to deliver up the country without further instructions from his master". This delay in the finalisation of matters, Verelst and Sykes believed was due to a private direction given by Janoji to his *vakil* "to endeavor to bring about an offensive and defensive alliance between him and the English." But the English gentlemen disfavoured such an alliance for the present, though they could realise that the "alliance with Janojee will greatly conduce to strengthen our arms and influence."[22]

In the month of August, 1767, the monopoly of salt trade became a point of argument between the Resident on the one hand and the Select Committee on the other. While the Resident insisted on this monopoly to lie in the hands of *zamindars* and higher officials of the government, the committee wanted it to remain in the hands of the common people, who "desired their subsistence from it." When the Society of salt Trade, the monopolistic cartel of the salt traders, was established, *parwanas* were circulated in different parts of the *subah* forbidding the inhabitants to deal in that article.[23] But this view of the Company was lator on modified and in their letter of 1 August, the committee informed the Resident that the right of trading in salt should remain

---

22. *Ibid.*
23. Sykes' letter to the Select Committee, 18 August (S.C.R., 2 September, 1767, pp. 285-288).

in the hands of the inhabitants. On this order, Sykes reacted sharply and in his letter to the committee he proposed his alternative plan : "that the Salt Lands should be worked on account of the Government under the particular inspection of the ministers....The *zemindars* and officers of the Government to oversee the making of the salt," and the whole stock might be brought to the grand marts. The salt might be disposed there at prime cost to the inhabitants of the country and a customary government duty be levied on the first sale The Resident also suggested that "an Account will be kept of the Names of several purchasers which may be laid before you from time to time, you will always be enabled to form a proper judgement of the manner in which the trade is conducted, as well as to check any tendency to abuse on Monopoly in its first growth."[24] But the Select Committee did not agree with the Resident's plan and resolved that the plan "ought not to be adopted". The Select Committee had their doubts that if the manufacturing of salt remained under the direction of the principal officers of the government "there will always arise suspicion that private views are answered under the specious pretext of public benefit." Hence "salt should be restored to those persons....who have no other means of providing for their families." As the collection of duties at different *chowkies* might open a door for abuse, the committee proposed that "the duties shall be collected at one established *chokey* only in every Route of Trade", and these duties would be rated "in the most equitable and moderate manner."[25]

In the above pass the Resident had to follow the resolution of the Select Committee, though he did it reluctantly. But when there were frequent complaints on the monopoly of inland trade, Sykes exerted his influence on the Nawab to issue a circular in favour of the Company's decision. Thus, the Nawab "thought proper to forbid all Europeans and foreigners of any nation" to carry on trade in salt, betel-

24. *Ibid.*

25. S.C.R., 2 September, 1767.

nut and tobacco.[26] In pursuance of this the Nawab issued a *parwana* throughout the *subah* of Bengal observing that "it has become our determined resolution that none but natives and merchants of this country shall be permitted in future to traffic in those articles and all foreigners whatever, whether English, French, Dutch, Danes or others, be excluded from dealing therein."[27] Reza Khan also immediately issued a circular to the *amils* and *zamindars* of the *subah* of Bengal that the trade in salt, betel-nut and tobacco "shal lbe entirely carried on by the merchants—natives of the country."

In spite of this decision of the Select Committee as well as the above *parwana* issued by the Nawab, Chevalier, a French merchant, carried on his private trade. This immediately came to the knowledge of the British Resident who informed the committee of this illicit trade, intimating that Chevalier, running his trade in rivalry with the English merchants had "established *Gomatahs* at many places for the purchase of rice, grain and other articles."[29] On the day following, the Resident again wrote to the committee that the French "are endeavoring to undermine our Trade" and an "earliest precaution" could only check their progress : that Chevalier even used to send clothes and other goods to Benares was something which went against the English interests.[30] In reply to these letters, the Select Committee resolved that "contrary to the tenor of our *Phirmaund*, oppressive of the Natives and destructive of the Peace of the country, it would be highly imprudent we should remain silent speculators of the progress Foreigners are making in the extension of their privileges." Therefore, the committee directed Sykes to use "the strongest terms" to impress upon the ministers to put

26. Sykes' letter to Select Committee, 8 October (S.C.R., 13 October, 1767, vol. 13, pp. 302-305)
27. Translation of a [*Parwana* from Nawab Saifuddaulah to the Chief of the French, Dutch and Danish factorie —7 October (S.C.R., 13 October, 1767, vol. 13, pp. 306-307).
28. Reza Khan's circular to the *Amils* and *Zamindars*—7 October S.C.R., 13 October, 1767 Vol. 13, p. 307).
29. Sykes' letter to Select Committee, 9 November (S.C.R., 17 November, 1767, Vol 12, pp. 405-407)
30. *Ibid.*, 10 Novemper.

an immediate stop to the trade of the rival traders as above, which "must deeply effect the revenues" and "frustrate all our endeavours for restoring the Natives to all their natural rights." The foreigners' trade must be confined to import and export only, according to the spirit of their *farman*. The President was also requested to direct Shitab Rai at Patna to restrain foreigners and stop their illicit trade in the province of Bihar, Directions might be given to Rumbold[31] also. as the committee directed, "to have the strictest eye over them" as it became easier to correct the evils in origin, than to remedy them after these had risen to a dangerous height.[32]

The Court of Directors also directed that the trade of the servants of the Company should be confined "to the articles of import and export only'. They were forbidden "to take part in inland trade." The court also could not help "condemning their salt monopoly". In lieu of their losses, the court observed "we are come to a resolution to give them a reasonable encouragement to exert themselves with zeal and alacrity in their several departments." In other words, they were to show their excel lence by serving the Company. The court further observed in the same letter :"That you draw out an annual account of the sums received from the *Dewannee*, deducting thereout the stipulated payments to the king and the Nabab, and the allowance of the Nabab's ministers, also the revenue of the provinces of Burdwan, Midnapur and Chitagong and Calcutta *pergunnahs* from which are to be deducted Lord Clive's *jaghire* and the ordinary charges of collection. Upon the amount of the said nett revenues, you are hereby indulged to draw a commission of 22 per cent."[33]

---

31. The English Cheif at Patna.
32. S.C.R., 17 November, 1767, pp. 405-407.
33. Letter from Court 20 November, 1767 (Firminger. *Fifth Report*, pp. 169-170 f.n.)

The sum so obtained was to be divided into 100 shares, which were to be distributed as under:

The Governor ... 31 shares

The rest of the Select Committee, not having

(conted.)

The Resident at the *darbar* had to perform a large variety of functions after the grant of *diwani*. Not only was the general supervision of revenues entrusted to him but in his capacity as a member of the Select Committee at Calcutta, he was also authorised to inspect the Courts of Justice at Murshidabad. Above all, he was the Chief of the English factory at Kasimbazar. It was realised that such multiplicity of functions should not devolve on the same person. Therefore, the Court of Directors wanted that the Chiefship of Kasimbazar might be bestowed on some other person, so that "the Resident at the *Durbar* may apply himself solely to the superintendency of the revenues."[34] But when the Company's authorities in Bengal did not carry out this direction within one year, the court again directed the Select Committee: "Being convinced that the Employs of Resident at the *Durbar* and the Chief of Cossimbazar cannot from the Importance and Extent of the Business of each department be properly executed by one person, we therefore direct that they be from this time forward separated, and that some other Member of the Council be appointed to the said Chiefship."[35] Thus, the Select Committee, after mature consideration, delinked the Chiefship of Kasimbazar from the Resident's post and informed the court in their letter of 13 September, 1768, about the appointment of William Aldersay, as the Chief of the Kasimbazar factory. By this appointment the powers of the Chief of Kasimbazar and the Resident at the *darbar* were made distinct from each other. It was decided that all applications to the Nawab should be made through

Chiefship	...	3 ½ shares
The rest of the Council, not having Chiefship	...	1 ½ shares
The Resident at the *Darbar*	...	4 ½ shares

The court reserved to itself the appropriation of the remaining shares, but the Select Committee disregarded it. In the benefit of the commission, the principal military officers were also included—Firminger, *Fifth Report*, p. 170 f.n.

34. Letter from Court, 21 November, 1766 (F. W. I. H. C.. IV, p. 221).

35. Letter from Court, 20 November, 1767 (*Ibid.*, vol. V, p. 59).

the Resident at the *darbar*. It was further decided that each of the two : the Chief of Kasimbazar and the Resident at the *darbar*, enjoyed the additional power to grant *dastacks* in their respective departments.[36]

In the month of January, 1768, Sykes again raised the question of inland trade in salt. As the Resident himself carried on private trade in the districts of Dinajpur and Purnea,[37] the regulations of the committee greatly hampered the progress of his trade. Naturally he was sorely disappointed when his recommendations were not approved by the committee. The Resident again pointed out to the committee that his concern was only for the "welfare and happiness of the people of these provinces" and as such he "always avoided interfering in any public act except where the Revenues were concerned." With regard to the deficiency of money mentioned in the sub-treasurer's letter to the committee,[38] Sykes informed the committee that he would make strict enquiry about it. The Resident further informed the committee about Reza Khan's proposed journey to Calcutta on 11 January with twelve lakhs of rupees.[39]

Sykes came to Calcutta and attended the meeting of the Select Committee on 10 February, where he placed an account of his transactions during his visit to Dinajpur and Purnea districts. In his visits to the two places his only motive was to enquire about the "just and stated revenues" of those districts. Dinajpur had long been "almost an independent Government of its own Rajah", while Purnea was "frequently in a state of actual rebellion". These created great disorder in both Dinajpur and Purnea, with almost a total ignorance on the part of the government about the "value of their collections" from the two districts. Notwithstanding the Company's utmost efforts, there was an unrealised balance of

36. B. p.p., Vol. LVII, 1939, pp. 32-33 (Banerjee, D.N., "The Resident at the Durbar (Moorshedabad)—His position and Functions".
37. *Transition*, p. 162.
38. Reed's (Sub-treasurer) Letter to the Committee, 31 December, 1767 (S.C.R., 5 January, 1768, Vol. 15, pp. 1-6).
39. Sykes' letter to the Committee, 9 January (S.C.R., 10 January 1768), Vol. 15, pp. 93-114).

no less than six lakhs of rupees in the previous year's account in respect of Dinajpur. While the President was at Murshidabad, in conjunction with the ministers and the Resident, he decided that the management of the Dinajpur district should be entrusted to its *zamindar*, and a person should stay there for superintending the collections. Accordingly, Saiyyad Muhammad Khan, on whom the ministers had confidence, was appointed with instructions to be vigilant about the activity of collections and remittance of revenues. But the said Khan, during five months of his stay at Dinajpur, did nothing but sent "complaints with representations of the poverty of the country". Neither could he send any paper or accounts to the Resident.[40]

This state of things forced the Resident to undertake a journey to Dinajpur in order "to determine whether the deficiency in the revenues was owing to real poverty and inability of the country to pay the amount at which it had been rated or due to the mismanagement of those on whom the "charge of collection had been entrusted". The Resident enquired about the real and actual receipts from the tenants for the last two years, i.e. after the Company's obtaining *diwani*. "I was much surprised to find on my entering the Dinagepore country", observed the Resident, "that it is in a most plenteous and flourishing situation, very well inhabited and the lands throughout cultivated and improved." These circumstances raised doubts about the authenticity of Saiyyad Muhammad Khan's representation of widespread destitution of the place. These doubts were more fully confirmed when Sykes examined the net amount that had been collected each year. The Resident found that between April 1765 to March 1766, the public statement with the government at the time of *puniyah* was Rs. 17,82,218 while including the *diwani nazranah* and other things, it stood at Rs. 19,27,744-7-2, which had been paid into the treasury at Murshidabad. But the actual collection of revenues was Rs. 24.05,483-12-15 out of which, after deduc-

40. Sykes' letter to the Committee, 10 February (S.C.R., 10 February, 1768, Vol. 15, pp. 93-114).

tion of Rs. 72,893-7-5 allowed for *batta* (commission/discount), there had been surplus collection of Rs. 4,04,845-14-8, a sum far exceeding the reasonable demands. The year 1766-67 exhibited a still more striking instance of fraud and abuse. In that year Rs. 14,00,340-1-5 had been paid into the treasury including the *diwani nazranah*. An additional balance of Rs. 6,51,188-11-7 had also been deposited, while the actual collection of the district was more than 24 lakhs of rupees. The Resident remarked that so large a surplus would be fully sufficient to prove "the rapacity of its collectors."[41] Huge embezzlements of money also stood proved in this way.

Sykes remained at Dinajpur for five weeks, but the necessity of his returning to Murshidabad obliged him to hasten his moving on to Purnea. For a more minute study of the situation the Resident posted William Rooke at Dinajpur for a short period. On his entry into Purnea, the Resident found "a scene widely different from that of Dinagepore". "This country though extremely beautiful, watered by many fine rivers and the lands in themselves rich and fertile", yet was almost universally waste and destitute of inhabitants or cultivation. He noticed, particularly so in town areas, that "the people bore evident marks of beggary and distress". During the two former years, Rajah Suchet Rai held the management of collections. The Rajah, however, pleaded his difficulties in collecting adequate revenues. But a study of the accounts changed the opinion of Sykes. He saw that during the years of the Rajah's being in appointment, from Aprii 1765 to April 1767, a sum of 38 to 40 lakhs had been collected from Purnea, whereas the Rajah had paid only Rs. 26,37,472 into the treasury at Murshidabad. So there was positive reason to believe that the Rajah had "reaped the fruits of heavy oppression and extortions." That the Rajah had taken Rs. 30,000 from one merchant, had been proved during the Resident's stay in Purnea. It was also proved that the Rajah had collected and misappropriated, no less than Rs. 1,40,000 from the current year's rent.[42]

41. *Ibid.*
42. (*Ibid.*

Upon the discovery of such an abuse, the Resident thought it absolutely necessary to recommend to Reza Khan that the principal actors of oppression should be put in confinement. On this occasion the Rajah of Dinajpur did not appear worthy of punishment as his "incapacity for business has rather rendered him the tool to carry on the wicked designs of others". At Dinajpur, those who stood guilty before the judgement of the Resident, were, Muhammad Jumna, the late collector of the district, with his agents and Hari Chand the *diwan* of the Rajah, with most of the Rajah's principal servants. In Purnea, the whole management of the district had been entrusted to Suchet Rai. Sykes acted with alacrity in this respect. The guilty people were kept under a strict guard "till such time as the ministers can come to a determination on the nature of the punishment they think proportionable to their crimes."[43]

The Resident could not remain at Purnea for a long time, and, therefore, had left such orders to the *faujdar* as would be "best calculated to remedy the progress of disorder". But as very little confidence could be "placed in the zeal and integrity of the people of this country", the Resident placed Redpearn, one of his assistants, as superintendent, till all things were brought to a satisfactory conclusion. The Resident, however, did not receive any report from his assistant at Purnea. But the affairs of Dinajpur were duly communicated to him "in a very full and particular manner" by Rooke, whose report the Resident placed before the committee.

While making his observations Sykes told the Select Committee that with regard to the first year, the misappropriations were in a great measure excusable, as the Company had just then obtained *diwani* and it was judged necessary "not to disgust the people". But before the commencement of the second year, proper directions had been given to the men on the spot: "the strictest orders were issued" by the ministers and the Resident that "no expenses were to be incurred without our knowledge and approbation". Still it was in

43. *Ibid.*

defiance of these orders that revenues had been misappropriated. As such the Resident recommended that effective and deterrent measures be taken to prevent these misappropriations, so that the Company could thereby gain rupees six to seven lakhs annually "without any additional burden".[44]

On his return to Murshidabad, the accounts maintained by Mirza Kazim Khan, the late *faujdar* of Hugli, were fully examined by Sykes. He placed these accounts before the Select Committee remarking that the accounts showed shortage of collection to the tune of more than six lakhs of rupees. The accounts also showed the difference between the actual collections and the remittance of money to Murshidabad. Whatever shortfall was there, minus Mirza Kazim Khan's salary, was undoubtedly due, which "must be paid by him to the Company."[45] Sykes forcefully maintained in his charges against the *faujdar*.

The Resident then submitted before the committee an account of his experiences and realisations during the course of his journey. He had found that it was the practice of the collectors to collect more money from the tenants than was actually due. This was undoubtedly a ruinous and destructive practice that needed no explanation. Though the tenants of Dinajpur had continuously suffered, they had been "governed by their own hereditary Rajahs" on whom nobody had exercised any control. On the other hand, Purnea and other districts had been exposed to the unrestrained avarice of the collectors. Sykes exhorted the committee : "this great and dangerous evil that requires your most serious considerations and demands that some immediate and effectual remedy should be applied". The Resident cautioned the committee by stating that what he deemed essential was that "we have regard before all things the welfare and happiness of the poor inhabitants of the country and to maintaining them in their just and natural rights." So he asked, "how far do they reap the benefits of our moderation and forbearance?" On his part, the Resident recommended that exemplary punish-

44. *Ibid.*

45. *Ibid.*

ment be given to the culprits : "I think it absolutely necessary we recommend to the ministers that a severe example according to the laws of the country be made of the most notorious of the present offenders as a tenor in future to the rest of our employment." The Resident concluded his statement by remarking that it was his business to see "that the Company as *Dewan* of the king have the full and just amount of their revenues."[46]

Upon such a strong representation from the Resident about the oppressions committed in Dinajpur and Purnea, the Select Committee debated this question at the next meeting and resolved "to take immediate notice of the malpractices of the *zemindars* and others complained of by Mr. Sykes." It was also agreed to "recommend to the government to inflict such severe Punishment as they may judge proper, on those persons who may be found guilty of embezzling the rents of that country, or of any other atrocious crimes they may have committed, in order to deter others from the like practices in future."[47]

In the next meeting Sykes himself came to Calcutta and occupied his seat as a member of the Select Committee. At this meeting the accounts of money borrowed by the Rajah of Dinajpur and his officers were discussed. It was resolved "that such sums as have been lent for the service of the Government and which stand registered at the *Cutcherry* Books. shall be paid out of the Revenues conformably to the Regulations of this Board, but with regard to Loans of money to the *zemindars* and others which do not appear in the register books of the *Cutcherry*, the Government are by no means to be responsible for and it is agreed that Mr. Sykes do adjust those accounts conformably to this Resolution". After this meeting, the Resident took his leave of the committee "in order to repair to his station at the *Durbar*."[48]

In 1768, the *puniyah* was held at Murshidabad on 14 May with the usual forms and solemnity. As the President

46. *Ibid.*
47. S.C.R., 23 February, 1768, Vol. 14, pp. 100-102.
48. *Ibid.*, 31 March, 1768, Vol. 14, pp. 175-176.

was unable to attend it personally owing to ill-health, Cartier went to the capital and officiated in his stead. The Resident also accompanied Cartier. There was much behind-the-stage activity before the *puniyah* was actually held. Cartier and Sykes tried to defer the holding of the *puniyah* as long as it could prudently be done, in order to bring in as much as possible of the outstanding balances of the previous year. The balances, however were small and in his report Sykes assured the Committee that these were in no way "deemed irrecoverable" The Resident proposed to pay every attention to them during the course of the ensuing season. Sykes seriously devoted himself to adjusting the accounts of the previous years, and preparing the one for the current year. He assured the Committee that he would transmit the statement of accounts to the Committee within a short time. Both Cartier and Sykes believed that the regulations of the Company would temporise the oppressors on the one hand, and on the other, would "convince the poorer inhabitants of the happy effects of English influence on the administration of their government.[49] However, Sykes carried over the balance of one lakh of rupees due from Dinajpur and assured the Committee that he would be able to collect the balance due against the Dinajpur Rajah. As it so happened at first the Rajah of Dinajpur seemed willing to pay the sum but later he turned *volte-face* and refused to pay unless he were reinstated the full management of Rangpur and Dinajpur. This insolent and arrogant refusal induced the ministers to dismiss the Rajah from all revenue managements. The Select Committee, on its part. began to try in every way to recover the balances due from Dinajpur.[50]

In the month of July, the Select Committee despatched to Sykes the extracts from the Company's general letter of 20 November, 1767, relating to the account of the *diwani* revenues. The Resident was asked to furnish a statement of all disbursements, along with the receipts thereof, brought

49. Cartier and Sykes' letter to the Committee, 15 May (S.C.R., 23 July, 1768, Vol. 14, pp. 329-330).

0. Letter to Court, 15 September, 1768 (F.W.I.H.C., V pp. 412-413).

up to 31 of July so as to send it to Europe on 1 September. The Committee also decided that all accounts of the expenses for the *parganah* sepoys should be brought to the book of the Military Paymaster General. The Resident was, therefore, to direct the paymaster to transmit all such accounts to the Military Paymaster General, right from the time of the *parganah* sepoys' employment at Murshidabad.[51]

Meanwhiie, Reza Khan informed the Governor that he had settled the quantity of *chunam* (lime made of shells or stones) to be provided at Sylhet, at quantity of three lakhs *maunds*, and had put the execution of business in the hands of the *amils*. But as per Reza Khan's report the Resident had pressed Khan to "hasten the *chunam* business", and had warned him that if less than three lakhs of *maunds* were supplied, Reza Khan would be considered negligent of his duties. In this regard the Khan informed the governor that the Resident's insinuations were unjustified as he was "never guilty of remisness in the management of the Company's concern."[52] In regard to *chunam* supply *bona fides* could not be doubted, he submitted.

In the month of August, reports on the extremely distressed condition of the Mughal Emperor had reached the Governor. As per the reports the Emperor was in great pecuniary difficulty and was managing his livelihood by taking loans from the *sahukars*. The Emperor himself informed the Governor that for a period of seven months no payment for the royal debts had been made to the *sahukars*, though the Governor had directed Reza Khan and the Seths to remit the money without any delay. The Company had not fulfilled its commitments for the payment of the royal tribute. The Emperor owed the *sahukars* nearly five lakhs of rupees. The Emperor had, therefore, sent to the Company's Calcutta office receipts for eighteen lakhs and some thousands of rupees through Dia Ram Pandit, the Emperor's *vakil*. The Emperor hoped that a positive direction would be given to Sykes and

51. S.C.R., 20 July, 1768, Vol. 14, p. 268.
52. Reza Khan's letter to the Governor, Rd. 28 July, 1768 (C.P.C., II, p. 289 No. 1062).

Reza Khan, to deliver the aforesaid sum to Dia Ram Pandit, so that the latters might pay the *sahukars* and send the receipts to the Emperor.[53] For the time being, however, the Emperor's request was kept in cold storage by the Calcutta authorities.

It gave much satisfaction to Sykes when he learnt that the plan adopted by him and Cartier, for the management of revenues had been substantially approved by the Select Commtttee. But at the same tlme, the Resident expressed his failure to obtain the account of the emoluments of the *faujdari* of Hugli. It eould be guessed from this that the relations between Sykes and the Hugli *faujdrr* were strained. About his appointment of Rooke to officiate at Dinajpur for sometime, the Resident informed the Committee that it was extreme necessity that had induced him to make this appointment. Still, in the light of the Committee's disapproval of the appointment of Rooke, Sykes observed in his letter: "you may depend upon it that your orders shall be obeyed and that he (Rooke) shall reside there no longer than when my apprehensions for the Company's revenue and the necessity of guarding against the frauds and malpractices of the *zemindars*, shall render it indispensable with the interest of our honourable employers."[54]

In the month of August 1768, as per directives from Calcutta, Sykes delivered the charge of the Kasimbazar factory to Aldersay, giving him such information as was necessary on the subject of the various investments already made.[55] But Sykes felt inconvenient in transacting the business of the *darbar*, when the Calcutta Council appropriated his Maidapur house for the use of the Chief at Kasimbazar. For reasons of the unhealthy surroundings at *Motijhil*, Sykes had been using the Maidapur house for sometime past. The Select Committee could not take this matter under

53. Emperor Shah Alam's letter to the Governor, Rd. 12 August, 1768 (*Ibid.*, p. 293. No. 1075).

54. Sykes' letter to the Committee, 25 August (S.C.R., 31 August, 1768, Vol. 14, pp. 495-497).

55. *Ibid.*

consideration and referred it to the Court of Directors for decision[56].

On 30 September, Sykes forwarded to the Select Committee the treasury account for the month of August. In the same letter he pointed out that a sum of two lakhs of rupees had been remitted to Calcutta during 1765 under the head of *nazranahs*. This sum had come from the ministers on account of the *diwani nazranah*, previous to the Company's obtaining the *sanad* for *diwani* and as such this amount was not included in the *pucca* statement of accounts. However, as it was a part of the Company's general recepit, Sykes desired its insertion into the Company's account for the sake of regularity.[57]

In the middle of 1768, the Select Committee decided to include the Collections from the Bhagalpur district in the collections made from Bihar and recommended to Sykes accordingly. The Resident took the opinion of the ministrs who acquainted him that in regard to Bhagalpur, the "revenues thereof had been paid at this place (Murshidabad) almost ever since the Behar province has been connected with that of Bengal." The ministers were thus of the view that the *status quo* should be maintained. So the Resident, communicated the decision arrived at by the ministers to the committee. As to the further remittance of money to the committee, Sykes pointed out that Aldersay, Chief of Kasimbazar, had demanded a further supply of three lakhs of rupees to be paid to him by the end of the next month, by Sykes. Despite such a heavy demand the Resident would try to remit to the committee "the sum you require."[58] But the Select Committee built up such an insistent pressure on Sykes for money that the latter had no "remedy left," but to hurriedly supply money to the Committee "by stopping the sum of four lakhs of rupees," collected for sending to Allahabad for Emperor Shah Alam. With this sum, the

56. Letter to Court, 15 September, 1768 (F.W.I.H.C., V, p. 413).

57. S.C.R, 6 October, 1768, vol-14, pp. 588-589.

58. Sykes' letter to the Committee, 5 November (S.C.R., 1? November, 1768, Vol. 14, pp. 625-627).

Resident observed he would add two lakhs more, and would send "the whole to Calcutta in a day or two."[59]

Sykes' health also began to decline, as, on the one hand, the climate of the country did not suit him, and on the other, the heavy pressure of his work as Resident had increased considerably. Sykes wanted to resign from his position and informed the Select Committee that the laborious business in which he had to struggle "has at length so far impaired my health, and brought on such disagreeable and repeated attacks, that I am under the necessity of looking for some department where so constant and vigorous an exertion wlll not be required." The Resident requested the committee to favour him "by looking out for a successor, in my present employment, and permit me resigning my charge to him."[60]

The Select Committee, in reply to his letter on 5 November gave clarifications on various points. They observed that at present there was no necessity for altering the channel of the revenue collections of the district of Bhagalpur ; since the change might prove dissatisfactory to the Nawab and the Resident that the ministers, "we shall not for the present desire any alteration," the committee observed. The committee also directed the small number of troops stationed at Mungher, might be paid from the Murshidabad treasury. About the appointment of Fateh Ali Khan under Reza Khan,[61] the committee informed Sykes that the final approval of this appointment still rested with the Court of Directors. In reply to his letter of 14 November, the committee informed Sykes, that the permission for resigning his post at the *darbar* "will be laid before President and Council in order that a successor may be nominated by the Board."[62]

The Select Committee again reminded Sykes about the depleted condition of the Company's treasury. They infor-

59. *Ibid.*, 14 November.

60. *Ibid.*

61. In view of his declining health, Reza Khan urged the Governor to appoint a person to assist him, who would act as his *naib.*

62. S.C.R., 17 November, 1768, vol., 14, pp. 631-633.

med him that the tribute to the Emperor had been paid up to October. So the sum of Rs.2,25,113, as had been claimed on the Emperor's behalf, would not be due to him on that account before 12 December next. Moreover, Cartier, Smith and Russell had prevailled on the Emperor, when they were at Allahabad, to accept part payments, and as such the Select Committee desired ; "we desire that no further sums be paid to him on account of the Tribute from Moorshedabad untill our further orders." About Udipuri Gossain, the Maratha *vakil*, a sum of Rs. 25,312 was due to him, which might be paid. But the Select Committee was little desirious of keeping the Murshidabad ministers in good humour. They held their posts by the Company's sufferance. Hence. Select Committee suggested that the ministers might be paid half of the sum in respect of their stipulated salaries during the term specified. The committee urged the Resident that these deductions in payment would bring about a favourable balance in Murshidabad treasury, up to 12 December, of Rs. 25,77,835. This would enable the Resident to make "considerable remittances to the Presidency for its immediate occasions."[63]

Sykes, in his reply dated 17 November to the Select Committee's letter, stated that it was not possible for him to collect so large an amount within a specified date, but collection of such a large sum might entail a long time and go on till the end of December "or possibly till the middle of January." About the committee's directions regarding the payment of the Emperor's tribute and the allowances of the Nawab's ministers, Sykes agreed to comply with them, yet, as he pointed out, it would take sometime to finalise everything in an effective manner. Sykes also indicated that the despatch of four lakhs of rupees to Allahabad would have to be held up. He pointed out further that the Kasimbazar factory had also urged for an immediate supply of money, and the President and the council had urged the Resident to supply Rs. 3,50,000 to the Dacca factory. Sykes felt that all these

63. *Ibid.*

demands were urgent and could not be postponed indefinitely. At Murshidabad itself the Nawab of Bengal was also in arrears, "his sepoys and servants being 5 or 6 months in arrears and very clamorous for their pay."[64] These circumstances, Sykes submitted, prevented him from supplying the necessary money immediately to Calcutta. But when the December payment would be obtained, Sykes hoped, he might relieve the difficulties of the committee.

In course of his ill-health, when the commitiee granted him permission to come to the Presidency, Sykes proposed to the committee that he would leave Murshidabad on the morning of 5 December. He would entrust the management of the affairs at Murshidabad to Rooke and Ducarel, two of his assistants, "till such time as you think proper to appoint others."[65]

Reza Khan lavished eloquent praises on Sykes. He described Sykes as a man of "unblemished character and with the greatest equity and prudence." The Khan further observed in the same letter to the Governor : "No act of oppression has ever been committed and the Company's affairs have been transacted in a proper manner during his residence here."[66] The Seths also saw prudence in Sykes in conducting the Company's business at Murshidabad.[67] But all these praises were not free from doubts, as in truth Sykes' character was not so unblemished. It was an open secret that he carried on private trade to the great detriment of the country merchants and the interest of the English Company. After the recall of Barwell from Malda, Sykes had no competitor in the districts of Dinajpur and Purnea, where he used his writ often to his own advantage. Besides when the orders came from England in November 1766 and

64. Sykes' letter to the Committee, 4 December (S.C.R., 13 December, 1768, vol. 14, pp. 697-699).

65. *Ibid.*

66. Reza Khan's letter to the Governor, Rd. 26 December 1768 (C.P.C., II, p. 328 No. 1234).

67. Seths' letter to the Governor, Rd. 26 December, 1768 (*Ibid.*, p. 329, No. 1238).

again in November, 1767, directing the committee to separate the office of the Resident from that of the Chiefship of Kasimbazar, it became essential for Sykes to appoint his own personal agents in Dinajpur and Purnea. He offered necessary excuses for sending there his own men. Very often Sykes appropriated for himself what did not belong to the Company.[68] About Sykes, Barwell wrote to his family: "It has been currently reported that Sykes' inordinate desire to be rich has made him to transgress decency in his acquisition."[69]

When Sykes gave notice of his intended resignation, the question was raised in the council. For the importance of the post, it should have automatically gone to the second in council—in this case, Cartier. But as no unanimity could be reached on the question, the members of the council were asked for their opinions, whether the second should be stationed permanently in Calcutta or should be posted as Resident at Murshidabad. Verelst, the Governor to whom Cartier was a thorn in the flesh at Calcutta, wanted Cartier to succeed Sykes and be posted at Murshidabad. But a majority of the members wanted Becher to be appointed to the post of the Resident at Murshidabad.[70]

On 2 January, 1769, Sykes sought permission from the President and the Select Committee to allow him to proceed to Europe, owing to the "present declining state" of his health. But at the same time, he reminded the committee that he had worked with dignity. "During the time I have held the station of Resident at the *Durbar*", observed Sykes "it has ever been my endeavour to support the system...of Hon'ble Employers."[71] The resignation of Sykes was finally accepted by the Select Committee on 4 January, 1769, and

68. *Transition*, pp. 159-162.

69. Barwell's letter, 28 February, 1768 (B.P.P. Vol. X, p. 30).

70. B.P.P., X, p. 34. Also, *Transition*, p. 147. Verelst, Becher and Sykes voted for Cartier's posting at Murshidabad, while Smith, Floyer, Alexander, Russell and Charlton voted for Becher—Letter to Court, 2 February, 1769.

71. Sykes' letter to the Committee, 2 January (S.C.R., 4 January, 1769, pp. 22-32).

on the same day Richard Becher[72] was nominated to the station of the Resident at the *darbar*. Becher was directed to proceed to Murshidabad with the instruction "to correspond with the Select Committee on the subject of the collections" as well as "other matters relative to the country government."[73]

Becher started from Calcutta on 6 and reached Murshidabad on 11 January.[74] He received the charge of the Residency from Maddison with a balance of the treasury up to 31 December, amounting to Rs. 6,66,067-6-17. After his arrival and taking over charge, Becher hoped that soon he would be able to despatch four lakhs of rupees to the Presidency.[75] The governor also informed Reza Khan, Durlabhram and the Seths about the appointment of Becher as the Resident[76] and urged them to follow his direction. As such Durlabhram sent four lakhs of rupees to Calcutta according to Becher's order.[77] The committee acknowledged the receipt of this money and requested the Resident to

---

72. Richard Becher was a man of experience. He joined the Company's service in 1743 and saw the rule of Nawab Alivardi. When Sirajuddaulah captured Calcutta in 1756, Becher was the Chief of Dacca. When the English recaptured Calcutta, he was chosen by the Directors as one of the three to be the governors of Calcutta by rotation. For the interest of the Company and his nation, Becher gave up his rights and jointly with Watts and Manningham, offered the post to Clive. Soon after, he left for home. When the Company obtained *diwani* he was sent again to Bengal as a member of the Select Committee in 1767. Previous to his appointment as Resident, he became the collector-general and supervised the revenue administration of 24 Parganahs, Burdwan, Midnapore and Chittagong.
73. Select Committee's letter to Becher, 4 January, 1769, pp. 19-21.
74. Letter to Court, 6 January, 1769 (F.W.I.H.C., V, p. 496).
75. Becher's letter to the Committee, 17 January (S.C.R., 25 January, 1769, pp, 60-62).
76. Governor's letter to Reza, Rai-Durlabh and the Seths, 26 January, 1769 (C.P.C., II, p. 338, Nos. 1282 and 1283).
77. Durlabhram's letter to Governor, Rd. 24 January, 1769 (C.P.C. II, p. 338, No. 1277).

"embrace every opportunity to send us the earliest supplies possible.[78] Again on 25 January, Becher remitted to Calcutta ten lakhs of rupees. whereof Rs. 7,43,001 was in cash under the care of the *jamadar*, Sheikh Abcdul Kader and 25 sepoys, while the remaining money he sent in bills.[79]

At its meeting held on 9 February, the Select Committee decided to revoke their order of 17 November and resolved that the arrears of tribute due to the Emperor, allowance to the Nawab and salaries to the ministers should be punctually discharged by the Resident at the *darbar* "previous to making any further remittance hither."[80] In consequence of the resolution, the committee wrote to Becher : "The sums which we shall have received from the city and from the Company's Lands will, we hope, for a time remove the evil which induced us to issue our orders on the 17th November for delaying payment of the allowances due to the Nabob and ministers. We therefore desire you will begin to discharge those arrears and to pay the Tribute which may be due to His Majesty previous to sending any further supplies of money to the Presidency."[81] At this time, the Select Committee had appointed Robert Maddison as the Deputy Resident, who would "greatly contribute to the relief of the Resident in the duties of his laborious employment.'. The committee had a very high opinion about Maddison, who had acquired a knowledge in the Persian language and in *diwani* accounts.[82]

At this meeting, the Select Committee also gave its judgment on the representation of Reza Khan for the disposal of salt within the districts of Mahisadal and Hijli,

---

78. S.C.R., 25 January, 1779, p. 57.
79. Becher's letter to the Committee, 25 Jauuary (S.C.R., 9 February, 1769, p. 84).
80. S.C.R.. 9 February, 1769, pp. 81-82.
81. Select Committee's letter to Becher, 9 February (S.C.R., 9 February, 1769, pp. 81-82). But meanwhile, before receiving this letter, Becher had sent Rs. 1,40,000 to Colonel Grant at Mungher for the expenses of his troops.
82. Letter to Court, 2 February (F.W.I.H.C., V, p. 514).

and directed the Resident that if, on enquiry, he found a just statement about the merchants' account of advancing money for salt, there would be no necessity of receiving further advances for the ensuing years. An annual interest of 12 per cent should also be allowed to the merchants.[83] In the next letter, Becher assured the Committee that regarding the disposal of salt produced within the districts of Mahisadal and Hijli, he would immediately consult the ministers. At the same time, the Resident informed the Committee that on the application made by Colonel Smith for a supply of elephants, Becher had sent him nine elephants a few days before writing this letter. The Resident, at the same time, sent to the committee, a bill of exchange on the Military Paymaster General for Rs. 44.400; the account of cash would be despatched from there to Mungher for the expenses for the maintenance of the troops there[84]. The Select Committee became surprised that some elephants had been sent to Smith by the Resident "withont having previously advised us on the subject". Therefore, the committee forbade Becher, not to comply with any such application in future, without the approval of the Select Committee. The committee further wanted to know the advances made by Becher to several factories and *aurungs*, for the investment of the present year, "and that no more be made until further orders."[85]

According to the direction of the committee, on 9 February, Becher discharged the arrears of the royal tribute in bills, amounting to three lakhs of rupees,[86] to Dia Ram Pandit—the *vakil* of the Emperor. The Emperor acknowledged the receipt of Rs. 2,50,000 urging that in future, the royal tribute might be remitted to the Emperor through the house of the Seths. But from Becher and Reza Khan, the Seths came to know that they (Becher and Reza) had remitted bills for

83. S.C.R., 14 March, 1769, pp. 153-154.

84. Becher's letter to the Committee 18 March (S.C.R., 21 March, 1769, pp. 199-200).

85. S.C.R., 21 March, 1769, pp. 188-189.

86. Letter from Dia Ram Pandit to the Governor, [Rd. 31 March, 1769 (C.P.C., II, p. 343, No. 1310).

three lakhs more to the Emperor and would shortly remit bills for a further sum of rupees two lakhs.[87]

Becher, at heart, was a very compassionate person. Within a short time of his appointment as Resident, he realised the wretched condition of the country and the oppression on its *raiyots*. On 24 May, he addressed a letter to Verelst and painted the factual picture of Bengal by observing: "It must give pain to an Englishman to have reason to think that since the accession to the *Dawanee* the condition of the people of this country has been wrose than it was before; and yet I am afraid the fact is undoubted"[88] The Resident then proceeded to state the causes of this decline. The first of these causes was the "mode of providing the Company's investment; the exportation of specie instead of importing large sums annually." The second cause, he pointed out, about the existing method of revenue collection. "The strictness with which the collections have been kept up", observed Becher in his letter, "and the destructive method of employing *aumils*." For instance, the Resident pointed out that during Alivardi's time, the amount of revenues paid into the treasury was much less, but still the *zamindars* and merchants were rich and at the time of emergency, supplied a large sum of money tc the Nawab. The *zamindars* had a natural interest in their districts and gave proper support and encouragement to their *raiyots*. During the time of the Maratha invasions the *zamindars* had paid the Nawab one crore of rupees at one time, and fifty lakhs at another, besides paying the customary *malgujari*. Becher remarked: "I mention this only with a view of showing what this fine country is capable of under proper management." But then he proceeded to show the glaring slide-down under the English management. Whereas, the first consideration of the English after *diwani* was to collect as large sums as they could. And when the *zamindars* were not willing or able to pay the huge sums required, *amils* had been sent to most of

87. Letter from the Seths to the Governor, Rd. 20 April, 1769 (*Ibid.*, p. 351, No. 1341).
88. Firminger, Fifth Report, p. 183.

the districts. These *amils* when appointed, agreed to pay a fixed sum for their districts and as such, they extracted the money forcefully from the people of Bengal. The Resident exclaimed with sorrow; "What a destructive system is this for the poor inhabitants.[89] The *amils* had no natural interest in the welfare of the district where they made the collections, nor had they any certainty of holding their posts more than one year. They had also no check upon them during the time of their employment; so that during the time of collections, their powers were absolute. This had given a pernicious encouragement to a continual demand for more revenues ever since the English obtained the *diwani.*

Becher then proceeded to suggest the reforms that might obviate the abuses and evils. "Permit me here, Sir," observed the Resident, "to assure you that I do not aim at acquiring credit to myself by an increase of revenue during the time of my residence at the *Durbar*, but to adopt such maxims as will relieve this country from its present oppressed state, and put the *ryotts*.in that state of ease which will encourage cultivation."[90] Becher then narrated his plan : "The plan to be pursued through the whole country should be the same as is now practised at Burdwan; viz. letting the lands out to farmers for at least three years, with an assurance that those who behave well, and give proper encouragement to their *ryotts* should always have the preference in remaining farms of those lands." Against the extortion of exhorbitant money by the collectors, the Resident proposed some regulations. "That the *ryott* may know as early as possible in the season, what the Collector has a right to demand of him, and no further demand should be made on any account whatever." About the illegal imposition of taxes on the *raiyots*, Becher proposed some urgent modifications. "The present destructive scheme of adding demand on demand under the name of *Matote*,[91] has been a material cause of the present distressed states of

89. *Ibid.*, p. 184.

90. *Ibid.*, pp. 184-185.

91. An illegal tax imposed by the Company after obtaining the *diwani.*

the country, and I wish the word could be abolished and never heard of more." In his opinion, the collection of revenue should be left to the *zamindars* of the districts. "I cannot help thinking the *zamindars* have a very natural interest in the welfare of their districts and are of course more likely to give encouragement to the *ryotts* than any *aumil* that can be sent." But the Resident. at the same time, did not want to take risk by banking wholly on the *zamindars*. He continued, "I wish every check to be put upon them that can consistently be; they should know that on proof of any oppression, they should forefeit their *zemindary* for ever." Becher then proposed that the *band-o-bast* with the *zamindars* might be made at a lower rate, "equal to what has been paid into the Treasury." And if this plan were adopted, "the Company would receive a larger real income from this country than they have already done." The Resident forcefully argued that if the plan would be a blessing to the people : "many families now in ruin would be relieved" and "it would greatly tend to enhance the name and credit of the Company."[92]

In view of such a criticism about the revenue administration in Bengal after *diwani*, as well as the statement made by the court of Directors, "to correct abuses of so long a growth require much time and industry." induced Governor Verelst to visit Murshidabad in the month of June. In collaboration with Becher, he drew up a lengthy letter by which they allowed reduction in revenues to the *zamindars* in view of the "distressed condition of the country". But despite this deduction, they were sanguine about realising an increased revenue. For the district of Purnea, they recommended that if a proper man was appointed to manage the collections, the revenue collections could be substantially stepped up without molesting the people. Accordingly, to set an example, after the recommendation of the ministers, they decided to transfer Muhammad Ali Khan, the *faujdar* of Hugli, to Purnea and hoped for a better prospect which would "under proper

92. Firminger, *Fifth Report*, pp. 185-186.

management admit of a large increase in a few years". Ducarel was appointed at Purnea to assist Muhammad Ali.[93].

At its meeting of 16 August, the Select Committee considered the joint letters of Verelst and Becher and were of opinion that the "present crisis of our affairs," as well as "the true cause of our declining situation", was due to various reasons. They began to analyse the causes and found that it was due to want of sufficient scrutiny and watchful control of the government. Secondly, it was due to the delegation of trust and authority to one or to a few for a work that required the abilities of many to execute. Thirdly, there was widespread ignorance of the real production and capacity of yield in the country. Fourthly, there were the numerous dependents and hangers-on whom the collectors entertained and whose demands were fulfilled from the spoils of the industrious *raiyots*. Fifthly, there were the clashes of interests between the collectors and the *zamindars*. Lastly, the subjection of the *raiyots* to the oppression of a number of *gomastahs* and their dependents had a very detrimental effect on the cultivators and the yield from their labours. The committee fully realised that much integrity and good conduct would be required "to raise the sinking heart of the *Ryot* from despair to confidence and hope; to re-people and settle the deserted and uncultivated tracts."[94]

---

93. Such hopes of increased revenues of the Governor and the Resident proved genuine in later years. In the district of Rajhsahi, which was divided in 1768 into twelve divisions of *zillas*, a three years' settlement had been made with Rani Bhawni and the Company obtained for 1769 Rs. 26,01,000, in 1770 Rs. 26,76,000 and in 1771 Rs. 27,51,000.
The district of Birbhum was left to the *zamindar*. He was given a warning that "on the least deviation he will forfeit his right". The Company received for 1769 Rs. 7,25,000, for 1770 Rs. 7,68,400 and for 1771 Rs. 8,11,879-3-10.
The district of Rajmahal had suffered much from the hunters and mountaineers. It was allowed an abatement of Rs. 12,140. The Resident and the Nawab requested the Governor to station there a battalion of sepoys——Firminger, Fifth Report, pp. 186-188.

94. S.C.R., 16 August, 1769. Also, Verelst *View* pp. 224-225.

The appointment of Ducarel at Purnea formed the precedent for the institution of supervisors in other districts of the *diwani* portion.[95] Thus the committee resolved "that in every province or district, a gentleman in the service be appointed, with or without assistance, in proportion of the extent of the district whose office or department is to be subordinate to the Resident at the *Durbar*[96] In view of this the Select Committee directed the Resident to issue a code of instructions to the several supervisors. Each supervisor had to work in each particular district "with a view to ascertain in a minute, clear, and comprehensive manner, a variety of circumstances which intimately concern the welfare of the country." This form of instruction provided the guideline for each supervisor. The instructions were as under :

Each supervisor would have to provide himself with a reliable and synoptic history of the district. The supervisor was to correct, under this head, the form of the traditional constitution of the district, compared with the present. He would have to collect an account of its rulers, the revolutions in their families, and their connections and the privileges which they had enjoyed and the material changes, if any, which they had effected in the district. Secondly, the supervisor was to enquire about the produce and capacity of lands. He would have to procure a complete rent-roll and the measures of lands in the district, as well as to fix the boundaries and divisions. Thirdly, the supervisor should know the amount of revenues and arbitrary taxes in the district which the government, *zamindars* or collectors had been conventionally collecting. In this connection the supervisor must keep himself fully informed about the activities of the *darogahs*, *kotwals* and *paiks* maintained for the protection of tenants, and also ascertain, as it was feared too often, how these officials had become the instruments of the tenants' oppression. An account of their number and expenses incurred on them should also be arranged. Fourthly, the supervisor was

95. Firminger, *Fifth Report*, p. 188.

96. Verelst, *View*, p. 226.

to look after the regulation of trade and commerce in the district. In this work, the supervisor must be careful as he might be opposed by private agents, *paikars* or *dalals*. The supervisor should estimate the production of every district and the number of manufacturers employed in each branch. And lastly, the supervisor was to see to the administration of justice. His conduct in all capital offences was to enforce justice "where the law demands it, checking any composition by fine....; and where any disputes arise in matters of property, you should recommend the method of arbitration to any other. The arbitrators should be men chosen by the parties themselves, and of known integrity."[97] The committee also sent to Becher, a list of supervisors, who had been ordered to be posted in the different districts of Bengal and Bihar.[98]

Ducarel, who had already been sent to Purnea as supervisor, gave a very deplorable picture about the excesses committed in the district, in his letter on 17 August to Becher. He stated "that the Company have received a very consi-

---

97. *Ibid.*, pp. 227-230.

98. Names of the supervisors corresponding with Murshidabad :-

Dacca	—Thomas Kolsall, who had a position superior to other supervisors. The supervisor of Sylhet, John Summer was under his control.
Hugli	– William Lushington.
Birbhum	– Alexander Higginson.
Trippara	– Walter Wilkins.
Purnea	– George Gustavas Ducarel.
Dinajpur	– H. Cottrell
Jessore	– Robert Wilmot.
Nadia	– Jacob Rider.
Rajmahal and Natore	– C.W. Boughton-Rous
Rangpur	– John Grose.

Corresponding with Patna :-

Saran and Champaran	– Edward Golding.
Shahabad	– Charles Lloyd
Tirhut	—James Inglish Keighly.
Rohtas	– Henry Palmer.
Munghyr	– Nathaniel Bateman.

– Firminger, *Fifth Report*, p. 188.

derable revenue from that country, but they have little known how it has been collected." About the intra-official as well as the public relations of the government officials. the supervisor was pained to report that "all industry is checked and all confidence destroyed; and neither labourer, farmer, collector, and so upward to the *fauzedars*, having any trust in each other."[99]

The resolution of the Select Committee, passed on 16 August, about the appointment of supervisors, was received by Becher on 7 September. Because the resolution embodied his own ideas, Becher readily agreed about the importance of the resolution. Still according to him, considering the gravity of the situation, the resolution required the most mature examination before it was actually implemented. Becher requested the committee to allow his personal presence at Culcutta for a short time when he would be able to discuss the matter in a thorough and careful manner with all others. He hinted that, for the present, "though the plan appears to me an excellent one" yet "it ought not to be proceeded on till present years collections are nearly completed" The Resident wanted to defer the execution of the plan till March next, when the annual collections would be completed,[100]

After despatching this letter to the Select Committee, Becher received another letter from the committee on the same day. wherein, he found the list of the supervisors as well as a letter of instruction which the committee directed him to be delivered to each supervisor. In his reply to this the Resident again stated the practical difficulties which he envisaged that the proposed plan would be of utmost importance but it could not be carried out immediately "without imminent risk to the present years' collections and, therefore, requested a delay till that business is nearly completed." Becher again requested the com-

99. Quoted in Caraccioli, III, pp. 535-536.

100. Becher's letter to the Committee, 13 September, September (S.C.R., 25 September, 1769, pp. 501-505).

mittee to permit him to go to Calcutta, where he would discuss the plan in details.[101]

In the mean time the news about the scarcity of rice due to the ravages wrought by drought in several districts reached Calcutta. The situation required emergent consultations with the Resident. So the Select Committee allowed Becher to come to Calcutta "as soon as you may judge your presence at the *durbar* can be spared with safety to the collections"[102]

Becher felt satisfied about Ducarel's conduct at Purnea. The Resident was happy that under Ducarel's supervision "the distressed condition of Purnea is in a fair way recovering its once flourishing state"; otherwise the district "would soon have been ruined had the former destructive system been continued". The Resident stated that he was rather looking for the future "than present increase of revenue from a conviction that I thereby act for the real interest of our employers."[103]

In the month of October, Becher came to Calcutta and took his seat in the committee. There, he put forward a lengthy statement, whereby he pleaded for delaying the execution of the plan, till the close of the year's collections, at least where *amils* were employed. He was in complete accord with the proposed plan which was excellent; he particularly commended "the instructions drawn with a masterly hand." But raised some points before the committee and wanted the latter to consider them. In the first place, the Resident argued that it was necessary to divide Bengal into *Zillas* or districts, "so that every part thereof may come within the inspection of one or other of the supervisors". An account of such a division he promised to lay before the committee for approval. Secondly, it was to be decided how far and in what

101. Becher's letter to the Committee, 14 September (S.D., 5 October, 1769, pp. 187-188).

102. Committee's letter to Becher, 16 September, (S.C.R., 25 September, 1769, pp. 501-505).

103. Becher's letter to the Committee, 22 September (S.C.R., 12 October, 1679).

manner the supervisors would apply the mode of collecting revenues for the ensuing season, what degree of power they were to be invested with and whether there would be others to assist them; all these matters were to be discussed and settled before the plan was put into practice. Thirdly, the records at Murshidabad, which might assist the supervisors in their enquiries, should be incorporated with the instructions. And lastly, the Nawab's ministers' participation and involvement in the scheme was "very essential for its success". The subordinate officials in the ministry would almost certainly try to frustrate the plan, "but their efforts will be weak and vain, if the ministers and Nabob in particular are hearty on our cause." Additionally before the introduction of the plan, Reza Khan must be taken into confidence and consulted, because the Resident believed that Reza Khan "has a claim to this from the indefatigable pains he takes and the services he has rendered to the Company."[104]

The Resident then began his argument, why according to him the supervisors should not proceed to the districts before the close of the year i.e. until April next.

The first reason, as Becher argued, was that in the instructions, the supervisors were forbidden to interfere with the collections. But since they would have to make enquiries relative to every branch of the revenue, they could not be expected to make any progress unless the records and account of collection were laid before them. This "cannot be done without their neglecting the respective parts of the revenues under their charge." Secondly, the people who had undertaken the payment of the revenues for the present years, were likely to be sufferers due to the unfavourable season. They would look for every opportunity to evade payment. The arrival of supervisors in the districts would give them a fair opening to create a divided power between the conventional machinery and the newly appointed supervisors and derive fiscal advantage out of it to the detriment of the Company's

104. Becher's statement before the Select Committee, 10 October (S.C.R., 12 October, 1769, pp. 526-431).

revenue. Thus "much inconvenienee must...arise and I fear loss of the revenue." Thirdly, the various revenue collection functionaries already in the district would look at the supervisors with jealousy and would withhold the necessary information. These collectors, if cooperative, might be of the most essential service to the supervisors in their enquiries. To ensure the success of the plan, it was essential to send the supervisors after the present season was over, so that the intervening period might be well employed in laying the ground for success. As the current season's collections were very near being finalised, Becher thought it necessary to go back to Murshidabad immediately. The Resident stated that the present season was so unfavourable that a famine was likely to prevail but he assured the committee that he would try his utmost "to prevent every ill effect."[105] Becher wished to see every district let out to be farmed and superintended by the officials in the Company's service. That way, he argued, the whole *subah* of Bengal, might be put on the same footing as Burdwan where Company's machinery was working effectively in harmony with the local and native officials. The Resident hoped that the appointment of supervisors should be permanent "and invested with such a degree of power as may be judged necessary for the well conducting the collections of the revenues". He stated that to ensure the plan's success the supervisors should be men of experience. About Ducarel in Purnea, the Resident had no doubt about his ability. About the supervisors nominated in Rajshahi and Nadia, the Resident had the same opinion. But the "other supervisors (should) be with the Resident at the *Durbar* at least six weeks before they proceed to their several stations and it shall be my business to prepare every information that can be procured." The Resident then requested the committee that the supervisors might be asked to remain with him at Murshidabad for their "knowledge in the Persian language". He added that Rooke might also remain with him for sometime more as he (Rooke) had begun a set of books "which he keeps in a very neat and correct manner", at least till the end of season.[106]

105. *Ibid.*

106. S.D.R., 26 October, 1769, pp. 216-226.

In the month of September, the question of Verelst's departure for Europe was raised in the committee. Naturally it was discussed that because Becher was the second in council, the posts of the Governor of Fort william as well as the President of the council should devolve upon him.[107] But Becher had given his opinion on 23 October to remain second in council even after Verelst's departure; his point was that "he was to remain in his present station of Resident at the *darbar*,"[108] because he (Becher) himself wanted to proceed to Europe the next year.

In the month of November, the Calcutta Council informed the Court of Directors about the "universal distress" in the *subah* of Bengal that was heading for a famine. As widely feared that this distress might increase, the Calcutta Council ordered for a reserve stock of grain "sufficient to serve our army". But at the same time, the council assured the home authorities that they would step up every measure in their power "to relieve the miserable situation" of the poor inhabitants in case the land actually came under the grip of famine.[109]

Becher had already stated on 10 October about the necessity of dividing the whole of Bengal into *zillas* or districts so that each *zilla* might come under the inspection of one or other of the supervisors. To transform his plan into reality, Becher, after his arrival at Murshidabad, divided the Bengal *subah* "into such *Zillas* or divisions by annexing to each principal Districts, all such small places as lay contiguous thereto" Accordingly, the salt lands of Hijli with several adjoining *taluqs* were added to the district of Hugli; Bishnupur was added to Birbhum; Edrakpur, Baharbund, Rangamati and some small divisions, to the district of Rangpur, and Sylhet

107. Letter to Court, 25 September, 1769 (F.W.I.H.C., V. p. 585).

108. Becher himself requested that he be allowed to continue in his present position as the Resident, as that station was "next in importance to that of the Governor" and that he thought himself "as qualified to conduct that branch, as any member of the Board that can be sent". – Bengal Public Consultations, 23 October, 1769.

109. Letter to Court, 23 Nomber, 1769 (F.W.I.H.C., V, p. 605).

was added to the district of Dacca.[110] But still there remained some districts which were not included under any supervisor. These districts were as follows. Chunakhally, with some small *taluqs* and villages was situated in the neighbourhood of Murshidabad and yielded a revenue of Rs. 7,81,496-12-2 annually. Rokunpur—a *zamindari*, some parts of which were bordering upon Purnea, others near Murshidabad, while the rest were bordering upon the district of Burdwan, yielded a revenue of Rs.4,35,992-1-8. A *Zamindari* adjoining Dinajpur, with a number of considerable *taluqs*, produced a revenus of Rs. 5,38,900-13-15. Fateh Singh, a *Zamindari* adjoining Murshidabad, yielded a revenue of Rs. 4,03,291-12-11. Jessore with the addition of Muhammad Shahi *Zamindari* and some considerable *taluqs*, yielded a revenue of Rs. 7,30,057-9-17.[111] For the management of the aforesaid districts, Becher suggested two alternatives: either to appoint more supervisors and allot the districts to them or annex those places to such districts as were under the supervisors. Becher recommended that some *talugs* adjoining Murshidabad might be placed under the supervision of the Resident at the *Darbar*. Some parts of the district of Rajshahi, which were adjacent to Murshidabad Becher suggested, might also be placed under the Resident, while the other part, which was on the other side of the Ganges, might be placed under a separate supervisor. The Resident recommended Jahangirpur to be added to Dinajpur. Becher thought these changes "essential" in "well conducting the intended plan of reformation". In concluding his letter Becher reminded the committee about the distressed condition of Sarfaraz Khan's family and the brother of late Rajah Rammnarain, and requested them to empower him to relieve their distress.[112]

In their meeting on 10 December, the Select Committee approved Becher's plan of dividing Bengal into *zillas* and were of the opinion "that the measure proposed by Mr. Becher for

110. Becher's lettar to the Committee, 26 November (S.C.R., 7 December, 1769, pp. 570-577).

111. *Ibid.*

112. *Ibid.*

fixing the several districts under the respective supervisors appears well calculated for conducting with regularity the business they are to be employed in." Hence, the committee appointed supervisors in each district and the gross amount of revenue that each supervisor would have to collect, was also indicated in their letter.[113] The committee also intimated to Becher "such degree of power" that had been invested on the Resident at the *Darbar* over the supervisors.[114]

It was Becher who had to give a practical shape to this plan and accordingly, on 20 December, he directed Jacob Rider to proceed to Krishnagar as the supervisor of Nadia.

113.

Names of the supervisors	*Districts and the amount of* revenue to be collected.
John Graham	Hugli, the salt lands of Hijli and the adjoining *taluqs*—Rs. 10,29,451-9-18-1.
Charles Stuart	Bishnupur, Birbhum and Panchet—Rs. 10,45,501-11.
John Grose	Rangpur, Edrakpur, Baharbund, Rangamati and dependencies—Rs. 9,23,052-5-2-3.
The Chief of Dacca	Dacca and Sylhet—*Rs.* 24,12,511-4-10-2.
William Hardwood	Bhagalpur and Rajmahal. The revenue of Bhagalpur was not estimated. From Rajmahal Rs. 3,74,029-0-9-3.
The Resident at the *Darbar*	Chunakhali and its dependencies, Fateh Singh, Lakhimpore and part of Rajshahi—Rs. 15,58,216-9-16-1.
George Vansittart	Jahangirpur and Dinajpur Rs. 20,38,900-13-15-2.
Boughton Rous	Parts of Rajshahi, eastward of the Ganges—Rs. 20,38,900-13-15-2.
Robert Wilmot	Jessore—Rs. 1,33,000 Rokunpur-Rs. 4,35,992-1-8-3, but none appointed till then.

—S.C.R., 10 December, 1769, pp. 596-598,

114. *Ibid.*

Becher sent him the instructions already transmitted to him by the committee and advised him to follow them accordingly. The Resident then acquained Rider about the position in respect of Nadia. From the year April 1769-April 1770, the Company had settled the Nadia district in favour of Rajah Nabkrishna and others. By the settlement which had been effected at Calcutta the lessee had been granted tillage rights over the land for a period of three years in lieu of payments made to the Company which included allowances for the *zamindar* of Nadia who had ceded his lands to the Company.[115] The farmers, i.e. Rajah Nabkrishna and others, were to made these collections and "by no means to charge either the *ryott* or trader with new taxation or assessment," over and above the terms of the settlement. Thus the farmers were entrusted with "the entire management of receiving" the rent from the tenants. The farmers were accountable to the Company's supervisor "for their agreement with the government." Rider was further directed to transmit the Nadia revenues from Krishnagar to Murshidabad. Becher wanted that "the payment of every *kist* should arrive at the city," i.e. Murshidabad. Becher also directed Rider that after the latter's arrival at Krishnagar, he should call all the *gomastahs*, whom the farmers had placed in several *parganahs* for the remittances of their revenues to Krishnagar. In case of any delay by the *gomastahs* in remittance of money, the supervisor was advised to send peons and *harkarahs* to oblige them to comply. The Resident then enclosed a list of the *parganahs* and also directed him that if the farmers desired to make any division of the *parganahs* amongst themselves, Rider "must

---

115. The following sums were agreed upon as payable by Rajah Nabkrishna and others, the lessees of Nadia :

Revenue to the Government	Rs. 8,00,000
Increased assessment	Rs. 58,000
Allowance for the support of the Rajah of Nadia	Rs. 1,00,000
	9,58,000

In the two succeeding years they agreed to pay an increase of Rs. 50,000 each year. S.C.R. 28 January 1770, pp. 9-16.

obtain this account from them with the rates of each *purgunnah* and transmit a statement thereof to me."[116] In other words, there should be no adverse effect of any expedient introduced by the farmers on the fiscs of the Company.

Becher further observed in his letter to Rider that the Rajah of Nadia had unjustly withheld a sum of Rupees one lakh and thirty thousand from the previous year's revenues, which might be good "by an annual deduction from his allowance." In the administration of justice, the Resident advised the supervisors to follow his method of justice at Murshidabad. His advice to them was : "Promote arbitration as much as possible" which was the most equitable way of deciding disputes. The supervisors were also to put a stop to arbitrary fines. Further, all the supervisors were to support the authority of the government's officers. At the same time, they were to recommend such regulations "as appear necessary for the welfare of the country."[117] After giving these directions to the supervisors, Becher also conveyed the same to Rider. Becher intimated to the Select Committee that he would send all the above instructions to the supervisors when the latter would be taking charge at their respective stations. Becher informed the Select Committee about his idea of governance : "That we should strictly keep up to the established form of the country government and suffer every act to pass in the names of the Rajah, *Aumil* or ministers." But at the same time, the Englishmen must learn "the real state of this fine country", and if the officials of the Company kept all this in view, "success will crown our endeavours to restore this country and its inhabitants to a flourishing and comfortable state." Becher also informed the committee about his unhappy relations with the supervisor of Dacca who showed symptoms of insubordination as well as arrogance towards Becher. Becher wondered how he was obliged to receive instructions from the Dacca supervisor who

116. Becher's letter to Jacob Rider, 20 December (.SC.R., 28 January, 1770, pp. 9-16).

117. *Ibid.*

should be under him and not *vice versa*. He thought that it was the committee which had the authority to instruct him and not any supervisor of any district. Becher had no thirst for power. He stressed that he wanted only "what is necessary for......well conducting the new adopted plan".[118]

In December, according to Becher's direction, C.W. Boughton Rous went to Rajshahi as supervisor of the district, with his headquarters at Natore, On the next day after his arrival, he assembled all the public officers and assured them that the object of the Company was "to relieve the country, to promote its commerce and manufacturers" and at the same time to prevent any "degree of oppression and Injustice, by the Establishment of a mild and equitable Administration".[119]

On 0 January, 1770, Becher directed William Harwood, the supervisor of Bhagalpur and Rajmahal, to proceed to his district, enclosing with his letter the instructions of the committee. Although Harwood's appointment at Rajmahal was deferred "till after the next *pooneah*", yet as the district had a very considerable unrealised balance of revenues, Becher was under necessity to direct Harwood to proceed there forthwith in order to use his "utmost Endeavors, to have the Excuse of this Ballance and to recover as much of it as possible." About the administration of justice, Becher instructed Harwood to follow his practice, by promoting arbitration as the means of resolving conflicts as much as possible.[120]

After the appointment of supervisors, Becher began to receive from them innumerable complaints of harassment, oppression, atrocities and even plunder, perpetrated on the people not only by the collectors but sometimes by the

118. Becher's letter to the Committee, 22 December, 1769, (S.C.R., 28 January, 1770, pp. 5-9).

119. Boughton Rous' letter to Becher, 30 December, 1769 (Letter Copy Book of the Supervisor of Rajshahi at Natore, Calcutta, 1925, p. 1).

120. Becher's letter to William Harwood, 20 January, 1770 (Copy Book of Letter of the Resident at the Darbar, 27 December, 1769-7 – August, 1770, Vol. I).

English soldiers. A serious complaint about the atrocities of the English troops at Rajmahal reached him through a letter of William Harwood—the supervisor, in the month of February, 1770. When the news of the arrival at Rajmahal of a division of English troops under the command of Colonel Winwood reached the supervisor, the latter personally went to the place to see whether the accounts of oppression and hardship of the people at the hands of the soldiers and sepoys, about which representations had been made to him, were exaggerated or not. But the supervisor became horrified and remarked : "I never before was witness to so distressing a sight", as the sepoys and camp-followers began to plunder "in all quarters of the town". By these frequent outrages of English troops, Harwood remarked in his letter to the Resident : "this once large and populous city is now reduced to a poor small thinly inhabited village". The inhabitants "were also persecuted by the travellers, plundered by the mountaineers and distressed by famine." The oppression and loot were committed not only by the detachment under Winwood's command, but every detachment from Calcutta to Patna, sent along this road almost customarily committed severe orgies and outrages. Consequently Harwood requested for remedies. He hoped for an immediate order for this purpose, so that he might use his "utmost endeavours to protect the inhabitants of Rajmahal, and by inflicting severe punishment on the plunderers."[121]

Becher forwarded this letter to John Cartier, the newly appointed Governor of Fort William as well as the President of the Committee, with the remark that the facts stated by Harwood "were sufficiently authenticated" and so the committee must stop such depredations and give positive relief to the inhabitants. The Resident also supported the fact represented by Harwood, that the inhabitants were oppressed continually by the English troops and their camp-followers on their march along the highroad from Calcutta to Patna. So he requested

121. Harwood's letter to Becher, 10 February (S.C.R., 29 March, 1770, pp. 165-168).

the committee to "issue such orders as shall be best adopted to prevent the like evils in future." As a suggestion to prevent such disorder, the Resident remarked that the troops should be provided with necessary supplies and "every officer commanding a detachment should receive orders to avoid encamping within two miles of any town or village." An officer from the government should aceompany every detachment. "The most severe punishments should be inflicted on those detected in plundering and distressing the inhabitants." Due to the unfavourable season, many of the *raiyots*, had to dispose of their ploughs, and Becher wanted that they should be given necessary advances of money that would "tend much to the general welfare of the country and the future increase of revenue". In such cases, the Nawab's ministers had assured Becher about their "attention to the distribution of what you may allow to be advanced". Abatements of impositions in several districts would be unavoidable, which appeared to the Resident absolutely necessary as a measure of relief and for the "general benefit of the Country."[122]

During this time, the President and the Select Committee came to know about the very risky development of "uncontrolled ingress and egress of French and other European ships into the river" and hence, they directed Becher "to apply to the Government for an order that all ships belonging to the European nations be obliged to come to Culpee and there undergo an examination." It was also decided that an officer of the Government with a proper guard be stationed at the place, i.e., Culpee, for that purpose. If any ship be found with a number of men exceeding 250 on board, the officer then must prevent the ship from advancing and make report to his superiors. Becher was further directed to request Nawab Saifuddaulah to issue orders to the governors of the European settlements to the effect that they should instruct all pilots to bring their ships at Culpee.[123] Two days

122. Becher's letter to the Governor and the Committee, 13 February (S.C.R., 29 March, 1770, pp. 161-164).

123. Committee's letter to Becher, 17 February (S.C.R., 17 February, 1770, p. 72 and pp. 74-75).

after, the Governor also sent similar instructions to Reza Khan, directing him to search the European ships at Culpee.[124] In reply, Reza Khan suggested to the Governorto appoint three officers for the inspection of ships, and further suggested that these officers be changed every four months.[125] Reza Khan's suggestion was approved by the Governor who informed him that a *darogah* with two other officers might be stationed at Culpee. These officers might be appointed in consultation with Becher.[126]

On 10 March, 1770, Nawab Saifuddaulah died of small-pox. His royal guardian, Muni Begam, immediately reported his death to the Governor and requested him that Mubarakud-daulah, another son of Mir Jafar, should succeed him.[127] Becher, in consultation with Reza Khan, recommended for the accession of Mubarakuddaulah to the *masnad*. This was approved by the Governor and the Select Committee and so, on behalf of the Company, Becher and Aldersay attended the installation of the new Nawab.[128]

In the month of March Becher informed supervisor Charles Stuart that besides Birbhum, the districts of Panchet and Bishnupur were also committed to his charge and he might proceed there as the supervisor of those districts. Becher told him that the instruction of the committee with its Persian and Bengali translations would be sent to him within a few days. Meanwhile, Stuart should impress on the people about "the humane intentions of your appointment" and to encourage them "to proceed cheerfully in the cultivation of their lands." As his residence would have to be at a central place within these districts, he was instructed to defer building

124. Governor's letter to Reza Khan, 19 February, 1770 (C.P.C., III Calcutta, 1919, p. 21, No. 87).

125. Reza Khan's letter to the Governor, Rd.13 March, 1770 (*Ibid.*, pp. 25-26, No. 105).

126. Governor's letter to Reza Khan, 12 March, 1770 *Ibid.*, pp. 28-29, No. 115).

127. Muni Begam's letter to the Governor, 14 March, 1770 (*Ibid.*, pp. 31-32, No. 123).

128. Letter to Court, 25 August, 1770 (F.W.I.H.C., VI, Edt. by Bisheswar Prasad, Delhi, 1960, pp. 214-215).

his residence "till such time as you know where your attendance will be most requisite."[129] In his letter of 17 March, the Resident sent his instructions to Stuart, as well as forwarded to him a statement of revenues of the districts of Birbhum, Bishnupur and Panchet. The Resident also informed the *zamindārs* and collectors of those districts about the nature of Stuart's appointment and asked them to extend the fullest cooperation to Stuart. When Stuart received the Resident's instructions, he assured the latter his due attention. The supervisor also informed Becher that the former would encamp in Birbhum, where he would encourage the farmers to cultivate the waste and jungle lands.[130]

The Chief of the Dacca factory, Thomas Kelsell, by virtue of his post, became the supervisor of Dacca and Sylhet. But he did not want to see his position lower than that of the Resident at the *Dārbār*. Hence, before taking over his duties as supervisor, Kelsell wanted to know from the President and the Select Committee that as he had been distinguished from other supervisors, he wanted to know his position on the hierarchy.[131] Kelsell became aggrieved when he came to know that he had been placed under the Resident. So he again represented the matter to the committee observing, "I do not see the force of the reasons which have determined you to place me subordinate to the Resident at the *Durbar*." The Chief of Dacca wanted to act in conjunction with Rajah Maha Singh, on the same footing as the Chief of Patna acted with Rajah Shitab Rai.[132] But the independent status of the Chief of Dacca was not allowed and it was confirmed that he would act as the supervisor of Dacca and Sylhet just like the other supervisors in the other districts. Kelsell was now left with no option. He wrote to Becher about his willing submission

129. Becher's letter to Charles Stuart—Supervisor of Birbhum, Bishnupur and Panchet, 14 March, 1770 (Resident at the *Darbar*, I).

130. Charles Stuart's letter to Becher, 22 March, 1770 (*Ibid.*)

131. Thomas Kelsell's letter to the Committee, 1 March, 1770 (*Ibid*).

132. Kelsell's letter to the Committee, 15 May, 1770 (*Ibid*).

and assured Becher that he would "hereafter represent and wait" on the direction of Becher.[133] And within a month, when Kelsell sought permission from Becher to coin Arcot rupee coins in the Dacca mint, his proposal was rejected by the Resident.[13]

Reports of cases of *zoolum* and oppressions on the tenants continued to come regularly from the supervisors. Becher received similar information from Rajshahi. The supervisor, Boughton-Rous, suggested to him to discourage the appointment of *paikars* and *dalals*, who had been found to be notorious oppressors. If they were eliminated, the supervisor intimated, the cultivator along with the manufacturer might "receive of his commodities at a more equitable valuation."[135]

Not only were there cases of oppressions by the collectors of revenue, but Becher also came to know about the illegal extortion of money by the Company's sundry officials from the poor inhabitants. These extortions were given the name of cesses, but they were illegally extracted and never any account of these were sent to the authorities of the Company. Sykes, the former Resident, used to extract them and kept all such acts secret, till Becher divulged everything before the Select Committee. Becher vehemently protested against these ignoble cases of extraction of money and sent his report and observations to the Select Committee in his letter on 28 March, 1770. He gave a detailed statement of the amounts collected under different heads of assessments till April 1769. These amounts were collected, right from the time the English had obtained the *diwani*, under the names of *mathut* and other similar realisations, and being unauthorised exactions, did not appear on the public records. Neither the *mathut* nor the sundry expenses were entered in the treasury

133. Kelsell's letter to Becher, 26 May, 1770 (*Ibid.*)

134. Becher observed : "I cannot acquiesce in your proposals for coining arcot rupees in the Dacca mint". Becher to Kelsell, 26 June, 1770 (*Ibid*).

135. Letter from Boughton-Rous to Becher, 26 March, 1770 (L.C.B., Natore, pp. 12-13).

accounts and both were left to the management of the ministers.[136].

Sykes, at the time of resigning the post of the Resident, had written a letter to Becher—his successor, pointing out the reasons why and how these cesses had been instituted. According to Sykes, these unlawful cesses had been established by Clive and the Select Committee, and these were not included in the Company's treasury out of the fear that the "Company would not permit such an expense". The *pushtabandy*, money collected on the plea of prevention of erosion of the river banks, was a necessary expense according to Sykes, though "*Resum nezarat* might be abolished", but, as he had added, because it was a custom of "an ancient standing, the abolition of it would have given disgust."[137] Thus Sykes had recommended the continuance of all these unlawful cesses. But Becher differed with Sykes and thought these impositions illegal. On this point Becher interrogated Reza Khan who also confirmed the attitude of Sykes in regard to these impositions. Becher thus thought it his duty to inform the Select Committee about the nature of these cesses which, he strongly felt, were illegal.

The cess called *chelat* had been greatly increased after the English had obtained the *diwani*. Formerly, the amount of this cess was collected for the official outfit of the *zamindars* and collectors at the time of puniyah. But since the Nawab had become a stipendary of the Company, he declined to have any part in this regard. According to Becher, either the Nawab should defray the expense of *chelats* or the system should be altogether abolished. But if the custom of giving dresses could not be abolished altogether, the expenses on this account might be drastically reduced. The cess called *pushtabandy* was meant for the charges of repairing bridges and culverts, repairing the embankment of the river etc. This cess on the people, seemed to Becher most unreasonable. Formerly the

---

136. Becher's letter to the Committee, 28 March (S.C.R., 28 April, 1770, pp. 197-215).

137. Sykes' letter to Becher, 16 Januara, 1769 (S.C.R., 28 April, 1770, 197-215).

expense of supporting these bridges etc. was vested in the *zamindars* whose lands were contiguous to them. But after the English obtained the *diwani* the *zamindars* neglected the matter completely and as such the banks of the rivers were soon in a state of great decay. Even the city of Murshidabad was in great danger in September, 1767, as a consequence of erosion caused by the river. So an assessment, which was levied on *zamindars*, was also forced upon the inhabitants of the districts. The cess known as *resum nezarat*—a fee of the *nazir*—was an old established custom. The post of *nazir*, in former times, was of great consequence. He had under him all the peons, *chobdars* etc. who on the pretence of collecting money, plundered the country. This office, seemingly burdensome, was abolished but the cess collections continued.[138]

"On my arrival here" continued Becher in the same letter, "I found that my predecessor had received from these cesses an allowance of 2000 rupees per month". Originally, these cesses were received by Sykes directly from the districts but due to personal inconvenience, he had entrusted the collections to Reza Khan. This allowance was continued during the time of Becher and when the Resident informed Verelst, the latter also did not disapprove the custom, "as he was sensible of the great expense attendant on my situation". The ministers also recommended the continuance of these cesses but Becher was doubtful about the legitimacy of these appropriations and wanted to know the view-point of the Select Committee.[139]

Becher thought that all the charges could be reduced greatly. The ministers as well as the Resident were of the opinion that if an arrangement for an additional sum of Rs. 3,50,000 were made, it might serve to bear all necessary expenses. If the proposed additional sum were added in the accounts of the general agreement, the *raiyots* might cheerfully accept it,

138. Becher's letter to the Committee, 28 March (S.C.R., 28 April, 1770, pp. 197-215)

139. *Ibid.*

for they would then know the amount they had to pay and, at the same time, be freed from arbitrary oppressions.[140]

In reply to Becher's letter, the Select Committee observed that "in a country where abuses of office are practised" by the collusion of the offenders with their associates, it became impossible to mark the offenders. However, about all the above observations of the Resident, the committee rather surprisingly remarked that before the Company had obtained the *diwani*, Rs. 83,000 had been collected from the cess called *chelat*. Thereafter the amount "each year has swelled the account till it has exceeded all bounds." Moreover, the committee could not abolish altogether the custom of giving dresses to the officials at the time of *puniyah*. So the committee directed that the *chelat* dresses be confined to "the members of the Board alone" and to those "who are entitled by their offices". About the new cess called *pushtabandy*, imposed with effect from 1767 "upon an extraordinary calamity", the committee saw no reason for its continuance after the banks of the river had been repaired so thoroughly. But the committee hoped to raise a fund earmarked for this particular purpose in order to meet any emergent situation in future. From the cess of *resum nezarat*, the *mutasuddies* and *mohorees* of the *cutchery* used to be the main gainers The committee wanted to know from Becher that in case this cess was discontinued partly or wholly, whether there would be a feeling of disgust among the concerned officials. On account of all such considerations, finally none of these cesses were totally abolished; but the committee on the one hand, wanted to limit the sums to be collected or defrayed and, on the other, tried equitably to distribute the sum throughout the whole *subah*. They also did not approve of fixing the additional sum of Rs. 3,50,000 which might be appropriated towards the payment of the debt of Rs. 2,29, 265-11-14. About *mathut*, the committee pointed out the great inequality in assessment. The extensive district of Dacca had paid only Rs. 5,000, while Nadia—a small district, had

140. An amount of Rs. 2,22,265-11-14 had been collected from all these cesses. *Ibid.*

paid heavily. Even Becher's proposal of adding *mathut* to the *band-o-bast*, was not approved by the committee and they observed, "our view is not so much to suppress the taxes," as to prepare a separate statement for them, independent of the *band-o-bast*.[141]

Becher entrtained strong hopes about the advantages that would be gained from the appointment of English supervisors in the management of affairs in different districts. The humane intention of the Company behind the appointment of the supervisors should be made public and hence the Resident wanted its publication in every village in the following terms: "The English *Sardars* taking into consideration the present state of these provinces whose welfare they have much at heart, are come to a resolution to send into the different districts English gentlemen whose business it will be to give the strictest attention to the ease and comfort of the inhabitants, to prevent oppression under every denomination, to give due encouragement to the *Ryotts* and prevent anything more being exacted from *Ryotts* either by *Zemindar* or *Talukdar* or *Aumil* or any one employed in the collection of the revenues." He also wanted to declare that "the gentlemen in the different districts will be ever ready jointly with the officers of the Government to contribute to carry into execution the humane plan formed by the Governor and Council for the relief, ease and comfort of these provinces."[142]

Accordingly, in the early days of April, Becher directed John Grose to proceed to Rangpur as the supervisor of the district. The field of his supervision was also extended to Edrakpur and some other adjacent *parganahs*. The Resident also enclosed an extract of instructions transmitted by the Select Committee and directed him to follow them strictly. From the cultivation and improvement of waste lands, in these areas, the Company estimated a considerable increase in revenues.[143]

141. Select Committee's letter to Becher, 28 April (S.C R., 28 April, 1770, pp. 197-215),

142. Becher's letter to committee, 30 March (S.C.R., 28 April, 1770, pp. 216-232).

143. Becher's letter to John Grose, 10 April, 1770 *Resident at the Darbar*, I).

On 20 April, John Grose arrived at Rangpur and informed the *zamindars* on the 23rd morning about the cause of his arrival. He examined the accounts and found that there was an unrealised balance amounting to Rs. 24, 837 due to the Company. Within a day or two, Grose realised the evil practices of collections. The *paiks* who were employed without pay, looted the "unhappy sufferers" over whom they were placed. He informed the Resident that if the monopoly of grain was not abolished at Rangpur, a famine was certain to break out. He further requested Becher to open grain *gollahs* (storage of grain) in different places[144] to tide over the situation. But the situation became worse. The English soldiers there also began to adopt their old practice of plundering the poor inhabitants. An *amil* of Govindganj complained to the supervisor of Rangpur about the predatory movements of the English troops. Grose himself found, after an enquiry, that "a company of seapoys from Moradbaug which were stationed at Rangamatty,.........moved to Govin Gunge," and went on a plundering spur. Hence the supervisor requested the Resident to recall those troops, who "can serve no end" but were plundering the district "under various pretence."[145]

About the employment of *paiks*, who molested the poor inhabitants, Becher informed Grose that the *paiks* solely depended upon extorting the weak and, therefore, their number should be curtailed. He assured the supervisor that the *paiks* would be prevented from practising oppressive measures.[146]

The news of these oppressions upon the poor people almost daily reached Becher from all corners of Bengal. Charles Stuart—the supervisor of Birbhum, Bishnupur and panchet, also informed him about the great drought in these places

144. John Grose's letter to Becher, 24 April, 1770 (*Ibid.*,).

145. *Ibid.*, 10 May, 1770.

146. Becher's letter to Grose, 21 May, 1770.

147. Letter from Charles Stuart to Becher, 17 March, 1770.

148. *Ibid.*, 28 May, 1770.

followed by the extortion of money by the *tahsildars*, over, and above their usual rents.[147] In the month of May, Stuart further informed Becher that he had received from the collection of Birbhum Rs. 1,25,000, but after an enquiry, he found that over and above this, there had been an excess collection of Rs. 29,078.[148] This amount had naturally gone into the pockets of the oppressive functionaries.

Becher's strong hopes of advantages to the country as well as to the Company, that he entertained in March, began to pale at the end of May. The condition of all the districts of Bengal looked gloomy, the harvest was very unfavourable almost everywhere. In his letter to John Grose, he drew a picture of the condition of Bengal as well as the Company's future plan of collecting revenues. The Resident observed in his letter: "The Districts placed under your Inspections have suffered little by the general calamity of drought in comparison with what may other parts of these provinces have done." The Resident believed that there would be "more considerable reduction of the Revenues of present year than of the last", and he feared that sufficient money could not be collected to pay the necessary demands of the troops and defray other expenses. But the duty of the Resident was "to suffer nothing to come in competition with securing such revenues under the present unfavourable circumstances." But under the "present calamitious Juncture", Becher advised Grose to interfere "as little as possible" in the collections. *Puniyah* was held at Murshidabad on 24 May, where Becher represented the Company.[149] And for the next season, the English authorities began to devise "a general system" to be established for the collection of revenues. Meanwhile, Becher recommended

---

149. Cartier – the Governor, wrote to Reza Khan that due to excessive heat, he could not attend the *puniyah* and it would be attended by Becher on behalf of the Company—Governor's letter to Reza Khan, 10 May, 1770 (C.P:C., III, p. 64, No. 207).

to Grose for the proper regulation of the functions of the judicial courts, the encouragement of cultivation and the promotion of free commerce, and at the top of all "carrying into Execution every well concerted plan to obtain the desired purpose."[150]

150. Becher's letter to Grose, 25 May, 1770 (Resident at the *Darbar*, I).

8

FAILURE IN REVENUE ADMINISTRATION, GREAT FAMINE IN BENGAL AND TRANSFER OF CAPITAL TO CALCUTTA

Bengal witnessed one of the severest visitations of famine from the middle of 1769, which reached its climax in the year following and ravaged the whole *subah* with its attendant train of death and devastation. The influx was abnormal because such was the fertility of soil and so genial the climate, that in normal times every year the *subah* was blessed with two good crops. Its little harvest came in April and the large one in October.[1] Early in 1769, the prices became high, owing to the partial failure of crops in 1768. In spite of the complaints of the local officers, Becher reported to the Select Committee, after assumption of his new post of the Resident early in February 1769, that the land tax was being rigorously enforced.[2] The rains of 1769, although deficient in the northern districts, on the whole seemed to hold out promises for relief. The September harvest of 1769 was sufficient to enable

1. Debrit, J., *Transactions in India* (London, 1786), p. 124, Hunter says that the lower Bengal produced three harvests every year: a scanty pulse crop in spring, a more important rice crop in autumn and the great rice crop in December. — Hunter, W.W., *Annals of Rural Bengal* (Reprint, Delhi 1975), p. 20.
2. Becher's letter to the Select Committee, 7 February, 1769.

the Calcutta Council to promise grain to Madras, notwithstanding the high prices. But in the same month, the periodical rains suddenly ceased and the young crops that depended on rain withered.[3] Thus a strong drought, that dried up the field of all moisture, converted the most fertile plains into sandy deserts. There was a complete failure of the large harvest of 1769 and of the little harvest of 1770. This failure was so general and extensive that notwithstanding some harvesting of rice on the high lands, the aggregate produce was not at all adequate to meet the needs of the inhabitants.[4]

The famine desolated almost the entire region of Bengal and Bihar. In the beginning of August 1769, rice became scarce in Calcutta. The report came from Bihar in July 1769 that the crops had been entirely spoiled and the famished cultivators had left their homes in search of livelihood. Becher from Murshidabad and Rumbold from Patna hinted about this famine and its sequel to the Calcutta authorities.[5] The Calcutta Council also reported this universal distress to the home authorities in London, with the remark that the whole *subah* was "threatened with famine." They could realise it well that the distress would continue the next year. As a precautionary measure the Calcutta Council directed a stockpiling of grain for their own army.[6] But they did not undertake any measure for the relief of the poor inhabitants. On the contrary they directed Becher to procure 40,000 *maunds* of rice from the districts of Dinajpur and Purnea. Though they also cautioned him carefully to know the wants of the districts, they emphasised that he should in no way allow the Company's interests to suffer. Without taking any relief measures for the poor, they only gave routine directions to the Resident and the supervisors of Bihar to prevent monopolies of grain and to encourage the cultivation of pulses, barley, and the grains that were grown in the dry season.[7]

3. Hunter, *Annals*, p. 21.
4. Debrit, *Transactions*, pp. 124-125.
5. Letter to Court, 30 September 1769 (F.W.I.H.C., V, p. 603).
6. Letter to Court, 23 November 1769 (*Ibid.*, p. 605).
7. Consulsation, 23 October, 1769 (Hunter, *Annals*, pp. 406-407).

Becher again narrated the story of the woeful plight of the Bengal people before the Calcutta authorities in the month of November, 1769, remarking that there was "an alarming prospect of the province becoming desolate in the ensuing season, from flight of the *ryuts* and want of cultivation". He delayed in communicating this condition "for fear of causing alarm", but duty and humanity required him to bring it to the notice of the concerned authorities. With the "rivers dry and tanks drained", observed the Resident, in extensive areas the rice crop was "totally lost". He feared serious loss of revenues, if the authorities could not find any remedy to the situation.[8] The Resident commented that the "collections are equal to those of former years, notwithstanding the drought, but this cannot be expected to continue."[9] This was an indication how the Company's agents and servants were extorting the pound of flesh from people who did not have the means to pay at all.

When the Calcutta authorities did not do anything to relieve the sufferings of the poor inhabitants, Becher himself came forward with a proposal to distribute rice at six different centres at the rate of half a *seer* per day for each person. It was further proposed that the Europeans and their *gomastahs* should be prohibited to purchase rice "till after next August." He added that the "Eastern districts of Bengal would supply rice to Calcutta". But even in the eastern districts the condition was hardly any better. To this suggestion of the Resident, the authorities in Calcutta, complacently ensconced on their Olympian seats, left the distribution of rice at Murshidabad, according to the Resident's "prudence and impartiality".[10]

As there was no foodgrain, the people began to "eat leaves of the trees and the grass of the field",[11] and this naturally was followed by great epidemics. Small-pox, one of the epidemics, broke out in a virulent form and 63,000 people of Murshidabad became victims of the great calamity. In the month of March, even Nawab

8. *Ibid.*, 20 November, 1769.
9. *Ibid.*, 6 December, 1769.
10. Consultations, 26 February 1770.
11. Hunter, *Annals*, p. 26.

Saifuddaulah and his brother, Saiyyed Asraf Ali Khan, two scions of the Nawab family, also became preys to small-pox and both of them died childless.[12] The epidemic was so great and alarming that the "streets were blocked up with promiscuous heaps of the dying and dead."[13]

Becher repeatedly wrote about the extremely distressed condition of the inhabitants of Bengal to the Governor and the Select Committee. In a long letter, written on 30 March, the Resident resumed his narrative and strongly urged the Calcutta authorities for quick practical measures so as "to bring this country again to a flourishing condition". As a necessary measure of preventing aggravation of the calamity, he proposed "a reduction of revenues" and at the same time suggested that the Company's collections should be made less oppressive to the *raiyots*. The Resident thought it his duty to narrate before the Company's authorities in Calcutta the "present miserable situation occasioned by the most extraordinary drought (ever known) for these two last years". To promote the "real interest" of the Company, Becher believed that the Company must be the catalyst for the "recovery of the country and the inhabitants from the present depressed state," without caring for loss of their revenues. The misery of the inhabitants was so harrowing that "little remains for me to add on this disagreeable subject", observed Becher in his letter. The Resident listed the names of the districts that suffered the most. Among them, Purnea, Rajmahal, Birbhum and a part of Rajshahi topped the list. The district of Bhagalpur had also suffered from drought. Besides, Bhagalpur had not only been oppressed by the former *amils* but as it had a direct road to Patna, the English troops had "reduced this fine country to a miserable State". As such, the Resident recommended to Harwood, the supervisor of that district, "to make a strict enquiry into the present state of the Bhagalpore province" and "be attentive to the interest of the inhabitants."

---

12. Letter to Court, 15.8.1770. Also, Hunter, *Annals*, pp. 26-27.
13. Hunter, *Annals*, p. 27.

The soldiers' depredations should also be stopped, he added. For the distressed districts, Becher recommended "the most lenient and moderate measures" to be pursued in right earnest. To restore these districts to their former glory, the Resident recommended two methods for immediate adoption. The one was to make advances of money to the *raiyots* so that they could purchase bullocks, ploughs, utensils etc, The other was to afford them relaxation from payment of their dues for a certain period of time. The Resident thus insisted on the Calcutta authorities to issue such orders as would enable the *raiyots* not to pay their revenues "till after the first of July next." In this way, he hoped, the *raiyots* would find themselves at ease, be encouraged to pursue their labour and, if better days prevailed, be able to pay their "rent in due time". After making these proposals before the Select Committee, the Resident seriously thought of undertaking "a tour round these districts," in the hope of directly assessing the situation and alleviating the distress of the *raiyots* as much as he could. Yet, fully posted with the gravity of the situation, he believed that very little would remain in his power "to contribute to their comfort." Just as food had become rare, the distress of the people had been further aggravated by the scarcity of drinking water, as owing to severe drought most of the tanks had been "entirely dried up".[14]

The Resident began to receive daily reports from the supervisors of different districts, about the calamity overtaking the inhabitants of Bengal. Boughton-Rous, the supervisor of Rajshahi, reported to him, in the month of May, about the critical situation caused by universal distress in his area. The supervisor observed in his letter that the provinces of Bengal and Bihar had experienced the "excessive drought", which was unknown "in the memory of the oldest inhabitants". His own district of Rajshahi had also fallen a prey to this universal calamity. By the long continuance of drought, and withering away of everything there was nothing left in the villages and no local means of redress was possible. Hence the proposal of relief had "almost entirely failed", i.e. no relief as

14. Becher's letter to the Select Committee, 30 March (S.C.R., 28 April 1770, pp. 216-232).

Becher envisaged was feasible in the situation. The Rajshahi officer added that the greatest part of the harvest "is totally parched and destroyed without even the possibility of recovery".[15] Reza Khan also made such a report to the Governor about the severe drought by observing that if so long the grain was scarce, subsequently, "it cannot be found at all". The tanks and springs had totally dried up. In addition, there had been a dreadful fire "destroying thousands of lives." The small stores of grain in the districts of Purnea and Dinajpur had been consumed by fire. The seriousness of the situation was escalating quickly. So long "each day furnished accounts of the death of thousands", observed Reza in his letter, "but now lakhs of people are dying daily."[16] The spectre of death was thus stalking a very large part of Bengal and Bihar.

To relieve the sufferings of the poor *raiyots,* as Becher suggested and the committee recommended, it was decided to reduce collecting the cesses— the "cess to be levied to defray the absolute necessary expenses". The Resident also tried "to lessen the charge of *Khelats*" and informed the Governor that it would be reduced during the famine year and "be collected in a less oppressive manner." At Murshidabad itself the situation was so bad, as the Resident also informed the Calcutta authorities, that eight *seers* of bad rice for a rupee had been purchased by the people at Murshidabad,[17] when in normal times a rupee could buy fifteen times more. In reply to this letter, the Governor and the committee expressed great anxiety for the distressed condition of the *subah* but remarked that "they have no consolation or resource but in the hopes of better and more favourable seasons." The Company thus offered only a faith-cure to the people. But to safeguard their own interest, the committee resolved to leave

15. Boughton- Rous's letter to Becher, 10 May, 1770 (L.C. Book, Natore, pp. 15-16).

16. Reza Khan's letter to the Governor, Rd. 15 May, 1770 (C.P.C.III, pp. 64-65, No. 209).

17. Becher's letter to the Select Committee, 23 May (S.C.R., 26 May 1770 pp. 303-305).

no stone unturned for their own necessities though apparently they proposed to reduce or stop the Company's "disbursements within the narrowest limit."[18]

There was no rainfall up to the month of June 1770, though the "inhabitants entertained daily hopes of rain", but, as observed the helpless Becher, "God was pleased to withhold the blessing." Thus the scene of misery continued unabated and it beggared all description. In several parts of the *subah*, the Resident was shocked to report that "the living have fed on the dead", and within a few months, according to his estimate of death, the figure stood as high "as six is to sixteen of the whole inhabitants." Yet in this situation of affairs *puniyah* which could be held in abeyance in that unusual situation, was held on 24 May and quite expectedly there was a balance due from several *zamindars*, *amils* and farmers, that amounted to Rs. 17,91,203-11-6.[19]

When such was the situation of affairs, and the severe drought and famine were ravaging a large part of the *subah*, Reza Khan, by his utmost effort "collected as much of the revenue for the year 1176 (1769-70) as possible." But the Khan also felt it "impossible to collect the balance without ruining the cultivators." So, when the Khan approached the *zamindars* for a *band-o-bast* for the ensuing year, the latter replied, "we have no power or footing in districts. How can we discuss the terms ?" In consequence each of the *zamindars* made a separate representation on the subject to Becher.[20] Commonly they were all under serious financial deadlock. Hence, Becher suggested to the Governor and the committee, "that innovations and changes in the mode of conducting the revenues should be gradual and tried in a few districts before it is undertaken in general." Yet it was realised that the terrible natural calamity demanded drastic

---

18. S.C.R., 26 May 1770, pp. 309-312.
19. Becher's letter to the Select Committee, 2 June (S.C.R., 9 June, 1770, pp. 348-360).
20. Reza Khan's letter to the Governor, Rd., 2 June 1770 (C.P.C. III, p. 71, No. 234).

revamping of the entire system of revenue collection. The Resident sarcastically remarked in the same letter that the "plans that carry every favourable appearance often fail in the execution." Referring to the situation as it existed, Becher stated that the *zamindars* and *amils* and the farmers were 'unwilling to enter into any engagements for the revenues of the approaching season unless they can be assured of being supported by their authority in the province and suffered to make their collections without interruptions from the supravisors or their people,"[21] But this difficulty was removed when Reza Khan came forward to "quiet the fears" of the *zamindars, amils* and farmers, and settled the *band-o-bast*[22] for the year 1770-71. The objections of the *zamindars* and *amils* were countermanded by assuring them that the supervisors would not interfere in matters of revenue, but if they did, the *zamindars* and *amils* would not be held responsible for advance balances.[23] This promise, which the *zamindars* wanted to get in writing, was accordingly done by Becher and Reza Khan.[24] In all these arrangements, as it was glaringly exposed, precious little was done to bring relief to the dying multitudes. On the other hand expedients were sought for to ensure inflow of revenue to the Company's coffers.

According to this settlement with the *zamindars* for the new years, Becher thought that there should be some changes in the mode of collections. He suggested two alternatives before the committee : either to "throw the collections into the hands of the supravisors in the different districts", or "to suffer the supravisors to interfere in the present year's collections." Between these two, Becher recommended the latter plan, because if the supervisors did not interfere in the collec-

---

21. Becher's letter to the Select Committee, 2 June (S.C.R., 9 June 1770, pp. 348-360).
22. When 35 per cent of the people died of starvation, Reza Khan added a land-tax of 10 der cent for 1770-71. Hunter, *Annals*, p. 39.
23. Reza Khan's letter to the Governor, 12 June 1770 (C.P.C., III, p. 75, No. 251).
24. Draft of the Pledge, 12 June 1770 (C.P.C., III, p. 76, No. 253).

tion within the year, they would establish a confidence with the *zamindars* and earn their gratitude. During the mean time, the supervisors might divert their energy to other useful spheres, they might find full employment "by exerting their abilities in the encouragement of trade, assisting the Government officers in the administration of justice, recommending the cultivation of waste lands and dressing jungles." This would enable them to obtain a greater knowledge of the country and "its capacity for improvement." So when the *zamindars* and some of the inhabitants were unwilling to lose their local influence, which they feared from the imposition of supervisors, Becher came forward with an argument in their support. In his clarification, the Resident observed in his letter whether the supervisors "with little experience, themselves attended by black dependants and *banions* chiefly from Calcutta and of course unacquainted in the affairs of collection, are capable to manage the revenues and counteract the various obstructions that will undoubtedly be thrown in their way." So, Becher pointed out that the supervisors should not be appointed indiscriminately for all the districts, but the experiment might be tried initially in one or two of the districts. In those selected districts, the supervisors should be appointed from among the men of experience in the affairs of collection, such as Graham, Vansittart, Stuart and Ducarel.[25]

When Becher suggested this regulation for the supervisors, which would make them abstain from interfering in revenue collections, Boughton-Rous, the supervisor of Rajshahi, protested against this decision. At first his complaint was relatively mild, when he accused Reza Khan for employing intrigue in restricting the authority of the supervisors. This restriction, according to Rous, would seriously hamper the supervisors in collections and also would go to generate other pleas for interfering in the conduct of the supervisors.[26] But when the Rajshahi supervisor came to

25. Becher's letter to the Select Committee, 2 June (S.C.R., 9 June, 1770, pp. 348-360).

26. Boughton-Rous' letter to Becher, 22 June 1770 (L.C. Book, Natore, p. 23).

know from Becher that it was the latter's point of view not to interfere with the *zamindar's* officers, Boughton-Rous wanted to know it clearly from the Resident, in what particular circumstances the supervisor's authority was impounded in matters of collections. As a matter of fact Rous put up a strong protest. He questioned the legality of such a step. He wanted to know how the supervisor's "controlling power formerly delegated by the Select Committee is annulled."[27] But when Rous again received the same direction from Becher, he appeared to be in a concilliatory mood and professed to comply with Becher's order. But at the same time, supervisor represented that in view of Becher's directions, it would be impossible for him to furnish "any genuine accounts" and his authority would be very adversely restricted in demanding such accounts as well. The supervisor launched a frontal attack on Becher by observing that he (Boughton-Rous) "cannot help regarding it as a severe and discouraging reflection upon those few, whose authority you have restricted...by a direct imputation of incapacity and ignorance, without proof of unworthiness, without trial of capacity."[28]

Not only from Boughton Rous of Rajshahi, but there were similar protests from John Grose, the supervisor of Rangpur, as well. Early in the month of June, Grose observed in his letter to Becher that denuded of his authority "I should be much embarrassed, even in the cognizance of judicial matters." that had a close connection with the matters of revenue.[29] Despite these protests Becher not only remained firm in his decision, but informed Grose not to repeat violent measures that had been unfortunately taken at Rangamati in the Rangpur district. Similar cases of abuses and oppressions also happened at Govindganj in Rangpur, when the inhabitants of that place represented before Grose that the *amil* of Govindganj directed "his *naib* to collect and remit him large sums of money." Thus the collection of Baharband

27. *Ibid.*, 29 June 1770, pp. 27-28.

28. *Ibid.*, 8 July 1770, p. 28.

29. Letter from John Grose to Becher, 10 June 1770 (*Resident at the Durbar*, I).

during 1769-70 amounted to Rs. 1,71,335-11-9- , which far exceeded the current rate of Rs. 1,19,702. Citing one of the many cases of inhuman oppression of the people by the, human sharks, Grose gave the following instance. Ramkanta-the original farmer had let out his land to Debicharan and got an earnest money of Rs. 10,000. Debicharan sent his brother Durgacharan to ransack the district in such a way that the "poor *ryotts* were forced to sell even their ploughs and bullocks to answer his exorbitant demand." Many of these totally impoverished *raiyots* complained about the severity practised upon them, before Grose,[30] but finding him incapable of settling the matter were bent upon a hunger march to Murshidabad to represent their grievances before Becher.

The settlement of the revenue collection of Rangpur during 1769-70 amounted to Rs 9,17,250 out of which Rs. 6,32,797 was remitted to Murshidabad and the remainder of Rs. 2,84,453 was shown as the amount of expenses incurred in course of collection. Grose observed that if he was allowed the controlling power, he would be able to remove many abuses and would be in a position to collect one lakh of rupees more and that would additionally enable him to maintain a proper check on the *amils*. Grose argued that from the ensuing year, there was no need of employing such *amils*. Even if the *amils* were retained, they might be given some monthly allowances, so that the *raiyots* would feel at least partially protected from the *amils'* oppression. If the cultivators were freed from the *amils*, Grose believed that the inhabitants would be able to bear an additional tax, answer the just dues of the government and at the same time, raise their harvest free from the exorbitant demands of the *zamindars* and others employed in collections.[31]

John Grose was in search of the *patwari* papers, just to have a knowledge about the "true sums collected" from his district and an exact measurement of all lands. But when he failed to obtain them, he solicited help from Becher to issue such orders to the concerning officers as would facilitate obtaining of the documents. In his view

30. Letter from John Grose to Becher. 15 June 1770 (*Ibid.*, I).
31. *Ibid.* 19 June, 1770.

the *zamindars* and *amils* had "for the series of years cheated the government and preyed on the poor *riots*, but as the relieving of those thus distressed securing the just dues of the government are the chief objects of my appointment", the information of the true worth of the district might help him in relieving the poor *raiyots*[32]. But Becher directed him in his letter of 30 June, not to interfere in the conventional modalities followed in the collection of revenues. This made John Grose greatly irritated against the Resident and in a long letter, he sent his protest to Becher observing that these officials "have no other motive to regulate their conduct, but self-in erest". This would oblige the supervisor, i.e. Grose himself, "to suffer those people to continue their former malpractices." Hence Becher's direction, Grose felt, was in contravention of the terms of the supervisors' appointments. Grose believed that his original appointment was "to prevent those abuses which have been so long and loudly complained of." Naturally Grose was highly offended with Becher. He was sore that when he was engaged in adding to the Company revenue to the tune of one lakh of rupees, he was denied "any credit that might be due from the attention" paid on his part. The supervisor argued in his letter to Becher by observing :"...you desire that I will permit the *aumils* to carry on their business without interruption, or giving them cause to complain, by which, I imagine that some complaints have already been preferred against me, which I should be glad to have an opportunity of answering to publickely. Am I then Sir, to shut my Eyes at their squandering and sequestering the Company's money, am I quietly to stand by and see them commit the vilest acts of oppression, without being able to render the aggrieved redress, a hard case indeed on the poor *Ryotts*, who must not look to me with hopes of having their cause enquired into, till such times as the *aumils zemindars* and other creatures of Government, have enriched themselves at their Expence, nay even their ruin." In his regard Becher informed Grose that Bengal had suffered much during the late

32. Letter from John Grose to Becher, 23 June 1770 (*Ibid*).

years, due to the oppressive measures of the English *gomastahs.* While admitting this point, Grose replied that it had not so much injured the country, "as the oppressions committed by the several persons" employed in the collections.[33] The fault thus was conveniently laid at the doors of the native major domos employed by the English masters.

Becher instructed Grose that during the course of the present session, he would acquire experience sufficient to enable him hereafter to discharge his duties "than what has been thought proper for the present to confer upon you". For the necessary collection of revenues, Becher had again appointed,Mirza Muhammad Husain as the *amil* of Rangpur with assurances that the supervisor would not interfere with him in the collection of revenues. But at the same time he insisted that the *amil* must show meek respect to the supervisor: "to pay a proper attention to any measures",[34] committed to him.

Becher also recommended the works of some supervisors in whom he had faith. So when the Resident learnt about the distress and miseries of the inhabitants of Bhagalpur district, he wrote an ecouraging letter to William Harwood, the supervisor of Bhagalpur and Rajmahal, remarking that the measures which Harwood had adopted to alleviate the "present miserable calamity", had the fullest approval of Becher. He advised the supervisor to secure the confidence and support of the people. The supervisor should be guided "by the advice and opinion of the most experienced inhabitants." About the highway robberies committed on the travellers, Becher thought it absolutely necessary to undertake some means to tame and control the desperadoes : "either to conciliate them to ours" or to "reduce them to obedience and subjection."[35]

After a mature consideration, Becher formulated a medium-size plan for conducting the management of revenue

33. Letter from John Grose to Becher, 14 July 1770 (*Ibid.*).
34. Becher's letter to Grose, 4 July, 1770 (*Ibid.*).
35. Becher's letter to William Harwood—Supervisor of Bhagalpur and Rajmahal, 10 June 1770 (*Ibid.*).

collection during 1770-71, which he intimated to Harwood. According to his plan "Districts nearly to the amount of Rs. 7,00,000 are left more immediately under the direction of the English supravisors", who had previous experience in that branch ; while in other districts the English supervisors' authority should be restrained "and leave the management of the collection in the hand of those appointed by the Government." In the latter districts, the *amils* should carry on their collections without interruption. However, the Resident further informed Harwood that he "would recommend every present Measure that can promote the ease of the *Ryots*, encourage cultivation...and restore the country to its former flourishing state,"[36]

Becher had words of praise also for the works of Charles Stuart, the supervisor of Birbhum, Bishnupur and Panchet. In the affairs of revenue collections stuart had already acquired a fair degree of experience at Burdwan. The supervisor advanced argument in favour of his system, which found support from the Resident. So reposing his confidence, Becher directed Stuart to exercise the controlling power in regard to the collection of revenues in his districts.[37] In reply Stuart informed Becher that he fully agreed with Becher about an adequate and honourable allowance to the *zamindars* of Birbhum behoving the latter's station. It was agreed between the two that the allowance which the *zamindar* "formerly received when his collections were managed by *aumils*,...was much too small to support." However, Stuart wanted time to settle the matter with the *zamindar*. At the same time he professed not to interfere in the collection of Bishnupur and Panchet.[38] In reply Becher directed Stuart not to make any hasty settlement with the *zamindar's* allowance, though "it ought to be adequate to his station." About the districts of Bishnupur and Panchet, Becher wanted to settle with the *zamindars* the question of malguzaris or, as an alternative, wanted the entire matter to be left to the committee. Becher would

36. *Ibid.*, 29 June, 1770 (*Ibid*).

37. Becher's letter to Charles Stuart, 13 June 1770 (*Ibid.*).

38. Stuart's letter to Becher, 19 June 1770 (*Ibid.*).

inform the supervisor, as soon as Becher heard from the committee about the settlement.[39]

But though the Resident tried to find out the best means for the maximisation of the revenue collections without being oppressive to the people, the terrible famine continued "to increase at a rate that baffled official calculation". The almost graveyard silence over vast stretches of the rural area, that had been reduced almost to a barren desert, began to make its impact felt in Calcutta by June 1770. The English settlement at Calcutta "awoke to find itself in the midst of universal and irremediable starvation." Throughout the summer and the unusually dry rainy season of 1770, the people went on dying. "The husbandmen sold their cattle, they sold their implements of agriculture ; they devoured their seedgrain ; they sold their sons and daughters, till at length no buyer of children could be found ; they ate the leaves of trees and the grass of the field", and in June 1770, many of them began to perish from malnutrition and disease.[40]

This severe famine, almost unprecedented in the history of mankind, could not create any sympathy in the minds of those who were in charge of revenue collections from the poor *raiyots*. As usual, the collectors and their agents began to oppress the inhabitants in order to extort money from the people who had been already reduced to utmost destitution. Many heart-burning accounts of oppression came to the knowledge of the Resident. John Grose reported from Rangpur on 14 July about the heinous practices of the rapacious *zamindars*. The district of Rangpur, though suffering, did not face such hardships as the other parts of Bengal, and as such, the local *zamindars* agreed to carry on their *band-o-bast* of Rs. 9,17,250, as in the previous year. They were allowed to pay Rs. 1,49, 292 less on account of drought. The supervisor reported that the *zamindars* had sent only Rs. 6,32,797 from the previous year's collections, to Murshidabad, and as such Rs. 2,84,453,

39. Becher's letter to Stuart, 22 June 1770 (*Ibid.*).

40. Becher's letter to the Select Committee, 2 June (S.C.R., 9 June 1770, pp. 348-360).

had been shown "under the heads of charges and deductions." But to his great surprise Grose noticed that the *zamindars* had not only collected, over and above the stipulated sums, Rs. 1,49,292 in the *muffasal*, but also an additional sum of Rs. 92, 752, under the head of the *mathut*. As such, no less than Rs. 10,10,003 had been collected in the previous year from the *raiyots*; but what was worse, still there remained a balance of Rs. 2,42,065 due from the *zamindars* and "as yet unaccounted for." Due to these irregularities the Company had suffered, "no inconsiderable loss of their property last year", the main factor responsible for this being the ill-management and oppression of the *zamindars*.[41]

When such was the naked orgy of oppression, the Resident reported to the Select Committee that his previous representations about the drought, famine and suffering were faint in comparison to the miseries of the present i.e. by July 1770. Within thirty miles of Murshidabad, rice sold at only three *seers* for a rupee, and "even at those exorbitant prices there is not nearly sufficient for the daily supply of half the inhabitants." In the city of Murshidabad alone, more than five hundred people starved daily and in the muffasal, "the numbers said to perish exceed belief." So the Resident exerted his utmost to impress upon the committee about quick and forceful measures "to lessen this dreadful calamity". At the same time, Becher was hopeful about the prospect of a good harvest in the next crop period when, he thought, the distress of the people would be greatly relieved. He even expected that within one month, the relief would come, at least in some of the parts, from the new harvest.[42]

But these hopes of Becher proved illusory in no time, for within seven days, he reported to William Harwood the melancholy devastation wrought by flood in the districts of Dacca, Sylhet, and a large part of Rajshahi, all these areas "being entirely overflowed by the sudden rise of the rivers". This sudden flood destroyed the crops on the ground and cruelly

41. Bengal District Records—Rangpur, Vol. I (Edt. by Firminger, W.K., Calcutta, 1914), p. p. 7.
42. Consultations, 19 July 1770 (Hunter, *Annals*, p. 419).

frustrated the expectations of the Resident. It became thus indispensable for him to know the exact accout of the other districts.[43] On the same day, Becher wrote a similar letter to Charles Stuart-the supervisor of Birbhum, Bishnupur and Panchet, intimating him to furnish the Resident with "exact accounts from the other districts".[44] Reports of high flood also came from Rangpur. From Rangpur Grose reported to Becher that the excessive rain had "done considerable damage to the paddy............a great quantity is entirely spoilt and other much damaged." Before this heavy rainfall, Grose also expected like Becher about the prospect of a good harvest. In consequence of this flood, the price of rice at Rangpur rose from twenty to twelve *seers* per rupee.[45]

On 4 August, Becher wrote a letter to Grose, similar to the one that he had written to Harwood on 19 June. In this letter, Becher informed Grose about his "medium plan". He let Grose know that for the current season, the districts that paid revenues of rupees seven lakhs or more would be placed under the English supervisors while the other districts should lie outside the jurisdiction of the English supervisors whose authority in respect of these districts would be restrained. "The district under your inspection being among those where the power of the supravisor is to be restrained", observed Becher to Grose; and he directed Grose "to permit the *aumils* to carry on their business without interruption."[46]

In reply, Grose informed the Resident that he would desist from pressing the *zamindars* of Boda and Baikuntapur for any paper or accounts, though these two places had long being annexed with Rangpur. These *zamindars* paid certain sums annually without giving any account of their collections.[47] But on the *amils*' representation, Becher directed Grose on 13 August to withdraw his people from Edrakpur and "to desist

43. Becher's letter to William Harwood, 24 July 1770 (*Resident at the Durbar*, I).
44. Becher's letter to Charles Stuart, 24 July 1770 (*Ibid*).
45. Grose's letter to Becher, 7 August 1770 (*Ibid*).
46. Becher's letter to Grose, 4 August 1770 (*Ibid.*)
47. Grose's letter to Becher, 20 August, 1770 (*Resident at the Durbar*, Vol. 2, No. 3).

from taking any accounts". As directed, Grose did not want to interfere in any respect with the collections; even so he requested Becher that his (Grose's) people might "be allowed to continue taking these accounts."[48]

But during the whole year of 1770, cruelly frustrating all hopes of nature's clemency, the famine continued unabatted. The little prospect of a paddy crop had been already shattered by excessive floods in the month of August in the eastern areas where paddy was the stable crop. While many of the English looked with sorrow and helplessness at the sufferings of the poor Indians, the Calcutta Council were aroused from their indolence by the critical situation in which they had been plunged. They sent to different districts their own agents to purchase whatever rice could be found on the Company's account and even seized the cargoes on the river. Their principal attention was upon preserving their own men. On the other hand, the Nawab and many of his officials, as well as the wealthy families of Murshidabad, displayed the most humane munificence by distributing rice doles to the needy, until their own granaries were exhausted. Thus, before long to these poor inhabitants, all the avenues of livelihood and subsistence were closed. The wretches vainly grappled with hunger and disease and called upon death for their relief. All over the city of Calcutta, as well as in the adjacent villages, thousands of human skeletons with their stomachs contracted to their back-bones, were seen fainting and dying under the pressure of intolerable anguish. As a matter of fact the whole *subah* looked like a huge charnel-house. The cottages, villages and even many of the market places were deserted and looked totally desolate. Debrit, a contemporary writer, observes that "there was not a corner in the city, or any lurking place in the vicinity of Calcutta, where the living, the dying and the dead, were not mingled or heaped together in melancholy confusion". He further describes that "the water of the Ganges became loathsome and corrupt from the loads of dead bodies which it daily received". As a result, disease broke

48. *Ibid.*, 30 August 1770 (*Ibid.*, No. 4).

out everywhere, and multiplied in proportion to the violence with which the famine raged. Thus Debrit continues: "No language can sufficiently exhibit the sudden and universal destruction produced by the ravages of these calamities." According to him, about three millions of people perished for want of sustenance.[49]

"Notwithstanding the loss the country has sustained in the number of inhabitants", observed the Select Committee in their letter to the Court of Directors, "We find the sum collected is *sicca* rupees 1,38,02,693-9-10", from which Rs. 8,03,321-15-0 had been remitted to the different famine-stricken districts to alleviate the distress of the wretched inhabitants and a balance of Rs. 6,14,219-8-0 remained to be collected from the previous years' agreement. The report added that during the commencement of the *puniyah* of 1770, the new settlement was made at Rs. 1,52,45,979-15-12.[50] Thus, it was seen that during the havoc of famine, the new settlement of revenues was considerably increased, which on the face of it, was a sad commentary on the principle which inspired the Company—everyman his own and devil take the hindmost.

The Court of Directors in London wanted to devise some new methods for the collection of the *diwani* revenues so as to augment the Company's income. As early as in June 1769 they had intimated their plan to the Company's authorities at Calcutta by observing that they had noted that the revenues of the ceded districts at Calcutta, Burdwan, Midnapore and Chittagong had been considerably increased, due to better regulations of affairs. Therefore, the same method might be applied in the other districts as well. "But a plan of reformation of so extensive a nature cannot be effected by one man, it must be the constant attention of many, and for this purpose we have resolved to establish a Committee of some of our ablest servants for the management of the *dewannee* revenue at Muxadavad for the Bengal province and at Patna for that of

49. Debrit, *Transactions*, pp. 127-130.

50. Letter to Court, 11 September, 1770 (F.W.I.H.C. Vol VI, P. 228).

Bahar." These Councils at Murshidabad and Patna were to have the control of all business relating to revenue, "but Muhomed Reza Khan or some other principal person of the country must be appointed *naib-dewan* for the Bengal province (that is, the Company's deputy) and all the business must be carried on thro' the *naib* and under his seal and signing and in like manner Shitabroy or some other principal person at Patna for the Bahar province."[51]

These instructions of the Court of Directors were sent to Becher in the month of July 1770, for his information and also intimating him about the mode of appointment of a Council of Revenue at Murshidabad for Bengal and another at Patna for Bihar. After a conflict between the council and the Select Committee over the question, it was finally decided by the former to establish such bodies. Accordingly, the Council appointed Becher as Chief of the Controlling Council of Revenue at Murshidabad, with Reed, Lawrell and Graham as its members.[52] Two months after, they addressed another letter to Becher, now as the Chief of that Council, wherein they further instructed him about the mode of revenue collections, as well as the rules and regulations by which this new body was to be guided. Under the new rules it became the duty of the Chief to inform the Calcutta authorities about the real state of Collections, about the actual payment of rents by the tenants and their previous payment, as well as the nature of cultivation in each district. In the implementation of this plan, Becher was to preserve and be guided by a spirit of enquiry. He must closely look to the "prevention of frauds in future." He was further authorized to control all the business of the *diwani* revenues. But Reza Khan would continue as *naib-diwan* and all

---

51. Extract from the Company's General Letter, 30 June 1769 (Proceedings of the controlling Council of Revenue at Murshidabad, Vol. I, pp. 4-6).

52. Letter to Becher, 13 July 1770 (P.C.C.P.M., Vol. I, pp. 1-2). For the Controlling Council of Revenue at Patna for Bihar they had appointed J. Alexander—the Chief, G. Vansittart and R. Palk as the members of the council. Firminger, Fifth Report, pp. 204-905.

the business must be carried through him. The *naib-diwan* must assist the Chief on the necessary measures. After the death of a *zamindar* in a particular district, the lands under him were to be settled for a term of years with another person. In the same manner, the waste lands were also to be settled. The authority which had so long been vested in the Resident at the *darbar*, would no longer remain with him but henceforth be exercised by the Chief and Council of Revenue. It was also decided that all the transactions with the government, so long carried on through the Resident, would cease to be as such and be with immediate effect conducted by the Chief and his Council. All the decisions must pass by a majority, but in case of equality, the Chief would have a casting vote. The Chief was to enquire into the character and conduct of the officers of government from the highest to the lowest. "Experience convinces us that without a proper degree of Authority all Researches will be fruitless and that it is in vain to send servants into Districts to detect Abuses", observed the Calcutta Council to Becher to whom they gave the further advice "that a servant who is unworthy of this confidence is unworthy of the station to which we have appointed him." The Chief was further to keep a record of all parleys and consultations, all letters to and from the supervisors and all those from the officers of the government. On all visits paid to or received from the officers of the government the Chief must be accompanied by one or more members of his council.[53] The officers were assigned their duties and allotted to their posts on 1 August, but they were to take formal charge from 1 September, 1770.

According to such orders, Reed, Lawrell and Graham went to Murshidabad as members of the Council of Revenue, but after their arrival on 17 September, they found Becher absent from the capital. Due to his illness, Becher had gone to Balasore for recovery.[54] In the meantime, i.e. on 5 September, he had written a long letter to the members of the

53. Letter to Becher, 11 September, 1770 (*Ibid.*, pp. 2-4).

54. P.C.C.R.M., Vol. I, p. 6.

Council of Revenue. In his letter, Becher wrote to the members about his illness and coming to Balasore for convalescence. He regretted his absence from Murshidabad. He further observed that his main object was fully to abide by the order of the Court of Directors and thus support the form of the country government. He lavished fulsome praise on Reza Khan whose abilities, experience and conduct had always been commended by the Company's London authorities. He also did a lot of self-praise. During the time of his Residency, Becher pointed out in a strong vein of self satisfaction, the collections had been well kept up. Previously the mode of carrying of the collections as well as the internal management used to be very defective, these were "originally imperfect", he added. But it was "by the advice and representations of the Resident," i.e. through Becher's good offices, that many improvements had been made in the older system. He also observed that the "settlement of the present year's Revenues has been made, and the Accounts transmitted to Calcutta", and as such, during this time, "I would recommend to your Attention previous to any other consideration is to support and Aid the Nabob on those collections as vigorously as possible." Becher further informed the members that besides the collections of the *diwani* revenues, Rs. 13,50,000 had been settled for the current year as charges for the *puniyah*, protection of the banks of the river near Murshidabad and small reforms. He further informed that as there were large balances due from the previous years collections, all such balances must be recovered on a top priority basis. From the district of Nadia alone Rs. 2,25,000 was still due. The revenue accounts of the districts of Birbhum, Jessore and Rajmahal had been ill-managed during the previous year, and as such Becher emphasised that these accounts must be strictly scrutinised. Besides there were large balances due to the Emperor Shah Alam II, Nawab Mubarakuddaulah, as well as the ministers, being their pensions, allowances and other charges, which must be settled as per the Company's covenants with them. "As I have

55. Becher's letter to Reed, Lawrell and Graham, 5 September, 1770 *Ibid.*, pp. 6-9).

neither seen the orders of the Court of Directors nor the Letter of Instruction framed by the Council for the conduct of the Board of Revenue", concluded Becher in his letter, "I can have little to say on that Head. But to regret that I cannot be present to assist in the Execution of such new Regulations as may have been pointed out sincerely wish success to those who can act.[56]

The Calcutta Council also informed Reza Khan about the establishment of this new office. The Governor observed in his letter that "as the office of the Resident at Murshidabad is of great importance and as the work there is so heavy that it has impaired the health of every gentleman who has held that office, the Company have thought it advisable to entrust the duties and the functions of the Resident to a Board of four gentlemen." The Governor also informed the Khan about the duties assigned to the incumbents on the new offices, but at the same time he conveyed to him that no order should be issued unless they were sealed and signed by the Khan himself. The members of the council must consult the Khan regarding the appointment of officials.[56] In this way, the Governor wanted to induce the influential and clever Reza Khan to help the revamped system of bureaucratic machinery.

At the end of September, John Grose wrote a letter to Becher and that way he was also not aware of Becher's absence from Murshidabad, in which he again narrated about the pathetic plight of the wretched inhabitants of Rangpur in the grip of famine. The district of Rangpur experienced a heavy rainfall, but this was of no avail as "the greatest part of the land is entirely uncultivated...owing to the great Scarcity of inhabitants." The villages were entirely depopulated and ruined. Those few who could not move and remained behind were incapaciated by disease and starvation. Thus to rescue the people from starvation and death Grose had decided upon relief operation. He had ordered distribution of rice worth

56. Governor's letter to Reza Khan, 18 September 1770 (C.P.C., III, p. 108, No. 372). On 1 October, Reed, Lawrell and Graham also acquainted Reza Khan about the instructions of the Calcutta Council – P.C.C.R.M., Vol. I, p. 14.

five rupees "amongst the most needy of them."[57] In their reply to Grose the members of the Council of Revenue fully endorsed the humane intention of Grose "of distributing a daily charity in grain to the amount of Rs. 5 to the relief of the poor."[58]

The oppression and torture of the people of Bengal had been further intensified by the rise of a number of robber bands that infested different parts of the *subah* and let loose a reign of terror. The members of the Council of Revenue came to know of such robberies from the districts of Rangpur and Jessore. But as they could not send reinforcement owing to the shortage of their own sepoys, they directed the respective supervisors of these districts to take prompt and effective measures against the robbers and to eradicate such nuisance from their districts.[59]

There was another factor responsible for the extremely sorry state of affairs almost all over the *subah*. The chaos and mismanagement of affairs in Bengal seriously eroded the effectiveness of the Company's administration. Quite substantially this was due to the appointment of those supervisors who had little experience in revenue administration and who were mostly corrupt and self-seekers. Becher struggled hard for the withdrawal of the supervisors, all Englishmen, from some of the different districts, but the Select Committee of Calcutta was bent upon carrying on with the scheme of supervisors at all costs and no withdrawal of anybody was allowed. Becher repeatedly pleaded for the withdrawal of the controlling power from the supervisors of every district, except Dacca, Dinajpur, Hugli and Birbhum. Despite his strong advocacy and advancing many arguments against the retention of the supervisors, initially Becher was frustrated by the Calcutta authorities. It was only his tenacity which gave him the reward in the end when the Calcutta

57. Grose's letter to Becher, 26 September 1770 (P.C.C.R.M., Vol. I, pp. 34-35).

58. Letter to Grose, 4 October, 1770 (*Ibid.*, p. 36).

59. Letters to Grose and Wilmot, 27 September, 1770 (*Resident at the Durbar*, Voi. 2, Nos. 14 and 16).

Council accepted the recommendation of Becher. The Select Committee in their letter to court, in the month of October, observed that they had been "induced to withdraw from some of the supravisors that controuling authority which the Committee intended should be vested in them all." As the Select Committee was not in favour of the establishment of the new system, as suggested by Becher, by which a division of authority and jurisdiction was envisaged, they observed in the same letter : "we thought an adherence to the original plan (of vesting power solely in the English supervisors) more suitable to the consistency and dignity of the government than a change." The reluctance of the Select Committee was too glaring to be ignored. They did not at all relish the idea of drastically cutting down the number of English supervisors, even though they had finally to fall in line with Becher's system. Therefore, the Select Committee at last gave their consent "that the controuling power should for the present be only vested in Messrs. Kelsell, Graham, Vansittart, Ducarel and Stewart."[60] Thus only five English supervisors retained their posts.

Becher was selected by the Court of Directors to succeed in the station of the President and the Governor of Bengal, which the former declined with many grateful thanks.[61] He did not like the governorship of Bengal but wanted to handle the revenue affairs directly from Murshidabad, so that he might establish peace and order in the *subah* of Bengal. Thus instead of filling up the coveted office, Becher went directly from Balasore to Murshidabad, where he reached on 12 November. At Murshidabad, he attended the meeting as the President of the Council of Revenue for the first time on 15 November. At this meeting Becher delivered his minute that he had "come with the resolution to give every assistance in his power to promote the intentions of the Company."[62] Then he resolved, with the consent of the other

---

60. Select Committee's letter to Court, 31 October 1770 (F.W.I. H.C., VI, p. 237).
61. Letter to Court, 1 November, 1770 (*Ibid.*, p. 244).
62. P.C.C.R.M., Vol. I, p. 184.

members, that the money that had been sent to Calcutta on 6 November during his absence, to the tune of rupees six lakhs in cash and one lakh in bill, should be reverted back to Murshidabad as he thought the Calcutta "treasury was in no immediate want". On the other hand, there were heavy balances due on the allowances of the Emperor, the Nawab and the others, besides the demands of rupees two lakhs for the factory at Kasimbazar.[63]

In consequence of this resolution, the Calcutta Council returned the above amount and the Council of Revenue at Murshidabad decided to disburse the sum as under :[64]

To His Majesty Shah Alam : His Stipend		Rs. 2,00,000
To the Nawab Mubarakuddaulah :		
Account Consumanny	Rs. 50,000	
Account Pay of Sepoys	Rs.1,00,000	1,50,000
To Muhammad Reza Khan		0,50,000
To Rajah Durlabhram's Estate		0,27,257-11
To Ahteramuddaulah		0,20,000
To Rukuddin Husain Khan		0,15,000
To Jagat Seth		0,30,000

The members of the Council of revenue also wanted to decide their own pays and allowances. Their total emoluments were also decided upon with the consent of Becher.[65]

At the meeting of the Council of Revenue at Murshidabad on 20 November, the controlling powers of the *amils* in differerent districts were fully discussed. The matter was urgent in view of various reports about their irregularity of functioning, their opressive methods and the deleterious effect on the Company's revenue collection on account of the *amils'* sharp practices. Becher called on the assistance of Reza Khan in the matter and sought his opinion regarding the necessity of continuing the *amils* under the changed circums-

63. Letter from the Couucil of Revenues to the Governor and Council, 15 November 1770 (*Ibid* , p. 183).

64. P.C.C.R.M., Vol. I, p. 196.

65. Becher as Chief would receive annually Rs. 60,000 (inclusive of all allowances), Reed as second would receive annual Rs. 45,000; Lawrell as third would receive annually Rs. 22,500; Graham as fourth would receive annually Rs. 22,500 – *Ibid.*

tances. The Khan also did not see any justification for continuing their servicees and observed that "no good effects are now to be expected," by keeping the *amils* in service on account of "the degree of authority delegated to the English gentlemen." Hence the *amils* were superfluous in the new set-up. Therefore, the council at Murshidabad wrote to the Governor and Council at Calcutta, confirming the controlling powers in the hands of the selected supervisors. On the question of continuing the *amils* the council posed the question "whether a necessity subsisted for continuing the *aumils* in different districts", and reached the consensus that as "our employees seemed to derive very little benefit from their services", they should be recalled.[66] The Calcutta Council accepted this recommendation and recalled the *amils* from different districts.

The withdrawal of *amils* was a wise decision on the part of the Council of Revenue. While the famine continued throughout the year of 1770, these *amils* oppressed the people and extracted money from them to their own advantage. Even during the latter part of 1770 serious compalints against the *amils* came regularly to Murshidabad and Calcutta.[67] But though the *amils* were withdrawn, the Calcutta authorities could not adopt any concrete measure for bringing relief to the famine stricken people. On the contrary, it was a wide-spread "belief that the famine of 1769-70 was largely due to the unscruplous commercial transactions of the Company's servants."[68] Becher had repeatedly urged advances of money

66. Letter from the Council of Revenue to the Governor and Council, 20 November 1770 (*Ibid.*, pp. 212-213).

67. Wilmot—the supervisor of Jessore, reported to Murshidabad on 29 October, 1770: "That besides the avowed wages to the *aumils* in our district, they had numberless perquisities." He stated that the *amils* of his district extracted mathut at Rs. 12,191,8 and *salamies* at Rs. 1579. George Vansittart—the supervisor of Dinajpur, stated on 31 December 1770: "That embezzlements there the year before, amonuted to no less than Rs. 1,69,662". In spite of such embezzlement, the total amount collected was Rs. 21,57,318—Caraccioli, III, pp. 536-538.

68. Firminger, *Fifth Report*, p. 203.

to the poor *raiyots*. But this was not granted by the Company's authorities at Calcutta.[69] There were some local efforts for relief. The Company's authorities imported rice from Bakharganj, for the benefit of their own dependents.[70] Becher himself had supplied rice from Barisal to the Company's dependents at fifteen *seers* per rupee.[71] Shitab Rai tried to alleviate the sufferings of the people of Bihar. He sent Rs. 30,000 to Benares for purchase of grains, which could be sold at low prices to the people. The boats loaded with grains came to Patna, three times a month. Shitab Rai sold the grains at Patna at the Benares rates.[72] But these individual and isolated undertakings were inadequate in view of the requirements of the millions of people. Hence the poor famine-stricken millions were by and large left to the mercy of their ownfate.

The health of Becher had been much impaired due both to the hardship of work as the Cheif and the hot, humid climate of Bengal. He desired to return home in the month of January, 1771. His resignation was accepted by the Select Committee, and they appointed Sammual Middleton[73] to succeed him as the Chief of the Council of Revenue at Murshidabad.[74] The governor immediately informed Reza Khan about the appointment of Middleton and asked Reza Khan to extend all cooperation and loyalty to him.[75] Middleton's appointment, however, placed Reza Khan in a very awkward position since there was no love lost between him and the new Chief. Still Reza Khan replied that he would spare no pains in

---

69. Hunter, *Annals*, p. 23.
70. Consultations, 14 December, 1770 (Hunter, *Annals*, p. 412).
71. *Ibid.*, 24 December, 1770.
72. *Seir*, III, pp. 56-57.
73. Middleton had been previously dismissed from the Company's service, but the court's letter of 23 March 1770 had pardoned him.
74. S.C.R., 17 January 1771, p. 51. Also, Letter to Court, 15 January, 1771 (F.W.I H.C., VI, p. 265).
75. Governor's letter to Reza Khan, 16 January, 1771 (C.P.C., III, p. 149, No. 557).

smoothly transacting the business of the government in conjunction with Middleton.[76]

On 10 April, 1771, a new Court of Directors (Sulivan group) had been elected. The new Court of Directors were biased against the Select Committee at Calcutta, of which Becher was a leading member. They appreciated the conduct of the Calcutta Council in opposing the Select Committee. Governor Cartier also earned the new Court of Directors' disfavour. The order did not take any long time to come. On 25 April, they sent order to Cartier to resign the governorship in favour of Warren Hastings.[77] "So alarming a disunion amongst our servants may be attended with consequences of a very serious nature," observed the Court of Directors in their letter, "we cannot omit the present opportunity of testifying our displeasure against those persons who have opposed the execution of our orders." This was evidently in reference to the earlier controversy over Becher's suggestion of drastically reducing the number of English supervisors and Becher's carrying the Select Committee along with him. The Court of Directors acted peremtorily by sending the order, which amounted to censure and punishment, that "Becher be dismissed from our Council at Bengal" and Russell and Floyer be immediately removed from Bengal to Madras.[78] But before this letter reached Bengal, Becher had already resigned from service and started for Europe.

In accordance with the order of the Directors, Hastings arrived in Bengal and took over charge of the Company's affairs from the hands of Cartier in the month of April 1772.[79] At Calcutta, he saw some familiar faces, who greeted him.[80]

76. Reza Khan to Governor, Rd., 20 January, 1771 (*Ibid.*, p. 151, No. 563).

77. Letter from Court, 25 April, 1771 (F.W.I.H.C., VI, pp. 109-110).

78. *Ibid.*, Also, Firminger, *Fifto Report*, pp. 205-206.

79. Hastings' letter to Nawab Shujauddaulah, 15 April, 1772 (C.P.C., Vol. IV, Calcutta, 1925, p. 1, No. 1).

80. His old *baniya* Kantu, his old creditor Khwajah Petrus, and the English civilian George Vansittart received him. Hastings became satisfied with Middleton—Feiling, *Hastings*, p. 80.

But, howsoever, heartening the greetings of his old colleagues were, Hastings fully realised the tough and onerous task before him. There were many ticklish and complicated problems which he had to sort out and solve. Just after his arrival, he received a letter written in August 1771, from the Court of Directors, in which the latter observed that in pursuance of the letters from Becher and Reza Khan, they had come to know that the English *gomastahs* had not only cornered and monopolished grain during the time of famine, but also compelled the poor *raiyots* "to sell even the seed requisite for the next harvest." Therefore, the court was pained to record that the "strictest enquiry into the names and stations of all persons capable of such transactions would have been the immediate consequence, and that the most exemplary punishment had been inflicted upon all offenders who could dare to counteract the benevolence of the Company, and entertain a thought of profiting by the universal distress of the miserable natives, whose dying cries, it is said, were too effecting to admit of an adequate description,"[81]

The Court of Directors in the same letter also expressed their surprise that "upon a general charge of this nature", no name had been mentioned by Becher and Reza Khan about the offenders, neither the Company's authorities at Calcutta had "entered into any enquiry at all about the matter." The court opined that it was none but only Becher who had suggested "of totally prohibiting all Europeans, in their private capacity or their *gomastahs*, from dealing in rice during the scarcity of that article." The monopolists of grain, the court suspected, "could be no other than persons of some rank in our service." The court thus directed that these charges should be examined impartially and "whoever may (is?) found guilty of a conduct which appears to us so unworthy be forthwith dismissed from our service, or deprived of our protection if not in our service, and sent to Europe."[82]

In 1771, the growing dissatisfaction of the Directors with the *naib-diwan*, Muhammad Reza Khan, came to a head.

81. Letter from Court, 28 August, 1771 (F.W.I.H.C., VI, pp. 119-120).

82. *Ibid.*,

Reza Khan seemed to have enjoyed the full confidence of all the Residents at the *darbar*, but it appeared that the Directors were influenced by the unfavourable reports sent by some non-officials advisers.[83] Thus in the same letter, the Directors recorded their censure of the conduct of Reza Khan and, therefore, announced their famous resolution to do away with the office of *naib-diwan* and "to stand forth as *Duan* and, by the agency of the Company's servants to take upon themselves the entire care and management of revenues." They levelled various charges against Reza Khan for his corrupt practices in connection with the monoply of salt and grain during the time of famine. Reza Khan was also charged with the balances of the Dacca revenues alleged to be left unadjusted. Therefore, the court further directed the Company's government at Calcutta "that notwithstanding we observe that Mahomet Reza Cawn complained of a monoploy of rice being carried on by other persons, we have received information that he himself, in the very height of the famine, has been guilty of great oppressions. That he has been guilty of stopping the merchants boats, loaded with rice and other provisions, intended for the supply of Murshidabad and has forcibly compelled owners to sell their rice to him at a price so cheap as from 25 to 30 *seers* per rupee and resold it afterwards at the rate of 3 to 4 *seers* per rupee." The Directors also suspected that the *naib-diwan* had, by oppressive means, extorted his share from *diwani* revenues, which he had put to his own use and also "distributed among the creatures of his own." The Court of Directors, therefore, gave the direction that Reza Khan and every person employed under him be put under arrest and brought to Calcutta for trial.[84]

The first work of Hastings' administration was to send order for the arrest of Reza Khan. On the morning of 24 April, Hastings sent a messenger to Middleton at Murshida-

83. Firminger, *Fifth Report*, p. 209.

84. Letter from Court, 28 August, 1771 (F.W.I.H.C., VI, pp. 121-122) Also, Khan, I.M., "Mohammad Reza Khan and His Trial", *Calcutta Review*, Vol. XVII, 1925, pp. 397-398.

bad, for the arrest of Reza Khan and Amrit Singh, Reza Khan's *diwan*, and directed them to be sent to Calcutta under a guard of sepoys. Hastings informed the Court of Directors that after the offenders' arrival at Calcutta an enquiry would be made in the persons' conduct "in obedience to your commands. But the Governor did not wish to arrest persons, other than the above two lest the action should cause "too great alarm."[85] At the same time, evidently giving the culprit a piece of his mind, Hastings wrote to Reza Khan that "those cordial relations which have hitherto subsisted...are to exist no more.[86] Hastings also informed Nawab Mubarakuddaulah through Middleton that "Muhammad Reza Khan has been charged with malpractices" and as such he stood suspended from the post of *naib-dewan*. As the Company already had maintained a friendly relation with the Nawab, it was the duty of the Governor to inform him about the matter. He added that Reza Khan, in addition to his office of *naib-diwan* of the Company, also held the post of *naib-nazim* under the Nawab. As the Company's interests were identical with those of the Nawab, the retention of Reza Khan in the post of *naib-nazim* would seem anomalous.[87] In reply, the Nawab enquired from the Governor about the offence committed by Reza Khan owing to which he merited such a severe punishment, especially when the Khan had served the Nawab as well as the Company faithfully. Upon this query Hastings did not commit anything in writing but expressed his displeasure at the conduct of the Khan and appealed to the Nawab that the latter should not disapprove of the action taken by the Company against the Khan.[88]

Middleton received Hastings' instruction to arrest Reza Khan on 26 April. On the following morning the Behram-

85 Hastings' letter to the Court of Directors, 24 April, 1772 (F.W.I.H.C., VI, pp. 407-408).

86 Hastings' letter to Reza Khan, 30 April, 1772 (C.P.C., IV, p. 3 No. 13)

87 Hastings' letter to Mubarakuddaulah, Rd. 13 May 1772 (*Ibid*, p. 4, No 22).

88 *Ibid* (*Ibid*, pp. 4-5, No, 25).

pore brigade of the English army took control of the city of Murshidabad lest there might erupt some disturbances. Middleton sent Anderson to the palace of Reza Khan to apprise him of the matter, while, he himself went to Mubarakuddaulah to prevail on him to accept the situation. Before the palace of the Nawab, Middleton delivered him the letter written by Hastings and himself argued against continuing Reza Khan in such an office of importance. The Nawab was fully convinced by these arguments and immediately dismissed Reza Khan from his post. The Nawab, at the same time, expressed his firm reliance on the friendship as well as protection of the Company.[89]

Reza Khan did not offer any resistance and on 27 April he was arrested[90] and sent to Calcutta for trial.[91] On the next day, Hastings announced in council that he had executed the Directors' secret order. Middleton, after the departure of Reza Khan from Murshidabad, immediately proclaimed at the *Kellah* and the *Khalsa* about the dismissal of Reza Khan from his station of *naib-diwan*. At the same time, he issued orders to all the supervisors for making it public in their respective districts[92] that henceforth Reza Khan would have no authority at all.

As per the wishes of the Court of Directors the Company was now determined to assume full powers as the *diwan* of the *subah* of Bengal.[93] The Directors, on their part, had only

---

89. Middleton's letter to Calcutta Council, 13 May (S.D. 16 May, 1772).

90. In Bihar, Shitab Rai was also arrested and sent to Calcutta for trial. Later on, he was acquitted.

91. In the trial, Reza Khan established his innocence. Middleton's verdict was in favour of Reza Khan.

92. Middleton's letter to Calcutta Councll, 11 May (S.D., 15 May, 1772).

93. The Company now realised that it was impossible to remain as the passive receivers of revenues. During the terrible years of famine, as Hastings pointed out in 1772, "notwithstanding the loss of at least one-third of the inhabitants of the province, and the consequent decrease of cultivation, the nett collections

(contd.)

announced their intention, but did not suggest any plan of action. To give a practical shape to the important changes to be brought about by the implementation of the idea, Hastings established on 14 May a Committee of Circuit, comprising himself, as the President, and four members of the council. The business of this committee was to make tours in several district of Bengal and to settle as well as to investigate the state of revenues[94] and to make a new arrangement for administration.

With this purpose in view, Hastings started for Murshidabad with the members of the Committee of Circnit[95] and remained there from the end of June to the middle of September. After their arrival at Murshidabad, Middleton joined them and shared their work. At a meeting of the Committee of Circuit at Kasimbazar held on 11 July, it was decided that after the dismissal of Reza Khan, a new *naib nazim* was not necessary. Hence the committee abolished this post. Then Hastings took up the work of remodelling the structure of the government. As the guardian and head of the Nawab's household, the committee selected unanimously, not any rival Prince, nor even the mother of the Nawab, but Muni Begam[96]—the Nawab's stepmother, who was to officiate until the Nawab attained majority. Hastings also appointed Gurudas—the son of Nandkumar

---

of the year 1771 exceeded even those of 1768." The net collections were as follows :-

1768-69	...	Rs. 1,52,54,856-9-4-3.
1769-70--the year of dearth, which ledof the famine in the year following...	...	Rs. 1,31,49,148-6-3-2
1770-71 -the year of famine and morality...		Rs. 1,40,06,030-7-13-2
1771-72	...	Rs. 1,57,26,577-10-2-1 .

--Firminger, *Fifth Report*, p. 213.

94. Debrit, *Transactions*, p. 143.

95. Among the four members of the Committee of Circuit, Dacres, Lawrell and Graham accompanied Hastings to Murshidabad. Middleton-another member joined them there.

96. As part of what was customary at the time, Hastings accepted from Muni Begam some £ 15,000 as "entertainment money".

as the *diwan* of the household with his brother-in-law Jagat Chand—who had been on bad terms with Nandkumar—as his deputy. This was an astute move. Nandkumar and his family, arch-rivals to Reza khan, would now be used to expose all the skeletons in Reza Khan's cupboard, the same as could be used against Reza Khan during the latter's trial. After finishing their task, when the commiitee members visited the Nawab and announced the changes they had effected, he accepted them with "unexpected calm."[97]

The Committee of Circuit began to consider whether the Council of Revenue at Murshidabad should be abolished and its functions brought directly under the management of the Calcutta Council. After spending some time in arguments, it was decided to put the scheme into execution.[98] After the abolition of the Council of Revenue at Murshidabad, Middleton was appointed Resident at the *darbar* in September 1772, with the duty of the Cheif of Kasimbazar as well. He was given the additional charge of regulating the collections of Rajshahi, which had been so long in the hands of the the local *zamindar*. His function as the collector was delimited only to receive the monthly instalments when due and to attend to the complaints of the *raiyots*.[99] With the council of Revenue at Murshidabad standing abolished, it was decided that as the administration of justice and the collection of revenues were, by far, the most important functions of the government, the transfer of the *nizamat adalat* from Murshidabad to Calcutta was also very necessary in this context. This was also agreed upon. Nawab Mubarakuddaulah also gave his consent on this point, and when the list of judges was sent to him by the Governor, the Nawab thought the judges well qualified.[100] All these steps were momentous inasmuch as the die was thus finally cast to shift the political nucleus from Murshidabad to Calcutta—a landmark in the history of the English rule over the country.

97. Feiling, *Hastings*, pp. 93-94.
98. Letter to Court, 3 November, 1772 (F.W.I.H.C., VI, p, 426).
99. *Ibid.*, pp. 425-426.
100. From Mubarakuddoulah to Hastings, Rd., 8 January, 1773 (C.P.C., VI, p. 24, No. 126).

This transfer of capital from Murshidabad to Calcutta would "afford great relief to the inhabitants" of the *subah* of Bengal in opening to them a more ready access to justice, as the appeals from the decisions of the lower courts might be made directly to Calcutta. This Change would also increase the number of "inhabitants and the wealth of Calcutta", observed the Calcutta Council in their note to the Directors, "which will not only add to the consumption of our most valuable manufactures imported from home, but will be means of conveying to the natives a more intimate knowledge of our customs and manners and of conciliating them to our policy and government."[101]

When the posts of *naib-diwan* and *naib-nazim* were abolished and when the Council of Revenue had been transferred to Calcutta, the old members excluded, the Calcutta Council formed a new Council of Revenue at Calcutta. They were employed in preparing the settlements of the districts of Hugli, Midnapore, Birbhum, Jessore, and Calcutta lands. These, together with the districts under the Committee of circuit, accounted for the whole of Bengal, except Burdwan, where the land had been given on lease for five years.[102]

The settlement of Bihar had been decided for a term of years, and, therefore. did not require any immediate change. Still the council decided to unite the collections of Bihar with that of Bengal and "to establish the same regulation in both the provinces."[103]

After making all these arrangements at Murshidabad, Hastings returned to Calcutta in the middle of September. The members of the Committee of Circuit proceeded to Dacca, in order to finalise the settlement of the district and the adjacent areas on the eastern side of Bengal. Middleton remained at Murshidabad to take charge of his new post as the Resident at the *darbar*, "without lessening the dignity of the country government". He had now very little business to do. In

101. Letter to Court, 23 November, 1772 (F.W.I.H.C., VI, p. 427).
102. *Idid.*, p. 428.
103. Ibid., p. 430.

addition to the duties of the Chiefship of Kasimbazar and the Collector of Rajshahi, the Resident was to superintend the transactions of the Nawab's court, to keep an eye over the conduct of the Nawab's guardian and his *diwan*, to furnish advances of the Nawab's stipend and to attend to the law and order and general welfare of the people of the city. The Governor believed that this could be done with the help of an efficient police and justice at Murshidabad.[104]

Thus, the office of the Resident at the *darbar* was reinstituted in 1772, though its duties were somewhat different from those of the original establishment.

---

104. *Ibid.*, 10 November, 1772 (*Ibid.*, p. 448).

CONCLUSION

The British Residents at Murshidabad played the most vital role in the consolidation of the English power in Bengal. It was due to their activities that the Nawabs of Bengal had to accept defeat, disgrace and final surrender before the English power. But this transition in Bengal politics did not come up all on a sudden, it gathered momentum for centuries. The disintegration of the Mughal Empire in the first half of the eighteenth century led to anarchy at the heart of the empire. As for the Britishers in India, the commercial spirit of Thomas Roe in the early seventeenth century had undergone a complete change by the middle of the eighteenth. From the end of the seventeenth century, the Company's servants carried on an independent traffic of their own. It was only some *subahdars* of Bengal under Aurangzeb, who prevented such inland trade of the Company's servants. Thus, interrupted and disturbed, the English soon directed their attention to the maritime trade and became successful in this diversion, to their superior skill in this field over the other merchants

During the last part of the seventeenth century when Bengal was disturbed by internal rebellion, the English became the *zamindar* of Calcutta. They, were authorised to receive revenues due from the inhabitants and to retain profits for themselves. This occupation of a *zamindari* created a gradual change in their outlook and by the mid-eighteenth century, their successes in the south, had developed among them a great power-thirst. On the other hand, the Nawabs of Bengal, after Ahmad Shah Abdali's invasion of Delhi, were left entirely on their own very limited resources to deal with these European attacks. Encouraged by their weaknesses, the English started fortifying their settlements, claimed trade privileges and extended asylum to the fugitives from the Nawab.

Sirajuddaulah was painted by the European historians in the blackest colours. They charged him with the strongest passion to drive away the English from Calcutta on the plea of the latter's having made unauthorised fortifications and sheltering political offenders; though some contemporary English officials gave a contrary report, saying that Sirajuddaulah was generous to the English at the beginning. It was only when the English disobeyed him that the Nawab captured Calcutta—the stronghold of the English, out of rage. Thus, there was no-denying the fact that the English provoked Sirajuddaulah for the caputre of Calcutta, while Sirajuddaulah provoked the English to take advantage of his mistakes.

In a false sense of security, Sirajuddaulah did not follow up his success in Calcutta by striking a further blow on the English at Falta. The Nawab minimised the number and strength of the English. Thus, his allowing the English to remain at Falta was the greatest blunder committed by the Nawab. For this blunder, the Nawab had to pay dearly. He had to accept Watts as the Britisth Resident at his *darbar*. So, in the diplomatic contest, the English gained ground. From now on, the Resident set himself against the Nawab at the very nerve centre of Bengal, which finally led to the overthrow of the Nawab.

On the appointment of a Resident at the Nawab's *darbar*, the English Company took the first firm step towards assuming power. As the Resident was on the spot, he was able to form an idea about the rumpus created by the disaffected nobles and formed a party of his own from among the Nawab's disloyal officials. Thus, Murshidabad became a hotbed of intrigues engineered by the Resident and the atmosphere of the capital became doubly tense owing to the diplomatic duel between the French and the English to gain a controlling hand in Bengal politics—Law on the side of the French and Watts on behalf of the English. In this duel, the *darbar* officers did not seem to have inclined particularly either way, till the diplomatic victory came to Watts. But Siraj was vacillating. He was afraid of openly siding with the French, though he secretly wanted their help. In the strategic game the French were soon caught on the wrong foot. Politically they lost all leverage, and after they had been practically ousted from the Bengal political scene the Nawab lost the opportunity of their assistance in time of need. Even so, the English capture of Chandernagore was the only military operation in Bengal by the English against the French. The rest was a deliberate intrigue fomented and successfully finalished by the British Resident behind the scene.

The Resident was committed to depose the Nawab of Bengal from the masnad; though he, as well as Clive, at the time of the treaty of 9 February solemnly declared in the presence of God that they would "inviolably adhere to the articles of the treaty." But at the same time, Watts, the Resident, framed the conspiracy and corresponded with Clive in cyphers. The Resident carried on the political intrigues by violating the norms of integrity and honour. In this most cunning spreading of the conspiratorial net, which Watts did from Murshidabad and Clive from Calcutta, no excuse or apology can be claimed by either of the two. In this pre-planned treachery, Omichand and Scrafton colluded with Watts. The correspondence between Watts and Clive was in no sense official and the whole responsibility of affairs rested with Watts who, it seemed, could make any move regardless of propriety. Admitting the fact that Sirajuddaulah was a tyrant, and that in all probability, his government might have been terminated by violence, yet the English Company had no right, after having courted the Nawab's alliance, to league with his subjects for the purpose of dethroning him. Even, if the treaty had never been entered into, it would have been impossible to reconcile such a proceeding with the recognised rules the game in any bi-partite political relation. Watts promised his faithfulness before the Nawab, availed the influence derived from the Nawab's impression of his character and employed it in lulling the Nawab into a fatal sense of security. Clive himself admitted that the Nawab had implemented almost every article of the treaty, paid three lakhs of rupees, delivered up the factory of Kasimbazar and hence, as the English themselves recorded: "little or nothing is wanting". But soon Clive wrote to the Governor of Madras that though the Nawab had complied with most of the articles of peace, yet no dependence could be placed on him. The Nawab was universally hated by the great men at the *darbar* which induced Clive to inform the Governor about the conspiracy against Sirajuddaulah. But, judged in the light of international behaviour, by waging a war against the Nawab, the English had usurped the sovereign rights of the Mughal Emperor. And as Watts became successful in his conspiracy against Sirajuddaulah, the English merchants sanctioned the illegal usurption of the *masnad* by Mir Jafar, the leader of the quislings against the Nawab.

In this conspiracy against Sirajuddaulah, the masses of people were most minimally affected. There was no question of national independence before them, for all parties were either the isolated elite or the foreigners : the Emperor, Siraj, the English and the French. Even the leading officials at the *darbar*, who joined in this conspiracy, could not understand the need for national integrity. They thought that some trade privileges would satisfy the English merchants. So the battle of Plassey was more a psychological than a military war[1]. Certain powerful individuals' mental articulations, right or wrong, were all that mattered.

In the fictitious treaty Watts and Clive deceived Omichand. This stratagem Clive applied guided both by his hindsight and foresight. And as Clive stated later on, due to Omichand's threat on Watts it had become necessary for him to set his foot down and put Omichand in his place. The fear of Omichand's divulgence of the plot before the Nawab was the cause of deceiving Omichand by the fictitious treaty. Though Clive professed to do the same hundred times if he had to deal with a professional plotter and traitor like Omichand, from the

1. Chaudhuri, N.C., *Clive of India* (London, 1975), p. 187.

examination of all popers, no such letter about the danger foreboded by Omichand was written by Watts to Clive before the battle of Plassey. This threat of Omichand was thus an invention of Clive later on, during the time of the parliamentary enquiry against him in 1772.

Watts also secured the private treaty from Mir Jafar in writing. As per this private treaty Mir Jafar had to make over Rs. 12 lakhs to the English army led by Clive, and Rs. 40 lakhs as presents to different English officials, over and above the actual treaty with the Company. This private treaty which was formed at the time of conspiracy, was misnamed presents. Later on, the demands set forth in the private treaty were regularly constituted as debts of Mir Jafar. But despite his doing all these mischievous acts and fomenting conspiracy against the established government, Watts was not found guilty. because as it appeared, his sole aim was to enhance the prestige of his own nation even though the means employed by him were ignoble.

The life of Siraj was one of constant alarm and suspense. Many of the acts of the young Nawab were also above reproach. But on the scale of honour, he was by far a superior man than Watts or Clive. He never betrayed his master, nor sold his country. "He was the only one of the principal actors in that tragic drama who did not attempt to deceive,"[2] In the battle of Plassey, had not Watts' intrigues secured the inactivity of Sirajuddaulah's generals, the English forces would certainly have been at the mercy of the Nawab. Hence, the battle of Plassey was won not so much by Clive's gallantry and generalship as by the intrigues of Watts.

Scrafton, the Resident at the *darbar* of Mir Jafar extracted the socalled presents from the Nawab. He was led on and helped by Watts and the other English officials. From this time on, the Residents began to dictate to the Nawab in regard to all matters, even in relation to his administration during the regime of Mir Jafar. As such, Mir Jafar became a puppet in their hands. The Residents now became free to do whatever they pleased. Scrafton began to advance loans to *zamindars* on high rates of interests. Warren Hastings—another

2. Malleson, Decisive Battles, p. 71.

Resident, was involved in the illegal trade in salt, opium, tobacco and timber through his partner. The constant threat of the Company's officials as well as the often highhanded dictates of the Residents, created tensions and agony in the mind of Mir Jafar. All the agonies of the preceding years of his life paled before those from which he suffered during his rule of three years in the usurped palace of his master.

Still, the much bewildered and helpless Nawab was deposed, allegedly on his breach of faith and contracting secrte correspondence with the enemies of the English. The protests of some councillors were of no avail. The Court of Directors approved hesitatingly his deposition and this letter of the Directors, Hastings did hot venture to translate before Mir Jafar, though the Resident also supported this deposition. Yet the voice of nemesis was spelled out before him and Mir Jafar had to quit. The destinies of the Bengal Nawabs thus remained completely under the mercy of the British Residents and the Company's authorities.

It was this mastery and preservation of their illegal rights that the English enjoyed after the battle of plassey, on account of which a war with Mir Qasim became inevitable. Free-passes, which were originally intended for the Company's trade, were extended to the company's servants and their *gomastahs*, trading in their individual capacities. The English adventurers who used forged passes, hired agents in the company's uniform and decorated their boats with the English flag. Hastings saw no boat without the Union Jack between Calcutta and Patna. This was due to Mir Jafar's grant of such free-passes as a favour to Hastings, Clive and some others. After the accession of Mir Qasim, these passes were considered as a matter of right instead of favour. Mir Qasim's protests were ignored and by 1762, the entire traditional internal trade of Bengal was threatened by the extension of this practice. Thus the battle of Buxar was fought by the Company against Mir Qasim in order to preserve their self-interests. Plunder rather than rights, wealth rather than glory were their main objects.

Thus, the Residency at Murshidabad became a guarantee of fortune. Middleton, whose chequered career brought him the office of the Resident during the restoration of Mir Jafar and the earlier phase of Najmuddaulah, began to trade on a large scale by land and sea. The Residents thus flouted the repeated orders of the Court of Directors. They now began to control even the household [affairs of the Nawab. In the Regency that was formed on the plea of Najmudddaulah's minority, Middleton occupied the pivotal place and controlled the Regency. And after the *diwani*, the powers of the Residents were considerably augmented and became operative in manifold directions. The Resident had to discharge the duties of the *diwan* under the direction of the select Committee, in addition to his former duties as the intermediary between the Compay and the *Nawab*. Thus the powers of the Nawabs of Bengal became virtually extinct. After the *diwani*, all the Nawabs of Bengal became pensioners on an annuity, while the real powers passed on to the Resident.

The Select Committee claimed after the *diwani* that the "security to the property, freedom to the trade and protections to the persons of the natural inhabitants" had been ensured. In their letter to the court on 24 January, 1767, Clive and the Select Committee wrote that the Resident "Superintends the whole collections, receives the monthly payments from the *zamindars*, disburses the stated revenues appropriated to the king and the Nabob, inquires into the causes of deficiencies, redresses, injuries sustained or committed by the officers of the Revenue and transmits the accounts of his office, the invoices of Treasure with every other occurrence of Importance to the President and the Select Committee."[3] The court, on its part, also clarified the duties of the Resident "who wouid stand between the administration and the encroachments always to be apprehended from the agents of the Company's servants." Thus, the practical operation of the office of the *diwani* devolved upon the Resident and the success or failure of the above office rested neither on the Governor nor his Select Committee. As the Resident was on the spot and the practical operator of the scheme, the whole scheme of dyarchy centred in him. But

3. Letter to Court, 24 January, 1767.

like Middleton, Francis Sykes—the new Resident after the *diwani* also did not follow the spirit of this ideal before his private gains. Though occupying an office of much weight, additionally acting also as the administrator of revenues, Sykes carried on his private trade and became a successful silk merchant at Kasimbazar. He received one lakh of rupees in jewels from Reza khan, when he became the Resident. Over and above this, he continued to levy extra cesses that went to his pocket. He continued to levy *mathut*, unofficially and secretly, through out Bengal and took two thousand rupees per month for his table and a further sum of two thousand rupees per month as commission for providing dresses issued at the time of the annual *puniyah*. He distributed Rs. 70,000 to 80,000 among the senior servants of the Company and at the end of his term he further distributed rupees three lakhs as part of the profits among the servants of the Murshidabad Residency. Thus, it was no wonder that the spirit of reform would surely miscarry under such morality of the Resident. As a consequence Bengal groaned under the burden of heavy taxation. The poor and industrious *raiyots* were taxed and fleeced to meet all these ignoble needs of the Company's officials. The poor *raiyots* were also regularly tortured by their *zamindars* and collectors. A child born, honour conferred, fines levied, and on many other such heads, the *raiyots* must pay to their *zamindars*.[4]

Among the Residents, it was Becher who tried to remedy this situation. He tried in vain to withdraw the controlling powers of the supervisors, when the supervisors failed to control the situation due to the enmity of the big farmers and the *amils* as well as for the lack of their own experience. It was only Becher who had the courage of conviction and conscience to say that since the Company had obtained the *diwani* the condition of the people of Bengal had become

4. One of the most formidable demands made on the *raiyots* by the *zamindars* was *mangan*. The enormous expenditure to which the *Zaminders* would go on such occasions as the funeral of parents, the marriage of children, or the adoption of heirs, was met on every occasion by cesses levied on their dependent *raiyots*.

worse than it was before under the Nawabs. He pointed out many defects in the system of revenue collections and suggested remedies. He proposed to follow the same policy everywhere, letting the lands to farm for three years. But these proposals could not materialise due to the dispute between the Council and the Select Committee. In utter frustration, Becher had to utter with surprise, "what a destructive system is this for the poor inhabitants!"

It was destined that Bengal should be the school of English administrators. The measure of appointing supervisors was a move in the right direction but it proved a failure as the supervisors themselves became tempted to share in the spoil. Though the *amils* were withdrawn on the representation of Becher, their rapacity could not be checked. The Residents failed to prevent the illegalities committed by the *amils* or those who replaced them. The *zamindars* had a permanent interest in the welfare of the *raiyots* beyond a certain limit, but this was not so when the *amils* collected the revenues. The man who offered to collect the most was generally appointed to the *amil's* post. Thus, the *amils*, uncertain of their office and without any desire for the people's welfare, ransacked the Bengal.

Bengal witnessed famine from 1769. Famines were no uncommon calamity at that time, but the savage spirit of monopoly and extortion occasioned anxiety and horror, destitution and helplessness. While many Englishmen lamented for the people who were in the grip of such a calamity, the Calcutta Council sent people to various districts to purchase whatever rice could be procured for their own men. They, were cruelly indifferent to the suffering of the people by such stockpiling. Becher vainly proposed for some relief measures before the unwilling ears of the Calcutta authorities. The belief that the famine was largely due to the unscrupulous commercial transactions of the Company's servants, gained a rapid and wide acceptance. Debrit, a contemporary English writer, shared this view. He observes : "This famine is an epoch in the history of Bengal which shall perpetuate while the world lasts, the sinister genius of mercantile policy, and record, beyond the ravages of time, to what a shocking excess of avarice have been extended against all that is most sacred and inviolable in the rights of humanity.[5] John Shore, in a note to his poem, writes : Ignorance and prejudice have attributed the famine to the avarice and machinations of the English, and Sir Francis Sykes, who left Bengal eighteen months before the famine commenced, has been culminated as the author of it. Whoever knows the country of Bengal, knows that no art can produce a famine there."[6] This opinion of the distinguished writers seemed true to a great extent.

During the famine, Reza Khan enhanced the assessment of land tax by ten per cent. The great famine took the life of a considerable number of people and rudely upset the socio-economic condition of Bengal. The Nawab had no influence except what he derived by the sufferance of the council ; and the council, on its part, was biased by a thousand considerations to give judgment and decide the mode of action without any regard for the spirit of humanity. In this way the British inherited a chaos. Thus, the great hope of the Select Committee in January, 1767, had been completely shattered by 1772 thanks to their own misdeeds. The unending rapacity and the attendent vices joined hands with nature's ravages and culminated in the terrible famine. Now it was beyond the power of the Resident or the Calcutta Council to provide even a ray of hope to the people of Bengal, groaning under heavy taxes and consequent despair that followed in its wake. The situation rumbled as for as England where it was realised that the administrative machinery in India required drastic changes. Hence, Hastings had to carry out the order of the Court of Directors that resulted in a complete change in the set-up of the system of administration. The Home Government of England became convinced about exercising a tighter control over the Company's activities in Bengal. This resulted in the rise of a new spirit and changed-ways of thinking which in the long run formulated their ideas of a colonial empire in India.

5. Debrit, *Transactions*, p. 131.
6. Firminger, *Fifth Report*, p. 203.

But in Bengal, the plot of extending an octopus control behind the thinly veiled pretence of dyarchy was universally discovered. The common men realised that the powers of the *diwani* so long exercised under dyarchy, were selfish and callous to the core. The Nawab was known to be a cypher, Reza Khan—a slave of the English, while the British Resident-an oppressor to the poor inhabitants. Though Hastings allowed a British Resident to continue at Murshidabad, the new incumbent lost all glory of his predecessors because the seat of power had already shifted from Murshidabad to Calcutta.

APPENDIX – A

Names of the Residents at the Darbar

1. William Watts (9 February 1757—14 June 1757)
2. Luke scrafton (July 1757—August 1758)
3. Warren Hastings (August 1758 – February 1761)
4. Thomas Amphlett (April 1763 – June 1763) Proposed Resident at the *darbar* of Mir Qasim.
5. William Watts (October 1763—May 1764). Absentee Resident at the *darbar* of Mir Jafar.
6. Stanlake Batson (May 1764—August 1764). Attended Mir Jafar at Patna.
7. Samuel Middleton (November 1764 – August (1765).
8. Francis Sykes (August 1765 January 1769).
9. Richard Becher (January 1769 – January 1771).
10. Samuel Middleton (September 1772—1774).

APPENDIX—B

Extract of a letter from Sykes, dated 10 February, 1768, narrating an account of his experience during his tour through Dinajpur and Purnea. He narrated fraud and malpractices among the revenue collectors of those districts.

"I now do myself the honour to lay before you an account of proceedings during my late journey to the provinces of Dinagpore and Purnea. I have already acquainted you in part with the reasons that induced me this undertaking; but as it was not in my power to be so explict at that time as the native of the subject required, I shall take the liberty before I enter into a detail of the conduct I have persued to point out more fully the motives by which I have been actuated upon this occasion.

The remisness and backwardness of *zemindars* as well as of those who were the immediate servants of the Government in remitting the just and stated Revenues from the larger jurisdictions has long afforded me full and sufficient cause of complaint nor has anything but the unwearied attention of the ministers, and an incessant threats and demands forced them to acompliance with this part of their duty. Of the districts depending on the city those of Dinagpore and Purnea are amongst the most considerable; the former has long been almost an independent Government of its own Rajah and the latter from its great distance and the weakness of the Nabob's authority frequently in a state of actual rebellion. These causes have introduced a more particular disorder and relaxation into the affairs of those provinces, with almost a total ignorance on the part of Government, either of the state in which they were or the respective value of their collections.

Notwithstanding our utmost endeavours and exertions there was a balance of no less than six lacks and upwards incurred in the Dinagpore province during the last year. The Honble President whilst he was at the city in conjunction with the ministers and myself recommended that the country should be taken from under the management of its *Zemindar*, and a person sent on the part of the Government, to superintend the collections and endeavour to improve the Revenue. Syed

Mohammed Cown a man in whom the ministers had much confidence was accordingly appointed and the strictest injunctions given to him not only to exact himself with vigilence and activity in the collection and remittance of the Revenues but also to endeavour to procure as such papers and accounts as might enable us to form a just idea of the true value of the province. This appointment however was productive of no real good effect. Syed Mohamed Cawn during five months of his stay did nothing but write the usual and ordinary excuses and complaints with representations of the poverty of the country, Distress of the tenants and oppression of the fromer collector. Nor were we able to procure from him any papers and accounts in which we could place the least confidence or that could in any respect afford us the light we designed to obtain by his appointment.

It was the result of these considerations and the satisfaction of having reduced the business of the city into a state of order and regularity that confirmed me in my resolution of undertaking this journey myself. being convinced that nothing but a residence on the spot could enable me to determine whether the deficiency in the Revenues was owing to real poverty and inability in the country to pay the amount at which it had been rated or the mismanagement of those to whose charge the collections had been entrusted.

……… ..After the representations of poverty and distress that had ever been made when the payment of the Revenues was in question I was much surprised to find on my entering the Dinagpore country that it is in a most plenteous and flourishing situation, very well inhabited and the lands throughout cultivated and improved. This circumstance so visible and striking in itself gave me stronger suspicions that I had before entertained.

These suspicions were more fully confirmed when I had been time enough on the spot to extract from the accounts the net amount which had been collected each separate year since the Company's appointment to the *Dewanee*. I found to my astonishment that between April 1765 and 1766 when the public statement with the government turned at the *pooneah* was

17,82,218-3-17 and that including the *Dewanee, Nuzzrana,* and other conditions there had been paid into the Treasury 19,27,744-7-2, there was a clandestine statement formed in the country of 26,34,760-6-13 and there has been actually collected 24,05,483-12-15 of sum out of Rupees which after the deduction of 72,893-7-5 allowed for batta exhibits a surplus of charges of collections to the amount of *sicca* Rupees 4,04,845-14-8, a sum for exceeding what might reasonably be allowed for the necessary demands and expenses of the province nor could anything but the weakness of the late Government either quietly put up with so great a loss or have suffered so unnecessary a charge to have been laid on the country and the Tenants. The year 1766-67 exhibits a still more striking instance of fraud and abuse for here there had been only 1,40,340-1-5 paid into the Treasury including the *Dewanee Nuzzeranah* and other additions to the statement and a balance of 6,51,188-11-7 incurred whilst we find that the statement made unknown to us with the country is 2,60,744-14-1 and that there has been actually collected upwards of 24 Lacks a difference too striking to need any remark or illustration.

.........Having gone through all such papers as were of any real utility and obtained the most material lights during a stay of five weeks at Dinagpore the necessity of my return to the city obliged me to hasten my departure to Purnea, but it appearing to me proper that a more munite extract should be made from the accounts in order for its being laid before you for your satisfaction. I determined on leaving Mr. William Rooke one of my assistants during a short time for that purpose, as also to superintend all expences made and prevent affairs being carried on upon the extravagant and ruinous system which has lately been practised, since I was convinced that without some precaution of this nature no order or injunctions would deter them from relapsing into the former mode immediately on my absence.

On my entry into the Purnea province it exhibited to me a scene widely different from that of Dinagpore. This country though extremely beautiful, watered with many fine rivers and the lands in themselves rich and fertile yet was almost universally waste and destitute of inhabitants or cultivation; and indeed in such villages as were to be met with, and particularly in the Town of Purnea, the people bore evident marks of beggary and distress. These appearances concurring so strongly with the lively representations made by Rajah Suchet Rai during the two former years he had the management of the collections secured in some measure to plead his excuse for the difficulties we had laboured under in procuring the Revenues ...Since I have the greatest reason to think that there has been collected during the two years of his appointment (viz. from April 1765 to April 1767) the sum of between 38 and 40 Lacks and we well know that there has been paid into the Treasury only 26 Lacks 37, 472 Rupees. The difference between these two sums after making a deduction for Batta short weight of Rupees in the amount at which we must rate his charges of collections and sorry I am to say that this is too great reason to believe that he has reaped the fruits of heavy oppression and extortions which do not come within the limits of this account. The sum of 30,000 Rupees taken from one Merchant only was proved against him by an equitable arbitration during my stay at Purnea as also another accusation of a very heavy nature that he has collected no less than 1,40,000 Rupees of the present year's rents since the dismission from the office at the time of last *poonea*."

—Select Committee Records, 10 February, 1768 pp. 93-114.

APPENDIX—C

—Extract of a letter from Richard Becher, dated 30 March, 1770, narrating the severities of famine and some measures for relief.

"My constant endeavours have been exerted jointly with those of the ministers to prevent as much as possible our honourable employers suffering by a reduction of the revenues, at the same time due attention has been paid that the collections should be made in a manner as little oppressive to the *Ryott* as the nature of the case would admit of and as you Gentlemen were pleased to allow me in concert with the ministers to take such steps as might to us appear absolutely necessary for the relief of the poor and the general welfare of the country and the real interest of the company, I have avoided giving you unnecessary trouble but affairs being now in that state as to require extra-ordinary efforts to bring this country again to a flourishing condition......I think it my indispensible duty to give you the best insight I can into its present miserable situation occasioned by the most extraordinary drought (ever known) for these two last years......... Permit me only here to give my opinion that ,the measures to be pursued the recovery of the country and inhabitants from the present depressed state they are in should be the object in view and that thereby the Company's real interest will be promoted, although to obtain this desired end an immediate loss must appear. It has ever been my idea of the management of the revenues that we should have an eye to the permanency of our possessions and that increase of revenue should be gradual and proceed from the efforts of encouragements......It has been my misfortune, Gentlemen, to be Resident at the *Durbar* under the most unfavourable circumstance and little credit can I except while the revenues decrease. However, from your candour I am sure not to meet unmanted censure that my own heart tells me. I have acted to the best of my judgement and abilities for the real interest of the Company and the welfare of these provinces.

...Extracts of letters which accompany this will point the real misery of the inhabitants in such strong colours that little remains for me to add on this disagreeable subject...... Only to assure you Gentlemen that from the strictest enquiry and the most undearable evidence there does not remain a doubt but these representations are the true picture of the distress.

......The districts that have more particularly suffered by the unfavourableness of the season are Purnia, Rajahmehal, Beerbhoom and a part of the Rajeshahy. Indeed the only district under this department from which complaints have not come of the want of rain, are Dacca and those low countries that are situated to the Eastward where the rivers have overflown and fertilized the lands even this remarkable dry season.

......You Gentlemen are acquainted that Bhagalpore is a distinct district whose revenues are not included in the general statement sent annually from hence soon after the *pooneah* but the *bundobust* is usually settled about the month of October or November. This district has particularly suffered by the drought, has been much oppressed by former *aumils* and being in a direct road of the march of our troops to and from Patna has been liable to many inconveniences and losses which have reduced this fine country to a miserable state and incapable to facilitate its inhabitants to pay their usual revenues. A large balance is outstanding. Mr. Harwood is now on his way to Bhagalepore and is directed by me to endeavour to obtain the most accurate account of what has been collected by the present *aumil* Sudder ul Huq Cawn and how the money has been disposed of. I have further recommended to that gentleman to make a strict enquiry into the present state of the Bhagalepore province, be attentive to the interest of the inhabitants in the settlement that may be made for the revenues.

......In the present distressed state of these provinces the most lenient and moderate measure should be pursued for a course of time. Such measures have been strongly recommended everywhere by the ministers and me but Gentlemen in order to restore this country to its former affluent state two points appear absolutely necessary. The one to make advances to assist the *Ryot* in providing of bullocks, ploughs and utensil of husbandry. The other to afford them a relaxation for a certain time from any demands on account of revenue. On the first you have been pleased to grant permission for such advances as might be judged necessary...The sum recommended by the ministers to be advanced for this purpose is much larger than usual as you will perceive by the accompanying account it is incumbent on me to assure you that I shall use my utmost endeavours that this sum be properly applied and as English Gentlemen will be in the districts and attend to recovering the money advanced on account Suceary (?). I flatter myself the Company run little risk of loss by this measure and I am very certain considerable benefit must accrue by enabling the *Ryotts* to pay their future revenues......Granting to the *Ryots* a certain relaxation from demands appears to me an essential point of the future prosperity of this country. In such seasons as the two last they must have been continually harassed for their rents and if restrictions are not laid will continue to be so. I have therefore proposed to the ministers that orders should be issued in all the districts composing the province of Bengal except Dacca and Eastern districts that no demands will be made on the *Ryot* till after the first of July next...Mahomed Reza Cawn approves of the measure and the orders will be issued next week to the effect unless you think proper to countermand them. The most statutory effects may in my opinion be expected. The season is at hand for planting, sowing and every degree of improvement. The *Ryot* finding himself at ease will be encouraged to pursue his labour and if it please God to grant seasonable weather will be better enabled to pay his rent in due time."

—Select Committee Records, 28 April, 1770, pp. 216-232.

APPENDIX—D

Accounts collected from the *zaminaars* of Rangpur

(a) Modungopaul Account collections of Tucker boondy for the year 1176 (i.e. 1769-70).

To amount collected which he has brought to account Rs. 2,70,933-11-16-1	By amount remitted to the city ......Rs 1,32,277-7-0
	By amount charges defrayed by home............51,594-15-16
To amount...... Ditto... not accounted for 5,320- 3- 0-0	By amount allowed by Mahomed Reza Cawn for Purgunnah charges... 37,037-15-0
2,76,253-14-16-1	By amount paid Md. Haussen in part of his Balance... 22,483-6-15
To amount borrowed of merchants...8,313-0-11-0	By Ditto 840-0- 0
	23,323-6-15
	By amount paid by merchants 8,313- 0-11
	2,52,546-13- 2
	By balance Rs. 32,020- 2-5-1
Narancy Rupees 2,84,566-15-7-1	Narancy Rupees 2,84,566-15- 7-1

(*b*) *Mahomed Haussen account*

To amount collected from the following Purgunnahs :—

Futtypore	... 14 annas	...	25,295- 2-10
Ditto	... 2 "	...	18,149-10-16
			43,444-13- 6
Cargyhaut		...	43,200- 1- 2
Cargyhaut Mushroot		...	28,077- 7- 1-1
Hoodassery		...	3,021-14- 0-0
Goraahdur		...	1,403- 4-15-0
Cahinoah		...	47,106-15- 7-2
Jipali		...	11,571- 5-10-0
Bausut		...	8,117- 8- 0-0
Bamindanga		...	32,936-10-12-2

Boda ...	61,927- 7-17-2
Pangah ...	22,568- 9-12-2
Bycuntpore ...	7,285- 0- 0-0

To amount collected for duties on opium 81-8

To amount collected from the following Talocks :

Abeersuder ...	2,004-10-19-1
Barbeille ...	7,852-9
Samnarain ...	30,200- 2-15
Adam ...	16,755-14- 7-2
Boubdabry ...	65,096- 5-12-2
Chaundconnah ...	10,821- 0-12-2
Huldabarry ...	18,857-13-10

To amount collected as follows :

Phousdary ...	1,977
butwally Rungpore ...	245
Mourtze Gunge ...	733- 4
butwally Tuzhaut ...	71-8

To amount collected from Purgunnah Coond ... 55,578 -5- 3

To amount borrowed of the following merchants :

Jaggut Seat ...	47,019- 3-15
Sibooram ...	66,097- 4
Consumanny ...	6,673- 7
Woodynaut ...	1,600
Bahadresing ...	39,025
Mahomed Tucky ...	4,000

Carried Over 1,64,414-14-15

Total of the total Rs. 6,39,039- 2- 5.

——Statement of John Grose—Supervisor of Rangpur
10 June, 1770
(Resident at the Durbar, Revenue, Vol. I)

GLOSSARY

Adalat (Arabic, means justice, equity) : A Court of Justice.

Amil (Arabic, From '*amal*', business, authority) : A Collector of revenue on the part of the government. An officer inferior to *Amin*.

Aurung (Hindi) : A place where any article of trade is manufactured and collected for wholesale disposal or export.

Band-o-bast (Persian, from *bastan*) : Agreement, settlement, adjustment. Settlement of revenue to be paid by the *Zamindar*.

Banian/Baniya (Hindi) : A Hindu trader, or shopkeeper.

Barkandas (Arabic/Persian. *barq*-lightning and *andaz*—one who casts) : A matchlockman, guard, or watchman, with shield and sword.

Bigha (Hindi) : A standard of measurement of land about 1/3 of an acre.

Buxbunder (Persian from *bakshi*-officer, *bandar*-port) : The Officer or office of customs.

Chauth (Hindi) : An assessment equal to one-fourth of the actual Government collections demanded by the Marathas.

Chelat (Arabic) : A custom of giving dresses to the *zamindars* and higher officials at the time of the *puniyah*.

Chobdar (Persian, *chob*—a stick, *dar*—one who holds) : A frequent attendent of Indian nobles or of Anglo-Indian officials of rank.

Chowky (Hindi) : A watch-house. Also a place appointed for the receipt of customs.

Dalal (Arabic) : A broker, a middleman.

Darbar (Persian) : A royal court.

Darogah (Mangolian) : The chief officer in various departments of the government. Later it meant the head of a Police Station.

Dastack (Persian, from *dast*—hand, signature) : A passport, permit or order in English Company's affairs. This privilege was enjoyed by the Company's covenanted servants.

Diwan (Persian) ; A minister, a chief of state. It was especially applied to the head official minister.

Diwani (Persian) : The office, jurisdiction of *diwan*

Farman (Persian, from the verb *farmudan*—to command, order) : A grant, order, decree or command of the emperor.

Faujdar (Persian, *fauj*—army, *dar*—one who has) ; An officer invested with the charge of Police and criminal matters. The chief of a body of troops.

Faujdari (Persian) ; The office of a *faujdar*.

Ganj (Persian) : A mart where grain and other necessaries of life are sold.

Gentoos : Hindus, natives of India.

Gollah (Hindi) : Storage of grain.

Gomastah (Persian, from the verb *gumashtan*—to commission) : An agent, an officer appointed by the *zamindars* to collect their rents. Also a clerk for vernacular correspondence.

Harem (Persian) : A family apartment for ladies in the palace of a muslim ruler or nobleman.

Harkara (Persian, *har*—every, *kar*—business) : A messenger, an emissary, a spy.

Hasb-ul-hukm (Arabic) : An order signed by the wazir of the Mughal Emperor.

Jagir (Persian, *ja*—a place, *gir*—taking or occupying) : An assignment of the Government share of the produce of a portion of land to a person generally for military services. Its holder was called a *jagirdar*.

Jamadar (Arabic/Persian, *Jamah*—a crowd, a troop, *dar*—one who has) : An officer of horse or foot. Also the head of the peons in the *sawari*.

Jiziya (Persian) : A poll-tax imposed on the non-Muslims.

Kanungo (Arabic/Persian, *Kanun*—law, *go*—one who speaks) : A village or district revenue officer.

Kazi (Arabic) : A muslim judge.

Kella (Hindi) : A Fort.

Khalsa (Arabic, from *khalis*—pure, sincere) The exchequer, the officce of government under the Mughals; as applied to lands it means those of which the revenue remains the property of government, not being made over to *jagir* etc. to any other parties.

Khazanchi (Arabic/Turki) : A treasurer, a cash-keeper.

Kist (Arabic) : Instalment.

Kistbundee (Arabic/Persian) : Settlement of the instalments of the revenue. Any document relating to fixed periodical payments of revenues.

Kotwal (Persian/Hindi) : The chief officer of police for a city or town.

Malgujari (Arabic/Persian, *mal*—property, land revenue, *gujari*—the act of paying a debt) : Revenue assessment, the payment of land revenue.

Masnad (Arabic) : A cushion seat, a throne.

Mathut (Hindi) : A poll-tax. An extra tax imposed on the cultivators.

Mohar (Persian) : A seal, a gold coin.

Muchelka (Turki) : A bond, a written obligation.

Muffasal (Arabic) : A rural area. A rural locality distinct from the *sadar* or principal town.

Munshi (Arabic) : A writer, a secretary.

Mutasuddi (Arabic) : A writer, a clerk. A general name for all officers employed in maintaining the accounts of the government.

Naib (Arabic) : A deputy.

Naib-diwan : A deputy-*diwan*.

Nazranah/Nazar (Arabic/Persian) : A present or offering from an inferior to a superior.

Nazim (Arabic) : The Lord Lieutenant, Viceroy or Governor of a province charged with administration of criminal law and police.

Nizamat (Arabic) : The office of the *Nazim.*

Nishan (Arabic) : A permit or privilege granted by a *Subahdar.*

Nazir (Arabic): A Superintendent, a commissary.

Omrah (Arabic) : The muslim nobles at the *darbar*, especially that of the Great Mughal.

Paik (Hindi) A footman, a village watch man employed as a guard at night.

Paikkr/Pikar (Hindi) : An agent through whose hands the articles of merchandise passed from the loom of the manufacturer to the public merchant.

Palkeen/Palki (Hindi) : A kind of litter or sedan—chair.

Parganah (Persian) : A sub-division of a district; the largest division of land in a *zamindari*; a tract of the country comprising many villages.

Parwana (Persian) : An order from a person in authority to a Subordinate: a warrant; a writ.

Peshkar (Persian) : An agent, or one exercising in revenue and custom affairs a delegated authority.

Peshwa (Marathi) : The Prime Minister of the Maratha State.

Puniyah (Hindi) : An annual collection day ceremony of the government revenues.

Pushtabandy (Arabic) : Money collected on the plea of preserving the river banks.

Raiyat (Arabic) : A cultivator, a farmar.

Rai-Rayan (Hindi) : A title of the financial minister and treasurer of the Nawab.

Resum-nezarat (Arabic) : An illegal cess as a fee of the *Nazir.*

Rawana (Arabic) : A custom-collector's permit.

Sahukar (Persian/Hindi) : A banker, a dealer in money and exchanges.

Salami (Persian): A fee paid to a superior as a mark of respect,

Sanad (Arabic) : A grant, a charter, a privilege or right from any great man of authority.

Sarkar (Persian) : An extensive division of a province under the Mughal Government.

Shahzadah (Persian) : The crown prince.

Sicca (Arabic) : A coining die, a stamp, a seal. It was used for the standard silver rupee.

Subah (Arabic) : A province of the Mughal Empire.

Subahdar (Arabic/Persian) : A Viceroy, a Governor of *Subah.*

Subahdari (Arabic/Persian) : The office of the *Subahdar.*

Tahsildar (Persian) : A collector of reveune. An officer collecting the revenue from a given tract under a *Zamindar.*

Taluq (Arabic) : A dependency, a division of a revenue unit. Applied to a tract of land usually smaller than a *Zamindari.*

Taluqdar (Arabic/Persian) : Owner of a tract of land.

Vakil (Arabic) : An embassador, a representative, an attorney.

Waddadar (Arabic) : An officer of the revenues. A contractor.

Wazir (Arabic, means one who bears a load) : A revenue and finance minister of the Mughal Government.

Zamindar (Persian, *Zamin*—land, *dar*—one who has) : An occupant of land. A landholder paying revenue directly to the Government.

Zamindari (Persian) : The office and rights of a *Zamindar.* The tract of land constituting the possession of a *Zamindari.*

Zilla (Arabic) : A district, a division.

Zoolum (Arabic) : Coercion, oppression.

BIBLIOGRAPHY

1. *Primary Sources*

(A)) *Unpublished*:

(a) Home (Public)

Letter to Court, 1755-57

(b) *Secret Department Records*

Secret Department (Feb-April) 1765

Secret Department (July-Oct.), 1769

Secret Department, 1771

Secret Department (May), 1772, vol. 22.

(c) *Select Committee Records*

Select Committee (Feb.-June), 1757.

Select Committee (June-Sept.), 1765.

Select Committee (May-Dec.), 1765.

Select Committee 1765, Vol. 2.

Select Committee 1765 Vol. 10.

Select Committee (January-Dec.), 1767, Vol. 12.

Select Committee (Feb.-Nov.), 1767, Vol. 13.

Select Committee (Feb.-Dec.), 1768, Vol. 14.

Select Committee (January-July), 1768, Vol. 15.

Select Committee (Aug.-Sept.), 1768, vol. 15 A.

Select Committee (January-Dec.), 1769.

Select Committee (January-June), 1770.

Select Committee (1771).

(b) *Published* :

Abstract of General letters to and from the Court of Directors, Vol. II (1765-1854), Calcutta, 1937.

Bengal District Records (Rungpur), 1770-1779, Vol. I, Edt. by W.K. Firminger, Calcutta, 1914.

Bengal and Madras Papers, Vols. II and III, 1688-1757, 1757-1785 : Calcutta, 1928.

Calendar of Persian Correspondence, Vol.I (1759-1767), Calcutta, 1911, Reprint. Delhi, 1970.

Calendar of Persian Correspondence, Vol. II (1767-1769), Calcutta, 1914, Reprint, Delhi, 1970.

Calendar of Persian Correspondence, Vol. III (1770-1772), Calcutta, 1919.

Calendar of Persian Correspondence, Vol. IV (1772-1775), Central Publication Branch, 1925.

Colonel Clive's Correspondence (1756-1758), Military Sundry Book No. 10 (*Vide* B.M.P., Vol. II).

Fort William India House Correspondence, Vol. I (1748-1756), Edt. by K.K. Datta, Delhi. 1958.

Fort William India Hruse Correspondence, Vol. II (1757-1759), Edt. by H.N. Sinha, Delhi, 1957.

Fort William India House Correspondence, Vol. III (1760-1763), Edt. by R.R. Sethi, Delhi, 1968.

Fort William India House Correspondence, Vol. IV (1764-1766), Edt. by C.S. Srinivasachari. Delhi 1962.

Fort William India House Correspondence, Vol. V (1767-1769), Edt. by N.K. Sinha, Delhi, 1949.

Fort William India House Correspondence, Vol. VI (1770-1772). Edt. by Bisheswar Prasad, Delhi, 1960.

Hill, S.C., *An Abstract of the Early Records of the Foreign Department*, 1756-1762, Calcutta, 1901.

,, *Bengal in 1756-57*, Vols. I, II and III, London, 1905.

Historical Introduction of the Bengal Portion of the Fifth Report Reprint, Calcutta, 1962.

Letter Copy Books of the Resident at the Durbar of Murshidabad (1769-1770), Vols. I. and II, Edt. by W.K. Firminger, Calcutta, 1919.

Letter Copy Books of the Supervisor of Rajshahi at Nattore (30 December, 1769,15 September 1772), Calcutta, 1925.

Proceedings of the Select Committee at Fort William in Bengal 1758, Edt. by W.K. Firminger, Calcutta, 1914.

Proceedings of the Controlling Council of Revenue at Murshidabad, Vol- I (1770), (Edt. by W.K. Firminger, Calcutta, 1919.

Selections from the Unpublished Records of the Government, Edt. by J. Long, Second edn., Calcutta, 1973.

The Fifth Report from the Select Committee of the House of Commons on the Affairs of the East India Company, Vol. I. Edt. by W.K. Firminger, Calcutta, 1917.

Vansittart, H. *Original Papers Relative to Disturbances in Bengal*, Vols. I and II (1759-1764), London, 1765,

Wheeler, J, Tolboys, *Early Records of British India*, New Impression, London, 1972.

2. *Contemporary Sources*

(A) *English* :

Aitchison, C.U., *A Collections of Treaties, Engagements and Sanads*, Vol. I, Reprint, Calcutta, 1909.

Bolts, William, *Considerations on Indian Affairs*, Second Edition, London, 1772.

Burke's speech at the Impeachment of Warren Hastings, Vol. I, Second Edition, Calcutta, 1909.

Caraccioli, C., *The Life of Robert Lord Clive*, Vol. III, London, 1775.

Debrit, J., *Transactions in India from 1756-1783*, London, 1786.

Holwell, J.Z., *India Tracts*, Third Edn., London, 1764.

,, *Important Facts relating to the East India Company's Affairs in Bengal*, 1752-1760, Third Edn., London, 1764.

Ive, Edward, *A Voyage from England to India*, London, 1773.

John, Moir, *Transactions in India*, London, 1786.

Orme, R., *A History of the Military Transactions of the British Nation in Indostan*, Vol. II, London, 1778. First Indian Reprint Edition.

Parker, Henry, *The History of War in India between Serajuddaulah and the English*, London, 1789.

Scrafton, Luke, *Reflections on the Government of Indostan*, A Miller, 1763.

,, *A History of Bengal Before and After Plassey*, London, 1763, Reprint, Calcutta, 1975.

Tavernier, J.B., *Travels in India*, 2 Vols. Edt. by V. Ball, London, 1889.

Vansittart, Henry, *A Narrative of the Transactions in Bengal* 1760-1764, London, 1766. Reprint, Calcutta, 1976.

Verelst, Harry, *A View of the Rise, Progress and Present State of English Government in Bengal* London 1772.

Watts, W., *Memoirs of the Revolution in Bengal*, London 1764.

Yule, H. (Edt.), *The Diary of William Hedges*, 3 Vols, London 1887-89.

(B) *Persian* :

Basit, Ghulam, *Tarikh-i-Mamalik-I-Hind* (Translated by Elliot and Dowson in the *History of India as told by its own Historians*, Vol. VIII, Reprint, Allahabad, 1964).

Blockmann, H., *Tarikh-i-Mansuri* (*Journal of Asiatic Society of Bengal*, Vol. XXXVI, Part I, No. II, 1867).

"Dastur-ul-Imla"—An unpublished Persian letter of Mir Qasim (translated by S.H. Askari in *Bengal Past and Present*, Vol. LVII, July-December, 1939).

Delhi Chronicle-an annonymous Persian Manuscript (Translated by J.N. Sarkar in the *Proceedings of Indian Historical Records Commission*, Vol. III, 1921).

Husain, Ghulam, *Seir Mutagherin*, Vols. II and III (English Translation by Hajee Mustapha, Calcutta, 1902).

Husain, Murtaza, *Hadikatu-I-Akalim* (Translated by Elliot and Dowson, Vol VIII)..

Khan, Muhammed Ali, *Tarikh-i-Muzaffari* (Translated by Elliot and Dowson, Vol. VIII).

Khan, Saqi Mustad, *Maasir-Alamgiri* (Eng. Trans. by J.N. Sarkar, Calcutta, 1947).

Khan, Nawab Muhabbat, *Akbar 1-Muhabbat* (Translated by Elliot and Dowson, Vol. VIII).

Muhammad, Fakir, *Jamiu-t Tawarikh* (Translated by Elliot and Dowson, Vol. VIII).

Rai, Harsukh, *Majmau-1 Akhbar* (Translated by Elliot and Dowson, Vol. VIII).

Salim, Ghulam Husain *Riyazu-s Salatin* (Translated by Abdus Salam, Reprint, Delhi, 1975).

Singh, Kalyan, *Khulasat ut Tawarikh* (Translated by Sarfaraz Husain Khan—*The Journal of Bihar and Orissa Research Society*, Vol. V, 1919).

(C) *French* :

Law, Jean, *Memoire Sur Quelques Affairs De L' Empire Mogol* (1756-1761) Edt. by Alfred Martineau, Paris, 1913 (Late G.L. Roy, National Library, Calcutta, translated the relevant portion for me. Also Hill, *Bengal in 1756-57*, Vol. III).

Memoire Sur L' Indoustan ou Empire Mongol (Translated by J.N. Sarkar in the Proceedings of Historical Records Commission, 1927).

Translation of extracts from a French Manuscript entitled "Revolutions in Bengal". (*Vide*, Hill, *Bengal in 1756-57*, Vol. III).

3. *Secondary Sources*

(A) *English*

Auber, Peter, *Rise and Progress of the British Power in India*, Vol. I. London, 1837.

Akhtar, Shirin, *The Role of the Zamindars in Bengal, 1707-1772.* (Dacca 1980).

Banerjee, B.N., *Begams of Bengal*, Calcutta, 1942.

Baden-Powell, B.H., *A Short Account of the Land Revenue and its Administration in British India*, Oxford 1913.

Beveridge, Henry, *A Comprehensive History of India* Vol. I, Reprint, New Delhi, 1974.

,, *Warren Hastings in Lower Bengal* (*Vide*, Calcutta Review, 1877).

Bhattacharya, S.K., *The East India Company and the Economy of Bengal*, Calcutta, 1969.

Broome, Arthur, *History of the Rise and Progress of the Bengal Army*, Vol. I, London, 1850.

Bruce, John, *Annals of the East India Company*, 3 Vols. London, 1810.

Busteed, H.E., *Echoes from Old Calcutta*, 2nd edn., Calcutta, 1888.

Carey, W.H., *The Good Old Days of Honourable John Company* New edition, Calcutta, 1964.

Chandra, A.N., the *Sannyasi Rebellion*, Calcutta, 1977.

Chatterjee, N.L., *Bengal under the Diwani Administration*, Allahabad, 1956.

Chatterjee, N.L., *Mir Qasim-Nawab of Bengal*, Allahabad, 1935.

,, *Verelst's Rule in India*, Allahabad, 1939.

,, *Clive as an Administrator*, Allahabad, 1935.

Chaudhuri, N.C., *Clive of India*, London, 1975.

Chaudhuri, N.G., *Cartier, Governor af Bengal*, Calcutta, 1970.

Chaudhuri, Susil, *Trade and Commercial Organisation in Bengal* 1650-1720, Calcutta, 1975.

Cotton, H.J.S., *Memorandum on the Revenue History c Chittagong* Calcutta, 1880.

Datta, K.K., *Alivardi and his times*, Calcutta, 1963.

,, *Studies in the History of the Bengal Subah*, Vol. I, Calcutta, 1936.

,, *Shah Alam II and the East India Company*, Calcutta, 1965.

Datta, K.K., *The Dutch in Bengal and Bihar,* Second Revised Edn. Patna, 1968.

,, *Sirajuddaula,* Calcutta, 1971.

Dani, A.H., *Dacca, A Record of its Changing Fortunes,* Dacca 1956.

Davies, A.M. *Clive of Plassey,* London, 1939.

Dodwell, Henry, *Dupleix and Clive.* Reprint, Gorakhpur, 1962.

Edward, Michael, *Battle of Plassey and the Conquest of Bengal,* London, 1963.

Elliot and Dowson, *The History of India as told by its own Historians.* Vol. VIII, Indian Reprint, Allahadad, 1964.

Elphinstone, M., *The Rise of the British Power in the East,* London, 1887.

Feiling, Keith, *Warren Hastings,* London, 1955.

Forrest G., *The Life of Lord Clive,* 2 Vols, London, 1918.

Foster, W., *The Embassy of Sir Thomas Roe to the Court of The Great Mugal, 1615-1619,* London, 1899.

Gatty, Reginald, *Robert Clive and the Founding of the British Empire,* London, 1927.

Ghose, N.N. *Memoirs of Maharaja Nubkissen Bahadur,* Calcutta, 1901.

Ghose, K.C., *Famines in Bengal, 1770-1943,* Calcutta, 1944.

Gleig, G.R., *The Life of Robert, First Lord Clive,* London 1907.

,, *Memoirs of the Life of Right Honourable Warren Hastings,* Vol. I, London, 1841.

Gupta, B.K., *Sirajuddaullah and the East India Company,* Leiden, 1966.

Habib, Irfan, *The Agrarian System of Mugal India,* London, 1963.

Hill, S.C., *Three Frenchmen in Bengal,* London, 1903.

Hunter, W.W., *Annals of Rural Bengal,* Reprint, Delhi, 1975.

,, *The Indian Empire,* Third Edn. Reprint, Delhi, 1973.

Huq, Mazharul, *The East India Company's Land Policy and Commerce in Bengal*, Dacca, 1964.

Irvine, William, *Later Mughals*, Vol. I, Calcutta, no date.

Kasim, A., *Murshid Quli Khan and his Times*, Dacca, 1963.

Khan, Abdul Majed, *The Transition in Bengal, 1756-1775*, Cambridge University Press, 1969.

Little, J.H., *The House of Jagat Seth*, Reprint, Calcutta, 1967.

Lawford, J.P., *Clive, Proconsul of India*, London, 1976.

Malleson, G.B., *The Decisive Battles of India*, New Edn. New Delhi, 1969.

,, *Rulers of India (Lord Clive)*, Oxford 1895.

,, *The Life of Warren Hastings*, London, 1894.

Malcolm, John, *The Life of Robert Lord Clive*, Vol. II London, 1836.

Majumdar P.C., *The Musnud of Murshidabad*, Calcutta, 1905.

Majumdar R.C., *Maharaja Rajballabh*, Calcutta, 1947.

Marshall, P.J., *East Indian Fortunes*, Oxford, 1976.

Marshman J.C., *The History of India*, Vol. I, London 1867.

Marx, Karl, Capital, 1906.

Mill, James, *The History of British India*, Vol. II, Reprint, New Delhi, 1972.

Mohsin, K.M., *Transition of a Bengal District : Murshidabad, 1765-93*, Dacca, 1975.

Mukhopadhyay, S.C., *The Carrer of Rajah Durlabhram Mahindra (Rai-Durlabh), Diwan of Bengal*, Varansi, 1974.

,, *Diwani in Bengal, 1765*, Varanasi, 1980.

,, *The Agrarian Policy of the British in Bengal, 1698-1772* Allahabad, 1987.

Nolan. E.H., *The History of the British Empire in India and the East*, London, No Date.

Ram Gopal, *How the British Occupied Bengal*, New York, 1963.

Roy, A.C., *The Career of Mir Jafar Khan*, Calcutta, 1953.

Roy, B.K., *The Career and Achievements of Maharaja Nanda Kumar*, Calcutta, 1969.

Sarkar . J.N. (Edt.), *The History oj Bengal*, Patna 1973.

,, *Fall of the Mughal Empire*, Vol. I, Calcutta, 1932.

,, *Bengal Nawabs*, Calcutta, 1952.

Spear, Percival, *Master af Bengal : Clive and his India*, London 1975.

Srivastava, A.L. *Shujauddaulah*, Vol. II, Lahore, 1945.

Stewart, Charles, *History of Bengal*, First Indian Reprint, New Delhi, 1971.

Syud, Hussain, *Echoes from old Dacca*, Callcutta, 1909.

Thompson, Edward and Garratt, G.T., *Rise and Fulfilment af the British Rule in India*, Allahabad, 1969.

Thornton, Edward, *The History of the British Empire in India* London, 1841-45.

Tolboys, W., *India Under British Rule from the Foundation of the East India Company*, London, 1886.

Verma, D.C., *Plassey to Buxar*, New Delhi, 1976.

Walsh, J.H.T., *A History of Murshidabad District*, London, 1902.

Wise, J., *Notes on the Races, Castes and trades of Eastern Bengal*, London, 1883.

Wilson, C.R., *The Early Annals of the English in Bengal*, Vol. II, Pt. II, Reprint, Calcutta, 1963.

(B) *Bengali* :

Bandopadhyay, K.P., *Banglar Itihas O Ashtadash Satabdir Nababi Amal*, 2nd Edn., 1315, B.S.

,, *Madhya Yuge Bangla*, Calcutta, 1330 B.S.

Chakraborty, Panchanan (Edt.), *Rameshwar Rachanavali*, Calcutta, 1965.

Haldar, Gopal, *Bangla Sahityer Ruprekha*, Pt. I, 2nd Edn., Calcutta, 1363 B.S.

Lahiri, Durgadas (Edt.), *Banglar Itihas*, Calcutta, 1316 B.S.

Maitra, A.K., *Sirajuddaulah*, lst Edn., 1304, B.S.

Marshman, J.T., *Banglar Itihas*, Calcutta, 1904.

Mitra, S.K., *Hugli Zelar Itihas O Bangasamaj*, Pt. II, Third Reprint, Calcutta, 1965.

Mukhopadhyay, Rajiblochan, *Maharaj Krishnachandra Rayasya Charitam*, Reprint, Calcutta, 1355 B.S.

Roy, Nikhilnath, *Murshidabad Kahani*, 2nd edn., Calcutta, 1310 B.S.

Murshidabader Itihas, Calcutta, 1309, B.S.

Sastri, Satya Charan, *Granthavali* (*Clive Charit*), New Edn., 1314 B.S.

(C) *Magazines and Journals*

Bengal Past and Present (January-June 1921, Vol. XXII). Little, J.H. "The House of Jagat Seth".

Bengal Past and Present. Vol. LVII, 1939. Banerjee, D.N., 'Residents' position and functions at the Darbar".

Bengal Past and Present, Vol. LVII, 1939. "Dastur ul Imla"-an unpublished letter of Mir Qasim.

Bharata Manisha Quarterly, Varanasi, Vol. III, 1978. Mukhopadhyay, S.C., "The English Wars against Aurangzeb in Bengal, 1686-90"

Calcutta Review, Vol. LXV, 1877. Beveridge, H., "Warren Hastings in Lower Bengal".

Calcutta Review, Vol. XVII, 1925 and Vol. XVIII, 1926. Khan, I.M., "Mohammed Reza Khan and his trial".

Indian Antiquary, 1914, Temple, R.C., "Documents relating to the first English Commercial Mission to Patna, 1620-21".

Indian Historical Quarterly, Vol. XVI, 1940. Datta, K.K., "Durlabhram a prominent Bengali Officer of the mid-18th Century".

Indian Historical Quarterly, Vol. XXII, 1946. Datta, K.K., "Sirajuddaulah and the English before 1756".

Journal of Asiatic Society of Bengal, Vol. XXXVI 1868. Blochmann, H., "Notes on Sirajuddaulah and the Town of Murshidabad taken from Tarikh i Mansuri".

Journal of Historical Research, Ranchi, Vol. IX, 1967. Mukhopadhyay, S. C., "Battle of Plassey and Durlabhram".

Journal of Historical Research, Ranchi, Vol. XII, 1970. Mukhopadhyay, S.C., "Influence of Hindu Officials in the Administration of Nawab Alivardi Khan".

Journal of Historical Research, Ranchi, Vol. XIV, 1972. Mukhopadhyay, S.C., "William Watts-the First British Resident at Murshidabad".

Journal of Historical Research, Ranchi, Vol. XV, 1973. Mukhopadhyay, S.C., Sirajuddaulah's Revolt Against Alivardi".

Journal of Historical Research, Ranchi, Vol. XVII, 1975. Mukhopadhyay, S.C., "Establishment of English trade in Bengal".

Journal of Historical Research, Ranchi, Vol. XXIII, 1980, Mukhopadhyay, S.C., "Job Charnock and 24 August, 1690—the foundation day of Modern Calcutta".

Journal of Indian History, Trivandram, Vol. LII, Pt. I, 1974. Mukhopadhyay, S.C., "Bengal Conspiracy of 1757—a Hindu Discontent."

Journal of Social Science, B.H.U, Varanasi, Vol. 4, 1984-85, Mukhopadhyay, S.C., "English trading privileges and Settlement in Bengal—a responsibility of Emperor Shah Jahen and Prince Shuja."

Journal of Historical Research, Vol, XLIII, Pt. I, 1965. Datta, K.K. "Delhi Restoration, 1772".

Proceedings of Indian Historical Records Commission, 1927. "Memoire sur L' Indoustan on Empire Mongol", translated by J.N. Sarkar.

Proceedings of the Indian Historical Records Commission, Vol. III, 1921. "Delhi Chronicle"—An annonymous Persian Mss translated by J.N. Sarkar.

The Journal of Bihar and Orissa Reasearch Society, Vol. V, 1919. Singh, Kalyan, "Khulasat ut Tawarikh", translated by Sarfaraz Husain Khan.

The Quarterly Review of Historical Studies, Vol. XXII, Calcutta, 1982. Sarkar, Jagadish Narayan, "Seeds of Economic decline in the century before Plassey".

INDEX
